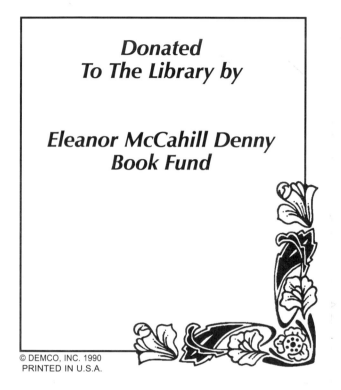

Claiming the City

A volume in the series

Cushwa Center Studies of Catholicism
in Twentieth-Century America
edited by R. Scott Appleby, University of Notre Dame

CLAIMING THE CITY

*Politics, Faith,
and the Power of Place
in St. Paul*

WITHDRAWN

MARY LETHERT WINGERD

CORNELL UNIVERSITY PRESS

Ithaca & London

First published 2001 by Cornell University Press

Printed in the United States of America

Title page photo: West Publishing management and workers at the 1916 carnival. Courtesy of the Minnesota Historical Society

Library of Congress Cataloging-in-Publication Data

Wingerd, Mary Lethert, 1948–
   Claiming the city : politics, faith, and the power of place in St.
Paul / Mary Lethert Wingerd.
      p. cm. — (Cushwa Center studies of Catholicism in
twentieth-century America)
   Includes bibliographical references and index.
   ISBN 0-8014-3936-1 (cloth : alk. paper)
   1. Saint Paul (Minn.)—Politics and government—20th century. 2.
Political culture—Minnesota—Saint Paul—History—20th century. 3.
Saint Paul (Minn.)—Social conditions—20th century. 4. Saint Paul
(Minn.)—Economic conditions—20th century. 5. Regionalism—Political
aspects—Minesota—Saint Paul—History—20th century. 6. Working
class—Minnesota—Saint Paul—Political activity—History—20th
century. 7. Industrial relations—Minnesota—Saint Paul —Historty—20th
century. 8. Irish Americans—Minnesota—Saint Paul —Politics and
government—20th century. 9. Catholic Church—Minnesota—Saint
Paul—History—20th century. 10. Christianity and
politics—Minnesota—Saint Paul—History—20th century.   I. Title. II.
Series.
F614.S4 W77 2001
306.2'09776'5810904—dc21

                                    2001002854

Cornell University Press strives to use environmentally responsible suppliers and materials
to the fullest extent possible in the publishing of its books. Such materials include vegetable-based,
low-VOC inks and acid-free papers that are recycled, totally chlorine-free, or partly composed
of nonwood fibers. Books that bear the logo of the FSC (Forest Stewardship Council) use paper
taken from forests that have been inspected and certified as meeting the highest standards for
environmental and social responsibility. For further information, visit our website at
www.cornellpress.cornell.edu.

Cloth printing   10 9 8 7 6 5 4 3 2

*for my mother,
an unsung hero*

Contents

Illustrations

Acknowledgments

Although, in the end, the writing of history is a solitary task, ideally it is a communal effort as well. During the years that I worked on this book, I was blessed with the best sort of scholarly collaboration, along with generous personal and institutional support.

A faculty fellowship from the Cushwa Center for the Study of American Catholicism at the University of Notre Dame and the Lilly Foundation provided the time to revise the manuscript and to participate in the Cushwa Project on Catholicism in Twentieth-Century America. Each member of the project expanded my knowledge in more ways than I can count. Center director Scott Appleby was unflagging in his support for the book, and the advice and friendship of Jim Fisher (fellow lover of St. Paul), Bruce Nelson, Steve Rosswurm, and Ellen Skerrett kept me on course during the last, long trek to the finish line.

In the earlier stages, funding from the Irish American Cultural Institute, the Mellon Foundation, and most unstintingly, from the History Department at Duke University, afforded the means for dedicated research and writing. A year as scholar-in-residence at the Minnesota History Center not only provided office space and support; it also introduced me to historians Rhoda Gilman, Lucile Kane, and Alan Woolworth, who so kindly shared their vast knowledge of Minnesota history and archival sources. Tracey Baker was an expert guide through the History Center's enormous photo archive, and Research Supervisor Deborah Miller offered intellectual acuity, enthusiasm, and warm friendship that revived me on many a weary day. I am also grateful for the assistance of Patrick Anzelc at the Archdiocesan Archives and Eileen McCormack at the James J. Hill Reference Library. Thanks also to the very talented Cory Barton for creating the maps that grace these pages.

I encountered scholarly generosity everywhere I traveled but must give special mention to historian William Millikan. With knowledge gained from his years spent researching and writing a history of the Minneapolis Citizens Alliance, Bill directed me to sources I could not have uncovered alone and shared the manuscript draft of his book, which was in itself a rich resource. I also am indebted to Jocelyn Wills for her insights on James J. Hill and for introducing me to the diaries of Michael Boyle.

At every stage of development, this volume benefited from thoughtful critiques by colleagues and friends. Derek Chang, Ann Claycombe, Paul Husbands, David Lanegran, Joseph McCartin, Bruce Nelson, Paul Ortiz, Steve Rosswurm, and Patrick Wilkinson all read and provided most helpful comments on parts of the work in progress. My brilliant friend, Mary Jane Morrow, saved me from despair when I could not find the path into my introduction.

John McGreevy, Peter Rachleff, Nick Salvatore, Margaret Steinfels, and George Waldrep all read versions of the entire manuscript and offered invaluable assessments. Arif Dirlik alerted me to theoretical implications of my analysis. And David Emmons not only read every page and shared his expertise on Irish American culture, he also gave much-needed encouragement to a junior colleague.

Many people touch our lives in ways that they may scarcely suspect. Sister Mary Regina, my high school English teacher, surely never dreamed what an impact she would make, but her love of the written word and formidable writing standards influence me still. And when I began my studies as a returning student at Macalester College, I am equally sure that my professors did not expect to change my life in the radical ways they did. James Brewer Stewart has been a staunch and inspiring mentor who fired my imagination from the first day I walked into his classroom. Peter Rachleff awakened a passion for working-class history, and later, when I was searching for a way to explore the questions that most intrigued me, he suggested that I might find the ideal topic in my own backyard.

St. Paul, Minnesota, is my hometown, but its fascinating dimensions only captured my curiosity from the vantage point of Durham, North Carolina. Some might say that perspective is everything, but it was more than distance that gave a new slant to the familiar. The community of professors, friends, and fellow graduate students I came to know at Duke University made my years there an intellectual adventure. Special thanks to Andy Arnold, Terry Bouton, Martha Jane Brazy, Derek Chang, Ann Claycombe, Alex Keyssar, Michael McQuarrie, Paul Ortiz, Eve Sterne, Susan Thorne, George Waldrep, and Peter Wood, for good times and great discussions.

When the time inevitably came to put words to paper, I was fortunate to work with faculty who were as generous as they are talented. John Thompson was a meticulous reader and provided valuable comparative insight; Leon Fink put my analysis to the test of his rigorous and uncompromising standards; and Nancy Hewitt read each chapter with an editor's as well as a historian's eye. On both counts, her attention improved every page.

My debts to William Chafe and Lawrence Goodwyn are incalculable. Both as a scholar and an adviser, Bill Chafe has been a crucial influence at each step along the way. What I learned from Larry Goodwyn cannot be put into words. While pressing relentlessly for clarity and focus, at the same time he somehow made me believe I could conquer the world.

For nurturing my spirit as well as my work, I am heartily grateful to lifelong friends Patti Brady and Cathy Flynn; to Larry and Nell Goodwyn for the haven they provided all those years I was away from home; to Leon Fink and Sue Levine for friendship and support that has extended across both years and miles; to Mary Jane Morrow for her historical imagination and unshakable loyalty; and to George Waldrep for his poetry, intelligence, and rare comradeship.

None of this would have been possible without the support of my family. The memory of my father's encouragement often kept me from faltering, and my sister and soulmate, Nancy Brill, has always cheered me on. Mark, Bill, and Caroline Wingerd never lost faith in their unconventional mother, with a confidence that often far exceeded my own. And for ultimate support, I could always count on my mother, Marguerite Lethert. Her roots are planted deep in the soil of St. Paul, and she gave us all our sense of place. This book is my small gift to her.

MARY WINGERD

White Bear Lake, Minnesota

Claiming the City

INTRODUCTION

May 22, 1934, was an unremarkable Tuesday in St. Paul, Minnesota. In its quiet neighborhoods, sunlight filtered through a pale green haze of leafing elms. The scent of lilacs infused the air. Housewives called to one another as they swept their porches or hung their laundry out to dry. And a scattered procession of milk-men, grocery delivery vans, and coal trucks made their expected way down the canopied avenues. The business district displayed its usual moderate bustle, as streetcars vied with trucks on city streets, transporting workers and goods along their regular routes.

Just across the Mississippi River in Minneapolis, the scene was decidedly differ-ent. Tension electrified the city. More than twenty thousand people crowded the market area, anticipating a confrontation between the city's striking teamsters and police. The strikers had shut down all commercial transportation in the city, but the chief of police had promised that his men, aided by deputized businessmen, would see that the trucks started moving that day. News photographers and movie men milled among the throng, ready to record the expected battle. They were not disap-pointed. A crate of tomatoes sailed through a window, and the fight was on. As the combatants pummeled one another with clubs, pipes, and blackjacks, an announcer from KSTP radio gave a play-by-play of the action from a nearby rooftop, "re-port[ing] the battle like a football game to listeners in all parts of Minnesota."[1] Some people in St. Paul may have followed the account with interest; others just as likely twirled the radio dial to another station. In either case, the civil war waging next door might as well have been in Spain for all it touched their daily lives.

The Minneapolis truckers' strike crested a wave of labor militancy that broke across the country in 1934. Mired in the Great Depression, working people united in unprecedented numbers to protest the injuries they endured—an uprising that would finally bring organized labor to a place of political power in America. The

Minneapolis truckers' strike was one of the most dramatic and historically significant contests of that year. In a four-month struggle to win union recognition, the truckers took on one of the most intransigent antilabor business establishments in the country, bringing Minneapolis to a state of armed chaos. The ultimate victory of the teamsters helped set the course for a new era in the fortunes of organized labor.[2]

Though the strike riveted the attention of state and federal authorities and the national press, workers in the "twin city" of St. Paul turned their backs on the conflict, offering only minimal support for their beleaguered fellow workers in Minneapolis. Chronicles of the strike, intent on capturing its heroic contours, offer little explanation for the unsettling lack of solidarity between Twin Cities unionists. The curious disengagement of St. Paul—an established union town, governed by a labor mayor, and separated from Minneapolis only by a municipal boundary—is a jarring note in an otherwise coherent saga. Consequently, it has been consigned to no more than a passing mention, a footnote, or complete erasure from the historical record. Rather than search for the forces that lay behind St. Paul workers' seemingly inexplicable behavior, both contemporary chroniclers and historians have been content to speculate that some sort of inherent conservatism stunted worker activism in St. Paul, probably due to the influence of the Catholic Church on its heavily Irish-Catholic working class.[3]

This book intends to challenge such assumptions. Taking St. Paul workers seriously on their own terms introduces a new complexity to the history of Minnesota labor and politics. More important, it also calls into question the prevailing models of labor history and class politics and demands a more nuanced inclusion of religion into the mix of social history. I argue that geography itself—and identification with place—is a critical if often neglected element of the social process. The contrasts between St. Paul and Minneapolis vividly illuminate the importance of place in the formation of identity and political culture. Neither ethnicity, religion, nor class can be understood apart from the social and physical geography in which they are experienced. Ethnic, religious, or even class commonalities notwithstanding, in the minds of workers in St. Paul, Minneapolis was another world.[4]

The economic and political structures in which people live their daily lives deeply influence the contours of identity. Geographer Alan Pred notes that "people do not produce history and places under conditions of their own choosing, but in the context of already existing, directly encountered social and spatial structures."[5] Once formed, these "ways of seeing" create chains of causation. Such chains are by no means inviolable; cultural understandings are constantly tested and renegotiated. But, as Charles Tilly has observed, "Past social relations and their residues—material ideological, and otherwise—constrain present social relations and consequently constrain their products as well."[6] The differences between St. Paul and Minneapolis are especially striking because of their proximity, but in every city and town similar place-based cultural processes occurred. Only by mining such differ-

ences can historians uncover what Tilly has called the "deep order of social processes"—the continuities that can be traced amid a welter of multiple contingencies
and causes.[7]

St. Paul and Minneapolis offer a particularly rich site to explore the formative
power of place. By the early twentieth century, the two cities had developed almost
polar cultural configurations—St. Paul characterized as an Irish, Catholic, Democratic stronghold, and Minneapolis noted for its Scandinavians, Protestants, and
Republican Yankee "progressives." Yet the cities were not nearly so demographically
different as the marked cultural differences would suggest. Irish immigrants poured
into both cities but became the principal ethnic group in neither; overwhelmingly
northern European, both cities were home to significant Scandinavian populations
(though St. Paul counted more Germans than either Scandinavians or Irish); and by
1918, Catholic churches were abundant on both sides of the river. More than simple
numerical predominance, then, a combination of social, political, and economic positioning gave a particular currency to Irish, Catholic, and Democratic affiliations in
St. Paul that disappeared when one crossed the river to Minneapolis.

The economic and social configuration that developed in St. Paul from its days as
a territorial outpost deeply influenced workers' choices in 1934. A particular set of
circumstances explored in the following chapters, fostered an intensely localistic
outlook that served as a barrier between St. Paul residents and people outside the
city—most especially Minneapolitans, their nearest neighbors. Ethnicity, religion,
and class assumed particular contours that were shaped and delimited by municipal
boundaries. Defense of those cultural values then generated a deep place-based loyalty—what I term *civic identity*—a common project to protect the territory that
housed the social understandings through which St. Paulites negotiated their world.

The concept of civic identity is a problematic one. Though recent scholarship has
explored national and regional identity formation in depth, the all-too-apparent in-
equalities of power in twentieth-century American cities have caused some skepti-
cism about claims of "civic community." The interdependencies that created accountability in a preindustrial age are presumed to have gradually withered with the
influx of a new immigrant population and the emergence of corporate capitalism. In
this analysis, by the onset of the twentieth century, claims of community had given
way to camps of competing interest groups.[8] In many cases, this was true. Thus, studies of urban America, for good reason, have focused most often on the city as a site of
internal conflict. But the struggles that characterized urban growth and decline operated within specific geographical boundaries—a social space with the capacity to
foster another, sometimes contradictory, group identity that was grounded in place.
Neither as intimate as the informal community of neighborhood nor as mythic as the
imagined community of nation, civic identity, as I define it, occupies a middle ground
between the two and can be understood only on its own highly contingent terms.

Although civic identity, like all identities, is socially constructed, the claims of
imagined fraternity that undergird nationalism or regionalism are put more closely
to the test in a local venue.[9] Municipal borders create a tangible container that in-

tensifies social processes. Three critical conditions prevail in the construction of civic identity: the geographical boundaries are immediate; the sources of power are evident; and the rewards of loyalty can be assessed on a daily basis. Thus, though city-builders, like nation-builders, might strive to construct a highly selective common past, because the project is tied to visible—and traversable—geographic space, the imagined elements that undergird nationalism or regionalism are more difficult to sustain. In short, the content of civic identity must rely much more closely on contractual elements than on imagined components. In common parlance, it must "deliver the goods." The claims of community must prove themselves in daily life.[10]

Whatever its specific configuration, a civic community bears only slight resemblance to the tight-knit social accountability of neighborhood. The informal affective bonds of kinship and neighborhood are attenuated, if not erased, when stretched across the urban terrain. But interdependence may yet sustain claims of "community" accountability—obligations brokered by religious or ethnic institutions that are socially accountable across class. Consequently, the task of crafting common civic loyalty among a diverse population depends heavily on cross-class institutions that are grounded in urban neighborhoods.[11]

The outcome of such a project depends on many variables. In major American cities, by the turn of the century, urban growth and the concentration of power in fewer and fewer hands made community accountability increasingly difficult to enforce. In many instances, civic identity had indeed become no more than the empty rhetoric of business boosterism. Minneapolis provides a case in point. There, a small cohort of powerful capitalists—families of the original New England settlers—jealously guarded control of the city, which had become the preeminent milling and manufacturing center of the Northwest. They dominated politics, finance, and business and successfully dictated the terms between business and labor. As a result of such closely held power and social exclusivity, class and ethnic tensions made Minneapolis a divided city, where claims of a common civic community rang increasingly hollow.

But for every such emerging industrial dynamo, a hundred other cities struggled just to keep pace. In these second-and third-tier cities, where power was more dispersed, accountability was more enforceable, and thus civic identity could play a real role in shaping politics and culture. One such city was St. Paul, where an uncertain economy and a more permeable stratum of elites created a different set of social dynamics. These dynamics in turn relied on negotiation and compromise among a broad set of players—including working people—to keep the city functioning.

This book examines the development of that "civic compact" and the political culture it fostered: the ways in which it was challenged, came apart, and eventually was reconfigured in response to state, national, and even global forces. In a complex dialectic, local identity formed, transformed, and became defined by the city's place in the region and the nation. At the same time, the meaning of nationalism itself was interpreted through the lens of everyday life, linking the global to the local in an interactive, if unequal exchange.[12] The story of St. Paul gives proof to Patricia

Limerick's bold assertion that "local history can inhabit at one and the same time, regional, national, and planetary levels of significance."[13]

The political culture that characterized St. Paul in 1934 had deep and complex roots that stretched back to the city's nineteenth-century origins as a trading post and its subsequent evolution as a transportation and distribution center with a commercial rather than an industrial base. Part 1 of this volume examines the opportunities that railroad development and a general shortage of capital created for German and Irish immigrants and the way ethnic and religious identities evolved within this context. As the city's fortunes began to decline, overshadowed by Minneapolis, St. Paul business-men struggled to find a way to compete. Because they lacked the means to unilaterally control labor relations, they turned to established intersecting religious and ethnic net-works to craft a negotiated settlement with organized workers. The Catholic Church, and Irish Catholics in particular, came to play crucial roles in brokering this civic pact. The formula they relied on was framed intrinsically in rhetoric of community and civic solidarity, which gained considerable intensity from an impassioned rivalry with Min-neapolis. Workers in St. Paul used these same constructions to further their own inter-ests. As a result, class tensions were mediated within a commonly understood set of rights and obligations grounded in loyalty to what they defined as civic community.

Part 2 focuses on the breakdown of the civic compact during World War I, when St. Paul business interests, in a rare alliance with their Minneapolis counterparts, seized wartime opportunities in an attempt to change the terms of the social con-tract. But the combination of state repression and a bitter intercity streetcar strike carried political, economic, and social costs that proved to be more than they had anticipated. The networks that undergirded the civic compact unraveled, and city workers shed old allegiances for a new coalition with farmers and Minneapolis workers, creating the seeds of the Farmer-Labor Party.

Part 3 examines workers' embrace and subsequent retreat from class-based poli-tics. Post–World War I St. Paul experienced a spiraling economic downturn that preceded the national depression by nearly a decade. As the local depression deep-ened, workers and employers, out of mutual weakness, once again turned to famil-iar, localistic modes of negotiation to resolve a city-wide crisis—a process that re-established the place of the Catholic Church and the Irish as the central brokers of civic peace. In my analysis, the pivotal cultural moment in St. Paul occurred in the aftermath of 1917—not in the 1930s, which proved so turbulent in Minneapolis. In St. Paul, by 1934, when this study concludes, the terms of negotiation had been reestablished and the settlement had been reached. The result was not a community of consensus, nor had it ever been. What was achieved instead was a locally circum-scribed arena in which opposing interests could bargain effectively, thereby rein-forcing cultural understandings that would influence politics and business in the city for years to come.[14]

Though the social evolution of St. Paul was the result of the specific history of a single mid-sized, Midwestern city, certain patterns emerge that are relevant for analyses of broader historical social and structural processes. The particular confluence of circumstances is unique to St. Paul, but its particular social landscape has much broader analytical utility when viewed in a comparative framework. The similarities and differences that emerge can provide essential building blocks for new syntheses of urban history. For example, late-nineteenth-century St. Paul, which prospered as the provisioner for the frontier, bears a startling structural resemblance to antebellum Buffalo, which served the same role in an earlier era. As described by historian David Gerber, Buffalo in the 1840s developed a culture of political pluralism that was remarkably similar to what emerged in St. Paul decades later. Other similarities can be seen in the case of San Francisco in the Progressive Era. Another city without an industrial base, San Francisco politics came to be dominated by the predominantly Irish building-trades unions. The era of American Federation of Labor (AFL) power in San Francisco had much in common with the contours of union influence in St. Paul. The circumstances that ended that era in San Francisco, when contrasted with labor's enduring vigor in St. Paul, offer a new perspective on the relationship between structural constraints and activism.[15]

In terms of understanding the contours of ethnic identity, a comparison with Butte, Montana, is also instructive. In that highly industrialized mining city, cross-class ethnic ties between Irish elites and workers accrued group benefits that reinforced the power of ethnic identity. In St. Paul, a city built on trade rather than industry, similar cross-class relationships nonetheless worked to produce somewhat comparable ethnic allegiances. In St. Paul, as in Butte, civic identity took on an Irish cast (somewhat akin to the German-influenced civic character that Kathleen Conzen described in nineteenth-century Milwaukee). Yet the content of Irish identity in St. Paul was quite distinct from its manifestation in Butte, or Boston, or even Minneapolis. This comparative frame of reference raises intriguing questions about the influence of place on ethnic consciousness.[16]

Until very recently, the role of religion in politics and society has been a neglected topic among social historians, one seldom subjected to the textured analysis accorded ethnicity, class, race, or gender. Faith, however, played a powerful role in shaping the identity and daily life of most of the ordinary folks who people social history. The Catholic Church in particular—with its highly articulated institutional structure and massive membership among the immigrant population—had the capacity to be a political player at least as influential as any political party. But despite its hierarchical organization, Catholicism did not speak with a single voice in every venue. Both its political presence and the interpretation of its doctrine were shaped far more by local conditions than by dictates from Rome.[17]

The Catholic Church, which came to have an enduring influence in St. Paul, also had significant roles to play in Buffalo, Butte, and San Francisco. In each case, neither religious practice nor institutional authority operated apart from the political, social, and economic context of the particular locales.[18] Telling evidence for local variation can be found in Paula Kane's study of Boston Catholicism. There, as Kane describes, the Catholic Church exerted leverage by maintaining what she calls a culture of separatism, fostering a bloc of concentrated Catholic power in opposition to the domination of a Protestant elite.[19] In contrast, Catholic influence in St. Paul derived from the church's integration into the broader culture and particularly through a Catholic presence in elite circles of power. While other denominations indisputably were voices of influence in the city, none had the unified hierarchical structure or the sheer numbers to match the Catholic Church in political leverage. Yet in Minneapolis, where a large Catholic population was confined primarily to the working class, the Catholic Church was an insignificant political player.

The most striking point of comparison, of course, is with Minneapolis. Neither contiguity nor a regional ethos allayed in any way the civic antagonism between the two rivals. To the contrary, the civic identity of St. Paul came to be self-consciously articulated in opposition to Minneapolis—a process that created barriers among all sorts of people who might otherwise seem to have been natural allies. Intercity rivalry was certainly not unique to the Twin Cities. Indeed, it would be difficult to discover a town or city that does not define itself in opposition to some real or imagined rival. Whether contiguous neighbors like Dallas–Fort Worth or separated by half a continent like Chicago and New York, such rivalries influence politics and social practices with varying degrees of significance that remain to be explored.[20]

In the case of St. Paul and Minneapolis, where cultural battles reflected real struggles for economic advantage and power, the stakes in civic rivalry were inordinately high. Thus, the cultural context of St. Paul cannot be understood apart from Minneapolis. Nonetheless, I make no claims to fully developed comparative analysis. My focus is the internal workings of St. Paul. Minneapolis weaves in and out of the story—central to the action at times, while at others merely a felt presence.

It is important to specify, as well, that while my goal has been to craft an integrative urban history that engages the evolution of ethnic, religious, and class identities in relation to structures of power, not every element of the social fabric receives equal attention. Certain prominent figures loom large in the narrative. With a background as a labor historian, I hadn't expected to examine the careers of the "great men" of St. Paul history. But I came to understand that the social text of the city was woven from multiple negotiations over power. To illuminate the nature of those negotiations, it was essential to explore the social and economic influence exerted by those individuals with the capacity to make an impact on ordinary people's lives. In no way does this undermine the role of ordinary people in shaping the narrative; rather, it creates a more nuanced context in which to understand their choices and acknowledge that they understood the contours of their world.

The ordinary people who are the primary actors in this account are the groups who participated most fully in the construction of civic identity and who gained the most from the compact it supported—the Old Stock Protestants, Germans, and Irish who were early arrivals in the city. Other immigrant groups who found their way to St. Paul somewhat later, though they created their own vibrant strains of community, either lacked the resources or the demographic mass to become major players in civic negotiations. Hence, they remained on the political periphery for most of the period I consider. Gradually, of course, this changed. By the 1930s, most of the city's ethnic groups had gained varying degrees of economic and political access to the larger civic community. The benefits of membership then encouraged a wide range of people to internalize the accouterments of civic identity, grounding the cultural markers by which they defined themselves in the particularities of place—a powerful incentive to invest in the localistic defensiveness that protected the place they called home.

Race remained a more insurmountable barrier to civic participation, though African American St. Paulites worked assiduously to claim their place in the larger urban community. Still, racial tension seldom broke the surface of civic peace. St. Paul's black population was exceedingly small—just over 1 percent of city residents at the turn of the century, increasing only to 2.5 percent by 1960. Other minorities numbered no more than a few hundred persons. Minneapolis was equally racially homogeneous. The relatively small number of African Americans minimized overt racial tensions, enabling the illusion of racial tolerance to go unchallenged in the public sphere for decades. In reality, however, though the black community in St. Paul was exceptionally diverse and relatively prosperous, it remained marginalized from the city at large until the 1960s. The absence of race as a central problem fundamentally differentiates the dynamics that shaped St. Paul—and Minneapolis—from the more complicated text of most other urban studies, but it also brings other sources of tension into sharper relief.

Tensions were always abundant in St. Paul, despite a population that was never less than 75 percent northern European. The political culture that came to characterize the city was the result of multiple clashes and compromises—social processes that are obscured by labels of parochialism or conservatism. My aim has been to reinterpret the politics and culture of St. Paul as an encounter between the place-based priorities of daily life and the larger forces of capital and power in a rapidly changing world. Inspired by Charles Tilly's call for an invigorated model of urban history that "attacks big questions, links large processes with local life, and takes the effect of time and place seriously," the story that unfolds in the following chapters represents an attempt to respond to that challenge.[21]

Fig. 1. St. Paul, Minnesota Territory, 1851. Courtesy of the Minnesota Historical Society.

I. STARTING FROM SCRATCH
The Construction of Civic Identity

Chapter 1

THE ECONOMY OF CULTURE:

City Building on the Frontier

On the evening of June 17, 1890, Deputy U.S. Marshal W. S. Daggett set off from St. Paul on a most unusual mission. Accompanied by a cadre of St. Paul police officers, his destination was a downtown Minneapolis office building where a committee of Minneapolis businessmen was "assisting" census enumerators in tabulating their city's population for the 1890 U.S. census. Though the trip was ten miles from courthouse to courthouse, the law enforcement team passed through only a few miles of open land between the two business districts. The cities were growing at such a rapid pace that by the end of the nineteenth century, it was apparent that soon only the boundary of the Mississippi River would mark where one city ended and the other began.

On reaching their destination, Marshal Daggett and his team thundered up the stairs of the Vandenburgh Building and battered down the Census Bureau's office door. The startled enumerators found themselves staring down the barrel of a gun. Producing warrants for the men's arrest, the marshal and his deputies herded them into a patrol wagon and spirited them off to St. Paul, where they were arraigned on charges of alleged census fraud.[1]

Minneapolis civic leaders were livid. The following day, two hundred of the city's leading businessmen and professionals convened an "indignation meeting" to compose a formal protest. According to the Minneapolis businessmen, the St. Paul citizens' committee had "for weeks patrolled our streets and dogged our census takers with paid Pinkerton detectives." With injured if disingenuous feeling, they declared that "these acts of insolence and violation of every principle of common decency and law are direct attacks upon the spirit of harmony so long publicly and earnestly encouraged by Minneapolis between the Twin Cities." More candidly capturing the relations between the two cities, one committee member observed, it "only goes to show how meanly and despicably St. Paul people can act."

The most damning assessment, however, may also have been the most accurate: "It looks as if St. Paul was in desperate straits."[2] In the clubrooms of St. Paul's posh Minnesota Club, the city's financiers and businessmen apparently had reached a similar conclusion.

In the spring of 1890, enumerators trudged up and down city streets and country roads across the United States, counting the population for the eleventh decennial census. Businessmen and politicians in cities throughout the nation anxiously awaited the results, for as one contemporary Minneapolis booster pronounced, "Population is the true test of a city's greatness. . . . Population brings wealth. Men are so much capital to a state." Population, he asserted, influenced every indicator on which new investment was based—commerce, industry, consumption, and the level of wages. Census figures also would determine apportionment in Congress and in the state legislatures.[3] Thus, the population count was no mere statistical endeavor. The outcome was directly tied to money and power.

For St. Paul and Minneapolis, squaring off against one another across the Mississippi River, the census enumeration was particularly charged, pitting the growing industrial might of Minneapolis against the wavering commercial dominance of St. Paul. In 1880, for the first time, the Minneapolis population had outpaced the capital city by some five thousand persons. Undaunted for the moment, St. Paul boosters continued to tout their superiority as the "metropolis of the Northwest— gateway to the Pacific and the depot and entrepôt of a commerce continental in its proportions." As for the troubling 1880 census report, they insisted that the two populations were "substantially equal," attributing the discrepancy to temporary fluctuations in the economy and alleged irregularities in the enumeration process. At the time, this explanation seemed reasonable. As the acknowledged transportation hub of the Northwest, Minnesota's capital enjoyed the role of preeminent wholesaling center of the region, recording sales of more than $46 million in 1881. By 1883, the city ranked ninth among the nation's commercial and financial centers, with the total capital in St. Paul banks tallied at more than $5.5 million.[4]

Nonetheless, in 1885, with the industrial engines of Minneapolis in full swing, the state census revealed that the population gap had widened to nearly eighteen thousand (despite Minneapolis allegations that St. Paul had counted the residents of its cemeteries in an effort to pad the returns). Not only had Minneapolis earned the title of flour-milling capital of the world and national ranking among the country's manufacturers; the "Mill City" also was rapidly chipping away at St. Paul's predominance in the jobbing and wholesaling trades.[5]

All this bad news was quite a blow to local pride, not to mention the potential effect on local pocketbooks. Grappling with the unhappy turn of events, St. Paul promoters suddenly found appeal in the idea of a combined metropolis, a proposition they had scorned while they held the upper hand. But revised circumstances required a revised scenario. With the astonishing rate of expansion, the city papers claimed, "Before too many years pass by, the two cities will be one." In 1888, one

Fig. 2. Bird's-eye view of St. Paul in 1890 on the eve of the census war. Photo by Truman W. Ingersoll. Courtesy of the Minnesota Historical Society.

St. Paul hagiographer confidently predicted a union of the two cities "not far in the distance, and with these combined elements a power will spring into existence here that will challenge the admiration of the world."[6]

Gloating Minneapolitans scoffed at the proffered olive branch. The Minneapolis press noted that "there is nothing in the figures to encourage the hope that Minneapolis will grow toward St. Paul." Quite the contrary, it noted; while St. Paul might be straining to expand toward Minneapolis, Minneapolis was developing away from St. Paul. As for the open land between the two cities (recently annexed by St. Paul), a grim future was predicted:

> The necessities of railroads for transfer and trackage facilities, for the joint use of the two cities, will fill the intervening territory with half-way houses, shanty neighborhoods, saloons, and a shifting, irresponsible population, recruited from the worse elements of both Minneapolis and St. Paul. . . . The inevitable tendency will be downward, and the indications plainly point to this state of things for the future.[7]

As one publication, endorsed by the Minneapolis mayor, Chamber of Commerce, and Board of Trade declared with typical disdain, "We do not have the heart to reproach the yearning of St. Paul to get nearer to her beautiful, stalwart sister;

but . . . [Minneapolis] would rather remain single than unite her fortunes with such an insinuating, patronizing suitor as St. Paul."[8] Working up to a rhetorical crescendo, the author declaimed that while "St. Paul (for the present) must be the capital of Minnesota," it would be useless for her to claim more: "She may aspire to [large things]; there's no law against a legitimate desire to want the earth, but the fates and the facts and the figures are all against her. . . . Minneapolis is the pet of the universe! She has the nerve and the enterprise to seize the reins."[9]

St. Paul residents swallowed such insults with poor grace, and the long-standing rivalry between the two cities escalated into outright hatred, particularly on the St. Paul side of the river. By 1890, the two cities made no pretense at cooperation. Any initiative that might benefit one city was automatically opposed by the other. When, in 1890, St. Paul sought federal funds to construct a hydroelectric dam, the *Minneapolis Tribune* declared it a "perfect absurdity" to support a scheme that would benefit its neighbor.[10] It seemed to St. Paul businessmen that Minneapolis interests blocked their every effort to regain parity. Their dreams of grandeur for St. Paul were rapidly slipping away. Thus, the result of the upcoming census count was an issue that merited drastic measures.

The "midnight raid" of the census office succeeded in discrediting the Minneapolis tabulations but, in the end, proved a somewhat hollow victory for its St. Paul orchestrators (though the negative national publicity it focused on Minneapolis was briefly gratifying). Minneapolis civic leaders countered the attack by accusing the St. Paul Census Committee of fraud in its own enumerations. By the time federal investigators had sorted out all the claims and counterclaims, they determined a recount was in order in both cities. According to the ensuing investigator's report, "There's every indication that St. Paul is as bad as Minneapolis."[11]

This was not at all what St. Paul civic leaders had in mind. Though the *Pioneer Press* railed against the injustice of coupling "scattered cases of error" in St. Paul with the "colossal" organized fraud of Minneapolis, such civic indignation proved to be more than a bit unwarranted. Among the "scattered cases of error," the investigation of St. Paul's enumeration turned up hundreds of nonexistent residences, numerous single-family dwellings that supposedly housed between 60 and 100 persons, 275 people residing in the Union Depot, 93 in the Market Restaurant, 25 in the barber shop of the Ryan Hotel, and 71 in the offices of the *St. Paul Globe,* where the paper's journalists were classified as "servants."[12]

When the recount was completed, the census war had turned out to be nearly a zero-sum game. The revised population figures demonstrated that both cities had engaged in creative tabulation practices. To be sure, Minneapolis had been a bit more successful than St. Paul, padding its total by 11 percent to St. Paul's 7 percent—thus outstripping its rival yet again. With Minneapolis' population figures reduced by 18,229 and St. Paul's by 9,425, Minneapolis still emerged the victor by a margin of more than 31,000 persons.[13]

Though the revised totals still demonstrated phenomenal rates of growth for both cities—251 percent for Minneapolis and 221 percent for St. Paul—neither

FOR HER HONOR'S SAKE.

There are cases where a brother must interfere in his sister's affairs.

Figs. 3a and 3b (following page). St. Paul editorial cartoonists took the moral high ground in exposing fraudulent enumeration practices in Minneapolis, *Saint Paul News*, 28 June 1890. When the recount was completed, Minneapolis returned the favor, *Minneapolis Journal*, 1 August 1890.

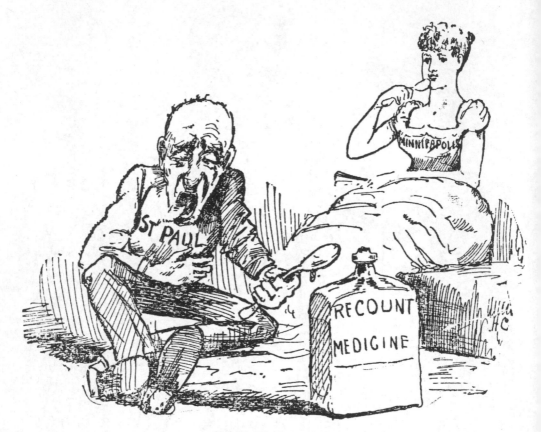

HOW IT WORKS.
JUST WHAT MINNEAPOLIS WANTED, BUT THE SAME MEDICINE MAKES ST. PAUL SICK.   HONEST
PEOPLE DON'T OBJECT TO INVESTIGATION.

city would experience such explosive growth again. The frontier period was ending, as was the moment of opportunity to become the queen city of the Northwest. In subsequent decades St. Paul would slip inexorably further behind. By 1910, Minneapolis outpaced St. Paul by more than 86,000 persons; by 1920, the disparity had increased to nearly 146,000. St. Paul's population stabilized at 234,698 in 1920 and edged only slightly upward over the course of the following seventy years.[14] By the end of the "census war," the men of the Minnesota Club were forced to recognize that St. Paul's glory days were on the wane.

They must have asked themselves how such a thing had come to pass. Only thirty years earlier, a spectacular future had beckoned. Located at the headwaters of the Mississippi, connected by the Red River Trail to the boundless wealth of the Canadian fur trade, and positioned to become the rail center for an emerging western agricultural empire, St. Paul had appeared destined for greatness. How had

Minneapolis—not even incorporated as a city until 1856—snatched the prize from their hands?

Though St. Paul and Minneapolis grew up practically within shouting distance of one another, their cultural and economic landscapes developed with distinctly different patterns. The focus on trade and transportation that had privileged St. Paul in the early days of settlement and crowned it as the state capital ultimately would doom it to fall behind industrial Minneapolis. In St. Paul's losing struggle for economic and political dominance, a cultural terrain was forged that would have a lasting impact on the city's subsequent history.

In the mid-nineteenth century, when eastern cities were already beginning to grapple with the complicated problems of urbanization, industrialization, and the influx of a new immigrant population, Minnesota was still an uninvaded land of forest and prairie, a jumping-off point for the frontier. No part of the territory was officially opened for settlement until 1837, when land-cession treaties were wrested from the Dakota and Ojibwe tribes. Even after the lands were opened, in-migration lagged, since popular opinion in the East held that the territory was too far north and too cold to sustain agriculture. Only a few adventurous souls initially dared to take the arduous trek up the river to stake out claims. But as glowing accounts of the "healthful" climate, bountiful resources, and economic opportunity made their way back to friends and relatives in the East, the trickle of migration began to swell; by mid-century, it had become a torrent.[15]

The new arrivals who disembarked at the St. Paul landing in the 1850s entered a world that was culturally unfixed and rife with possibilities. A traveler's account, published in 1850, colorfully described the "most peculiar feature of the capital of Minnesota, which in respect to its inhabitants differs from any place I have visited in the west":

> A motley group of human beings, gathered from all parts of the Union, the Canadas, the Indian lands, and Pembina, besides the curiously mixed up race of natives. . . . Being an old settlement of French and half-breeds, and the present seat of government for the territory. . . . All the different classes, however, mingle together, forming a singular mass, variously habited, speaking different languages, and distinguished by a variety of complexions, features and manners.[16]

The settlement had been founded in 1838 in the most haphazard fashion by men with no thought of city building on their minds. On the contrary, their common bond was an aversion to the constraints of "civilization." Primarily French Canadian and mixed-blood voyageurs, they had made their way in the northwestern wilderness as trappers, traders, guides, and interpreters for the American Fur Company and the military outpost of Fort Snelling, established on the western heights of the Mississippi River to protect the fur trade. A footloose and independent lot, many engaged in a thriving whiskey trade with the Indians and the soldiers at the fort. By 1838, "beastly scenes of intoxication among the soldiers of this garrison and the Indians in its vicinity" drove post commandant Joseph Plympton to expel all civilians from the military reserve.[17]

Unfazed, the whiskey entrepreneurs simply removed themselves across the boundary line of the reserve to the eastern shore of the river and reestablished business as usual. Plympton's edict also evicted a handful of impoverished settlers who had clustered near the fort. Refugees from the hardships of the ill-fated Canadian Selkirk settlement, these weary Swiss and German immigrants had no heart for further travels and followed the traders across the river. Together, the traders and displaced settlers informally founded the rough settlement—soon known to the Dakota as "the place where they sell Minne-wakan [alcohol]." French and English speakers dubbed the outpost "Pig's Eye," in recognition of Pierre "Pig's Eye" Parrant, its most notorious whiskey trader, until, thanks to the urging of its first Catholic priest, in 1848 the infant town was christened St. Paul.[18]

The very name "Pig's Eye" attests that these early settlers had no urban pretensions. Nor did they yearn to accumulate and capitalize on the rich lands around them, more closely sharing the *mentalité* of the Native Americans they moved among than that of the land-hungry settlers who would follow. Though a few formed families and established homesteads, the value of land claims for most of St. Paul's first residents lay in their usefulness as a medium of exchange rather than as an opportunity to put down permanent roots. With bewildering rapidity the settlers staked claims, traded them away for a barrel of whiskey or a few dollars, then claimed other sections of the seemingly limitless land.[19]

For some soldiers at the fort, including a number of Irish immigrants, this untrammeled lifestyle was an alluring prospect that drew them to settle among the voyageurs when they received their discharges. Not only were they beyond the reach of formal mechanisms of order, but here was a place where social distinction was based on physical strength and courage rather than on ethnic or social pedigree—no small attraction for Irish immigrants familiar with discrimination in the cities to the east. Other racial differences also blurred; many of the settlers were of mixed blood, and marriage with Dakota or Ojibwe women was a commonly accepted practice among all.[20] James Thompson, a freed slave who had been an interpreter at the fort, made a home in this circle, married a Native American wife, and became a builder and ferry boat operator. One early St. Paul biographer, himself an "old settler," described Thompson in terms that suggest a certain fluidity of racial boundaries. According to this contemporary, Thompson was "fully equal both to the white or the Indian when [the Indian was] a free man. . . . [and] played an important part in the history of our city and our state," with "nothing to mar a well-earned reputation."[21]

Still, this was no utopian, egalitarian society. Among the frontier adventurers was a coterie of well-situated Old Stock Americans and Anglo-Canadians who wielded considerable power and influence as agents and traders for the American Fur Company. Though they were not conventional mercantile capitalists and had

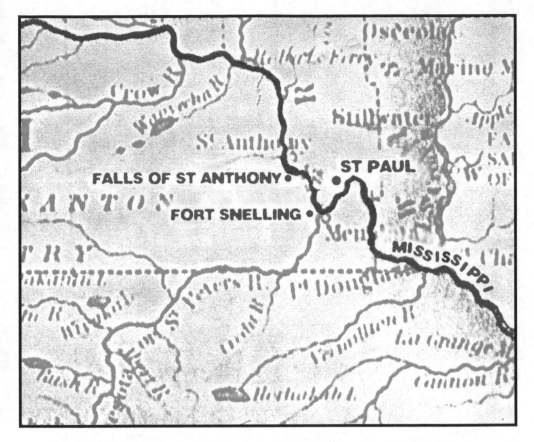

Fig. 4. Detail of Minnesota territorial map in 1849. Land west of the Mississippi River remained part of the Fort Snelling Military Reserve and closed to settlement until 1856, when Minneapolis was established at the site of St. Anthony Falls. Created by Cory Barton. Property of the author.

taken to the frontier for the adventure and "refuge from puritanism" it offered, ✓ they also had the acquisitive entrepreneurial instincts of their English forebears. Backed by association with a company described by one historian as "almost as powerful in the region as the government of the United States," these agents took full advantage of the opportunities frontier development provided. Henry Sibley, a partner in the "Western Outfit" of the company and the most prominent among the group, reminisced that he and his contemporaries did not take up the life of Indian trader for "love of money . . . for rarely could or did a trader accumulate or become wealthy," but rather to be "liberated from all the trammels of society, independent, and free to act according to his own pleasure."[22]

More often than not, however, their pleasure to act as they chose brought the fur trade agents personal gain and, in the process introduced "civilization" to the frontier. Though they dressed the part of frontiersmen and mingled with the traders, guides, and Natives, they were in fact the bridge that would carry Minnesota to statehood and transform Pig's Eye into the urban center of St. Paul. For example, Sibley, his fellow agent Henry Rice, and Indian agent Charles Flandrau (all three with some training in the law) actively participated in Indian removal from Minnesota, speculated in land acquisition, and rose to prominence in state politics. Among them, they held an array of influential public offices. Sibley served as territorial congressman and as the state's first governor, Rice as senator, and Flandrau as a justice of the territorial and state supreme courts. From these positions of power, they were able to lobby for statehood and for public land grants to spur railroad development and migration into the territory.[23]

By the 1850s a substantial cohort of former fur traders had settled permanently in St. Paul, where for the following three decades they energetically engaged in real estate speculation, set up businesses, sat on company boards, and held numerous positions in local associations and municipal government. Though in his memoirs Sibley mourned the disappearance of the frontier and the "noble savage," at a testimonial dinner held in St. Paul in 1885 the old trader and former governor sounded more like Babbitt than Natty Bumppo. He thanked God for "the transformation of this region from a howling wilderness, tenanted alone by wild beasts and savage men, into a proud and powerful commonwealth."[24]

By the mid-1840s, the former fur company agents were stoking up the engines of change, but the multicultural vagabonds who had settled Pig's Eye as yet had little indication that they were sitting on a future metropolis. Formal governance was at a minimum.[25] Disputes were most often settled informally and immediately, with fists, knives, or guns, and the only enterprise carried on with some consistency was a booming traffic in the liquor trade. In 1846, the settlement claimed only twenty families, "not more than three or four of whom were white," along with perhaps a half-dozen traders. Nonetheless, change was in the air. A stream of migration had begun, originating in all parts of the East and South but most often funneled through Prairie du Chien, Wisconsin, the provisioning point for the fur company's Western Outfit, where rumors abounded that fortunes were to be made in St. Paul.[26] Granted the title of territorial capital in 1849, the settlement formally established itself as a town, with proper lots surveyed and platted. The newcomers who snapped up the lots had a different design for the town's future than had its *Canadienne* founders. Backed by the powerful Sibley and Rice, and most often with fur trade connections of their own, these adventurers also had the means to impose their vision.[27]

The influence of fur-trade capital was everywhere apparent, and the north–south axis of the fur-trade routes, rather than western expansion, fueled St. Paul's first burst of growth. Mercantile and transportation entrepreneurs capitalized on its strategic location, where the Mississippi River trade met the Red River Trail leading to the settlements of the Hudson's Bay Company across the Canadian border. More than one hundred Red River carts, loaded with furs, made the 448–mile trip to St. Paul in 1851, then returned north overflowing with goods purchased from local provisioners. By 1863, though the quantity of furs had decreased, the value of the pelts marketed at St. Paul peaked at more than $250,000, which fed directly into the local economy. The furs continued their journey down the Mississippi by steamboat, which, by 1853, made dockings at St. Paul thrice weekly, laden with goods and hopeful new residents—sometimes more than one hundred in a single steamer. In 1855 one local packet company declared a dividend of $100,000 on the season's business; hotels and boarding houses were bursting at the seams, with people even camping in the streets; every sort of business was "fairly coining money." Skilled workmen could almost name their wage, and the local paper bemoaned the scarcity of mechanics to keep up with the building demands.[28]

Men on the make were everywhere. An 1850 traveler's account noted that, along with the multiethnic mosaic "may be seen another class, which by the way is too numerous for so small a community. . . . This is composed of a host of lawyers, politicians, office-holders and office-seekers . . . refugees from other States . . . actuated by the hope of gaining some honorable position and a share of the public spoils. . . . The character is decidedly Eastern."[29] By 1855, the population had quadrupled to nearly 5,000 residents; five years later, it had more than doubled again, soaring to 10,401. St. Paul had become a boom town.[30] With the opening of the lands west of the Mississippi, the possibilities for growth appeared limitless. Perched at the trading nexus of the Northwest, some local boosters began to dream that St. Paul might even challenge Chicago as an entrepôt.

Social pretensions among the nascent elites grew even faster than their fortunes as they strove to produce a frontier version of fashionable society, replete with "brilliant" parties, balls, fairs, and musical soirees. Pedigrees, though most often brief, were highly valued. Of one new bride, the gossip went: "'Tis said her father was a mechanic in Hartford and that she has been a governess. Too bad to let such a rumor get about."[31] The fragile upper crust vigilantly guarded its dubious credentials. Matilda Rice, wife of civic leader Henry, recounted an occasion when, due to a shortage of ladies, a chambermaid was recruited as a dancing partner. Unfortunately, the gentlemen—including the one who had brought her—"jealous of their social standing," refused to dance with the young lady. The problem was resolved only when a politician stepped in to claim her as his partner. In Mrs. Rice's cynical opinion, he "saw the opportunity of a lifetime. He would show the people that he was democratic, that he drew no social lines, that his sympathies were with the struggling masses."[32]

The masses were indeed a problem for the incipient civic leaders. If St. Paul was to realize its destiny as a great urban metropolis, they first had to grapple with the problem of social order. It was one thing for brandy, oysters, and champagne to flow at upper-class affairs, but quite another for the French Canadian original settlers and growing numbers of Irish immigrants to entertain themselves in the town's more disreputable saloons. Growth had so far outpaced institution building that the booming town found itself with few mechanisms of social control, and the al-

Fig. 5. A caravan of Red River carts rolls into town in 1857 to exchange furs for provisions purchased from St. Paul merchants. Courtesy of the Minnesota Historical Society.

ternative culture of Pig's Eye vied with Yankee mercantilism to define its emerging character.

With only rudimentary forms of law enforcement to manage the polyglot population, the aspiring elites leaned on the cultural authority of the one institution that wielded influence among the town's first residents—the Catholic Church. The timely arrival in 1841 of French missionary Father Lucien Galtier, had woven the church immediately into the developing social fabric of St. Paul. The early establishment of a Catholic presence served an instrumental purpose that would grant the church and its clergy an enduring status in the life of the city. Never marginalized as it was in eastern cities, Catholicism was welcomed here by Catholics and Protestants alike, though for quite dissimilar reasons. For the Catholic population, it represented cultural continuity; for the Protestant urban entrepreneurs, it provided a much-needed mechanism to achieve social order.

Though probably few of the French Canadian and Irish first residents were punctilious in performing their religious duties, Catholicism was an integral element of their cultural identity.[33] The rare arrival of a Catholic priest at Fort Snelling had been invariably "a cause of great joy to the Catholics." According to a report by Father Galtier, "They manifested a great desire to assist at divine worship, and to approach the sacraments of the Church." When the priest proposed to establish a permanent church at Pig's Eye in 1841, he was received with open arms. French Canadian settlers Vital Guerin and Benjamin Gervais donated a commanding site on the river bluff for a church, garden, and graveyard, and Catholic communicants provided the materials and labor to erect the "Chapel of St. Paul." So delighted were the residents of Pig's Eye with their first community institution that they rechristened the river settlement in its honor.[34]

By the time the first Protestant church was erected in 1848, the Catholic Church had already become an established community institution. When Father Galtier turned his ministry over to Augustine Ravoux, another French missionary, in 1844, he had recorded 454 Canadian and Irish worshippers at St. Paul and another 130 at Fort Snelling.[35] Three years later, the growing number of communicants required an addition to the chapel, and in 1851 the diocese of St. Paul was formally established. According to the *Minnesota Pioneer,* the arrival of St. Paul's first bishop, French-born Joseph Cretin, "was hailed with considerable enthusiasm by our Catholic fellow-citizens." The chapel overflowed with people eager to receive his blessing, the bishop addressed his new flock in both French and English, and as the familiar strains of the *Te Deum* and the *Magnificat* echoed across the river, the entire congregation was moved to tears. The event was greeted with anticipation rather than alarm by the non-Catholic population as well. The *Minnesota Chronicle and Register* noted, "This will insure the building of a splendid Cathedral here, to supply the religious wants of the numerous members of that denomination, and incidentally add to the architectural beauty of the growing town."[36]

The pioneer priests of St. Paul were uniquely credentialed to be accepted by the budding upper class. By mid-century, in most of the United States, the Catholic Church had begun to take on a distinctly Irish character, which only fueled growing nativist sentiment. But the priests who journeyed to the wilds of the Northwest were a different strain of Catholic. These missionaries were drawn from the French bourgeoisie—sons of bankers, merchants, and prosperous artisans who set off for the North American wilderness as a great adventure, much like the young men who had followed the fur trade. Many of them tempered by years of hardship on the frontier as missionaries to the Native Americans, the priests had the ready respect of hard-bitten veterans like Sibley and Rice as well as the Catholic voyageurs. The nouveau elite of St. Paul regarded the educated Frenchmen as dashing aristocrats and welcomed them into their social circle. Moreover, the ambitious town builders recognized that the clerics shared their interest in bringing civilization to the rude hamlet. Imbued with vivid memories of Catholic persecution following the French Revolution, the French missionaries were fiercely devoted to establishing an unassailable Catholic institution, a project that required the social and material uplift of their unlettered congregants.[37]

By the time Protestant churches began to appear in St. Paul, Father Ravoux was a prominent citizen of the growing town, and Catholic institution-building was poised to take off. Bishop Cretin, on his arrival in 1850, wasted no time in laying the foundation for the centerpiece of his new diocese. He had persuaded seven clerics and seminarians—six French and one iconoclastic Italian—to join him in the enterprise and promised he would "neglect nothing to promote education and morality in St. Paul."[38]

The settled Catholics, especially the early French Canadian landholders who had formed families, also shared this social agenda.[39] In January 1852, French Canadian community leaders met with Bishop Cretin to organize the Catholic Temperance Society of St. Paul. Eighty-five French Canadians and thirty-six Irish Catholics signed the temperance pledge and promised to "daily recite the Lord's prayer for the promotion of the cause of temperance." Despite its impressive membership list, the society appears to have had a short life, perhaps because many of its hard-pressed members were attracted more by the sick and funeral benefits it promised than by a desire for moral uplift. At any rate, the attempt to tame the boisterous town surely did not go unappreciated by its civic leaders.[40]

The "civilizing" effect of the Catholic church was everywhere apparent in the loosely organized settlement. Within a year of Bishop Cretin's arrival, backed by financial support from the French Society for the Propagation of the Faith, the log chapel had been replaced by a three-storied combination cathedral and school for boys. Three years later, the city's Catholics had outgrown the new building, and an even larger and more imposing edifice was constructed. The log chapel became a school for girls under the direction of four French nuns, from the order of St. Joseph of Carondelet, whom the bishop had induced to relocate from St. Louis. The sisters soon took on the added responsibility of caring for the town's orphans and running St. Joseph's Hospital, which Cretin erected on land donated by Henry Rice. When devastating cholera epidemics struck the town in 1854 and 1855, residents had yet another reason to appreciate the Catholic presence. Local editors increasingly rhapsodized over the selfless devotion of the nuns, "those angels of mercy, the Sisters of St. Joseph, to whom the care of the distressed is a joyful trouble."[41] The community's esteem for the Catholic Church clearly owed as much to the work of these dedicated nuns as to the efforts of the bishop.

In the boom years of the 1850s, the fortunes of the Catholic Church rose on the general tide of prosperity. Of course, not all St. Paul's citizens viewed the Catholic presence as a blessing. As native-born easterners swelled the ranks of St. Paul residents, many inevitably carried with them acculturated fear and dislike of the Catholic Church; such opinions made little headway, however, in a social world where the established elites already had determined the social value of the Catholic clergy. As the editor of the *Minnesota Democrat* declared in 1855, though he was "no believer in the Catholic religion," he was willing to do them justice" and abhorred those who would "attack some of our best citizens and represent them as criminals of the deepest dye." Thus, social pressure from the town's most prominent citizens, buttressed by the press, soon relegated anti-Catholicism to no more than a disgruntled murmur on the political fringe.[42]

The late-coming Protestant clerics were quite dismayed to find papism so firmly ensconced in the community and worked assiduously to make up for lost time—fostering rivalry among the various denominations to outdo one another in providing service to the community. This competition for the hearts and minds of St. Paul residents provided a municipal boon, creating an exceptional number of charitable and educational institutions—a dense, privately managed social welfare net that significantly reduced the demand for public relief. As the city grew, the proliferation of parochial and private schools also would ease the financial burden on the public education system and grace St. Paul with four private colleges by the turn of the century.[43]

Catholics were in the forefront of all these initiatives. From the outset, Bishop Cretin and his confrères recognized what was at stake. In a letter to the Society for the Propagation of the Faith, Cretin warned that the Presbyterians and Methodists were building colleges, with "subscriptions collected with the avowed purpose of stopping the progress of Papism in the State of Minnesota. Nothing therefore must be neglected to found educational institutions." The editor of the *Minnesota Pioneer* tried to spur Protestants forward in an editorial that decried the state of "little untaught brats . . . along the streets and along the levee in utter idleness. . . . All this in a town that boasts half a dozen steepled churches. If St. Paul is not a priest-ridden town, it is in a fair way to be."[44]

Still, to most St. Paulites, the obvious benefits of Catholic institution-building far outweighed the liabilities. By 1867, the Catholic schools' enrollment of more than nine hundred children greatly reduced the demands on public education. Indeed, as one disgruntled Catholic complained, non-Catholics enjoyed double their share of the school fund, since parochial schools, which operated without public monies, cut the public school population by half. Nonetheless, as Baptist minister Lyman Palmer ruefully pointed out, "The elite of St. Paul Protestants send their daughters to the Catholic School."[45]

Indeed, Protestant St. Paul derived significant benefits from Catholic initiatives. The church fueled development of the city's institutional infrastructure and used its authority to discipline the Catholic masses, leaving the Yankee entrepreneurs free to concentrate on making their fortunes. As their wealth increased, the emerging elite then contributed liberally to the churches where they worshipped. Thus, in a convoluted manner, the Catholic clergy indirectly helped secure the wealth of the emerging Protestant congregations. Prosperity among the city's Catholics, however, did not grow in tandem with the church's increasing prominence. Seminarian Daniel Fisher (the sole Anglo-Saxon Catholic cleric in the city) noted in 1852 that "the Catholics are very poor here . . . Half-breeds, Canadians and Irish. The Yankees have all the influence, the wealth and the power, although they are not near as numerous as the others."[46]

The enduring prominence of the Catholic Church in St. Paul was ensured because the institutional structure preceded rather than followed the waves of Irish and German immigration that would inundate the city in the following half century, which transformed the cultural makeup of its Catholic population. As for the original congregants, the Native Americans were soon to be legally "removed" from the territory, and most of the French Canadians (and the majority of the early Irish settlers as well) gradually disappeared from the city census rolls. The extensive lands they had once claimed quickly slipped into the hands of Yankee developers with more acquisitive instincts. The ethos of "progress," development, and accumulation of wealth was culturally alien to the former voyageurs, who gave away land with generous disregard or sold it for a fraction of its potential worth. Some, no doubt, were cheated and reduced to poverty by canny speculators, but others simply found city life distasteful.[47]

The original French Canadian settlers set off no ensuing chain migration of friends and relatives. Theirs had been an occupational migration. As the fur trade declined and St. Paul evolved into an urban center, French Canadians retreated north in a return migration rather than toward the urban magnet. Of those who stayed in the vicinity, most moved beyond the reach of the city. By 1870, nearly eight hundred French Canadians were living in the rural enclave of Little Canada, northeast of St. Paul. By 1900, less than five thousand first-or second-generation French Canadians remained in the city—a mere 3 percent of its residents.[48]

But for every old settler who left, a hundred newcomers arrived to take his or her place. From 1850 to 1857, the city experienced manic growth. On a single day in 1854, six steamboats arrived, landing more than six hundred passengers. Twenty-eight thousand visitors registered at the city's four hotels in 1856. And by the summer of 1857, St. Paul was said to be

> the fastest and liveliest town on the Mississippi. . . . The hotels and boarding houses were crowded to overflowing. The principal business streets fairly hummed with the rush of busy life. Business was never so brisk; an army of workmen and mechanics labored night and day to keep up with the demand for dwellings and stores. . . . Saloons, of course, throve as they always do. . . . The city was continually full of tourists, speculators, sporting men and women and even worse characters, all spending gold as though it was dross.[49]

Fueling all this activity was a real estate mania driven by "a mad, crazy, reckless spirit of speculation," vividly described in an eyewitness account:

> Everybody seemed inoculated with the mania, from the moneyed capitalist to the humble laborer who could merely squat on a quarter section, and hold it for a rise. The buying of real estate, often at the most insane prices, and without regard to its real value, infected all classes, and almost absorbed every other passion and pursuit. . . . Agriculture was neglected, and breadstuffs enough for home consumption

were not raised. . . . Farmers, mechanics, laborers even, forsook their occupations
to become operators in real estate, and grow suddenly rich, as they supposed.[50]

In August 1857, the bubble burst. A world away from the burgeoning outpost,
the Ohio Equitable Life Insurance Company failed in spectacular fashion, setting off a national financial panic. The reverberations from the crash of the eastern money market brought this frontier paper kingdom tumbling down. Real estate was suddenly "valueless and unsaleable at any price." Banks closed their
doors, business was paralyzed, and hard currency virtually disappeared. The city
lost half its population, and not one in five businesses survived the crash. Most
of the fledgling elites found themselves with empty pockets once again. Four
years after the crash, survivor Henry Rice ruefully assessed the damages: "One
thing I do see . . . is that *all* of the Old settlers in Minnesota are *ruined* hopelessly." As the city struggled to pull itself out of the wreckage, the playing field
had been leveled, and Yankee dominance would never be quite so monolithic
again.[51]

How did Minneapolis fare in this scenario of boom and bust? That future dynamo
had barely been etched on the map in 1857; it had been incorporated just a year before the crash. The west bank of the Mississippi, where the city would be established, had remained part of the Fort Snelling military reserve and off limits to settlers until 1855. But despite its delayed development, there was never any doubt
that a city would eventually rise on the spot. St. Paul gained its strategic value as
head of navigation for the Mississippi River, but seven miles upstream lay the Falls
of St. Anthony, the only major waterfall on the length of the great river and, in the
age of industrialization, a most valuable resource on which to found an aspiring city.
Ambitious entrepreneurs had long marked the falls for investment and were poised
to make their move. Well before the lands officially opened for settlement, certain
influential men had parlayed political connections to gain first advantage in capturing the waterpower of the falls. Though soldiers periodically evicted squatters from
the reserve and burned their cabins, a few select individuals, by special permission
of the fort commandant, were allowed to stake out land there.[52] That game of influence, patronage, and friendship assured that Minneapolis, from the outset, would
have a markedly different character from that of St. Paul.

St. Anthony Falls was well known throughout the country, thanks to artists' ren-
derings and travelers' accounts. As industrialization took off in the East, curious
capitalists ventured westward to assess the potential of the fabled waterpower. In
1849, Illinois congressman and businessman Robert Smith used his influence in
Washington to lease the land and the army's sawmill at the falls from the War Department. He was joined in the enterprise by fellow congressman Cadwallader C.
Washburn. Neither man became a resident of Minnesota but, nonetheless, their political position and capital resources allowed them to set the tone for the city's development.[53]

By the time the reserve was officially opened for settlement in 1855, Smith and Washburn had consolidated their mills and lands into a partnership of twelve men, including Washburn's younger brother William and cousin Dorilus Morrison (who would become the city's first mayor). Washburn shrewdly had recruited trusted family members to oversee the investment on the ground. The partners moved first to organize the Minneapolis Mill Company, which would control access to the water power of the falls. Next, they established sawmills to harvest the forests on the upper reaches of the river. These enterprises garnered immediate profit. But the partners recognized that the opening of the agricultural hinterland promised even greater returns for future flour milling operations, and they poised themselves to capture this lucrative market. Within ten years, the development of the milling empire had begun. William Washburn and Morrison, as the resident partners of this ambitious enterprise, aggressively positioned themselves to become the most powerful men in Minneapolis.[54]

The success of the Washburn dynasty was a foregone conclusion. Not only did Cadwallader Washburn have access to deep capital reserves—he had already amassed a fortune in timberlands in Wisconsin and eastern Minnesota—but his family had unparalleled political influence. By the mid-1850s, three Washburn brothers served in the U.S. Congress: Cadwallader from Wisconsin, Elihu from Illinois, and Israel from the family home base in Maine.[55] Three other brothers, involved in banking and private business in Maine, provided invaluable sources of capital reinforcement.[56]

The panic of 1857 caused the Minneapolis Washburn combine to tighten its belt temporarily, but the three family members had the reserves to ride out the storm. In the long term, the panic worked to their advantage, enabling them to squeeze out their other partners. In setting up the partnership, they had inserted a clause requiring the partners to lend the company money through assessments against their shares. When the panic hit, the nine outside partners, lacking the capital reserves available to the Washburns and Morrison, either sold out their shares or defaulted on their assessments one by one, leaving the three men from Maine as sole owners of the single most valuable property in Minnesota.[57]

The critical importance of capital reserves in a frontier economy is displayed vividly in the contrasting fortunes of the village of St. Anthony, located on the east side of the falls. Franklin Steele, a sutler at the fort, had literally run a footrace to claim the water-power site on the Mississippi's eastern bank the very day the lands were opened in 1838. Steele had no less vision than the Washburn brothers about the potential for development; he simply lacked the money to put his plan into action. Forced to cobble together a broad collection of investors, his efforts to develop the site were stymied by chronic cash shortages, squabbling among the partners, and a seemingly endless series of litigation. The financial disaster wrought by the 1857 panic was a blow from which Steele's enterprise never fully recovered. The village of St. Anthony languished along with his milling company until St. Anthony was incorporated as part of Minneapolis in 1872.[58]

Incorporation 1856

Although St. Paul was devastated by the 1857 crash, the setback was not nearly so severe for Minneapolis. Incorporated for less than a year, it did not have as far to fall. The panic drove out fly-by-night speculators and investors, leaving the development of the new city in the hands of a small group of New Englanders who had the resources to survive the immediate disaster and, in the long term, to profit from the crash—gobbling up land at rock-bottom prices. William Washburn, as chief partner of the water-power company, quickly became the preeminent power in Minneapolis, buttressed by a close-knit cohort of like-minded men who, from their base at the falls, would parlay eastern banking and political connections into lumber and grain-milling fortunes. This milling fraternity created a closed circle that would dominate banking, business, politics, and civic culture in the city for nearly a century. Almost all New Englanders—60 percent of the population in 1857 had migrated from Maine—they were products of a chain migration based on previous friendships and on business and family connections.[59]

Thus, Minneapolis differed from St. Paul at its very foundations, both culturally and economically. Its early population was remarkably homogeneous. The rolls of early settlers and residents display a notable lack of ethnic diversity. Primarily Protestant New Englanders, they were not hampered by the internal tensions of a multiethnic society. Proudly declaring themselves the "New England of the West," by 1859 the civic elites had established the New England Society. Even more select was the membership of the Sons of Maine and the Bowdoin College Alumni Association.[60]

The debate surrounding the naming of this little New England illustrates its fundamental difference from St. Paul. Anticipating the imminent release of the reserve lands and readying themselves to launch their metropolitan project, boosters vigorously debated the question of a name for their city-in-the-making even before they had title to the lands on which it would stand. Whereas St. Paul had casually been christened "Pig's Eye" for its most notorious whiskey trader, early industrial visionaries in Minneapolis suggested it be named in honor of Lowell, Massachusetts, since they intended to build their city on the model of that eastern manufacturing dynamo. Where St. Paul acquired its formal name in recognition of the arrival of a Catholic priest, the Yankee enclave on the western side of the river had no such papist leanings. For some time, the settlement had been informally called "All Saints"—intended as a prediction that it would surpass both St. Paul and St. Anthony put together. Though the future civic leaders no doubt agreed with the sentiments behind the title, they wanted no part of the Catholic taint that went with "the miserable misnomer." As newspaper editor Charles Hoag noted, "It is a name that is applicable to not more than two persons in the vicinity of the falls, and of doubtful application even to them." Indeed, two years after incorporation, Minneapolis was home to five Protestant congregations, but not a single Catholic steeple marked its skyline. The name finally settled on was a combination of the Dakota word *minnehaha*, "laughing waters," and the Greek *polis*, or city. To the city's architects, the name perfectly expressed their grand design to transform the wilderness.[61]

While the panic of 1857 wiped out most of St. Paul's original precarious fortunes, making room for a diverse group of small-scale entrepreneurs to get in the game, in Minneapolis the financial collapse cleared the way for a few solidly positioned capitalists to found an empire in milling and manufacturing. For the moment, thanks to its strategic location, St. Paul still held the advantage as a trading and transportation center. It would rebuild its economic viability based on those advantages, though the slender fortunes left in the aftermath of the crash required new coalitions and compromises with German and Irish newcomers. The financial lessons learned in 1857 also fostered a more cautious business outlook that would become part of the enduring culture of the city. The difficult days following the real estate debâcle fostered another cultural imprint as well—that of the Catholic Church. By providing critical services to the struggling citizens, the Church further solidified its position as a part of the civic entity.

In contrast, the men of capital who held the reins in Minneapolis emerged from the panic only slightly bruised. Whatever short-term financial hardships they suffered were more than made up for by the elimination of small-time competitors and those who did not share their design for progress. New Englanders to the core, they set about shaping the city in their image. In the next two decades, the opening of the western lands and the rush of immigration that followed created a hinterland that would fill the city's grain elevators and make Minneapolis's fortune as the milling capital of the world. It would also create an insatiable demand for lumber sawed in the Minneapolis mills and goods produced in its factories. The major beneficiaries of this explosion of growth remained the few dozen men who had capitalized on the water power of the falls in the 1850s. For them, and for Minneapolis, the future was secured.

The battle lines between St. Paul and Minneapolis were drawn—commercial versus industrial capitalism, trade versus manufacture, independent enterprise versus corporate combination. Though the outcome may now seem foreordained, none of this was clear to the participants at the time. For most of Minnesota's short history, the capital city had reigned as its economic leader. By 1872, according to business historian Jocelyn Wills, it had claimed the prize of "undisputed hub for transportation, finance, and wholesaling in Minnesota, Iowa, Dakota, and Manitoba."[62] But less than a decade later, the industrial engines of Minneapolis had propelled it into the lead, leaving St. Paulites shaken. In this contest for economic supremacy and survival, though they were geographic neighbors, the cities increasingly regarded themselves as worlds apart. Their civic identities became predicated on more than the internal elements of ethnicity, religion, and culture; they were defined self-consciously in opposition to the "other"—an other that, at the same time, looked to outsiders to be a nearly identical twin. But for those engaged in the escalating rivalry, whatever common ground they shared was shrinking by the day.

Chapter 2

MONEY, STATUS, AND POWER:

The Making of an Irish-Catholic Town

$\mathbf{M}$innesota won the prize of statehood in May of 1858, but the capital city, reeling from its financial crash, could muster neither the funds nor the enthusiasm to celebrate the event. City papers glumly reported "no immigration," and not one in ten of the old settlers who had gone down in the panic would recover from the disaster.[1] Still, in the estimation of those who managed to ride out the storm, the long-term prospects for St. Paul were undimmed. The fur trade remained a profitable venture; immigrant farmers had begun to fill the hinterland to the north and west, creating a market for enterprising merchants; the harvest had been abundant; agricultural prices were high; and Minnesota had begun to export grain. To make the most of these opportunities, the new state's entrepreneurs and politicians agreed that Minnesota urgently needed a rail network, both to carry new settlers into the state and to transport goods and resources to the market. Local and outside investors held federal land grants to finance railroad building, but the economic collapse had quashed the undertaking overnight. Faith in the enterprise as well as investment capital had disappeared. In 1860, not a mile of track had been laid in the state.[2]

Most Minnesota boosters eagerly courted railroad development, but for some St. Paul capitalists the dearth of rail service spelled personal profit, by granting a reprieve to their established transportation networks. Stagecoach, wagon train, and steamboat operations were saved from obsolescence long enough to give investors time to rebuild their capital reserves. Many of the most substantial and enduring St. Paul fortunes were established in this manner. While railroad development foundered, confining city merchants and wholesalers to a limited market, transportation entrepreneurs reaped substantial rewards.[3] Despite the temporary lull in immigration, settlers in the hinterland needed provisions. Most important, the government had profitable contracts to let—for mail delivery and to supply its western troops and Indian agencies. The political connections nourished in the quest for government contracts proved equally useful in acquiring valuable timber from Indian reservation lands. While national attention was focused on the waging of the Civil War, a small group of Anglo and Anglo-Canadian residents of St. Paul, many connected by blood or marriage, made the most of these opportunities. They then leveraged the cash accrued from these ventures into wide-ranging investments in timber, mining, water power, insurance, and railroads.[4]

By 1862, with war chests replenished, these millionaires on the make were positioned to take full advantage of the passage of the Homestead Act. Though ostensibly the act was designed to attract frontier smallholders, well-heeled investors covertly took title to vast tracts of land by manipulating the terms of the act and using hired preemptors to stake spurious claims. St. Paul financier Amherst Wilder was one among many who profited from such stratagems. Described as a "shadowy merchant prince of the prairies," Wilder's holdings had made him a millionaire by the 1870s. A number of Wilder's business associates—all friends or relatives—enjoyed comparable success in their endeavors.[5]

The important insight to be gained here is that the fortunes of St. Paul's wealthiest elite depended on operations and investments that radiated outside the city. St. Paul served as the base of operations and as financial headquarters, but the source of capital accumulation resided in trade and transportation networks that did not require the services of a large local labor force, nor did city politics impinge significantly on these entrepreneurs' designs for profit. Thus, the men who had the capacity to wield the most power and influence in these early years paid scant attention to the internal workings of the local economy or to the imposition of social order. As the town's foremost citizens, they engaged in hometown boosterism to be sure, promoting St. Paul as a wondrous metropolis in the making; they also supported civic causes and were particularly enthusiastic about developing the municipal infrastructure—sewers, roads, and other improvements that made their lives more pleasant and also increased the value of their real estate holdings. But, though they made St. Paul the banking center for their myriad investments and speculated in local property, their business ventures primarily operated far to the west and north and only indirectly spurred the local economy. The timber harvest that helped make many personal fortunes in St. Paul was transformed from raw material to finished product in the sawmills of its rival. In 1865, Minneapolis produced sixty-two million board-feet of lumber; St. Paul's two small mills were not able to supply even the local demand for building materials.[6]

Minneapolis capitalists, unlike those in St. Paul, built their fortunes on an industrial base that was geographically centered in the city proper. Minneapolis lumber barons fed their harvest to Minneapolis sawmills, which held sway as the state's primary industry until surpassed by flour milling in the 1870s. Both industries were dominated by local combines that channeled their profits into other industrial and manufacturing ventures also located in the city. These operations demanded a large

Fig. 6. While railroad building languished, river trade enjoyed greater prosperity than ever, evident in this view of the lower levee ca. 1865. Photo by Whitney & Zimmerman. Courtesy of the Minnesota Historical Society.

and tractable local labor force, which ensured that those at the pinnacle of power were deeply invested in the maintenance of industrial and social order.[7]

At the time, the problems of economic growth and social order in St. Paul were left primarily to a lower echelon of mercantile entrepreneurs. The collapse of the local economy had deeply injured the emerging Old Stock merchant class. Many small proprietors closed their doors and pulled up stakes. Those who managed to hold on were left with only minimal capital with which to rebuild. As they cast about for an infusion of cash, social snobbery and ethnic or religious prejudice were set aside in the effort to cobble together new business alliances. Irish or German dollars were as green as those of any Anglo-American. By 1860, when migration into the city began to gather steam once again, ethnic newcomers encountered a providential moment of opportunity to mingle easily with the Old Stock in forging a reinvigorated mercantile economy. Even a small stake of capital provided entree into the mainstream economic and social life of the city.

In 1860, more than 50 percent of the city's adult population was foreign born— 23.5 percent German and 26 percent Irish. Even these impressive figures fail to measure fully the ethnic presence, since the 1860 census made no tally of second-generation ethnics, who swelled the Irish contingent considerably.[8] Newcomers to the city, whether Irish, German, or Yankee, discovered quickly that the dream of "rags to riches" was as elusive in St. Paul as anywhere else in the fabled land of opportunity. The promised wealth of the frontier could be purchased only with capital already in hand, either in the form of savings or skills that could generate cash. But for those who could pay the price of entry, neither religion nor ethnicity were exclusionary bars.

As a group, German immigrants had a distinct advantage over the Irish. Most of the Germans had arrived with some combination of necessary skills and capital, as well as a familiarity with the workings of a capitalist economy. Political upheaval, religious persecution, and the impact of industrialization on regional economies in the loose-knit German empire had set off an exodus of artisans, shopkeepers, and farmers rather than a flight of peasants or proletarians. As a result, even most of those who arrived in St. Paul directly from their homeland were armed to compete, culturally as well as economically. As an added advantage, by the close of the Civil War whatever nativist sentiment that had existed toward Germans had largely dissipated throughout the nation.[9] In St. Paul, where their skills and capital were sorely needed, the Germans—whether Protestant, Catholic, or Jewish—found a particularly warm welcome. If some German immigrants tended to cluster apart from the rest of the population, it was from a decided sense of cultural superiority rather than any forced exclusion.[10]

By 1860, German St. Paulites already had made a place for themselves in the economic life of the city. Fully 26 percent of German-born males were engaged in trade and service; another 27 percent were employed in some sort of manufacturing, while only 14 percent worked as common laborers. In 1856, the brothers Ferdinand and Gustav Willius had opened a banking house to serve their enterprising fellow countrymen, one of only two private banking houses to survive the 1857 panic.[11]

Germans moved quickly up the social and economic ladder in St. Paul. While some German businessmen preferred intraethnic partnerships or independent enterprise, a remarkable number of German–Old Stock partnerships soon made an appearance. City business directories displayed a noticeably interethnic character; firms such as Auerbach, Finch, and VanSlyck and Lindekes, Warner & Schurmeier (wholesale drygoods), Foot, Schulze & Co. (boot and shoe manufacturers), and Field, Mahler & Co. (retail dry goods) took their place among the city's most respected and profitable establishments.[12]

Such fluidity may not seem unusual in a rapidly expanding frontier economy, but as late as 1895, interethnic business alliances were a rarity in Minneapolis. In that New England stronghold the Yankee middle and upper classes stubbornly held themselves apart from immigrant newcomers, both in business and in social interactions, fostering the development of separately functioning ethnic subeconomies. The upper echelons of power almost invariably were reserved for the closed club of Yankee

Fig. 7. The Athenaeum, established in 1850, was one of many German organizations dedicated to the celebration of German *Kultur*, as in this 1885 gathering. Photo by Truman W. Ingersoll. Courtesy of the Minnesota Historical Society.

capitalists, who had less need than their St. Paul counterparts to turn to outside sources of investment.[13] The barriers to power, once in place, were not easily over-come. In 1936, *Fortune* magazine noted that although the city had become the nation's largest Scandinavian enclave, "socially and financially Minneapolis is still dominated by the New England families that settled it, and, with three or four exceptions, there are no Scandinavians in positions of importance outside of politics." The author of the article might have added, "and few Germans or Irish, and certainly no Jews." As late as 1946, journalist Carey McWilliams dubbed Minneapolis "the capital of anti-Semitism in the United States." In contrast, McWilliams found St. Paul "relatively free from the odious social restrictions and limitations . . . in Minneapolis."[14]

The distinct social climates that developed are perhaps most sharply delineated by the contrasting history of Jews in the two cities. St. Paul's relatively small contingent of German Jews were early arrivals; nearly all were merchants who brought with them at least a small stake of capital. While some devoted their energies to the establishment of Mount Zion Temple and the maintenance of a vibrant Jewish culture, those who chose a more assimilationist course found easy acceptance among the city's cash-poor merchant class. Merchant Moritz Auerbach took advantage of what historian Gunther Plaut has described as the city's "early tradition of total Jewish acceptance and integration." Auerbach anglicized his name to Maurice; established a wholesale drygoods partnership with George Finch and William VanSlyck; married Matilda Rice, daughter of prominent pioneer Henry Rice; and, as his fortune grew, blended into the ranks of the city's elites, maintaining only tenuous ties with his Jewish heritage.[15]

The economic imperatives that opened this window of opportunity had long-term cultural consequences for all St. Paul Jews. Though hints of anti-Semitism began to appear with the influx of eastern European Jews in the 1880s, it was an identifiably class-based prejudice. German Jews themselves had ambivalent feelings about the culturally alien eastern Europeans. But because Jews were prominent among the city's civic leaders, anti-Semitic sentiments, though an undeniable undercurrent, were not expressed in institutionalized forms of exclusion, leading St. Paul Jews to congratulate themselves and their Christian neighbors for what they deemed an exceptionally broad-minded spirit. In classic St. Paul fashion, Jewish attorney Hiram Frankel attributed this social phenomenon primarily to the superior character of St. Paul's Jews, especially in comparison to their coreligionists in Minneapolis.[16]

In Minneapolis anti-Semitism had deep institutionalized roots, but the character of the city's Jews had little to do with it. Rather, anti-Semitism was simply a particularly overt component of a larger pattern of exclusivity in place from the city's earliest days. Cultured German-Jewish merchants were no less disdained than the more "rustic" eastern European Jews who arrived in later years. As the Jewish population grew, anti-Semitism only became more embedded. Minneapolis Jews were excluded from all sorts of businesses, employment, and organizational memberships, and were unwelcome residents in the more affluent neighborhoods. Just as St. Paul's culture of integration had grown out of a particular economic configuration, anti-Semitism in Minneapolis can be traced to the cultural authority of the city's major capitalists. Once in place, the patterns tended to reinforce themselves, creating radically different social landscapes. For example, by the 1920s, when Jews were denied membership in the Minneapolis Automobile Club, the St. Paul chapter was headed by a Jewish president.[17]

The origin of St. Paul's relative openness toward Jews was not wholly economic. German Jews also benefited from the presence of a burgeoning German Christian population. The commonalties of language, *Kultur*, and social class helped to mediate differences of religion in the new alien environment. While German Protestants, Catholics, and Jews built separate organizations defined by religion, they also collaborated on a variety of German cultural enterprises that reinforced ethnic networks across religious lines. In addition, the Catholic Church and the German-Jewish community maintained a particularly sympathetic relationship, viewing any tendency toward exclusionism as a threat to Catholics and Jews alike.[18] Thus, Jewish St. Paulites were knit into the fabric of the community through intricate threads of economic, ethnic and religious interdependency.

The social web of the city was complex, but its benefits were far less accessible to those who lacked the all-important initial capital stake. Irish immigrants, most of whom arrived with empty pocketbooks, were at a singular disadvantage, both as individuals and as a group. Not only did they have less capital than their German counterparts; they also had to contend with commonly held derogatory Irish stereotypes that migrated with them from the East. Moreover, overwhelmingly Catholic, the Irish had borne the brunt of nativist attacks, culminating in the rise of Know-Nothingism in the 1850s. In freewheeling frontier St. Paul, the force of nativism was considerably blunted, but when combined with the group's overall lack of resources, it worked to provide the Irish a considerably less cordial welcome than that accorded German artisans and merchants. In 1857, the *Daily Minnesotian*, in reporting on heavy immigration from Ireland, commented, "We hope to gracious none of the Paddies will hear where St. Paul is."[19] Yet, despite these undeniable economic and cultural disadvantages, and even though by the 1880s they were outnumbered by both Germans and Scandinavians in the city's population, the Irish rose to exceptional prominence.

How did this come to be? In 1860, of the 1,903 Irish-born males of working age in St. Paul, more than 50 percent were employed as unskilled laborers; no more than 12 percent were engaged in trade.[20] Early city directories reveal few Irish involved in interethnic commercial enterprises. No ethnic banks existed to serve the Irish community. Without access to the avenues of mobility employed by German immigrants, who outpaced the Irish in sheer numbers as well as in tangible assets, the Irish were unlikely candidates for upward mobility. Yet, though statistics demonstrate that the group lagged behind the general population economically through the turn of the century, a small cohort carved a niche of power and influence that, in time, against all odds, turned Irish identity itself into a capital asset and influenced the city so deeply that St. Paul came to be known as an "Irish town."

Politics more than commerce provided the Irish with an initial avenue to influence in St. Paul, which they parlayed into upward mobility and prominence in the city's social structure. As early as the 1850s, when the Irish briefly numerically dominated the immigrant population, Irish candidates regularly won election to city offices. Joseph Cretin, the politically astute bishop, noted in 1852 that already "the Catholic vote is beginning to hold the balance in elections. They do not dare to disregard it."[21] The chief architect of growing Catholic political influence was Irish-Protestant lawyer William Pitt Murray. Seizing the political moment, Murray claimed kinship with his fellow Irishmen, defended their Catholicism, and built a political career (together with French Canadian Louis Robert) by delivering the immigrant Catholic vote in city and state elections. Cut in the mold of the classic Irish politician (despite his Protestant lineage), he was described as "sympathetic, a real friend of the poor, kind-hearted, plain, blunt, smiling 'Bill Murray.' "[22] All this would seem a typical blueprint for the founding of a nineteenth-century urban Irish political machine, a system fashioned on ethnic and class separatism.[23] But in St. Paul, Irish politics (broadly conceived) were much less clearly delineated.

The profile of Irish migration to St. Paul was quite distinct from that to urban centers in the East. Not only were social barriers more permeable in the unformed city, where the Irish were early arrivals, but the very nature of Irish migration also had a different cast. By 1860, a swelling chain migration from Ireland to the United States had been operating for more than a quarter century. For a small but pivotal group of St. Paul Irish, the city was the final destination in a search for prosperity, a staged westward migration from the eastern seaboard. Along the way, they had accumulated skills, particularly in the construction trades, and perhaps even a bit of capital. A number of St. Paul Irish were second-or even third-generation Americans. Moreover, many of those classified as first generation had arrived in the United States as children. As a result, they were far better equipped to negotiate the frontier city than were bewildered, often illiterate, adult immigrants.[24] Census data confirms that these "Americanized" Irish were in the minority; nonetheless, however small, the upwardly mobile cohort played a critical role for the group as a whole, securing jobs, crafting political leverage, and providing a cachet of respectability that softened the contours of anti-Irish prejudice in the city at large.[25]

As the state capital, St. Paul was a particularly fertile field for politicians and lawyers, and the Irish, many of whom had acquired political savvy in eastern enclaves, took full advantage of the opportunities presented. By 1880, 35 percent of the city's lawyers were Irish-born. Partnerships between Old Stock and Irish attorneys became quite common, even among the upper echelon, fostering other interethnic investment partnerships and further blurring the lines of ethnic separatism.[26] Thus, in St. Paul ethnicity did not in itself bar social and economic mobility for the Irish immigrant population. Still, for the majority of the Irish clustered at the bottom of the economic ladder, the material gains they reaped from this cultural openness were slow to materialize. In 1900 30 percent of the city's foreign-stock attorneys were Irish-born, and first-generation Irish held 15 percent of the city's government jobs. But fully 43 percent of the St. Paul Irish remained unskilled laborers—when unskilled labor constituted only 20 percent of the total labor force. The Germans, in contrast, who had the advantages of skills and capital from the outset, had settled comfortably into trade, manufacture, and commerce.[27]

Despite the economic disadvantages that plagued St. Paul's Irish community, Hibernian influence continued to grow. In other cities with strong Irish political machines, such as Boston, San Francisco, or Chicago, working people had overcome similar obstacles by virtue of sheer voting power; St. Paul's demographics did not support a similar strategy, however. Though the majority of the city's early immigrants had Irish origins, by the turn of the century their numbers had fallen far behind those of Germans and Scandinavians (principally Swedes). In 1910, the first- and second-generation ethnic population of the city was led by Germans (25%), followed closely by Scandinavians (15.8%). The Irish had slipped to a mere 7.8 percent of city residents. The German presence was so dominant that it lagged only slightly behind that of the Old Stock American-born (28.7%).[28] By all rights, if the city was to reflect a particular ethnic character, it should have resembled St. Louis more than Boston.

In truth, by the turn of the century it looked like neither. A striking cultural landscape was taking shape that belied the city's demographics. Though a distinct ethnic character was apparent in certain wards where working-class Germans or Scandinavians clustered, the city as a whole was commonly considered an Irish enclave.[29] However, the contours of its Irish character were quite peculiar. Unlike other strongholds of ethnic power, St. Paul had no "Irish" wards. Instead, the Irish population was dispersed more or less evenly throughout the city; in 1910, no ward had more than 3 or less than 1 percent Irish-born residents. This pattern of residential dispersion was a key element of Irish influence, which relied on integration as well as ethnic solidarity. The Irish had moved into every quarter and social stratum of the city, including its most elevated ranks, while still maintaining ethnic ties. Without the numbers to build a self-sustaining political machine, solidarity among the Irish was not enough to bring them to prominence as a group. Instead, they built a complex web comprising both interethnic alliances and ethnic loyalty. Through these networks, the Irish became the power brokers of the city. This was not typical political bossism; the Irish not only had leverage with the elite but they also had entered its ranks.

This was quite a feat. It was one thing for Old Stock Yankees to make political or business partnerships in the name of expediency but quite another to admit Irish-Catholic upstarts into their social realm. The entree of Irish Catholics into elite society and the leverage derived from it were fundamentally supported by the rise to prominence of the Catholic Church, as overseen by Irish archbishop John Ireland. The Catholic Church, in turn, owed much of its prestige to Protestant Canadian mastermind James J. Hill, the architect of the Great Northern Railway—a man with his own somewhat inscrutable Irish preferences. Jim Hill and John Ireland, each an empire builder in his own way, would become intimately linked and the future of the city profoundly affected by their relationship with Mary Mehegan, a modest Irish-Catholic girl with no pretensions to grandeur at all. The emerging cultural terrain of St. Paul can only be understood as it conjoined with the saga of these pivotal historical actors.

Among the crush of immigrants who thronged the St. Paul levee in the 1850s, the arrival of the undistinguished Irish families of Timothy Mehegan and Richard Ireland went largely unnoticed. Scarcely more noteworthy was the appearance of an eighteen-year-old Scotch-Irish Canadian Jim Hill, a boy with few apparent assets other than a bit of bookkeeping experience and a head for figures. But thirty years later, the railroad dynasty created by Jim Hill would rule the St. Paul economy and shape the course of western development, and Richard Ireland's son John, engaged in episcopal empire-building of his own, would direct one of the most powerful Catholic dioceses in the country. Devoutly Catholic Mary Mehegan, childhood playmate of the Ireland brood and future wife of Jim Hill, would play a powerful if less visible role of her own in shaping the social landscape of St. Paul.

Mary's father, Timothy Mehegan, had set out for St. Paul with his wife and two daughters in 1850, clutching the same dreams of prosperity that drove most of the city's new residents. His inauspicious history paralleled all too many immigrant tales. As the Mehegans' introduction to St. Paul, a fraudulent town official absconded with most of the family's worldly goods within hours of their arrival. Left with little but the clothes they were wearing, the family struggled along for three years until Timothy suddenly took ill and died, leaving a young widow and two fatherless daughters. As a result of this family tragedy, Mary Mehegan grew up one of the ragged Canadian and Irish children of whom the town fathers despaired. Mary recalled that, only the assistance of the Sisters of St. Joseph and the local French priests saved the family from utter destitution, which engendered in her a fierce devotion to Catholicism and an unshakable loyalty to the priests and nuns who, she believed, had been her salvation.[30]

When James Hill met Mary Mehegan in 1863, he was already a man with a future, while she was a waitress at the local Merchant's Hotel, where he took his meals. On arriving in St. Paul, Hill had immediately entered the booming river trade, using his bookkeeping skills to land a position as a steamboat agent. From his vantage point on the bustling levee, Hill set out to learn every aspect of the transportation economy that fueled the city's growth. A quick study, young James soon impressed local entrepreneurs with his unusual business acumen. Within seven years, he had come to be a figure to be reckoned with on the levee, with investments in river transportation, wholesale merchandising, and the buying and selling of commodities—forging partnerships with some of the city's elites along the way. But Hill's ambition outpaced them all. Not content to profit from his already substantial enterprises, Hill had his eye on the future—one driven not by river transport but by rail. Confident that he could construct the best-built and -managed railroad in the United States, James J. Hill watched and waited for the opportunity to jump into the railroad game.[31]

This was no idle dream. Hill became a self-taught expert on railroad construction, financing, and management and monitored closely the progress of Jay Cooke's Northern Pacific Railway (NP), which had mapped out a route through Duluth—bypassing St. Paul and Minneapolis, to the dismay of businessmen in both cities. The development of the Northern Pacific was a classic example of "robber baron" railroading. The profits from its outrageously watered stock offerings went into the bank accounts of the chief investors while the road was plagued by shabby construction, broken-down rolling stock, and management decisions that displayed fla-grant disinterest in the long-term viability of the railway. As Hill would later assure his partners, the Northern Pacific was not really a competitor. "The selection of the routes and grades is abominable," he wrote. The NP was not "an honestly capital-ized, well-constructed road."[32]

By the mid-1860s, already absorbed in profitable transportation enterprises, Jim Hill envisioned a much bolder scheme: to marshal the expertise he had acquired and construct a road paralleling the Northern Pacific. His grand objective was nothing less than to run the NP out of business. On the ground in St. Paul, Hill recognized what New York-based railroad tycoons missed, that the real riches lay in the long-term development of the Northwest, not in quick profits to be gained from stock manipulation and land speculation. This vision became James Hill's single-minded life's passion and differentiated him from other contemporary rail-road entrepreneurs. Alone among them, Hill became a "railroad man," personally overseeing the smallest details, inspecting every mile of track, calculating grades and rates, and ultimately making the securities of his roads "the bluest of blue chips in the Northwest."[33]

However, as Hill laid out his grand plan in the 1860s, his vision far exceeded his means. For ten years he refined his calculations and built up his assets. In 1873, the moment to strike at last arrived, a chance to snatch up the stock of the bankrupt St. Paul & Pacific, which had laid less than a hundred miles of track but retained valu-able assets in its land grants, rights-of-way, and state incentives. Unfortunately, de-spite Hill's undeniable business savvy, he had neither the personal resources nor the Wall Street connections to launch a career as a railroad baron. Eastern capital-ists snubbed the proposals of this unknown upstart from the provinces. Unde-terred, Hill turned to Canada. Drawing on connections he had made in the Red River trade and promising rail connection between Manitoba and St. Paul, he per-suaded Canadian financiers to enter into the partnership that would create the Great Northern Railway, financing the venture with British rather than New York capital. Fifteen years later, Hill not only had completed the Great Northern to the Pacific Ocean; he also held working control of the Northern Pacific as well, giving him unparalleled influence over the fortunes of the Northwest and nearly supreme power to make or break the mercantile economy of St. Paul.[34]

Because of the towering role Hill came to play in the city, his romance with Irish-Catholic Mary Mehegan had significance for the status of all Irish Catholics in St. Paul. In enterprise as well as affection, Hill bestowed his favor on the city's Irish. The railroad magnate engaged in numerous business and political relationships with local Irishmen, helping to create fortunes for some lucky Hibernians and suc-cessful political careers for others. Thus, to understand the making of St. Paul as an Irish-Catholic town, the complicated cultural and pragmatic roots of Jim Hill's Irish connections bear some scrutiny.

Considering Hill's single-minded determination to launch his railroad venture and the lack of connections and capital that held back implementation of the plan, a logical strategy would have been to "marry up" into one of St. Paul's fortunes, a common practice among ambitious young men. As an up-and-coming business-man, he was invited to the city's best drawing rooms. Surely, he might have courted one of the local daughters. Instead, in 1864 he determined to wed Mary Mehe-gan—Irish, Catholic, and poor—a surprising choice that would make a notable im-pression on St. Paul's social terrain.

A Canadian with Scotch-Irish roots, James J. Hill's ethnic self-identification—or whether he held any ethnic allegiance at all—is difficult to determine. Andrew Carnegie would hail him as a fellow Scot, while the Ancient Order of Hibernians embraced him as one of their own. No evidence exists that Hill disputed either claim.[35] In the seventeenth century his family, Protestant dissenters, had migrated to County Down in northern Ireland. Two hundred years on Irish soil probably had considerably weakened their Scottish ties. In 1819 the Hills emigrated once again, this time to Ontario. Thus James Hill, born in 1838, had only a tenuous connection to Ireland and even less to an ancient Scottish past.[36] Perhaps Mary Mehegan's slight Irish accent had a comfortingly familiar ring to a young man many miles from home. But just as conceivably, this self-made man had little faith and less interest in ethnic background or religious affiliation, and Mary's gentle nature alone captured his heart. There is no way to be certain. But, at the very least, his choice of bride in-dicates that he did not share widely held Protestant Scotch-Irish antipathy for Irish Catholics.[37] Neither, however, did he identify himself with the immigrant Irish. But, once wed to an Irish-Catholic wife, Hill had a personal stake in countering Irish slurs.

Most plausibly, neither ethnicity nor social background were relevant categories to this self-constructed as well as self-made man—quite unlike his Minneapolis contemporaries, who self-consciously defined themselves and others by these markers. He chose his friends and associates on the basis of confluence of interests without regard for pedigree. Snubbed as a provincial by Wall Street financiers when he went looking for initial investment capital, Hill found more amenable partners in old acquaintances, Canadian veterans of the fur trade. The lesson remained with him, though within years Wall Street eagerly backed his operations. Throughout his life, Hill's few close friends remained those he had made when they were neigh-bors and "young men on the move" together in St. Paul's early days: Henry Upham, a Massachusetts native and president of the First National Bank; Conrad Gotzian, a successful German shoe manufacturer; and, closest of all, Patrick Kelly, an Irish-Catholic wholesale grocer and Democratic Party boss who, with Hill, came to control Minnesota's Democratic Party.[38] Quite conceivably, Kelly, who directed day-to-day Democratic politics in St. Paul and oversaw dispensement of patronage, significantly influenced the steady stream of Irish into jobs with the railroad. By the 1890s, the Irish constituted fully a third of railroad employees in the city—both as managers and workers. Thus, the favor that the Irish gained from Hill derived most probably from an intersection of personal relationships with political and prag-matic priorities.

Whatever the sources that underlay Hill's employment practices, his railroads provided undeniable opportunities for enterprising Irishmen to climb the employment ladder. One of the most notable careers was that of William Kenney, who, as a boy, worked the streets of Minneapolis as a newsboy, sleeping in the corridor of the newspaper's printing offices. After migrating to St. Paul, Kenney secured a job with the railroad, rose from the ranks to become "the trusted assistant of James J. Hill," and eventually won the ultimate prize—President of the Great Northern— an exceptional rags-to-riches tale that inspired fellow Irish and enhanced the stature of the group as a whole.[39] Other promising opportunities for Irish advancement lay in the construction of the great transcontinental road. Unlike railroad barons such as Jay Gould or Collis Huntington and his partners, who acted as contractors as well as financiers of their lines, skimming the profits from construction as well as from stock offerings, Hill contracted the construction of his railway with independent firms, primarily Irish-owned.[40]

Construction was one area of enterprise where the Irish excelled, schooled as they were as "human steamshovels" in cities across America. Though St. Paul's unskilled Irish population traveled a rough road to upward mobility from their jobs as low-paid construction laborers, those who managed to acquire trade skills found an opportunity for real advancement with Hill. The immigrant Foley and Butler families, to name two examples, built nationally recognized construction firms on the reputations they earned in forging the Great Northern across the plains. With their companies established and the equipment in hand to take on major projects, they then leveraged their connections with the Irish-controlled local Democratic Party to win most of St. Paul's major civic construction projects as well. In 1897, Butler Brothers achieved the ultimate coup, obtaining the contract for the $4 million state capitol building.[41]

For most of their fellow countrymen, the success of the Butlers and the Foleys generated no more than access to reasonably steady work on the company's projects (in itself a significant benefit when, after 1880, unemployment in construction trades sometimes rose as high as 40 percent). But skilled Irish workers had a greater advantage, enjoying preference from the Irish contractors. As a result, Irish occupational concentration in the trades more than doubled between 1860 and 1895. For some resourceful Irish railroad men, the rewards could be even more substantial as they utilized ethnic connections and the knowledge they acquired working on Hill's roads to found ancillary enterprises. For example, Joseph Shiely, son of a hard-pressed St. Paul teamster, went to work for Butler Brothers at the age of sixteen, moved on to become a supervisor for the Great Northern nine years later, and eventually, with a thousand dollars of capital, established a sand and gravel company, which accrued for Shiely and his brothers one of St. Paul's most substantial fortunes.[42]

The ethnic network stood Shiely in good stead. He recalled that "Bill Butler was my idol" and helped him get his job with the Great Northern. Pierce and Walter Butler assisted him in starting his own business, and Butler Brothers became one of his first customers. Shiely also liked to recall his association with the legendary

Fig. 8. The section crew, such as the one pictured here in 1900, illustrates the range of employment opportunities that railroad development offered Irish jobseekers, from common laborers to skilled workmen to management. Courtesy of the Minnesota Historical Society.

Hill, telling his grandchildren that he and James J. Hill "built the Great Northern Railway."[43]

In St. Paul, where almost every aspect of the economy was linked in some way with the railroad, Hill was connected at least indirectly with countless successful Irish careers, though most less dramatic than those of Kenney, Shiely, or the Butlers. His hand seemed to be everywhere. If not immediate riches, Hill's enterprises offered at least a chance for Irish toilers to make their way forward in a slow but steady progress. For instance, John McCarthy, born on a steamboat in 1860 as it carried his family to an unknown future in St. Paul, recalled that his father, a common laborer, worked hauling bales in Jim Hill's warehouses. John himself ascended several rungs up the economic ladder as a railway postal clerk, a secure position that he probably acquired through the offices of his uncle, already a stalwart in local Democratic politics. The family finally reached the pinnacle of success with John's son Fred, who earned a law degree, married into a prominent St. Paul Protestant family, and became general counsel for the Northern Pacific Railway. For this Irish family at least, the iron rails of Hill's roads carried them steadily upward.[44]

In politics as much as in business, St. Paul's Irish found James J. Hill a powerful ally. Politics and patronage served up abundant benefits for the Irish in St. Paul. They were consistently over represented in civil service jobs, and the most typical avenue for Irish advancement was through politics and the law. Making all this possible was a Democratic machine that dominated city politics, its workings liberally supported behind the scenes by Jim Hill. A typical "Bourbon Democrat," Hill had no interest in pursuing political laurels for himself. Nor was it particularly important that Democrats be elected to statewide office—never an easy proposition in heavily Republican Minnesota. Instead, the aim of Hill and his fellow Bourbons was to forestall farmer or labor insurgents from gaining a foothold in the Democratic Party. In short, the goal was to make both political parties serve the interests of business and choke off avenues to effect fundamental economic reforms.[45]

This strategy was highly successful in Minnesota, as witnessed by the frustrated political career of populist Ignatius Donnelly. Donnelly, who championed the interests of Minnesota farmers and workers for nearly four decades, frequently railed against Hill as the power behind the Democratic Party who had "taken a contract to wipe me out." "Scratch the Democratic Party of this state," the battling Donnelly charged, "and you will find Jim Hill." Though Donnelly persevered, serving multiple terms in the state legislature, the powerful Bourbons, along with conservative Republicans, kept him from realizing higher political aspirations at either the state or national level. They also repeatedly beat back his efforts to effect agrarian or labor reforms in the legislature.[46]

Bourbon control of the Democratic Party did indeed stifle the political voice of farmers and workers throughout the state, but in St. Paul working people derived singular benefits. As the lone solid Democratic district in the state, St. Paul voters provided the critical swing votes in determining the party's slate. Thus, the Bourbon power brokers, led by Hill, his closest friend Patrick Kelly, and political boss Michael Doran, lavished favors and jobs on St. Paul's loyal Democrats, both through municipal government (which Democrats consistently dominated) and through their private business connections. The beneficiaries of this political largesse then spread the riches to an even broader Irish constituency—to young men like railway postal clerk John McCarthy.[47]

It is important to note, however, that the political system that developed inside the city limits differed from classic Irish political machines in that while the Irish were highly visible as party brokers, they were not the dominant voting constituency. Opponents decried "Irish control" of St. Paul politics, but in fact the city's politicos played a delicate balancing game. Though the most reliable corps of voters was the Irish working class, Irish politicians had to guard against the appearance of unduly privileging fellow ethnics and shrewdly worked to enfold a diverse voting public under the Irish banner.[48]

As early as the 1850s, St. Patrick's Day was orchestrated to be a civic as well as an ethnic celebration. The organizers invited "their countrymen of all nations" to join the "warm hearted sons of Erin" in the day's festivities. The endless toasting that topped off the day invariably praised local dignitaries and the city's other immigrant groups—"naturalized citizens of the United States now celebrating their day with us." The strategy proved so successful that a local Republican paper, dismayed by the popularity of the event, declared that it should confine itself to "addresses from their own speakers, their national and characteristic music, &c. . . . The requisite talent can be found without going out of their own ranks."[49] This, of course, would defeat the purpose of the day—to emphasize the all-embracing nature of "Irish" politics. Leading Irish politicians carefully tended interethnic relationships and made it their business to contribute—both in dollars and participation—to non-Irish ethnic celebrations throughout the city. When, in 1889, a slate top-heavy with Irish candidates was rejected by the city's voters, Democratic politicians scrambled to recoup, enlisting the aid of wealthy German brewer William Hamm to reestablish the inclusive panache of the party.[50]

Democratic power in St. Paul derived from a complex web of ethnic and working-class alliances—enhanced in this heavily Catholic city by a Republican reputation for anti-Catholicism.[51] But other compelling local economic issues also brought many middle-class St. Paulites along with working-class voters into the Bourbon Democrats' fold. One of the most hotly debated issues in late nineteenth-century American politics was the question of the tariff. Manufacturing centers, such as Minneapolis, embraced the protectionist stance of the Republican Party. But in a city like St. Paul, where the proportion of jobs in manufacturing actually declined by 8 percent between 1884 and 1890, protectionism primarily spelled high prices for consumers. The city's economy was overwhelmingly dependent on trade, wholesaling, and transportation—all forms of enterprise that profited from the greatest possible flow of goods at the lowest prices—making the free-trade stance of the Democrats attractive to the city's businessmen.[52]

Furthermore, the Republicans favored regulation of railway rates. Naturally, railroad magnate Hill abhorred the idea. The substantial number of St. Paul voters employed by the railways, who regarded their jobs as dependent on the railroad's profitability, also opposed regulation.[53] But many of the city's mercantile class, who on the surface would have benefited from regulation, opposed it as well owing to the strategic genius of Jim Hill. To the enduring frustration of Minneapolis businessmen, Hill consistently set rate schedules that favored St. Paul at the Mill City's expense.[54] By the 1880s, with St. Paul struggling to maintain its hold on the single realm in which it dominated Minneapolis, the city's mercantile class was willing to pay Hill's price, provided the price for Minneapolis was greater.[55]

A final issue that cemented Democratic loyalty in St. Paul was the growing temperance movement. As the Republican Party moved to embrace issues of social reform in the late nineteenth century, it became closely associated with the temperance cause. As numerous historians have noted, immigrant voters regarded this as a cultural assault. Certainly, this was the general opinion in St. Paul. But, in a departure from the norm, most local civic leaders were no more amenable to sumptuary regulation than were working-class voters. Partly this was due to the complicated interethnic social web of the city, which required careful consideration of ethnic sensibilities. But far more compelling was the integral role that production and consumption of alcohol played in supporting the city's economy. The brewing industry was the single area of production in which St. Paul surpassed Minneapolis and one of the city's most important employers. In 1880, eleven breweries had a combined capitalization of $371,500, second only to the city's printing industry.[56] In addition, by 1886, St. Paul was home to more than eight hundred saloons and taverns that provided a livelihood for numerous small proprietors and employees, supported a thriving business for liquor distributors, and generated more than $80,000 for the municipal coffers, through licensing fees.[57]

Most important to the city's respectable merchant class, St. Paul's reputation for a lively nightlife was a critical draw in attracting buyers and traveling salesmen to do business in St. Paul rather than Minneapolis. Moreover, as the railroad system developed, St. Paul also found itself in increasing competition with suppliers in Chicago for the role of provisioner to the hinterland. In 1880, local salesman Michael Boyle, employed by the city's most prominent wholesale drygoods firm, confided in his diary: "We have to sell some stuff very cheap now in order to meet Chicago prices. More merchants want to go to that City of Wickedness this fall to buy goods than ever before."[58]

The St. Paul market was undeniably shrinking. Salesmen prowled the train depot for potential customers, hoping to get the jump on local competitors. In Michael Boyle's words, a promising prospect might find "a dozen drummers who were laying for him in the lobby of the Merchant's [Hotel] while he was at breakfast." Increasingly, business firms turned to courting customers with wine, women, and song to give themselves an edge. As Boyle recounts it:

> Wholesale merchants of St. Paul have been on the *qui vivre* this week over the presence of a firm from Pembina who are going to open a large store there. There has been a drawn battle between us [Auerbach, Finch and VanSlyck] and Lindekes for their bill, which resulted today in victory for us, through the fine generalship of George R. [Finch]. Champagne dinners, choice cigars, a gala night at White Bear Lake and Mr. Finch's gentlemanly courtesy did the business 5 or $6,000 and honor & glory are the spoils.[59]

Such lavish entertainments were reserved only for the largest accounts. More typically, customers were lured by the bright lights of the downtown saloons, gambling dens, and red-light district—all tacitly endorsed by the upright members of the business community. Even the most respectable firms counted on the vice economy to attract buyers to the city.[60]

Between 1870 and 1883, disapproving reformers and Protestant churchmen launched no less than five reform campaigns, but community resistance remained entrenched. Temperance advocate Christopher O'Brien briefly held sway as mayor, swept into office unopposed in 1883 on his Irish-Democrat credentials and promises to clean up the city. However, when O'Brien shocked his Democratic backers by actually attempting to implement his pledge, his actions were met by loud protests from merchants who claimed the mayor was ruining business in the city. O'Brien, a man of staunch and straitlaced principles, refused to back down, but he wisely did not run for re-election. His successor, Edmund Rice (brother of city father Henry Rice), quietly allowed the vice economy to return to business as usual, without vocal opposition.[61]

For all these reasons, then, even though contemporaries characterized St. Paul Democratic politics as driven by an Irish machine, that label masks a far more complicated intersection of local cultural and economic interests. The different strains of the city's Democratic constituency, though fraught with internal tensions, all gained benefits from party loyalty. Few would have endorsed Jim Hill's underlying agenda to constrain the parameters of political choice, but neither did they identify with farmers' issues that translated into attacks on the railroad, the lifeblood for St. Paul's jobs and economy. The Republican Party, with its endorsement of protectionism, sumptuary reform, and the attendant taint of anti-Catholicism, affronted ethnic sensibilities and local economic interests at the same time—a lethal combination. Irish political bosses in St. Paul used all this to their advantage, successfully playing on the particular configuration of the city's social and economic landscape to craft a party loyalty that was nearly impenetrable.

The Democrats seldom managed to elect their candidates at the state or national level. In fact, identification with the anomalous and defiantly self-serving St. Paul was nearly always deadly for political hopefuls.[62] But that hardly mattered to the city's voters since, in or out of office, the Democrats delivered the goods where it mattered—in the city proper. Furthermore, at the municipal level, where city jobs and contracts were distributed, they were seldom out of office.

As Richard Oestreicher has observed, political and labor historians have been "reluctant to confront the extent to which values, opinions, and behavior are shaped by power rather than free and rational choice." Quite clearly, power limited the landscape of political possibility in St. Paul. But within those limits, in which real lives were played out, the choices that shaped a tensile cross-class coalition supported self-interest as well. This does not indicate either an erasure of class consciousness or a leveling of social hierarchy. Rather, the peculiar configuration of the city's economy fostered an interdependent culture in which even competing class interests often appeared best served, at least in the most immediate sense, by the city's Democratic brokers. As Oestreicher acknowledges, "Cultures are vast and internally contradictory . . . susceptible to a range of ideological interpretations."[63]

The volatility produced by those internal contradictions differs with circumstance and location. At its most effective, a constructed community, grounded in place, creates a system of accountability through which the "range of ideological interpretations" are negotiated. Loyalty to community—and place—develops and is internalized in direct relation to how effectively the system operates. In St. Paul, it operated extremely well, and St. Paul's Irish Democrats functioned as cultural as well as political brokers, perfecting a system that, once in place, would prove highly resistant to change.

General opinion in the rest of the state was that the Capital City was a veritable den of corruption. Farmer radicals focused on the hated Hill as the deus ex machina of Democratic Party politics (and were equally frustrated by the grain trust that dominated the Republicans). During the 1884 presidential campaign, Ignatius Donnelly, the farmers' steadfast ally, had tried to leverage support from St. Paul's ethnic political network, tirelessly canvassing the state on behalf of Democrat Grover Cleveland. However, once Cleveland was in the White House, Donnelly discovered the limits of Irish brotherhood. To his dismay, his fellow Hibernians shut him out from any political appointment. Donnelly protested directly to President Cleveland that the Minnesota Democracy "is going to the devil . . . with P. H. Kelly at its head." His protest was to no avail, since Jim Hill, the real power behind the Minnesota Democrats, had directed that the antimonopolist Donnelly be left out in the cold. In a disingenuous move, Kelly offered Donnelly a mission abroad, which would effectively remove him from Minnesota politics. The disappointed and angry populist understandably declined.[64]

The Minneapolis press regularly excoriated the "Irish ring" that dominated St. Paul politics. During the Cleveland administration, Minneapolis papers turned up the volume of their indictments, decrying the "Kelly-Doran office-broking agency" as Patrick Kelly and Michael Doran lavished patronage on their fellow Democrats. The tone of the critique played heavily on negative stereotypes of Irish politicians, in the process casting St. Paul as little more than a corrupt Irish slum.[65] Such characterizations affronted civic as well as ethnic pride. As a consequence, St. Paul residents of every sort had reason to rally in defense of the city's Irish.[66]

Political bossism or even elected office does not necessarily translate into social credentials. In many cases, quite the reverse has been true. Nineteenth-century Minneapolis elites, for example, viewed politics and politicians, below the rank of senator or governor, as beneath their social station.[67] For the Irish, the disreputable taint of politics often added yet another unpalatable element to negative cultural stereotypes, strengthening a tendency for Irish-Catholic separatism.[68] In St. Paul, however, by the 1880s the Irish had moved easily into the upper echelons of society, which smoothed their integration into the fabric of the city at the same time that it enormously enhanced the range and value of Irish ethnic networks. This dual identity uniquely positioned them to broker city tensions. Successful Irish-Catholic merchants, contractors, lawyers, and bankers maintained cross-class relationships through ethnic and religious associations. But they also mingled with their Yankee and German counterparts in the city's best drawing rooms—hardly a surprising circumstance, since the most coveted invitation in the city was to the home of James and Mary Mehegan Hill.

It was in this critically important social realm that Mary Hill played a central role. Surprisingly unassuming despite her husband's rise to power, the empire

DOING BUSINESS AT THE SAME OLD STAND.

Fig. 9. Minneapolis editorial cartoons labeled St. Paul a sink of political corruption run by seamy Irish politicians. *Minneapolis Journal*, 14 November 1893.

builder's wife set wide parameters for St. Paul social credentials, in ways that may have been largely unconscious. Her diaries reveal a woman who never became quite comfortable with her elevated status. After a trip to a posh Lake Minnetonka resort, summer enclave of the Minneapolis elite, Mary confided to her diary, "So glad to reach home. Went right into the kitchen to finish some jelly." To the discomfiture of her servants, the lady of the house had a habit of regularly invading the backstairs domain. Legend has it that, remembering her working days, Mary Hill insisted that wooden floors be laid in the mansion's kitchen; the proposed marble flooring would be too hard on servants' feet. When her long-time cook gave notice, she wistfully recorded in her diary, "I shall miss her often."[69] From her servants' perspective, however, the lady of the house was "on our necks" and an unwelcome intruder in their territory. Downstairs maid Celia Tauer complained in a letter that "the old lady was preserving for two days and she smired everything up with syrup & sugar so that I was afraid she'd stick to something & that I'd have to keep her down in the kitchen all together."[70]

In truth, as the wife of the powerful James J. Hill, Mary was out of place among her servants, but neither was she quite at home as the grande dame of St. Paul society. As a result, she clung with intense loyalty to family, old friends, and her Catholic faith. With Hill absent much of the time, either conferring with financiers in New York or overseeing the management of his far-flung network, Mary spent as much time as possible with her nine children at the family farm outside the city, especially after Hill constructed the new family mansion in 1892—a brooding pile of stone that dominated the apex of fashionable Summit Avenue.[71]

Most of the city's upper class summered on the shores of nearby White Bear Lake. But Jim Hill, to whom leisure was a foreign concept, established a working farm as the family retreat. Although the rambling farmhouse was comfortable, it was no gentleman's lavish estate. In the assessment of unimpressed maid Celia Tauer, "The farm is allright but ghee if I was a big bug like Mr. J. J. Hill I wouldn't stay out there in that shack."[72] But then, Jim Hill was no ordinary financial baron. At North Oaks, as the farm was called, he experimented with pure-bred cattle and agricultural innovations that he then persistently touted to the farmers who had settled in the Great Northern's hinterland. He also marketed the products of the small-scale farming operation—meat, fruit, vegetables, eggs, grain, and firewood— to local consumers. It must have seemed somewhat peculiar to city elites, straining for sophistication and polish, that the man whose favor they universally courted produced the butter on their breakfast trays.[73]

Nonetheless, socially prominent St. Paul dutifully made the pilgrimage to North Oaks to pay homage to the butter-making railroad tycoon and his wife. Mary's diaries record a litany of daily visitors that included nearly every figure of substance in the city. As they gathered on the porch or around the dining table or were dragged by Hill to admire the results of his scientific farming experiments, they took note of who was present in the inner circle. If Hill himself was present, the group was almost certain to include railroad officials and business associates, since the farm was merely an extension of the railroad magnate's office, and subordinates were regularly required to trek to the farm on his command. Mary's favored guests, however, those who received the coveted invitations for extended visits, included only trusted old friends and neighbors, such as the Irish McQuillans and Kellys along with the Yankee Uphams, German-Catholic Gotzians, and her spiritual adviser, Father Caillet.[74] The lesson here was self-evident. If St. Paul society hoped to lure the truculent Hill, on whom they were all dependent in some fashion, and the almost reclusive Mary to grace their soirees, then they had best keep aristocratic airs in check and shed any vestige of condescension toward either Catholic clergy or Irish Catholics—at least those of the proper class.

Minneapolis elites were seldom among the welcomed guests at North Oaks. It

Fig. 10. Mary Hill, posing with three of her nine children in 1888, was most comfortable in the sheltered circle of family and close friends. Courtesy of the Minnesota Historical Society.

was common knowledge that no love was lost between Hill and milling tycoon William Washburn, and Hill did not take forays into the enemy's camp lightly. In fact, the enduring rivalry between Minneapolis and St. Paul, and St. Paul's eventual decline, may be traced in no small part to the feud between Hill and Washburn. It might have been predicted that the two would become natural allies; the fortunes of the grain trust and the railroad monopoly were so closely intertwined. Indeed, for a time such a combination appeared imminent. In a confidential letter in 1882, Washburn offered Hill stock in Minneapolis Milling. Probably hoping to leverage more favorable treatment in shipping rates, Washburn suggested that "as there is no possible antagonism between us and so many things in common, it seems to me that it would be desirable for you to have an interest with us."[75] Hill initially seemed to rise to the bait, investing in Minneapolis enterprises, and enthusing publicly, "The time has come when the cities of Minneapolis and St. Paul can work together for

Fig. 11. James J. Hill, pictured here at Havre, Montana, in 1913, never tired of extolling the benefits of diversified farming and scientific stock management to farmers along the Great Northern's line. Original photograph in the Louis Hill Manuscripts, James J. Hill Reference Library, St. Paul, Minnesota.

their mutual advantage and advancement. . . . The future of these cities will be greater if we work together."[76]

If such a plan had been followed, the cultural distinctiveness that divided the cities possibly would have dissipated over time as their economic interests intertwined to craft a combined industrial/transportation metropolis. However, attempts at cooperation abruptly came to a halt after 1883, when a group of Minneapolis investors, with Washburn at its head, invaded Hill's terrain. Frustrated by the favorable rates that Hill continued to maintain for St. Paul and increasingly uneasy that Hill might ship grain to Buffalo via Duluth and the Great Lakes at a more favorable rate than to Minneapolis, the concerned businessmen determined to establish a competing road, with Minneapolis as its railhead. When Hill learned of the incorporation of the Minneapolis, St. Paul & Sault St. Marie (Soo) line, he was outraged, particularly when he discovered that Washburn and his partners were financing their venture through the Bank of Montreal, whose president, George Stephen, was Hill's associate. Stephen, caught in a most uncomfortable position, disingenuously denied involvement and promised to put an end to any Canadian financing that might be behind the operation. As he assured Hill, "Washburn or his friends will get no help from . . . me for any schemes inimical in any way to [Hill] interests."[77] The Soo Line's financing quite suddenly dried up, forcing the investors to scramble to keep the venture afloat.

Washburn and his fellow millers attempted to use the Soo as a bargaining chip to persuade Hill to grant them lower rates than those set for Duluth. Perhaps this was the strategy from the beginning, rather than to make a serious run against the powerful Hill. If so, Washburn had made a grave miscalculation. In Hill's estimation, Buffalo would soon overtake Minneapolis as the nation's milling center, and that was fine with him.[78] As Hill's lieutenant, Henry Minot, confided to one of the railroad's directors, "Minneapolis . . . is no longer of great importance. . . . It must be remembered that Minneapolis is simply a manufacturing city, and not a trade centre as St. Paul is. It is St. Paul that distributes merchandise and supplies to all the local points on our line. . . . If Minneapolis should be destroyed to-day, people elsewhere would none the less go on eating bread and demanding flour made from Red River Valley wheat."[79] Apparently, Minot's assessment reflected company policy; Hill evinced little further interest in Twin City cooperation, keeping his hand in Minneapolis banking operations but just as likely to use his influence to oppose Minneapolis interests as to further them. Though he had purchased a controlling interest in the St. Anthony Water Power Company in 1880, the usually profit-minded railroad tycoon made no move to promote attendant industry on Minneapolis's languishing east side.[80]

The breach between Hill and the Minneapolis business establishment never healed, and apparently the antagonism worked both ways. Hill had begun to develop the resort area of Lake Minnetonka, preferred summering spot of the Minneapolis elite. The residents banded together to oppose the development at every turn and refused to grant a liquor license for the posh residential hotel Hill had constructed. Hill took the rebuff as another personal affront and abandoned his interest in Minnetonka, agreeing with his engineer who commented, "It appears to me that if they believe you favor electricity, they will pray for steam."[81]

The result of this personal feud was a much wider rift. Other St. Paul financiers and businessmen, wary of offending Hill, were hesitant to participate in Minneapolis investments when the occasional opportunity arose. Nor did they wish to appear too cozy with Hill's antagonists. In this way, St. Paul society and its corridors of power developed their striking contours and boundaries—exceptionally open to religious and ethnic diversity within the city limits but wholly separate and nearly closed off from Minneapolis. Thus, as the result of Hill's economic and political power, the personalities of James and Mary Hill left an indelible stamp on the emerging social landscape of St. Paul.[82]

Archbishop John Ireland, the third key player in the making of this Irish-Catholic enclave, left a striking imprint of his own. In terms of cultural roots, Ireland was the male counterpart of Mary Hill, having grown up on the streets of pioneer St. Paul, Irish, Catholic, and poor. In terms of goals and ambitions, however, he more closely resembled James J. Hill in his passion to construct an episcopal empire. The combination of his impoverished roots and vaulting ambition made Ireland a complicated mix of democratic and authoritarian leanings—qualities that he drew on with great effect to mediate the city's social tensions.

Ireland never shed the childhood memories of Irish discrimination that had followed his family as they trekked across the continent in search of a home—from the eastern seaboard, to Chicago, and finally to St. Paul, where the Irelands put down permanent roots. But perhaps most painful were the eight years he spent as a seminarian in France. In 1853, Bishop Cretin had plucked the fourteen-year-old Ireland from the ranks of the town's "dirty little Irish boys" to be trained for the priesthood. Overwhelmed by the responsibility of administering a diocese that encompassed 166,000 square miles and unable to attract clerical reinforcements, Cretin had persuaded the French Society for the Propagation of the Faith to underwrite seminarian training for two local boys. Recognizing a rare intelligence beneath Ireland's ragged exterior, Cretin informed the boy and his parents that Ireland had a vocation; within months, John Ireland and his friend Thomas O'Gorman found themselves bound for France.[83]

Thousands of miles from his family and separated by language, class, and ethnicity from his fellow seminarians, young Ireland's loneliness and confusion can only be imagined. Deposited at the diocesan minor seminary in the town of Meximieux, he felt the familiar sting of prejudice or, at least, condescension. Fellow students accused him of "placing the worst construction" on what they described as "quite innocent remarks." To defend himself in this new alien environment, Ireland self-consciously emphasized his *American* rather than his Irish identity, tiring his classmates with his boasting about the "grandeurs of America." Determined to prove his worth, he also dedicated himself to his studies and embarked on a furious self-improvement campaign.[84]

Though in later years, Ireland spoke with nostalgic affection about Meximieux, he maintained a conspicuous silence about the following four years spent at the major seminary of Montbel, under the supervision of the Marist Order. Social distinctions in French religious orders, far more than in the diocesan structure, self-consciously replicated those of French society. Quite likely, this heightened hierarchy of class made Ireland's position as an Irish-American "charity case" even more painfully apparent. These formative experiences provide a subtle context for the role Ireland later played in national Catholic politics; they also informed the way he managed his diocese in St. Paul.

During his long tenure as archbishop, Ireland displayed an enduring antipathy toward male religious orders and only reluctantly allowed them into his diocese. Furthermore, he mandated against internal hierarchies within the women's orders he supervised. As one St. Joseph sister asserted, "This classification was a custom which Archbishop Ireland could not abide. It was European to his mind and utterly opposed to American practice and principle." A group of aristocratic French Visitation nuns had arrived in St. Paul in 1874 to found a school for the daughters of the city's elites. When Ireland was appointed bishop the following year, he promptly informed the mother superior that in his diocese the order's distinctions (based on social class) between contemplative and active nuns must be abolished.[85]

In the public man who returned to Minnesota to be ordained in 1861, no trace of the ragged little Irish child could be discerned. Elevated to bishop in 1875 and to archbishop thirteen years later, John Ireland appeared an urbane and supremely confident figure. But, clearly, the memories of discrimination were not forgotten. The same experiences that fostered the archbishop's democratic leanings filled him with fierce patriotic fervor and paradoxically led him to privilege Irish Catholics above all others in the cause of uplifting the race. They also imbued him with an intense ambition for both personal advancement and the development of a powerful Catholic diocese.

Ireland's commitment to the interrelated projects of Irish uplift and Catholic institution-building was by no means unique. In nineteenth-century America, similar efforts were underway in nearly every urban center with a significant Catholic population. Indeed, the pioneer French priests in St. Paul had clearly understood that the security of the church depended on their ability to advance the material well-being of their Catholic flock. Ireland stands out not for the originality of his strategy but because of the unparalleled energy and resources he devoted to Irish advancement—a passion that drew as deeply on personal pain as on political savvy. Among his initiatives as head of the St. Paul diocese, Ireland launched an ambitious colonization effort to resettle poor Irish immigrants in rural Minnesota; passionately crusaded for Irish temperance; and unabashedly privileged the training and promotion of Irish diocesan clergy. As one non-Irish St. Paul priest ruefully recalled, "With Ireland . . . it was all completely Irish."[86]

Long before he attained a position of power in the diocese, the savvy Ireland saw the advantages to be gained from the impending union of James J. Hill and Irish-Catholic Mary Mehegan. He was not alone in this insight. The good French fathers wholeheartedly approved of Mary's engagement to the Protestant Hill, even though ordinarily the Catholic Church deeply disapproved of interfaith marriages. As Hill's biographer shrewdly notes, "This ambitious young man, who clearly would be one of the most important citizens in St. Paul . . . was about to found a family which would be an ornament of the Catholic Church in St. Paul, in the Northwest, and perhaps in the United States." Mary's protector, Father Caillet, actively promoted the marriage, advising her that she "must educate [herself] to become his companion and "must always try to follow him in his career." Just as Mary's childhood acquaintance, John Ireland, was dispatched to France to prepare him for his future role in the church, in somewhat similar fashion Father Caillet packed Mary off to a convent in Milwaukee to acquire the social graces required for the wife of a substantial businessman. It would not do for this Catholic wife to be a social embarrassment.[87]

Thus, the Catholic courtship of Jim Hill was well underway by the time that Ireland returned to St. Paul from the battlefields of the Civil War where, as a natural outgrowth of his patriotic fervor, he had served as a chaplain. Drawing on his long acquaintance with Mary, the ambitious young priest lost no time in seeking to ingratiate himself with Hill. On the surface, the project appears to have been an unqualified success. As Hill's fortunes rose, so did his contributions to the Catholic Church, culminating in a $500,000 gift to underwrite the establishment of the St. Paul Seminary in 1890. The railroad magnate regularly contributed modest amounts to other denominations in the city, but his Catholic donations far exceeded the sum of all the others combined.[88] The common perception in St. Paul thus was that Hill was deeply sympathetic to Catholicism. Hill himself chose to attribute his generosity to the influence of his devoutly Catholic wife, but the historical record casts doubt on such a simple explanation. In fact, the relationship between Hill and Ireland seems to have flourished despite a lingering coolness that Mary Hill displayed toward her old acquaintance.

Mary's strained relationship with Ireland is apparent when contrasted with her other social interactions. Throughout her life, she relished visits with "old settlers" from all walks of life who shared her history in frontier St. Paul, noting them with pleasure in her diaries; she retained close ties with her confessor and former protector, Father Caillet; she regularly visited the convents of the Visitation, Good Shepherd, and St. Joseph sisters (maintaining a friendship with Ireland's sister, Ellen, who had become mother superior of the St. Joseph order); and she urged her husband to donate funds to a wide range of Catholic causes. But John Ireland, whom she had known nearly all her life, was an infrequent visitor in her home and was never among the circle who gathered at North Oaks. Even after his investiture as bishop of the diocese in 1875, Ireland was mentioned only rarely and without particular enthusiasm in Mary's diaries.[89]

What lay behind Mary Hill's coolness toward Ireland is something of a puzzle. She left no written assessment of the archbishop. But quite likely she suspected that opportunism tinged his proffered friendship—a suspicion that may have taken root on the occasion of her wedding. When she and Hill appeared at the church sanctuary to take their vows in a private ceremony, Mary was dismayed to find John Ireland waiting for them rather than her cherished Father Caillet, whom she had expected to officiate. Ireland, perhaps hoping to have the honor himself, explained that he had "forgotten" to inform Caillet of the occasion and offered to perform the marriage in his place. The deeply disappointed Mary snubbed his suggestion and asked for the Alsatian-born Father Oster instead.[90]

While she never publicly voiced suspicions about this unfortunate affair, subsequent events suggest that Mary Hill, in her quiet way, was fully her husband's equal in holding a grudge.[91] Throughout her life, she continued attendance at Father Caillet's Church of St. Mary's rather than the more prestigious cathedral where Ireland held forth—though the cathedral sat just across the avenue from her home. Indeed, it was also at St. Mary's, under the supervision of Father Caillet, that her nine children received their religious education and took their first Communions.[92]

Nonetheless, another sort of relationship between John Ireland and James Hill developed, one that was grounded, quite simply, in mutual self-interest rather than affection, faith, or friendship. Though Hill agreed that his children be raised in the Catholic faith and on rare occasion accompanied his family to mass, his support for Ireland's institution-building had little to do with theology and much to do with his twin interests in business and social control. For instance, Ireland's Catholic colonization project neatly fed into immigration efforts promoted by Hill's railroad. The Irish-Catholic settlements the bishop founded were located conveniently along Hill's railroad lines. Ireland acted as land agent for the railroad, and the railroad acted as banker for the colonies—an arrangement that suited both men's ambitions.[93]

The serendipitous confluence of their individual goals often linked the two empire builders together, along with a mutual appreciation for the grand scale of their vision. Nonetheless, despite John Ireland's growing stature within the hierarchy of the American Catholic Church, his was never an equal partnership with Hill. It was a lesson brought home to him most painfully in the early 1890s, when the archbishop, without the endorsement of Hill, concocted an elaborate land-development scheme in collaboration with Minneapolis streetcar mogul Thomas Lowry.

As part of his grand archdiocesan plan, Ireland embarked on an ambitious building campaign, establishing the St. Paul Seminary and the College of St. Thomas, with preliminary plans for the women's college of St. Catherine in the works as well—all to be located at the far western edge of the city. A decade earlier, in partnership with Irish real estate developer Thomas Cochran, Ireland had begun to acquire extensive holdings around the proposed building sites, anticipating a tidy return for the archdiocese as Catholics flocked to settle near the impressive new institutions. In short, the archbishop expected to finance his church-building through land speculation. The success of both enterprises relied on construction of transportation links to the city center, and streetcar magnate Lowry (who held exclusive franchises for both Minneapolis and St. Paul) was the key. Ireland paid Lowry a $250,000 "incentive bonus" to make his properties a priority in streetcar route extension plans. He also personally assumed an additional $50,000 in indebtedness for the line. His partnership with the streetcar magnate was both potentially profitable and highly public. On the 1890 inaugural run of St. Paul's first electric streetcar, the archbishop sat in the place of honor at Tom Lowry's right hand. In 1892, when Lowry was feted in Minneapolis, Ireland, Lowry, and the governor of the state stood together to greet the guests in the receiving line.[94]

Unfortunately for the archbishop, his trust in Tom Lowry's good faith proved to be misplaced, bringing Ireland's real estate adventures to an ignominious conclusion. Lowry had his own Minneapolis real estate to sell and devoted his resources to Minneapolis expansion at the expense of St. Paul, despite his promises to the archbishop. By 1885, Minneapolis counted forty-seven miles of track in comparison to a mere twenty-five miles laid in the capital city. A Minneapolis publication loftily declared that "President Lowry will undoubtedly extend the system in Saint Paul as rapidly as the growth of the city will justify . . . but no one who understands the situation in both cities will for an instant doubt that the necessities in Minneapolis will keep ahead of Saint Paul in the extension of the railway system." Boosters across the river saw the situation somewhat differently. In 1890 a "large delegation of the leading business men of St. Paul" charged the streetcar magnate with "pushing the work" in Minneapolis to intentionally disadvantage St. Paul.[95] In either case, the result was that the lines inched only slowly to the city's western edge, and before Ireland could profit from his venture, the bottom had fallen out of the real estate market in the panic of 1893, leaving him, in his words, "simply crushed down by this load of debt." Ireland desperately promoted his properties to the city's Catholics, but despite his exhortations, in the depths of the depression, the lots remained unsold.[96]

Facing imminent financial ruin and public humiliation, the archbishop frantically begged his long-time patron Hill to save him: "I entreat you, do something. Matters nearing an end. I can do nothing without you."[97] Hill must have savored the moment. Ireland's speculations had allied him with a man Hill privately detested, and Jim Hill did not forgive such transgressions easily. In addition to his streetcar interests, Lowry was part of the business combine that had established the Soo line and the road's current president—which earned him Hill's abiding antagonism. The 1893 financial panic plunged Lowry as well as Ireland into financial trouble, and Hill ordered his son-in-law, a director of the Minneapolis Trust Company, to provide Lowry no aid. "If his load crushes him, it is his matter," Hill declared. "We have nothing at stake." The railroad king was slightly more merciful to the archbishop. Hill grudgingly saved Ireland from his woes but not before he exacted a full degree of penitence from the humbled archbishop, insisting that Ireland's properties be placed in a trust supervised by Hill's son-in-law. The price for salvation put the archbishop into the role of permanent supplicant to James J. Hill.[98]

Despite serious doubts about the archbishop's business judgment, Hill did not withdraw his $500,000 gift to the seminary, already under construction. That project served other priorities of the railroad tycoon. Convinced that the public schools failed to instill the "proper" values in an industrial workforce, Hill was a vocal critic

Fig. 12. To his later chagrin, in 1890 Archbishop John Ireland played a very public role at the inaugural run of St. Paul's first electric streetcar. Thomas Lowry is seated at far right, wearing top hat, with Ireland to Lowry's immediate right. Courtesy of the Minnesota Historical Society.

of public education and regularly contributed to private, church-related schools of every denomination. Since the majority of the working class (and his employees) were Roman Catholic, his greatest investment naturally was in the institutions of the Catholic Church. John Ireland's commitment to "Americanization" and Catholic uplift fit neatly with Hill's ideas, and though Hill declared that his establishment of the St. Paul Seminary was in honor of the "earnest devotion, watchful care, and Christian example of [his] Roman Catholic wife," his generosity was driven more directly by his belief that priests trained under Ireland's watchful eye (overseen by Hill) would impart the proper sort of religion to a Catholic working class. To ensure the continued appropriate management of the institution, he crafted a trust agreement that kept dispersal of the funds under close supervision of Hill and his designated trustees.[99]

Thus, the fortunes of the Catholic Church became tied in multiple cultural and material ways to James J. Hill. In terms of real financial support, Hill sought to use the church to advance an agenda that was disconnected from any personal attachment to the Catholic faith. At heart, his donations to the Catholic Church were motivated by business considerations. Nonetheless, at the level of general *perception*, regardless of Hill's underlying motivations, his strong support for Ireland as well as his own "Roman Catholic household" enhanced the church's already favorable position in the community and imparted it a truly unassailable stature. Thus, in St. Paul by the end of the nineteenth century, the combination of Irish and Catholic affiliations had attained a local cultural currency that matched or even exceeded the power they carried in other, much more dominant Irish strongholds in urban America.

If James Hill was deemed a political deus ex machina, the same might be said of his social role in St. Paul. Though only marginally interested in the comings and goings of socially prominent St. Paulites, he and his Irish wife set the tone that opened the door for Irish Catholics to move easily into elite society, a position that greatly enhanced the vertical range and value of Irish and Catholic networks. Those networks remained intact because even from the vantage point of posh Summit Avenue, Irish Catholics sustained a collective memory of past discrimination—a strong incentive to maintain and support group advancement. The result was a complex culture of integration and separatism that operated in tandem and made Irish Catholics uniquely equipped to act as the city's social brokers, a function that reverberated in neighborhoods well removed, both socially and geographically, from the sprawling homes of city elites.

A vivid reconstruction of the workings of this social web is revealed in the diaries of Michael Boyle, an unremarkable salesman in late-nineteenth-century St. Paul. In 1875, at the age of nineteen, the young, Irish-Catholic Michael was left as sole provider for his mother and sister after his father fled back to Ireland to escape persistent creditors. Casting about for a means to support the family, Michael turned to his Catholic support network to help him find work. As he records in his diary, within days, "through the instrumentality of the Sisters of the Good Shepherd," he had secured a position with Auerbach, Finch, and Culbertson, the city's leading wholesale drygoods concern. Michael quickly rose from the position of delivery wagon driver to salesman, thanks in large part to the support of Catholic Constantine McConville, Auerbach's "right-hand man," "intimate and life-long friend of Archbishop Ireland," and husband of Michael's old friend and fellow parishioner, Mary Corrigan. In the meantime, prominent Irish community leaders helped to extricate him from his father's financial woes. By 1880, Michael was optimistic enough to consider building a home with a loan from a local building society, made possible through the intervention of St. Paul Democratic boss Patrick Kelly. The Irish-Catholic network was in full and efficient operation.[100]

But the world of Michael Boyle was no simple ethnic enclave. Though he gravitated to the pomp and social cachet of the cathedral and Bishop Ireland, his strict

Catholicism (and his love for any social occasion) led Michael to make the rounds of churches throughout the city—the "French church," the "German church," and the "Bohemian church," where in 1880 he attended daily mass. Nor was his world a strictly Catholic one. Along with the Catholic (and Irish) Fortnightly Literary Club, he joined the German gymnastic club at the Turner Hall and the St. Paul Boat Club, where middle-class sons of every ethnic and religious affiliation mingled convivially. Striving for social acceptance and respectability, Michael's circle increasingly became defined by class rather than by ethnicity or religion. He was as likely to attend a strawberry festival at Methodist St. Luke's Hospital or a musicale sponsored by the boating club as an oyster supper for the benefit of Catholic orphans. Yet, despite this apparent social fluidity, occasional notations in Michael's diaries of encounters with "hatred for the Catholic Church" convinced him that "the spirit of Know Nothingism abideth with us yet," and caused him to retain a certain cultural defensiveness (whether from real or imagined sources) that bound him to his Irish-Catholic roots even as he sought to enter the ranks of elite society.[101]

The sensibilities of Michael Boyle reflected the mixed emotions of many other Irish Catholics, even those who had reached the upper rungs of the social ladder. Mayor Christopher O'Brien, though married to a member of the Old Stock establishment, "hated the English with a hate that knew no ending"; his brother Thomas, thoroughly integrated into the city's upper echelon, nonetheless recorded aspersions against the Irish in the memoir he dictated at the end of his life. Ignatius Donnelly, renowned as a scholar as well as a politician, regarded his accomplishments as a vindication of his race, since "a good many people believe that the proper occupation for a person of Irish blood is digging a ditch"[102] Defensively burdened by vestigial baggage of ethnic stereotyping, even those who had achieved status and success tended to retain a heightened investment in the image of the group as a whole. Thus, a complicated system of ethnic preference, in the name of "uplift," worked in tandem and sometimes in contradiction with class loyalties.

Whatever private reservations the rest of St. Paul may have held about its Irish Catholics, publicly at least, those with credentials of class and respectability appeared to be seamlessly absorbed into the social mainstream. John Ireland was a prominent figure at every civic occasion, and a series of lectures he delivered in 1881 attracted "an extremely large" audience, "about half of which was Protestant." Similarly, events to publicize the cause of Irish nationalism drew support from prominent non-Irish St. Paulites. An elaborate reception held for the Irish patriots Charles Parnell and John Dillon in 1880 was attended by the mayor and St. Paul's most respected citizens; Bishop Ireland made a stirring address; and the German-Jewish merchant Maurice Auerbach was moved to donate $150 to the cause.[103]

Michael Boyle's diaries offer a unique window on both the possibilities and the limits of social and economic mobility in late nineteenth-century middle-and upper-class St. Paul. Though he remained optimistic nearly to the end, the social and financial success to which Boyle aspired finally eluded him. He was welcomed in the best homes on Summit Avenue, joined the most elite clubs, and squired the daughters of the city's socially prominent businessmen, including Nellie Auerbach, daughter of his employer, but he never advanced from pleasant dinner companion to son-in-law. Michael chose to lay the blame at religion's door, but it was not his Irish Catholicism that stood in his way. To the contrary, the Irish-Catholic network had first opened the door of social possibility. Instead, a poor money manager, Michael never achieved the financial success that was the most essential credential for an "outsider" to marry into St. Paul society.[104]

Given the measure of fluidity in St. Paul, Michael's dreams were not unattainable, though they never materialized fully. Hamstrung from the outset by his father's debts and family responsibilities and unable to resist the attractions of the St. Paul social whirl, whose glitter never dimmed in his eyes, Boyle devoted most of his energy to honing his social rather than his business skills. A charming and competent salesman, he remained with his firm for fifty years but never moved into its management ranks, though his Irish-Catholic mentor, Constantine McConville, eventually became a partner in the firm. As approaching old age diminished Michael's value as a dinner guest, the Catholic Church and a shrinking circle of old friends once again became the focus of his bachelor social world. Always a staunch worker for the Democratic Party, he was rewarded for his loyalty when other resources dwindled. At the age of seventy-four, he went to work as a clerk for the county assessor, a post he held until his death eleven years later. In the end, living alone in bachelor quarters at the University Club, he was sustained by the same Irish-Catholic connections that had launched him as a youth.[105]

Though in Boyle's estimation the social world in which he traveled was the height of sophistication and refinement, his path never crossed that of James J. Hill, who seldom bothered to socialize with the mercantile civic leaders who invited Boyle into their homes. The set so admired by Michael on its part was equally in awe of Hill and his favored friends. With Hill as a model, mercantile society opened its doors to respectable young Irish men and women, many of whom were more successful than Michael at marrying into the "best" Protestant families and entering the ranks of the city's elite. Still, tales of discrimination continued to circulate in the Irish community, even among its upper class. Whether the stories sprang from real or imagined slights, they served to preserve and reinforce ethnic sensibilities. The tenacity of such claims of discrimination gives testimony to the power of the myth of mournful exile that bound the city's Irish together.[106]

St. Paul native F. Scott Fitzgerald, a member of the Summit Avenue crowd in the 1910s, felt marginalized in his social set and blamed it on his Irish Catholicism. That he genuinely believed this to be so is unquestionable. Indeed, volumes have been written about the ways in which his Irish-Catholic status anxieties informed his work. Nonetheless, the historical record suggests that the source of Fitzgerald's discomfiture was rooted in economic rather than ethnic circumstance, much like the case of Michael Boyle. Fitzgerald gained entrance to fashionable society through his Irish-Catholic grandfather, Philip McQuillan, who had been a promi-

Fig. 13. By the turn of the century, Irish, German, and Old Stock St. Paulites mingled as members of the elite Town and Country Club. Photo by Sweet. Courtesy of the Minnesota Historical Society.

nent St. Paul wholesale grocer, and through the social connections of his Aunt Anabel, a close friend of Mary Hill. If Fitzgerald felt confined to the social fringe, it was more likely because his father was a failure in business than for ethno-religious reasons.[107]

The city's "smart set," as delineated by the 1915 roster of the fashionable Town and Country Club, included Hill's sons and daughters, Old Stock Protestants, Irish Catholics, and German Catholics, Protestants, and Jews. Fully 20 percent of the members of the Town and Country Club had recognizably Irish surnames. Another 20 percent were of German origin.[108] In sum, an unusually diverse class of elites had coalesced to become St. Paul's civic leaders.

Of course, this group represented only a thin stratum of the city's population. Few working people achieved the financial credentials required for admission to the Town and Country Club. Still, the cross-class nature of ethnic and religious networks connected them in limited ways to city elites. As St. Paul's glory days drew to a close and the local economy began a slow decline, the capacity of these networks to cross class as well as cultural lines assumed an enhanced importance. Following the fiasco of the 1890 census war, St. Paul businessmen soon came to realize that for the city to remain economically viable, working people as well as the country club set must be enlisted in the civic project to save St. Paul, an endeavor that required careful mapping of a considerably broadened social landscape. It was one that would promote civic loyalty in the name of a common community of interests—interests that were inevitably and invariably threatened by enemies lurking just across the river in Minneapolis.

Chapter 3

DELIVERING THE GOODS:
The Social Geography of a Declining Economy

The Town and Country Club perched on a hill at the far western edge of St. Paul, overlooking the river that demarcated the city's boundary. Ironically, it seemed to fix its gaze longingly on Minneapolis rather than on St. Paul. This was no accident. Built in 1890, it stood as a memorial to St. Paul's final effort to wed its fortunes to those of its sister city. As one of the club's founders recalled, members had favored the site, "a good drive from either city," with specific hopes to draw members from Minneapolis, "thereby cementing the social relations, which were then and have been ever since rather frigid."[1] Not surprisingly, the victors of the census war were unmoved by this gesture of conciliation, and all but a few Minneapolis elites declined the invitation to join the Town and Country Club. Instead, they pointedly established their own exclusive Minikahda Club on the shores of Lake Calhoun—at the far southwestern edge of their city, geographically and socially removed from contact with St. Paul. The thrust of Minneapolis development consistently followed this pattern, moving ever westward and more distant from its less impressive twin.[2]

But the evolving urban geographies of St. Paul and Minneapolis were a function of internal workings far more than of intercity rivalry. The social ordering of the cities inscribed itself in their spatial ordering. Geographically, as in every other way, the contours of the two were more different than alike, and the social realities that shaped the cities cannot be understood apart from the built environment in which they occurred. Thus, as prelude to the politics about to unfold, a brief tour of these early twentieth-century urban spaces is in order.

Minneapolis elites demonstrated a distinct preference for distancing themselves from the common folks at home as well as from the city of St. Paul. In a pattern shared with most major urban centers, the city's mushrooming growth propelled rapid development of middle- and upper-class neighborhoods, followed by an equally speedy decline. As the city expanded, prosperous Minneapolitans moved steadily away from the core. The enormous wealth accumulated by the milling and lumber barons and their peers allowed them to erect lavish mansions, only to abandon them a decade later as the city encroached on their preserve. Attracted by the magnet of the picturesque lakes that lay to the southwest, each relocation increased their distance from the city's working class. By 1900, the addresses of prestige were located increasingly in Kenwood, overlooking Lake of the Isles, then distant from the city center, where protective covenants insured the "quality" of its residents; even more exclusive was Lowry Hill, where the mansions of city leaders peered down from inaccessible heights. The arrival of the automobile only accelerated this elite migration until by the 1920s, most of the families of the city founders had abandoned Minneapolis altogether, forming a self-contained enclave of country homes and estates in the village of Wayzata, twelve miles to the west on Lake Minnetonka, where they were far removed from social contact with the working city, which served to diminish accountability between employers and workers.[3] This spatial reordering thus was fraught with social consequences.

Older middle-class neighborhoods evolved in a similar pattern. The Oak Lake Addition, platted in 1880 near the city center as an "exclusive" middle-class neighborhood, had been largely abandoned by the Protestant middle class by 1910, fleeing the advance of the business zone (and Jewish and black residents) on their formerly pristine environment. Following the trail blazed by Tom Lowry's streetcar routes, middle-class Minneapolitans then moved en masse south and westward within the city limits, settling in new subdivisions conveniently owned and platted by Lowry and his associates. These migration patterns had a notably destabilizing effect on community identities.[4]

Working-class neighborhoods in the city were considerably more stable, since residents usually lacked the means to relocate at will. Nor could they afford long commutes to their jobs. In addition, working people were reluctant to stray far from the churches and social institutions that formed their primary social and economic support network. Though economic uncertainty might drive working-class families to change residences more frequently than middle- or upper-class Minneapolitans, the distance logged in their migrations was most often measured in blocks rather than in miles. Thus, in working-class Minneapolis, the primary composition of community was grounded in stable neighborhoods and fundamentally defined by class—socially, economically, and geographically separated from and in opposition to upper-class city leaders.[5] In sum, the geography of the city was both cause and effect of its social tensions.

In contrast, the urban geography of St. Paul developed in a distinctly different manner. While Minneapolis, by the turn of the century, was fueled by a spirit of economic exuberance, the luster of the capital city was already beginning to dim. In the economic heyday of the 1870s and 1880s, affluent St. Paulites had begun to relocate to Summit Avenue, a grand residential boulevard constructed along a bluff that overlooked the bustling, commercial center below and the river beyond. Such boulevards were common conventions in the Victorian cities of America. Summit Avenue was St. Paul's answer to Prairie Avenue in Chicago, Euclid Avenue in Cleveland, or Park Avenue in Minneapolis. But while Park, Prairie, and Euclid succumbed to encroaching industrial growth and elite migration, St. Paul seemed to stop dead in its tracks. The commercial center, hemmed in by hills and the river, never scaled the bluff to threaten the gracious vistas of the avenue. Moreover, St. Paul's slowing economic climate fostered fiscal conservatism among the upper class, resulting in a decided tendency to remain in place, protecting their considerable investment on the avenue, rather than drain their limited capital in extravagant new residential construction. Thus, unlike their peers in Chicago, Minneapolis, or Cleveland, St. Paul society stayed put on Summit for generations, anchored by the imposing residence of James J. Hill and, just across the boulevard, by the mammoth St. Paul Cathedral, dedicated in 1915. Claiming on the city's most commanding site, the cathedral dominated the city skyline, as indeed it does today.[6]

Summit Avenue endured as the most fashionable address in St. Paul, but the few large fortunes that remained in the city did not have the critical mass to create a milieu of glittering high society. Out of necessity, the badge of social prestige came to rely on pedigree rather than wealth. "Old money" (which, in St. Paul terms, meant about twenty-five years old) as often as not meant diminished wealth as well. As a result, elite St. Paul came to display a relatively modest appearance, a social sphere where the wealthy residents of Summit Avenue mingled with somewhat less affluent neighbors who resided in the immediately adjacent neighborhoods of Crocus and Cathedral Hills.

St. Paul native F. Scott Fitzgerald was a member of this crowd. Though Fitzgerald's family was continually in financial straits, moving from one rental unit near the avenue to another, his grandfather McQuillan had once been one of the city's most prominent wholesalers and his grandmother and aunt remained close friends with Mary Hill. Socially if not financially they had the proper credentials, and the family was admitted to the "best" society. At the Ramaley Dancing Academy just off Summit, where Fitzgerald and other proper young St. Paulites were schooled in the social graces, the somewhat ambiguous nature of the city's upper crust was quite apparent. Vividly described by Fitzgerald's biographer, "The wealthiest children came to Ramaley's in black limousines with monograms and coats-of-arms on the doors and liveried chauffeurs in attendance. Those less wealthy drove with their mothers in the family electric, and those not wealthy at all rode the streetcar or trudged through the snow, swinging their patent leather shoes in a slipper bag."[7] Though this hardly represents a broad leveling of society, it does indicate a far more elastic circle of elites than that of the clique who defined "society" in Minneapolis.

As the city grew, upper-class St. Paulites found themselves in intimate daily contact with a much broader range of people. The real estate developers who laid out

Fig. 14. In a departure from the typical urban pattern, fashionable St. Paulites did not abandon Summit Avenue, which retains its cachet as an address of prestige and appears today much as it did in this 1886 photo. Courtesy of the Minnesota Historical Society.

Summit Avenue had plotted a peculiar course. After winding along the scenic bluff for half a mile, the street abandoned its picturesque route and took a sharp right turn to plow across the plain in a straight line west to the city limits, where it again met the river, which bowed back to meet it. The planners had good reason for making this detour. By routing the parklike boulevard across the flatland, they boosted the real estate value of miles of otherwise unremarkable properties.[8]

This scheme did not quite live up to expectations. The developers had envisioned miles of finely appointed neighborhoods blooming in the shade of the avenue, basking in its reflected prestige. In 1884, the trustees of fledgling Macalester College, hoping to benefit from the anticipated land boom, relocated the college to what was then the outlying reaches of the boulevard. Their aim was to build the institution's endowment through the development of some forty adjacent acres of curving lanes, promoted as an exclusive, pastoral suburb—a plan that paralleled Archbishop Ireland's speculative venture two miles farther west. Unfortunately for all concerned, both projects fizzled. First, Minneapolis streetcar magnate Thomas Lowry delayed construction of the all-important streetcar lines; then, the boom of the 1880s gave way to the depression of the following decade. St. Paul never recovered its former economic ebullience, and new fortunes in the city were few and relatively modest. The market for country estates proved to be almost nil, and most of the college lots remained unsold for decades.[9] Other development plans met a similar fate. As a result, Summit Avenue, which retained its élan, became bounded by considerably less pretentious neighbors.

Crowded out of the commercial district, middle- and working-class St. Paulites followed the exodus up the bluff, resulting in a geographic intimacy between ordinary citizens and elites. Though St. Paul developed primarily as a city of single-family residences, the slow population growth and stagnating housing market after the turn of the century fostered a heterogeneous mix of properties. The mingling on nearly every block of substantial two-story dwellings with more modest cottages, duplexes, and an occasional apartment building established neighborhoods of a somewhat mixed economic and occupational character. The neighborhoods that sprouted within walking distance of Summit Avenue typically included tradespeople and skilled workers along with middle managers, professionals, and prosperous businessmen.[10]

St. Paulites of every class came to consider the Avenue as something akin to a public park. Sunday afternoons saw servant girls and mechanics, dressed in their Sunday best, strolling past the lavishly appointed mansions as they enjoyed the amenities of the boulevard.[11] Working people also mingled with elites in neighborhood establishments that grew up on the streetcar commercial strips on either side of the Avenue. In 1910, the soda fountain at nearby Frost's Drugstore was a favorite haunt of diverse groups of young people that included both the sons and daughters of privilege and domestics employed in the Summit Avenue mansions.[12]

None of this is to suggest that proper young ladies sipped sodas with servant girls or that mechanics and businessmen mixed socially. Nonetheless, the intimate scale of the city fostered an interclass proximity that required daily interactions on many levels. Where the line most notably blurred was between the tradesmen, skilled workers, and middling white-collar professionals, clerks, and managers who shared the neighborhoods on either side of Summit Avenue. These would become the central players in the construction of the civic compact.

The solidly working-class neighborhoods were ethnically and economically more homogeneous, often defined by their parish churches. For instance, in the large German enclave in Frogtown, a mile north of Summit, unpretentious homes clustered around the beloved magnet of St. Agnes Church, the center of much of the neighborhood's social activity.[13] For many of the working people who lived in Frogtown, economics as much as preference proscribed their social circle. The prohibitive cost of a five-cent streetcar fare determined that people like blacksmith Peter Theis and his family kept outings within walking distance. Others, such as young Maude Pohl, the daughter of a modest bookbinder, had so many social commitments in the neighborhood that she seldom found time for travels around the rest of the city. In 1909–10, daily letters to her fiancé described a calendar of events that kept Maude in constant motion but seldom took her more than a few blocks from home. A seamstress for a neighborhood milliner, Maude divided her evenings between card parties and dances at Tschida's Hall, sewing club with other German young ladies, choir rehearsals at St. Agnes, and the occasional treat of a play, sometimes performed in German—a schedule so full that she was "all in by the end of the week." Besides these organized activities, several nights a week family and friends gathered around the table for conversation and heated games of Hasenpfeffer. Her "lonesome Joe," posted to Chicago by the railroad, lamented to "Darling Maude," "Gee won't I be glad when I'll be back in good old St. Paul again."[14]

In Frogtown, the biggest event of 1909 was the laying of the cornerstone for the new St. Agnes church, with the dedication sermon delivered by the German bishop from St. Cloud rather than the archbishop—an occasion that drew German St. Paulites from every class and neighborhood to celebrate the event with the more than one thousand German families the parish served. The ethnic character of the parish quite evidently created a center that nurtured interclass relationships among German-speaking St. Paulites.[15] But the practice of Catholicism also fostered other sorts of cross-class and cross-ethnic mingling.

Though Catholics displayed fervent loyalty to their particular parishes, which worked to create enduring neighborhood stability, they also shared a devotion to the cathedral, the physical manifestation of Catholic power in St. Paul. For ten years, the city's Catholics faithfully contributed their hard-earned dollars to the building fund, many of them laboring on the project. On completion, the magnificent edifice welcomed all Catholic worshippers to the rarefied heights of Summit Avenue. The church also encouraged its members to participate in services with their confreres in other parishes, as well as in special occasions at the cathedral—a testament to Catholic universalism. The mass, at least in theory, was celebrated in an identical manner in churches everywhere. Evidence abounds that a tradition of "church visiting" was a long-standing practice in St. Paul that encouraged ethnic, class, and neighborhood interaction. When the French church of St. Louis was dedicated in 1868, the occasion was celebrated by a procession of "the various pious associations of the German parish with their banners [and] the music of their band," who then were hosted by the French Canadians at the ensuing celebration. In the 1880s, Irish salesman Michael Boyle recorded regular travels about town to attend Mass at the German, French, and Bohemian parishes. Mary Hill, the grande dame of St. Paul, recorded a similar pattern of church visiting, as did her downstairs maid Celia Tauer in 1910. As late as the 1950s, for some St. Paul Catholics, proper observance of Holy Thursday (three days before Easter) included visitation at a minimum of six different churches in the city. Parish festivals and fund-raisers also occasioned such city-wide visiting.[16]

On a more regular basis, Catholic organizations created other venues for diverse citizens to come together. Maude Pohl and her brother John occasionally hopped the streetcar to attend card parties at the Knights of Columbus Hall, the bastion of respectable Irish Catholics. Celia Tauer also participated in interethnic Catholic socializing, attending parties at the local Hibernian Hall. This multilayered Catholic

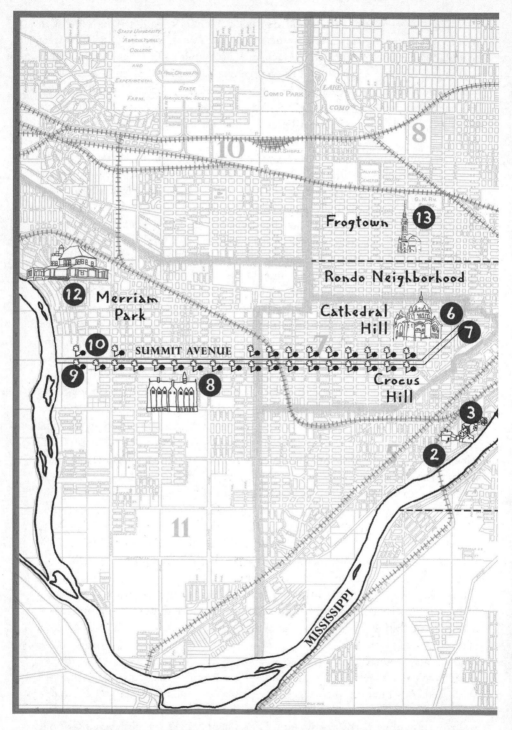

Fig. 15. Map of the city in 1905. Created by Cory Barton. Property of the author.

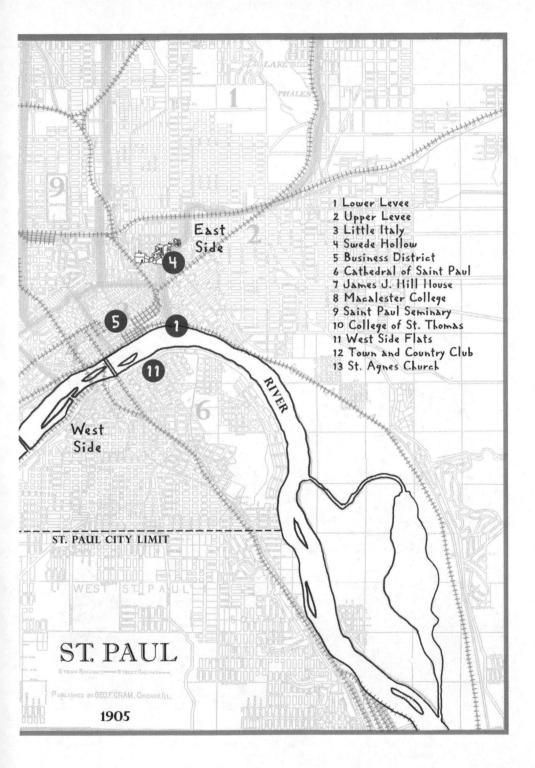

1 Lower Levee
2 Upper Levee
3 Little Italy
4 Swede Hollow
5 Business District
6 Cathedral of Saint Paul
7 James J. Hill House
8 Macalester College
9 Saint Paul Seminary
10 College of St. Thomas
11 West Side Flats
12 Town and Country Club
13 St. Agnes Church

East
Side

West
Side

RIVER

ST. PAUL CITY LIMIT

WEST ST PAUL

ST. PAUL

Steam Railway — Street Railway

Published by GEO.F.CRAM, Chicago, Ill.

1905

LAKE PHALEN

Fig. 16. When completed in 1917, the cathedral towered above surrounding neighborhoods, the visible symbol of Catholic power in St. Paul. (The roofline of the Hill mansion is visible on the right.) Courtesy of the Minnesota Historical Society.

world served to shrink the space that separated neighborhoods, creating another set of linkages that crossed class, ethnic, and geographical boundaries.[17]

Set in the midst of these multiple border crossings was one neighborhood where boundaries were distinct and quite impermeable, though no map marked their coordinates. By the turn of the century, St. Paul's small contingent of African Americans had begun to coalesce in a narrow sixteen-block area bounded on the north by German working-class Frogtown and by the mixed neighborhood north of Summit Avenue on the south. Within these confines, the city's African Americans created a thriving self-contained community that became, according to historian David Taylor, the "center of Black social and cultural activity in the state, well into the 20th century." The Rondo district, as it was called, was home to black professionals, businesses, cultural and political clubs, a newspaper with a national audience, and no less than six churches. This was no mere pocket of poverty. Quite to the contrary, blighted housing was relatively rare. The black community had its own social and spatial hierarchy that extended from the socially proper Oatmeal Hill on the western edge to the poorer district of Cornmeal Valley to the east.[18]

The racial fluidity of frontier St. Paul had been of short duration. In fact, by the mid-1850s, St. Paul legislators had attempted first to pass a bill discouraging black in-migration and, when that failed, a measure that would restrict black residency to Minneapolis—hardly gestures of either interracial or intercity fraternity.[19] In St. Paul's early years, interracial marriages scarcely raised an eyebrow, but by 1888, the attempted elopement of an interracial couple landed the two in the county jail.[20] Still, for several reasons, such racial tensions seldom broke the surface of civic peace. Most important, blacks constituted a tiny minority of the total population. In 1910, only 3,154 African Americans resided in St. Paul—less than 1.5 percent of city residents. Second, local blacks had successfully recruited a wide range of professionals to relocate to the city—doctors, dentists, lawyers, teachers, newspaper editors—that created a leadership contingent who assiduously worked to guard community interests. As early as 1887, for instance, local citizens had established a state civil rights league to advance black industrial and civil rights.[21]

Though racial prejudice enforced residential segregation and limited job opportunities, the political configuration of St. Paul provided a certain amount of leverage that African Americans used to their advantage. Black voters were Republican voters. In this city of Democratic dominance, Republican leaders sometimes were driven to cultivate African American voters, who might mean the margin of victory in close city elections. Maximizing these opportunities, before the turn of the century members of the black community had secured positions in the police and fire departments, served on local juries, and established an African American company of the city militia.[22] Thus, the place of African Americans in the civic community was fraught with ambiguity. As the most startling example, in 1900 Charles James, a light-skinned black artisan and member of a long-established St. Paul family, presided as president of the St. Paul Trades and Labor Assembly.[23]

Clearly, then, the black community was not wholly marginalized. Nor was segrega-

Fig. 17. The ladies of the Minnesota Federation of Negro Women, posing on the steps of Pilgrim Baptist Church in 1907, reflect the middle-class leadership that influenced St. Paul's African American community. Courtesy of the Minnesota Historical Society.

tion strictly observed, though black-white interaction was a highly unequal exchange. In 1892, Archbishop Ireland, always attuned to opportunities to expand Catholic influence, established St. Peter Claver parish as a Catholic beachhead in the Rondo neighborhood. In the fluid environs of pioneer St. Paul, the Ireland family had lived for years next to black and racially mixed neighbors. That intimate contact had imbued young John with racially progressive ideas that outdistanced those of most of his contemporaries. As early as 1863, he had attempted to start a school for the town's African American Catholics.[24] Thirty years later, he was still struggling against the tide. Preaching the doctrine of racial equality, he declared, "I would open to the Negro all industrial and professional avenues—the test for his advance being his ability but never his color." Sending a succession of Irish, Polish, and German priests to serve the parish, he hoped to create a racially integrated enclave and thereby "blot out the color line." But, despite his efforts, few white Catholics extended their church visiting to St. Peter Claver, and reluctantly, "as a temporary expedient," the archbishop declared St. Peter Claver a national parish—which in this case, of course, meant a segregated parish.[25]

Missionary efforts were not the only white incursions into the Rondo neighborhood, which was never purely a racial preserve. As late as 1930, no more than 48 percent of its population was black. Though most white St. Paulites held themselves aloof from African American fellow citizens, those who chose to live in the Rondo neighborhood encountered little resentment. For instance, German Catholic siblings, Henry and Ann Houck, resided contentedly for more than fifty years on Rondo Avenue in harmony with their black neighbors. This permeability of racial borders was a one-way street, however. Though the Houcks could choose to reside on Rondo, their neighbors would have been decidedly unwelcome either in Frogtown or in the Macalester Park neighborhood where Ann and Henry's siblings made their homes.[26] African American professionals mainly lived and worked inside the neighborhood. Wage workers, of course, ranged across the city, laboring for the railroads or working in hotels, restaurants, and private homes; but at the end of the day, they returned home to the community they had created—a part of the city and yet a place apart.

Scandinavian St. Paul built another sort of separate world. This ethnic enclave was both culturally and geographically disconnected from the rest of the city. The relatively late arrival of the Scandinavians had excluded them from opportunities that had benefited German and Irish immigrants who had preceded them. In 1880, no more than twenty-five hundred Swedes and another one thousand Norwegians of foreign-born or mixed parentage resided in Ramsey County. Most had arrived without capital and found work as common laborers. Initially, they huddled on the city's undeveloped East Side, separated from the rest of the city by a series of deep ravines and a tangle of railroad tracks and shops. As their financial stability and numbers grew—by 1905, the combined Scandinavian population of the county had exploded to more than forty-seven thousand persons—most chose to stay on the East Side, creating an ethnic enclave that was almost a city in itself, with its own thriving main street, Payne Avenue, and its own somewhat self-contained subeconomy, where Swedish was the common language of commerce. As the Scandinavians began to prosper, they created new neighborhoods to the east and north rather than melting into other areas of middle-class St. Paul, "making it possible to move up the social ladder without leaving the community."[27]

The Scandinavians held fast to their churches and ethnic associational ties and usually voted Republican, abhorring the free-wheeling practices of the Catholic-dominated Democrats. Politically, though they became a force in statewide politics, they were marginalized at the municipal level, particularly after 1914, when the city replaced ward-based representation with a commission style of government, the six commissioners elected on an at-large basis—a reorganization that probably was not unrelated to the growth of the Scandinavian population.[28] Thus, by both choice and circumstance, Scandinavian St. Paul remained cut off—geographically, culturally, and socially—from the intercourse among neighborhoods that characterized other areas of the city.

Then there was "invisible" St. Paul, the pockets of poverty that had no place in

Fig. 18. View of the East Side, 1910. Both deep ravines and a welter of railroad tracks created barriers between the East Side and the rest of St. Paul. In some places, people had to negotiate sixteen sets of tracks to cross to the city center. Photo by Albert Munson. Courtesy of the Minnesota Historical Society.

the emerging civic vision. Hidden away from the public gaze, the city's poor could count on little support from official sources. Those who populated "Little Italy" on the river flats on the east bank of the river, the eastern Europeans who claimed the flats on the western side, the down-and-out Irishmen who battled Swedes and Italians for scarce resources in "Swede Hollow," a deep ravine below Hamm's Brewery on the East Side, or the mixed population of Connemara Patch, stashed away amidst the tracks and trestles of lower Payne Avenue—all were left largely to find their own means of survival.[29]

Though they provided an essential source of unskilled labor, these city residents received no commensurate share of public resources in return. In Swede Hollow, for example, a ramshackle cluster of jerry-built houses, the city never saw fit to extend either running water or sewers to its residents, though for more than seventy years it housed a succession of immigrant workers—Swedes, Italians, Poles, and, fi-

Fig. 19. Secluded below the High Bridge, Little Italy (pictured here in 1889) was relatively hidden from public view, which allowed city leaders to ignore the needs of its residents. Courtesy of the Minnesota Historical Society.

nally, Mexicans. Nils Hokanson, who lived in the hollow in the 1890s, recalled that his father had climbed the long, narrow stairway out of the ravine each morning to work a ten-hour day on the streetcar tracks for one dollar's pay (a job he had obtained by bribing the Irish crew boss). His mother also made the trek to work as a laundress in city homes. Residents of the hollow supplemented such meager incomes by raising chickens, goats, ducks, and pigs, and tried to keep the filth at bay by organizing community cleanup days—a futile effort, since people living above them had a habit of dumping their garbage down the steep banks into the ravine. In 1892, an article in the *Pioneer Press* described the culture of the hollow as quaint, "a little world all of its own, and drunken Saturday night brawls failed to disturb the people far overhead." In the summer of 1900, the city health department briefly took notice of the abominable living conditions. A sweltering heat wave had elicited flurries of complaint from surrounding residents, "disturbed" for once by the odors emanating from below. Public interest evaporated, however, when a fortuitously heavy rainfall brought citizen complaints to an end, permanently shelving plans to begin a sewer project.[30]

Despite the colorful names that characterized these impoverished neighborhoods, they were not the ethnically homogeneous enclaves that might be found in certain working-class neighborhoods. The city's poor were of mixed origin, and out of necessity, their sense of community often derived from common economic condition as much as from ethnic bonds.[31] For instance, in the Badlands, a humble district near the railroad tracks populated by common laborers and their families, Italians mingled with Irish, Jews, and African Americans in neighborly confusion and mutuality. According to Angelo Vruno, who vividly recalled his boyhood in the neighborhood, "You could go into anybody's house. They'd never chase you out. There'd never be no hard feelings. . . . Everybody got along and people were good to each other." When Angelo's mother was facing childbirth, her African American neighbor, Mrs. Beasley, came from next door to assist her. If a birth was particularly difficult, the Vrunos called on Dr. Williams, another African American, to aid in the delivery. Similarly, Gentile Yarusso declared that in Swede Hollow, people were closely attached to the community and "all nationalities got along very well together."[32] The interethnic mingling that characterized St. Paul's upper and middle classes was even more apparent at the bottom of the economic ladder.

Official city policy was to regard these hidden enclaves of poverty as "picturesque," asserting that the immigrant residents lived according to "old-world custom" purely by choice. This was a sustainable myth because several factors combined to keep the city's poverty problem "under control." First, the size of any one of these immigrant hamlets was relatively small. Swede Hollow had only seventy houses, and less than one hundred families lived in what was called Little Italy. In 1900, only slightly more than one thousand first- and second-generation Italians lived in all of St. Paul. Twenty years later, despite a national explosion of Italian immigration, their numbers locally had increased to just five thousand. Without a substantial industrial economy, St. Paul's job opportunities were too limited to attract great numbers of immigrants to the city. Minneapolis, on the other hand, had an insatiable demand for industrial labor; moreover, it was the acknowledged recruiting center for the casual labor that fed the harvest fields and lumber camps of the Northwest. Given the relative labor markets, it well may be that St. Paul's most flourishing export in these years was its unemployed and working poor to the labor markets of Minneapolis.[33]

Those who remained sustained themselves through a combination of resourcefulness and privately funded aid. Most important, though they had precious little cash, the immigrants had access to land, unlike the urban poor in many other cities. Even the meanest of these local enclaves was made up of single- or double-family dwellings. Though the living quarters might be rude and inadequate, families had the space to keep livestock and plant gardens or lovingly tended grape arbors that flourished somehow, despite the harsh Minnesota winters. Salvatore and Phylla Vruno, who raised a family in a one-bedroom house, could not begin to feed their thirteen children from the wages Sam received as a ditch digger for the local power company. Instead, they relied on home production and Sam's resourceful forays into the countryside, where he netted fish, rabbits, pheasants, and even an occasional raccoon. Thus, though wages were meager and uncertain, through their own resourcefulness families like the Vrunos somehow managed to have something nourishing bubbling in the pot when the family sat down to dinner.[34]

As a last resort, the immigrants could turn to a complex network of aid supported by local ethnic or religious charitable organizations. A combination of ethnic sensibility and denominational competition had cultivated an array of associations dedicated to the somewhat inconsistent aims of Americanization, cultural maintenance, uplift, and social control. The Catholic Church was the engine at the head of this social-welfare train. The twin projects of uplifting and ministering to the poor were familiar responsibilities, and by the turn of the century, Catholic institutional support covered the full spectrum from infant care to old folks' homes. In addition, by 1896, nearly every settled parish had established a chapter of the St. Vincent de Paul Society, dedicated to relief of the poor. The Protestant churches, not to be outdone by the Catholics, had mustered their own army of institutions. Germans and Scandinavians, true to form, created yet other support networks, based on ethnic association as well as religion—a project that foregrounded cultural maintenance as an integral element of assistance. In contrast, the city's German Jews, dismayed by the arrival of rustic coreligionists from eastern Europe, instituted an energetic Americanization campaign, supplementing material aid with the establishment of the Neighborhood House on the West Side flats, which focused on teaching the English language and "explaining the customs and ideals of their adopted country."[35] Thus, in a variety of ways and means, private organizations competed with one another to win the hearts and minds of the poor.

The reaction from the intended beneficiaries predictably was mixed. Italians, Poles, and Bohemians wrangled with Irish clerics over attempts to reshape their culture and religion; hard-drinking Swedes sometimes snubbed the missionary efforts of straitlaced, fellow ethnics; and Jews on the river flats often stubbornly clung to their traditional ways.[36] Moreover, the immigrants, though poor, "had a lot of pride" and turned to charity only as a last resort. According to Angelo Vruno, when his family and their neighbors were forced to accept temporary relief measures, they attempted to hide it from one another, ashamed to admit their need.[37] Still, when all else failed, these institutions of support could at least temporarily keep the family afloat. The support offered was never generous enough to improve living conditions substantially. Nonetheless, given the relatively small size of these pockets of poverty and the quasi-rural nature of the settlements, private charitable efforts contained the poverty "problem" well enough to keep it from intruding unduly on the public consciousness.

The physical terrain of the city also acted to maintain the invisibility of its poor. Little Italy on the upper levee, "isolated from the rest of the city by bluffs and railroad tracks"; Swede Hollow, buried in a deep ravine; and the West Side Flats on the far side of the river—all were spatially as well as culturally disconnected from the city proper.[38] Workers emerged from these neighborhoods every morning to dig the ditches, stoke the fires, and wash the clothes of their fellow St. Paulites but were quickly forgotten when they disappeared at the end of the day. In working out the complicated negotiations and compromises that underlay St. Paul's civic relationships, the city's poor were truly out of sight and most definitely out of mind.

The great irony of St. Paul was that a city built on networks of trade extending across the continent and beyond would come to stake its survival on a parochial localism based on narrow spatial and imaginative boundaries. Though at the end of the nineteenth century St. Paul was deeply enmeshed in the world economy, its citizens did not experience their city as part of a global framework. Their perspective was ineluctably local. But neither were they seeking a return to a set of pre-modern, idealized relationships. Only gradually, out of a complex interaction of economic, social, and cultural contingencies, would the various architects of civic identity construct the protective fortress of community insularity. As they searched for some way to redeem St. Paul's stature at the close of the nineteenth century, in their minds, the future course of the city was as yet undetermined.[39]

In the summer of 1893, quite evidently metropolitan dreams had not yet expired. The city of St. Paul, hoping to publicize itself as a national trade center, orchestrated a spectacular celebration to fete James J. Hill and the completion of his transcontinental railway. The last spike of the Great Northern had been driven the previous January in the Cascade Mountains but without any of the hoopla that had surrounded the completion of the Northern Pacific (now in receivership) a decade earlier. In fact, the truculent Hill had stayed home in St. Paul, nursing a bout of rheumatism.[40]

Local boosters were not about to lose such an opportunity to publicize their city and its most famous son. They determined to celebrate the momentous feat in style, reminding all the world that St. Paul was the headquarters and heart of the remarkable Great Northern. Five months in the planning, the three-day extravaganza unfolded as a spectacle that commingled civic pride and homage to Hill. Four triumphal arches, miles of flags and bunting, and countless portraits of the Great Man transformed the city's business district. From a reviewing stand, the Empire Builder himself nodded approval as floats representing the states and cities linked to St. Paul by the Great Northern paraded past, together with those of St. Paul manufacturers, wholesalers, and jobbers whose prosperity was equally tied to Hill's transportation network. The rich and famous gathered that evening to honor Hill at a testimonial banquet held in the elegant Aberdeen Hotel. Ordinary St. Paulites were invited to pay tribute the following evening at a reception "in no sense of a private character," where they might shake the magnate's hand and witness the presentation of an intricately wrought silver punch bowl, commissioned by the city to commemorate the momentous occasion.[41]

The fervent lionization of Hill was understandable. Not only was he St. Paul's most powerful resident and its greatest claim to fame; as the financial panic of 1893 inexorably crushed the nation's economy, the Great Northern alone among the rail carriers continued to show a profit, so much so that, according to Hill's biographer, it was something of an embarrassment. Hill had foreseen the coming crisis and was well prepared when the panic struck. For this, his employees and all those who depended on his roads were exceedingly grateful.[42]

Within the year, however, they realized that their gratitude was somewhat misplaced. Despite the Great Northern's sound financial position, Hill nonetheless cut wages to the level of the other rapidly bankrupting roads. As he saw, it the depressed wage market provided a golden opportunity to divert labor costs into capital improvements. Not surprisingly, his employees saw the situation differently. In April 1894, after wages had been slashed for the third time in less than three months, Great Northern workers appealed to Eugene Debs, president of the fledgling American Railway Union (ARU), to intervene. Only months earlier, the ARU had successfully negotiated a new wage schedule with the ailing Northern Pacific, which accrued the union new prestige and confidence among railroad workers. Flushed with success, Debs welcomed the opportunity to test the union's strength.[43]

As the strike attested, Hill had seriously underestimated his employees. Perhaps the great celebration held in his honor had deceived him about the degree of personal loyalty he commanded. More likely, he believed he had enough inside influence with the railroad brotherhoods and the Knights of Labor to keep workers from defecting to the ARU. His donation books reveal regular dispersal of funds to injured workers and widows of men killed on the job, contributions to the railroad brotherhoods, and most intriguingly, an unspecified gift of $250 to the Knights of Labor. Apparently confident about his ability to negotiate with his employees, Hill had refused to tie his wage rates to those of the other roads, informing a receiver for the Northern Pacific that "different methods of treating with the men should be pursued by the different roads."[44]

The railroad baron initially believed he could break the solidarity of the ARU by calling on the loyalty of "faithful employees," negotiating separately with the skilled brotherhoods, and firing known members of the ARU. He quickly discovered his mistake. Workers all along the line, inflamed by Hill's high-handed tactics and impressed by the ARU's success against the Northern Pacific, flocked into the union by the hundreds. The Knights of Labor also temporarily reversed its decline in membership by throwing its support to the striking railroad workers. As the strike raced along the line, the Great Northern ground to a standstill.[45]

To his consternation, Hill found that he had few supporters in the struggle as his expected allies defected, one after the other. His fellow railroad magnates took the opportunity to repay his earlier refusal to join in association with them, by declining to handle freight routed in Great Northern cars. Political connections also failed him. Despite Hill's substantial past support for Grover Cleveland, the president refused to deploy federal troops, advised by federal judge (and St. Paul resident) Walter Sanborn that the strikers had violated no federal law.[46] As for local businessmen, they were desperate to end the strike on any terms. Few of the manufacturers in the city had the capital resources to stockpile large quantities of raw materials, nor could the city's wholesalers or retailers afford to carry extensive inventories. St. Paul's economy demanded a constant traffic of raw materials and consumer goods in and out of the city to sustain itself in the best of times. In the present depression, an extended transportation shutdown could easily have been fatal.[47] Finally, the Minneapolis grain trust had a long-standing antagonistic relationship with Hill and, more immediately, feared that the strike would foster an alliance between workers and farmers along the line that might have dangerous political consequences. In short, while labor displayed unprecedented unity, capital could not have been more disunited than in this struggle.[48]

Hoping to split the union's ranks by granting concessions to the running trades, Hill attempted to negotiate privately with Debs, but Debs held firm in representing the interests of the unskilled as well as skilled workers. The pragmatic Hill finally had to admit defeat. He agreed with Debs to submit the dispute to a panel of St. Paul businessmen for arbitration. With the city's economy imperiled by the transportation shutdown, immediate self-interest won the day. The panel voted to grant the strikers 97.5 percent of their wage demands, thus concluding the only major strike against Hill's railroads in his lifetime.[49]

The strike lasted just less than two weeks, but the lessons it conveyed would make an indelible imprint on labor relations in St. Paul. Though James J. Hill grudgingly accepted the terms of arbitration, even congratulating Debs on his "shrewd management" of the strike, he must have been galled. As Debs's train pulled out of the St. Paul yards, the men of the Great Northern, who had cheered Hill on so many public occasions, doffed their hats in silent gratitude to the man who had bested him.[50] The railroad titan had learned that even he could not rely on personal authority and back-room negotiation to keep order among his thousands of employees. Not a man to make the same mistake twice, at the urging of his associate, financier J. P. Morgan, Hill set about rationalizing labor relations.[51]

The first order of business, as all the railroad managers agreed, was to rid themselves of the dangerous industrial unionism advocated by the ARU. In July, when a major strike broke out in Chicago against the Pullman Car Company, they made their move. Hill and his fellow railroad executives across the country, marshaling their collective political and economic influence, clamored for federal intervention. The troops denied to Hill three months earlier swept into Chicago, destroying the strike. The subsequent prosecution and imprisonment of Debs and other ARU leaders for supposedly conspiring to interfere with interstate commerce and the mails dealt a mortal blow to the fledgling ARU.[52]

That task completed, Hill then agreed to join in association with the other transcontinental roads to regularize rates and labor negotiations, a combination made considerably less distasteful after he gained a managing interest in the Northern Pacific in 1895, effecting a virtual transportation monopoly between St. Paul and the Pacific coast. Since the efficient and continuous operation of rail service was dependent on the skills of the engineers, firemen, conductors, and trainmen—

the members of the "Big Four" brotherhoods—the railroad systems were willing to work with the "responsible unionism" of these skilled workers as a palatable alternative to industrial unionism. The brotherhoods accepted the bargain. As a result, workers in the running trades achieved what historian Shelton Stromquist has described as "an unprecedented level of security and recognition" that eluded most American workers, including unskilled railroad laborers, until the 1930s.[53]

The benefits of this pact were not lost on St. Paul businessmen. The Great Northern strike had brought home to them, as never before, the city's dependence on the railroad. It also demonstrated the havoc played on their balance sheets by even a short disruption of business. Thus, the model of rationalized railroad labor negotiation prepared them to consider the possible advantages of "moderate" unionism at the local level. Compromise and negotiation seemed a small price to pay when the alternative was financial disaster. If even the powerful James J. Hill thought it prudent to negotiate with organized labor, they would take their cue from him.

Other considerations also worked to create a pact between local business and labor. Ironically, the completion of the Great Northern, which the city had celebrated so extravagantly, would hasten St. Paul's decline. The local economy had been powered for years by railroad expansion. The constant flow of men and supplies through the city's command post had generated jobs orders, and cash for the local economy, as well as created a number of significant fortunes in construction and correlative industries. All this was coming to an end. The building of trunk lines and maintenance of the roads assured that established major firms, such as Butler Brothers and Foley Brothers, would endure; new opportunities in construction began to fade, however, as did many of the jobs they had provided. Moreover, with enhanced cooperation among the rail carriers and technological advances, such as refrigerated rail cars, by the turn of the century St. Paul had lost its pivotal position as a distribution point. That crisis was exacerbated by the growth of mail-order retailers and national chain stores along with the slowing of westward migration. The local consequences of these larger trends became apparent only gradually, the final blow delivered by the opening of the Panama Canal in 1914. But even by the turn of the century, the city's economy had begun to slow perceptibly. Local wholesalers, jobbers, retailers, and manufacturers—indeed, every sector of the city's economy—felt the pinch. The city had tied its fortunes in a thousand ways to the railroad, and the boom years were over. The problem now became less one of growth than of survival.[54]

The city's working people also took lessons from the Great Northern strike and its aftermath. Organized labor already had put down deep roots in the city, transplanted from the East with its Irish and German ethnics and supported by the city's Democratic Party, which relied on the grace of working-class votes to keep it in power. The *Minnesota Union Advocate*, established in 1886 by an Irish-Catholic union typographer, Cornelius Guiney, flourished as the official voice for organized labor in the city.[55] But the future trajectory of the labor movement was as yet uncertain in 1894. Union membership split between trade unionists affiliated with the American Federation of Labor (AFL) and the more inclusive Knights of Labor. In 1885, the city counted fifteen hundred trade unionists and thirteen assemblies of the Knights. Dual unionism was tolerated without friction, and the Trades and Labor Assembly, established in 1882, served as an umbrella organization for both the Knights and the AFL.[56]

The aftermath of the Great Northern strike occasioned a notable realignment. During the strike the Knights had welcomed Eugene Debs and thrown their whole-hearted support to the ARU, while the craft unions, following the lead of AFL president Samuel Gompers, sided with the brotherhoods and stayed out of the fray. In the euphoria following the ARU victory, the Knights experienced a brief upsurge in membership, but the subsequent collapse of the railroad union took down the Knights of Labor in its wake, ending St. Paul's flirtation with industrial unionism. The Knights' demise in turn solidified the position of the trade unions. Skilled former Knights took their union consciousness—and a new sense of caution—into the AFL, leaving their unskilled brethren behind. Unionism in St. Paul from that point forward modeled itself on the strategies of compromise and negotiation that characterized the success of the craft-defined railroad brotherhoods. Just as the brotherhoods viewed their interests as dependent on the well-being of the railroads, so the city's trade unions became deeply invested in maintaining a healthy economic climate in St. Paul. The greatest threat to their well-being, as they assessed it, was not from employer abuse but from forces outside the city that might eradicate their jobs and their community altogether. Thus, the stage was set for a long era of compromise between business and organized labor. Though their interests were not identical, they had a common stake in the economic well-being of the city, and when they came to the bargaining table, both sides understood that compromise was essential to keep the city's increasingly precarious economy intact.[57]

As the century turned, both business and labor were coming to regard St. Paul as a city under siege. The Minneapolis industrial dynamo emerged from the depression of the nineties stronger than ever. Its sawmill industry was on the verge of becoming the largest producer in the nation; it had become the country's largest primary wheat market; and it was eating away at St. Paul's already shrinking wholesaling market. The capital city was rapidly being reduced to no more than a regional distribution center and struggled mightily to maintain even that modest position. The total value of its manufacturing output in 1900 was less than one third that of Minneapolis. By 1907, when bank clearances in Minneapolis had reached the billion-dollar mark, St. Paul lagged far behind at $250 million.[58]

Faced with such hard facts, St. Paul civic leaders were forced to discard metropolitan aspirations and focus their energies on a defensive strategy to keep the city's position from eroding further—a project that would require interclass investment in civic loyalty. Boosterism was redirected at a new audience—the residents of St. Paul—in a campaign to turn the city's liabilities into virtues. Smaller was better, so the rhetoric went. St. Paul, unlike its rival across the river, cared about its citizens. St. Paul was not a heartless industrial machine; it was a community. The bonds of

Fig. 20. By the 1890s a strong union culture was well established in St. Paul, as displayed by the United Brotherhood of Leatherworkers at this 1894 gathering, the year of the Great Northern strike. Courtesy of the Minnesota Historical Society.

community then logically demanded that St. Paulites patronize local businesses, support the Democratic Party, and keep their dollars and their votes out of the grasping hands of Minneapolis. The other side of community accountability required business to make considerable concessions to working-class residents of the city. Both business and labor had much to gain from such a pact, and they worked together to construct a fortress of localism that would engage St. Paulites, across class and ethnic differences, in a common loyalty to the city.

The insular civic identity that became St. Paul's most distinctive characteristic derived from a logic based on complicated material and cultural underpinnings. With pretensions to national prominence gone aground, the city's economic life depended primarily on small businesses and manufacturers. With the exception of the railroads, few operations employed more than fifty workers, only a handful more than one hundred, and not a single employer had a payroll of five hundred workers.[59] As a result, employers most often interacted face to face with their employees, increasing accountability on questions of wages and working conditions. Shared ethnicity or religious affiliation often constrained employers in other, complicated ways.

The economic and social landscape of St. Paul had little in common with that of Minneapolis where the milling, manufacturing, and machine tool industries that powered its economy served a national rather than a local market. These industries depended on a large-scale industrial work force—people primarily of immigrant stock who shared few common bonds with their employers. The corridors of power in Minneapolis remained the exclusive province of the Old Stock families. All of this fostered economic and social priorities quite unlike those of St. Paul and created a distinctively different set of labor relations.[60]

The first years of the twentieth century marked a nationwide explosion of growth for organized labor. In St. Paul, union membership increased by nearly a third between 1900 and 1902. Fully 31 percent of the city's wage earners—more than seven thousand workers—belonged to the seventy-six locals of the Trades and Labor Assembly. A similar burgeoning occurred in Minneapolis, but there the numbers hid a functional weakness that profoundly inhibited the effectiveness of the Minneapolis labor movement.[61] In St. Paul, the closed shop was rapidly becoming accepted practice and union membership carried genuine clout; but in Minneapolis, where powerful business interests opposed unionism, workers often found that a union card was at best a meaningless piece of paper; at worst, it was a ticket to the unemployment line.

By 1901, Minneapolis business leaders, alarmed at labor's growing strength and unwilling to make concessions to employee demands, had embarked on a campaign to drive organized labor out of the city. That year, a unified employer initiative established the principle of the open shop, crushing the machinists' union, which had been the strongest and most well organized of the trades. The employers followed up their victory in one industry after another, capping the campaign with the defeat of more than three thousand striking members of the flour-mill unions in 1903. As recounted by the corporate biographer of Washburn-Crosby (later to become General Mills), "The unions, failing to carry their point, were practically eliminated and never regained their former strength in the mills." The devastating effect of this defeat for organized labor in Minneapolis cannot be overstated.[62]

Orchestrating the employer offensive was the Citizens Alliance, a business association backed by the city's major financial interests. The avowed purpose of this organization was to establish and maintain the open shop in Minneapolis. The Alliance employed an impressive arsenal of weapons to combat union efforts—political influence, blacklisting, employee incentive plans, financial support for strike-bound employers, and financial pressure on those who were less militantly antiunion. When all else failed, they relied on the deployment of a cadre of quasi-official "deputies," funded and armed by the organization. Thus, in a multitude of coercive ways, the Citizens Alliance policed the city, proudly publicizing Minneapolis as the "Open Shop Capital of America"—a distinction it claimed for more than thirty years.[63]

St. Paul businesses could not afford such an offensive against organized labor. Protracted disputes could easily drive many of the city's marginally profitable businesses into bankruptcy. Besides, it was becoming apparent that when industrial turmoil erupted in Minneapolis, St. Paul firms were likely to experience an upsurge in orders and profits. Moreover, the city's economy had become heavily dependent on the local market. The working people of St. Paul were not only employees; they were critical consumers as well. With the diverse commercial attractions of Minneapolis only a nickel streetcar ride away, St. Paul businesses had to rely on less tangible incentives to keep consumers at home. Civic loyalty became the catchword of their promotional strategies—a loyalty that carried with it clearly understood mutual obligations. St. Paul business interests energetically boosted a "buy at home" campaign that equated local consumption with local pride. St. Paul manufacturers claimed to concentrate on "the idea of giving not quantity but quality." The city's comparatively small manufacturing output was the result of "the care used in the manufacture" of its goods. In addition, working people were reminded that the manufacturers "favored the use of St. Paul labor" as well as St. Paul products.[64]

St. Paul labor meant organized labor. Indeed, business weakness translated proportionally into union strength. Thus, both business and labor had a stake in maintaining what they termed the "live and let live plan," an unwritten agreement that situated resolution of economic issues within a social context of community rights and responsibilities.[65] The unions made the most of the leverage they derived from this compact. The language of labor negotiation was framed always in the terms of community accountability—mutual obligations owed to fellow citizens. This negotiation required a certain amount of compromise on either side but, as union officers reckoned, the numbers told the tale. St. Paul wages equaled and often exceeded those in Minneapolis. In negotiating hours and working conditions, the claims of community responsibility proved even more effective.[66] Thus, the labor press had good reason to consistently play down class divisions, emphasizing instead that labor negotiations were "harmonious and pleasant throughout, and the best feeling prevails between employers and employees."[67]

When infrequent disputes disrupted industrial "harmony," the unions drew on the claims of community accountability to buttress their cause. As a typical example, unionized workers instigated a boycott of a local department store for betraying "old time residents" by hiring "migratory and often incompetent worker[s]" (all non-union men) who had "no interest in Saint Paul or the community." As labor argued, such hiring practices betrayed the civic compact and forced legitimate members of the community to leave the city. In the confines of St. Paul, this was a powerful argument, and labor most often won its point.[68]

The unions used the same rhetoric of civic responsibility to uphold wage rates and improve working conditions. But they also shored up claims of community accountability with potent reminders that working people were consumers as well as

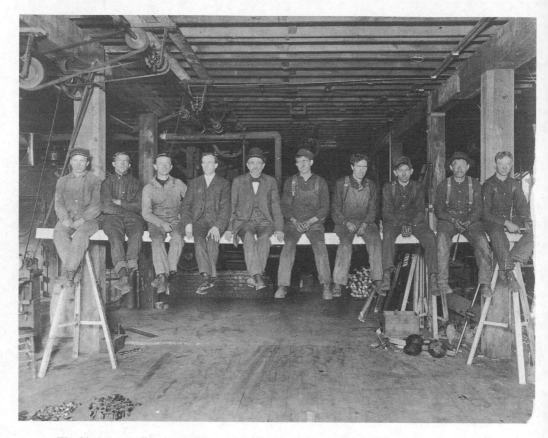

Fig. 21. As part of the logic of live and let live, St. Paul employers took pains to foster the appearance of democratic relations between themselves and their workers. In this 1910 photo of the H. B. Fuller Company, owner Fuller situated himself literally on a level plane with members of his production crew. Courtesy of the Minnesota Historical Society.

wage earners. The *Union Advocate* regularly reminded local merchants that a generous union wage scale meant more consumer dollars to fuel the local economy. By upholding union scale, it argued, they would be "making a bid for a share of this vast amount of money."[69] Concurrently, the paper encouraged union members to "buy in our home town." Prominent among a long list of reasons for local consumption were: "Because the community which is good enough for me to live in is good enough to buy in"; "because every dollar I spend at home stays at home and works for the welfare of St. Paul"; and "because the man I buy from helps support my schools, my church, my lodge, and my home."[70]

Businessmen and union leaders carried on the public discourse about the meanings and obligations of community that underlay this economic pact. But the emphasis on community and consumption positioned women at the center of the ongoing civic drama, as both the moral guardians of home and community and the chief household consumers.[71] Men laid out the rules of civic reciprocity, but women put them into action. Thus, working-class women played an essential economic role in upholding the civic compact. They also could serve as the most compelling symbol of the democratic nature of the civic community, as was evident in the summer of 1903, when city leaders planned a municipal carnival to raise funds for civic improvements. As part of the festivities, city residents were invited to vote for a carnival queen, to be chosen from a diverse field of candidates. The contest waxed as heated as any political campaign, but organized labor ultimately swept union dressmaker Miss Helen Marks onto the throne. "St. Paul has a union queen," crowed the *Advocate*. The business leaders who orchestrated the carnival, for compelling commercial reasons, also applauded this working-class "queen of the city." As Miss Marks was escorted through the streets in a flower-bedecked carriage drawn by six white horses, the pomp and ceremony confirmed in very public fashion the cross-class scope of civic identity—and all the mutual obligations carried therein.[72]

Organized labor might well take pride in its union queen, but relatively few women in St. Paul carried union cards. In 1902, the Bureau of Labor Statistics reported just over five thousand women in the city working in occupations other than domestic service. Only a few hundred of these claimed union membership—so few that the bureau did not even bother to tally their numbers. Judging from the pages of the *Advocate*, the Trades and Labor Assembly spent precious little effort working to increase their presence. However, the union paper did expend considerable energy in wooing the wives and daughters of workingmen to labor's cause. The *Advocate* equaled if not exceeded business efforts in its campaign to court the support of working-class women and thereby direct their consumption habits. In every issue, the paper featured fashion layouts, advice columns, recipes, and romantic tales of working-class girls who rose to fame and fortune by remaining true to their principles. In the editor's calculation, the column space was well invested. Capturing the attention of this key audience with housekeeping hints and entertaining fiction, the paper then had the opportunity to school them in the ideology of labor solidarity as well. Thus, though few women joined the ranks of organized labor, both business and labor depended on them to help maintain the civic compact.[73]

The ideology of hometown loyalty had obvious benefits for workers, small businessmen, and those who relied on local consumers. But for the city's few large-scale employers who were linked to broader markets, the claims of civic mutuality were somewhat less compelling. Accordingly, in the summer of 1903, the city's largest wholesalers, its three major manufacturers, and an officer of West Publishing (which had attained a national monopoly in the publication of law books) met privately with representatives of the Minneapolis Citizens Alliance to explore the possibility of establishing a similar organization in St. Paul.[74]

These open-shop advocates crafted a carefully worded invitation for "concerned citizens" to join the newly minted St. Paul Citizens' Association. They admitted that "it may be a surprise" to learn St. Paul had a labor problem but warned that "the difference is one of degree only." If not checked, the "obnoxious principles" of labor autocracy would become "a menace to the business of this City!" That summer seemed to provide a propitious opportunity for the open-shop contingent to enlist support from the broader business community. The city's plumbers were engaged in an unusually contentious dispute with local plumbing contractors, a strike that showed no sign of early settlement. As the strike wore on, the plumbers called for the "friends of organized labor" to boycott firms that have "imported men from other cities . . . to fill our places"—the tried-and-true language of community accountability. The businessmen pointed to this proposed action as a dangerous precedent that might very well lead to a wider boycott. As they argued, "It is probably a fair presumption that the next step will be to serve notice on the merchants that if they have any business relations with these unfair firms, organized labor will in turn boycott them."[75]

The men of the Citizens' Association claimed that, far from creating divisions in the community, they had the best interests of labor at heart, as well as those of business. In a wildly creative justification for their organization, they patronizingly declared:

> The largest possible benefit to the labor unions will result from finding themselves confronted by a power able and willing to hold them accountable to the law for the acts of their representatives. The discreet use of this power will tend to drive from office in the labor movement the dangerous and unprincipled leaders who are bringing shame and confusion upon it, and to make room for the more wiser and conservative men who have been so largely pushed aside and silenced during the past three years.[76]

Although this argument was unlikely to appeal to any but the already converted, the "menace" of a working-class boycott of city businesses carried real weight. The question was how to deal with the problem. For obvious reasons, the local plumbing contractors signed on with the association, as did a few other members of the Builders' Exchange. Two of the major mercantile figures tentatively gave their support as well. But as department store magnate Albert Schuneman warned, most members of the Retail Merchants Association would be "reluctant to affiliate themselves with the [Citizens'] Association."[77]

Schuneman's assessment proved to be correct. In the absence of significant labor strife, most of the business community balked at disturbing the civic compact. Those who were most dependent on working-class patronage sided most firmly with the unions. In the brewing sector for example—one of St. Paul's most important industries and one that relied heavily on a working-class customer base—the wealthy German brewers made their position unmistakably clear. In a resolution passed by the St. Paul Brewers Association and forwarded to the *Union Advocate*, they declared that not only did they accept unionism in their industry, but they also resolved to buy only locally produced—and union-made—fixtures, boxes, or packing crates. Nor would they contract work with outside shops that employed nonunion labor. This clear break in business ranks alarmed the Citizens' Association enough to have the resolution read in entirety into its minutes.[78]

In the meantime, despite attempts of the Citizens' Association to keep a low profile, the *Union Advocate* had discovered that something was afoot. Rather than bring the opponents to a point of public conflict, however, the union paper elected to attack the problem indirectly, with a series of articles castigating the views of "the unspeakable" D. M. Parry, president of the National Association of Manufacturers (NAM). At the same time, the paper began running a feature entitled "St. Paul Industries," which praised and urged the patronage of businesses who were "friends to labor." As if to emphasize labor's reasonable—and pivotal— political role, the paper also stepped up its denunciations of socialism as the "parasite and enemy of the labor movement." Without directly confronting the challenge to unionism that was brewing locally, the *Advocate* nonetheless managed to make its point—that organized labor was vigilant, powerful, and eminently reasonable; and that business was better off with labor as a friend than as an enemy.[79]

It was a point well taken by city businessmen, who were increasingly uneasy about the costs of disrupting the social and economic status quo. An invitation to participate in the founding convention of a national employers' federation set off a debate among Citizens' Association members. Though the association ultimately decided to send a delegation to the Chicago convention, it was with the strict understanding that attendance did not commit them to join the organization. As two of the founding members of the St. Paul group argued, "Our Organization was not yet sufficiently strong to openly commit ourselves to any plan which might be favored by older Associations in communities where they had had more labor difficulties than we have had."[80]

The report the delegates brought back from the convention only added to the growing reservations. Describing themselves as "ultra-conservative" in comparison with other delegations, the St. Paul men, though lured by the open-shop aims of the newly inaugurated Citizens' Industrial Association of America (CIAA), were somewhat alarmed by the "radical" antilabor strategies under consideration. The election of NAM president David Parry (detested by organized labor) to head the new venture further convinced the St. Paul group to proceed with caution. Before announcing publicly their affiliation with the national association, the group agreed they must substantially increase their membership base and convince the public that the "welfare of the city" was behind their actions.[81]

Their cautious strategy went awry, however, when only two weeks later Parry arrived in St. Paul to deliver a speech, his visit previously arranged by the Minneapolis contingent of the Northwestern Manufacturers' Association. The audience of 150 businessmen sat in uneasy silence as Parry unveiled his organization's agenda for a full-scale offensive against organized labor, the text of which was reprinted in full in the *Union Advocate*. At the close of Parry's remarks, the audience, as described by the *Advocate*, literally fled, making for the doors without pausing even to applaud.[82]

As the old adage goes, they could run but they could not hide. Parry's inflammatory remarks went against the grain of accepted codes of labor relations in St. Paul, and the St. Paul Citizens' Association (its name unfortunately mimetic of the national organization's) was guilty by association. The *Advocate* warned, "We tell those employers of St. Paul who are responsible for this man's leadership in their organizations that they are in a fair way to make themselves accomplices in industrial crime." The potential consequences of this breach of the social contract soon became glaringly apparent as the *Advocate* set about sorting labor's friends from its enemies. With the Christmas shopping season about to begin, the most critical time of the year for the city's retailers, the paper urged its readers to patronize only the "merchants, business and professional men who have . . . sympathy for and faith in organized labor. . . . They do not belong to the Parry gang, or no such thought would ever enter their minds." Unlike the members of the Citizens' Association, labor's friends did not betray the community welfare: "They are liberal with their employees and live up to the principle of live and let live." In turn, as the *Advocate* reminded them, the union man had a reciprocal obligation: "As he buys . . . FOR his friends, so let him in all cases buy FROM his friends."[83]

The Citizens' Association backpedaled as fast as possible. Its officers assured the public that though the names were unfortunately similar, "in no way was the St. Paul Association a branch of the other." They strained to mute the open-shop agenda endorsed by their organization with claims of friendship and community. According to its platform published in December, the St. Paul group pledged to "promote and encourage harmonious relations between employers and employes [*sic*] upon a basis of equal justice to both" with a "platform so fair and . . . intentions so praiseworthy that to declare them publicly is to merit the unqualified indorsement and co-operation of all good citizens."[84]

The good citizens of St. Paul's working-class community had their own notions of civic cooperation and, as voiced by the *Advocate*, refused "to accept the complacent theory of the Citizens' Association that it and its members represent all there is of civic virtue or influence in the community." As tensions mounted, business support for the organization weakened—and fell apart completely when the national CIAA announced a plan to boycott union-made goods. Even the staunchly pro-business *Pioneer Press* condemned the proposal on its editorial page. In St. Paul, the boycott was labor's most feared weapon. Adoption of the tactic by the employers, the *Press* presciently noted, would serve as a "formal endorsement . . . of the iniquitous and vindictive destructiveness of the boycott as a legitimate weapon in the conflicts of labor and capital." In short, it would serve to strengthen labor's arsenal.[85]

The radical suggestions that had alarmed the St. Paul delegates in Chicago were intruding uncomfortably close to home. With David Parry at the helm, the national

Citizens' Industrial Association proved too militant for the vulnerable businessmen of St. Paul. In their estimation, public opinion would not stand for such blatantly antilabor tactics.[86] While the Minneapolis Citizens Alliance applauded each aggressive initiative and became a key influence in formulating the national organization's policy decisions, the St. Paul group collapsed in confusion.[87] The affluent businessmen who had formed the Citizens' Association had discovered the limits of solidarity between "big capital" and small-scale business. In St. Paul, where industrial strength was the exception rather than the rule, local considerations were paramount. For most city businesses, the civic compact was too valuable to discard, and the costs of confronting labor proved more than they were willing to pay. Accordingly, the St. Paul Citizens' Association slipped quietly out of existence.

This pivotal moment in St. Paul labor relations reveals the local considerations that fostered closed-shop unionism in the city. The interdependence of business and labor demanded a careful negotiation of their separate interests. Each side chose its words carefully, with an eye always fixed on community opinion, pushing its agenda as far as possible without allowing the contest to break out in open conflict. The critical insights to be gained here are twofold: First, both business and labor, for different reasons, were deeply invested in maintaining the common constructions of a shared civic identity; and second, civic identity equaled consensus only at the level of rhetoric. The meanings, rights, and obligations embedded in this community compact were constantly tested, challenged, and negotiated, not only in the realm of economics but in cultural terms as well. Yet claims on "community" required that outright conflict be avoided if at all possible, to keep the construct—and the economy—intact. This created a crucial niche in the power structure of the city for those institutions and groups that acted as brokers in maintaining the civic compact. In St. Paul, the Catholic Church and particularly its Irish Catholics stepped in to fill this role. A tangle of cultural as well as economic circumstances had situated the Church and its Irish members in the right place at exactly the right time.

The critical importance of local relationships had fostered an intense parochialism that came to be a central feature of St. Paul's cultural landscape. Unquestionably, this localistic outlook derived much of its power from the interdependence implicit in the particular configuration of the city's economy. But civic identity sprang from more than material considerations alone. The people of St. Paul felt themselves to be under both economic and cultural siege, an island in a sea of enemies represented most visibly by the overpowering presence of Minneapolis, just next door. Not only did Minneapolis civic leaders unceasingly gloat over its dominant economic position; they also claimed cultural superiority. Journalist Harrison Salisbury, a Minneapolis native, recalled his boyhood perception of St. Paul as "a haunt and a dive, populated in large part, by politicians (a very lowly breed indeed), Democrats (even more lowly), Irish (another step down), and drunks . . . a region of dismal slums, alien people, narrow streets, saloons, and God-alone-knew what evils."[88] To this litany of disrepute, he might have added "Catholics" as yet another distasteful element of the St. Paul population. In Minneapolis, the heart of the Minnesota progressive movement, reformers viewed St. Paul as the model of all that was wrong with the American city. The reform platforms so common in Minneapolis, especially the temperance movement, carried with them disturbing reverberations of nativism and anti-Catholicism.

None of this went unnoticed. Though progressive reformers may have intended their speeches and proposals as a class-based critique, the sting of their words struck at every stratum of St. Paul society, where sons and daughters of immigrants shared power with Old Stock Americans; where Catholics were among the most distinguished of its citizens; where its greatest claim to fame was as the state's political center; and where, not least in importance, the consumption of alcohol was an integral part of the cultural fabric and its production a pillar of the city's economy. The Minneapolis combined penchant for nativism and reform thus considerably heightened the cultural stakes of civic rivalry, providing the ideal foil against which to generate an unflinching defense of civic identity and interests.

The Catholic Church and Irish Catholics in particular derived singular benefit from St. Paul's growing insularity. The city was the seat of the archdiocese, overseen by John Ireland, a figure of international renown who conferred with presidents and heads of state—which fostered civic pride in the Catholic archbishop from all quarters. No important event was complete without Ireland's affirming presence. As for the Irish Catholics who had achieved singular success in the city, they were well aware that Irish Catholicism carried a cultural currency within the boundaries of St. Paul that disappeared when one crossed the river to Minneapolis.[89]

A scandal that erupted in Minneapolis in 1877 became part of the lore that attested to the benefits the Irish enjoyed in St. Paul—a tale that lived long in popular memory. As the story went, Kate Noonan, a young Irish-Catholic domestic, was seduced and abandoned by the son of a prominent Minneapolis banker. The distraught girl, "taking the law into her own hands," shot and killed her betrayer. When the murdered man's grieving father "employed the best legal talent in Minneapolis to assist the county attorney" in securing a conviction and no Minneapolis lawyer would take on the girl's defense, it seemed poor Kate's fate was sealed. But an incorruptible St. Paul attorney (and future mayor), Christopher O'Brien, came to the rescue. Foregoing legal fees, O'Brien constructed a masterful case, exposed the girl's former lover as a "libertine," and won acquittal on the charges. According to O'Brien's brother, the celebrated case made the future mayor's reputation in St. Paul.[90]

The text of this narrative and others like it, as they were passed on through the years, carried considerable cultural weight with Irish Catholics, as a reminder of the multiple ways that membership in the civic community of St. Paul conferred status and protection across class, apart from its economic returns. The Catholic Church and its Irish constituency thus had a considerable investment in maintaining the social relations that characterized the city. Penetrating into every stratum of its social world, they also were uniquely positioned to mediate its tensions. The skill with which they negotiated this balancing act enhanced their stature even further.

Archbishop John Ireland, the most prominent of the city's Irish Catholics, was a master at the game. As described by one historian, "He had a genius for espousing causes which met the approval of effective public opinion . . . a typical American of his times—a war veteran, a hustler, and a western booster"—all of which endeared him to the business establishment. His efforts at episcopal empire-building had meshed neatly with those of James J. Hill to populate the hinterland of the Northwest. Moreover, his devotion to Catholic institution-building provided St. Paul with hospitals, schools, two colleges, and a major seminary, projects that increased the city's prestige while coincidentally raising surrounding property values. These privately funded institutions also relieved the drain of public services on the municipal budget. After his disastrous flirtation with Minneapolis financiers in the 1890s, the archbishop poured his resources and energies primarily into St. Paul, where his base of support was centered. By the turn of the century, John Ireland had become the city's most ardent booster. For all these reasons, city leaders were exceedingly grateful to the archbishop and, following the example of James J. Hill, provided generous support for his episcopal endeavors.[91]

To city leaders of whatever denomination, the Catholic Church had a social value that outweighed even its investment in bricks and mortar. They looked to the church to enforce social order among St. Paul's predominantly Catholic working class—a mandate that, in their estimation, John Ireland admirably fulfilled. Long before he received the bishop's miter, young Father Ireland had achieved local fame for his commitment to the temperance cause, which became a life-long crusade. The miseries of the city's poor Catholics, especially his fellow Irish, could be traced directly to the evils of drink, he believed. Establishing local chapters of the Father Mathew Society (a temperance organization transplanted from Ireland), the future archbishop worked tirelessly to enlist Catholics as total abstainers. That was no easy task in a city where saloons proliferated on every street, where alcohol and sociability went hand in hand, and where the production and sale of liquor was an integral part of the economy.[92]

In his temperance crusade, Ireland demonstrated the complicated motivations and political acumen that made him such a pivotal political figure in St. Paul. Unquestionably, his focus was on working-class drinking habits, not those of the "respectable" middle class—a project endorsed by both Catholic and non-Catholic civic leaders. The city's most successful Irish Catholics, concerned about the image of the group as a whole, were among his staunchest supporters.[93] Though the Father Mathew Society was publicized as a Catholic project, its membership rolls reveal that its mission focused exclusively on Irish uplift. Every member had an Irish surname. While the city's German Catholics may well have applauded the effort to curb Irish excesses, they considered it a cultural affront to lump them—"moderate beer drinkers all"—with the intemperate Irish, and they kept their distance from the organization.[94] Moreover, the city's thriving brewing industry was a German monopoly, both in terms of brewery owners and the majority of brewery employees. The temperance crusade not only offended their cultural sensibilities, but it also threatened their livelihoods.

Civic leaders, though they approved the taming of the unruly Irish working class, had no desire to limit let alone abolish the production or sale of alcohol. Ireland's voluntarist organization offered a felicitous middle course. The archbishop understood clearly the limits of his mandate. When asked to sign a petition to close city saloons on Sundays, the head of the Father Mathew Society declined, stating that volunteerism rather than legal intervention was the preferred way to proceed.[95]

As for the Irish who were the subject of the endeavor, Archbishop Ireland soon discovered that only a minority were willing to keep the pledge for more than a short time. At every meeting of the Father Mathew Society, after recording the names of new members, the secretary dutifully noted the expulsion of those who had publicly broken the pledge—and the considerably longer list of those who were unaccountably "absent," week after week. Though Ireland's authority grew in many ways as he ascended the episcopal ladder, the temperance problem continued to elude resolution. Even among his clergy, total abstinence remained an unattainable goal, driving the archbishop in 1901 to institute a special organization, the St. Paul Clerical Total Abstinence Society, with membership required of all seminarians and strongly urged for priests of the diocese. Clearly, both the culture and the economy of St. Paul presented particular problems for Ireland's temperance crusade.[96]

He addressed the problem with admirable ingenuity by a slight rewording of the abstinence pledge. In the reconstituted Crusader's Total Abstinence Society, temperance was obligatory but total abstinence discretionary. As stated in italics at the head of the pledge card, "The basis of this society is *a union on perfectly equal terms between those who use moderately and those who abstain entirely from intoxicating liquors as beverages*"—a position designed to suit nearly everyone. As further incentives, the society offered its members a literary and debating society, free library, gymnasium, and a club room with pool, checkers, chess, and a cigar stand, "the real pleasures of the saloon with none of the pains." Open to the general public, the society regularly produced musicales and plays in its assembly hall. Thus the temperance crusade had evolved into an Irish social club that served several useful purposes beyond the cause of temperance. It provided "uplifting" entertainments at which a wide range of city residents mingled with the "respectable" Irish. It also provided a social milieu for Irish-Catholic young people to gather and for emerging Irish politicians to make themselves known. How effective any of this was in changing the drinking habits of St. Paul's Catholics is debatable. (By the turn of the century, more than $2.5 million was expended annually on alcoholic beverages in the city.) That it supported cross-class socialization among Irish Catholics is without question. But perhaps the greatest effect was to confer on John Ireland the public persona of moral arbiter and guardian of the social order.[97]

James J. Hill had such faith in the moral suasion of the church that he donated $500,000 to build and endow the St. Paul Seminary. He had never made before—

nor would again in the future—a gift of comparable magnitude. At the dedication ceremonies in 1895, Hill piously declared that he had "undertaken the building and endowment of a Roman Catholic theological seminary [because] almost all other denominations have members who are able to help their church work in every material way, but the Catholic church, with its large number of working men and women" (coincidentally, the bulk of Hill's employees), "have little else than their faith in God and those devoted men who have been placed in charge of their spiritual welfare." Praiseworthy sentiments to be sure, but a congratulatory telegram from a fellow Protestant financier captured more succinctly the underlying logic of Hill's philanthropy: "That the Roman Catholic church is bound to have a most potent influence on the future of the United States is certain. That an educated priesthood—educated in America, in touch with the life of America—will be a factor for good, I do not doubt."[98]

Ireland did indeed attempt to instill in his priests and parishioners principles that won the approval of the employing class—temperance, diligence, respect for authority—all the attributes of model workers. But it would be a mistake to see him and his church as simple tools of business interests. The support of city elites was a great boon for the church, but the wellspring of Catholic power was its working-class communicants. Ireland's genius lay in his ability to balance the two constituencies.

The archbishop had won the hearts of the working class in 1886 by championing the cause of the Knights of Labor. At the time, the Catholic clergy was deeply divided over the right of labor unions to exist; some priests even denied the sacraments or the rite of Catholic burial to members of the Knights. But Ireland attained international attention as an advocate of their cause, even traveling to Rome to plead the Knights' case before the pope. His argument was practical rather than theological. By the mid-1880s, the Knights had more than seven hundred thousand members, two thirds of whom were estimated to be Catholic. To make them choose between their church and union might lead to wholesale rebellion and alienation, a risk the church could not afford. Such pragmatism ultimately won the day, and the Vatican removed the Knights from its list of forbidden secret societies.[99]

Ireland earned wide acclaim in working-class circles for his part in the negotiations and happily accepted the appellation of "the socialist bishop," which, as he interpreted it to the press, simply meant that he desired to "eliminate social evils." On a rare occasion in 1889, he pressed the issue further, declaring that socialism was, "in its first outburst, the shriek of despair from the hungering souls upon which presses the heavy hand of greed and injustice. . . . The human race does not exist for the benefit of the few."[100] In terms of real policy, however, he was far from socialistic. As Ireland's biographer acknowledges, over the course of his career the archbishop "exhibited less enthusiasm for organized labor than did many of his colleagues." During the Pullman strike in 1894, he endorsed the use of federal troops, declaring that "the fatal mistake which has been made in connection with this strike is that property has been destroyed, the liberty of citizens interfered with, human lives endangered, social order menaced."[101] This pronouncement (judiciously delivered in Detroit rather than at home in St. Paul) must have pleased James J. Hill immensely; the Saint Paul Seminary, which Hill had funded, was nearing completion, and Hill was also in the process of extricating the archbishop from his financial embarrassments. Quite clearly, Ireland understood the limits of the bargain that underlay Catholic power.

Politically, the archbishop walked a fine line, but that is not to say that his concern for working people was insincere. Rather, as he assessed the limits of working-class agency, compromise rather than conflict seemed a more effective strategy in negotiating the structures of power. Anti-Catholicism was a looming specter that had not been laid entirely to rest. If the church was to protect its working people, he reasoned, the first priority must be to safeguard the institution. As Ireland asserted repeatedly over the years, "The Church must be kept before the American people as the great prop of social order and law—all the more so that Catholics are numerous in strikes and riots." On a practical level, he understood the necessity of straddling the class divide in St. Paul. Although he supported workers' right to organize and spoke out for just relations between capital and labor, he also condemned strikes and boycotts and insisted on the preeminent rights of private property—all of which was roundly applauded by the city's employers. With Catholics well represented among employers, judges, and local lawmakers, Ireland optimistically relied on the moral suasion of Catholic doctrine to obviate resort to outright conflict.[102]

In St. Paul, this strategy seemed to prove its worth. By 1903, employers across the nation increasingly were turning to the courts to suppress labor protest, and injunctions against striking workers seemed to issue from courts in every part of the country. During the 1903 plumbers' strike, St. Paul plumbing contractors sought to take advantage of this highly effective weapon, encouraged by a similar injunction recently granted against building trades workers in Minneapolis. However, to their chagrin and workers' jubilation, the strategy did not play in St. Paul. Ramsey County District Court Judge William Kelly ruled against the employers, stating that "in no case has any violence or threats of violence or intimidation been used" by the striking plumbers. Most tellingly, as justification for his decision, Judge Kelly cited the teachings of Pope Leo XIII and quoted from the papal encyclical *Rerum Novarum*. In his concluding remarks, the judge advised that "if all the owners of capital and all the owners of labor would pay heed to the simple and beautiful lessons of justice taught in the encyclical from which I have quoted there would be no labor troubles, for the occasions from which they arise would cease to exist."[103] John Ireland could not have said it better.

The judge's decision was a source of local pride to the city's working people and only increased their confidence in the value of the civic compact. Union officials, rank-and-file members, and unorganized workers all read the victory as unique to the culture of St. Paul. For a local janitor, the judgment reassured him that "be a man rich or poor, [he] is beyond all doubt, absolutely sure of receiving absolute justice" in the St. Paul courts. Miss G. C. Seyfried, a member of the Salesladies'

Union, found it a "grand decision. . . . So few judges have favored the wage-earners that it is a source of deep pleasure to find a judge in our home city that does recognize the rights of those who have to work for a living." Perhaps the strongest reinforcement to workers' sense of community exceptionalism came in comments from beleaguered union members in Minneapolis, where the injunction was becoming standard practice in labor disputes. As one Minneapolis union man mournfully attested, "The iron hand of the law has been laid upon us so heavily and so unjustly in Minneapolis that I think we appreciate a decision like that of Judge Kelly more than you do in St. Paul. Organized labor only asks justice, and that Judge Kelly has given us, which is something we didn't get in Minneapolis."[104]

Workers were not unmindful that their victory had been armed by the legitimating power of Catholic doctrine, an authority that dissipated outside the boundaries of St. Paul. Cornelius Guiney, the Irish-Catholic editor of the *Advocate*, gave thanks that Judge Kelly had upheld the "enunciated truths and principles of justice" of "Pope Leo the Beloved." In soaring biblical language, he proclaimed that the decision was to organized labor "what an oasis in the desert is to a man perishing with thirst" and that unions were "athirst for a decision that abounds in justice."[105]

Given the particular social and economic configuration of St. Paul and both business and labor's resultant desire to avoid direct confrontation, the Catholic Church emerged as a critical mediator. Thus, despite the archbishop's tendency to hedge his support for labor's rights, he remained enormously popular with the city's working people. Catholics and non-Catholics alike understood the legitimating power of the archbishop's presence at labor's side, never more than in the wake of the plumbers' victory. Accordingly, they invited Ireland to be the honored speaker at the upcoming Labor Day celebration. As the planners agreed, "If the archbishop will lend his presence on the occasion and deliver an address . . . it will be a noteworthy event in the history of the labor movement in the Northwest."[106]

Ireland took the occasion to give a speech that was described in the same sentence as both "conservative in tone" and "plainly sympathetic with the cause of the masses." According to the *Advocate*, he somehow managed to argue for the rights of capital and labor at one and the same time. Arbitration and reciprocal respect would win labor far more than strikes "which harmed the strikers more than anyone," so he urged. Perhaps in light of recent events in the city, workers were inclined to agree and were willing to consider his claim that "the best friend of labor is . . . Christ and his church . . . the preacher of eternal justice."[107] If not labor's best friend, at the very least, the archbishop's audience was prepared to concede that the church had the capacity to be a most powerful advocate on their behalf.

Power, of course, is relative and always under negotiation. Despite his imposing presence, the archbishop was continually pulled from both sides. He was acutely aware that his authority over working class Catholics would be sustained only if the church stood for justice as they perceived it. But, paradoxically, his influence as a community leader derived in large part from his close connections with the elites, particularly with James J. Hill. Working people seemed to understand this conun-

Fig. 22. St. Paul celebrated Labor Day as a major civic holiday in the early twentieth century. Union workers used the parade to claim their place in the civic polity as throngs of spectators cheered them on. In the 1904 parade, pictured here, more than seven thousand marchers turned out in style. *Minnesota Union Advocate*, 9 September 1904.

drum and regarded Ireland as an empowering ally despite his sometimes less than idealistic proclamations. As for the autocratic Hill, even he could not impose unilateral control, as the evolution of the St. Paul Seminary was to illustrate.

The terms laid out for the seminary endowment made provision for close financial supervision by Hill and his heirs. Nonetheless, the archbishop directed the most critical elements of the institution: recruitment of seminarians and the course of study. From the time he had assumed direction of the diocese in 1884, Ireland's priority had been a diocesan-run seminary that would train native Minnesotans for the priesthood, boys whose "training could be tailored to meet local needs." Ireland's aim was to educate an army of clerics whose first loyalty would be to their archbishop. Hill's gift, intended to support the railroad builder's interests, coincidentally promoted the archbishop's plan to concentrate diocesan power in his hands.[108]

In less than twenty years, the project was complete. By 1915, the city's priests were a homogeneous lot: 74 percent American-born; 55 percent Irish ethnics; 52 percent Minnesota-born; and 78 percent graduates of the St. Paul Seminary. Ireland had achieved his goal of a personally selected clergy trained under his direction. He allowed priests from religious orders to enter his diocese only grudgingly, to serve a handful of ethnic national parishes. As a result, according to one Catholic historian, "The cohesiveness of the Minnesota Catholic community was greatly enhanced." Its priests had been thoroughly acculturated from boyhood to the archbishop's authority.[109] Thus, when push came to shove, Ireland's clerics seldom raised their voices in public opposition to ecclesiastical policy.

Ecclesiastical policy, however, was a nuanced and multilayered text. In addition to the quality of his seminarians' loyalty, Archbishop Ireland shaped the content of their theological training. Within the seminary classrooms, a philosophy held sway that was significantly more liberal than Ireland's public statements betrayed. In 1902, Ireland appointed his protégé, Minnesota-born Father John P. Ryan, as professor of moral theology at the seminary. By the time Ryan left the post for Catholic University in 1915, he had become the foremost champion of social justice (and organized labor) in the American Catholic Church. Ryan declared himself opposed to socialism and even debated Morris Hillquit on the issue in the pages of *Everybody's Magazine*.[110] But his speeches and writings, quoted regularly in the *Union Advocate*, called for a minimum wage, an eight-hour workday, protection for picketing and boycotts, public ownership of utilities, and a progressive income tax, among other reforms. As his biographer observes, "Ryan's ideas were more radical than the program of a good many moderate, dues-paying socialists."[111]

His ideas certainly appeared more radical than the archbishop's. Yet, Ireland made no move to restrain his subordinate. According to Ryan, "[Ireland] did not even once declare or intimate that my teaching was unorthodox, or too 'radical,' putting dangerous ideas into the heads of the young men who . . . would be elevated to the priesthood."[112] Perhaps the archbishop allowed Ryan free rein simply to assuage workers' doubts about the church, while he reassured business interests with a considerably more conservative official Catholic position. But it is equally plausible that Ireland privately endorsed Ryan's passionate embrace of social justice, a position that was politically untenable for the archbishop himself to take. Perhaps the truth lies somewhere between the two. But the incontrovertible result was that the Catholic social justice movement, which was nurtured by John Ryan and which came to fruition in the decade of the 1930s, can be traced directly to the St. Paul Seminary—Jim Hill's single most substantial investment in social control.

Locally Ryan's radical proposals had a decidedly undramatic effect—but therein lay their value. The insular compact that upheld the social and economic fabric of St. Paul required that internal relationships—the content of civic identity—supersede any other broader and potentially divisive alliances, particularly those based on class. The Catholic Church, with its remarkable elasticity, proved exceptionally adept at negotiating the tensions that were always just beneath the surface of civic harmony, a service valued by St. Paulites of various classes and denominations. Though other individual ministers and particular Protestant congregations were voices of influence in the city, only the Catholic Church had the centralized, hierarchical structure to exert *unified* influence across neighborhoods and class. Every ward was anchored by at least one Catholic parish, often more. Thus, the archbishop's influence stretched into every corner of the city in a way that no Protestant cleric could match. Nor could any one Protestant denomination compare in numbers to the city's Catholics.

No group benefited more from Catholic influence than did the Irish. Conversely, the Irish were the pillar of Catholic power. The fortunes of the two were fundamentally intertwined. The archbishop's decided preference for his Irish congregants provided them with exceptional opportunities to rise within the clergy, a career path that automatically imbued them with a degree of prestige. Of broader value, the priests and nuns of the archdiocese, as well as the archbishop, frequently used their connections to secure jobs for Irish petitioners. On the other side of the coin, the prominent role the Irish came to play in the city added to the stature of the church. Out of this complicated and symbiotic relationship, the Irish and the church together became the central brokers of civic peace.

The church derived much of its power from its centralized, articulated structure, but Irish influence flowed from a dispersed negotiating network of key individuals linked by common ethnicity. By 1900, it seemed that Irish influence was everywhere, though demographically the Irish ranked a distant fourth behind Germans, Scandinavians, and Old Stock Americans. But what the Irish lacked in numbers, they more than made up for with a political savvy that utilized ethnicity in complicated ways.

While the numerically predominant German St. Paulites participated in the public and business life of the city, they also maintained a parallel closed cultural world in German neighborhoods, buttressed by a dense network of German-language newspapers, churches, and fraternal and cultural organizations. German Catholics, to the continuing frustration of the archbishop, continued to show a decided preference for national parishes, where German ruled as the lingua franca and Catholic practice was inseparable from maintenance of German *Kultur*. The German parishes, though technically not geographically configured, in practice supported the maintenance of insular ethnic neighborhoods, as German Catholics settled in homes nearby these national parishes.[113]

Even those Germans who resided outside the ethnic enclave and integrated themselves more fully in the life of the city tended to maintain their closest private ties within a separate social world. The wealthy Weyerhaeusers, Lindekes, Schulzes and Schurmeiers, while they socialized frequently with their Summit Avenue neighbors, confined their intimate circle most often to other German elites.[114] The German brewing magnates maintained even more complicated ethnic connections. The brewers built mansions near the breweries, surrounded by their workers—a paternalistic model with its own peculiar set of inherent account-abilities. This residential arrangement also fostered multiple ethnic, cross-class ties based on shared church and associational memberships.[115] With such broad and deep cultural attachments, it was a rare German indeed, even among those who had most thoroughly assimilated, who did not retain a certain aura of ethnic exclusivity.

Scandinavian St. Paulites remained even more geographically and socially aloof on the city's East Side. The network of Swedish, Norwegian, and Danish ethnic associations, churches, and foreign-language newspapers rivaled that of the Germans. Though national differences divided them among themselves, they also participated in a pan-Scandinavian culture of separatism that derived from the more significant cultural, political, and economic chasm separating them from the rest of St. Paul. Churchgoing Scandinavians, whether Lutheran, Baptist, Methodist, or Reformed, had no love for the Catholic Church. Furthermore, they decried the drinking, dancing, and gambling that the Irish and Germans so loved and that, to the Scandinavians, made St. Paul seem a den of iniquity. Almost to a man, "respectable" Scandinavians voted the Republican ticket and supported the futile cause of municipal reform, all of which only reinforced ethnic separatism.[116]

Irish ethnicity, in contrast, operated quite differently. In some ways, it created an exclusive club of insiders with cultural signifiers that accrued them special benefits among themselves, but it also became the critical linkage on which civic negotiation hinged. As a minority group in St. Paul, the Irish could not rely on ethnic solidarity alone to maintain their influence. Nor did they favor the creation of an ethnic enclave. Rather, the Irish had a grander vision; St. Paul itself was to be an Irish domain. Unlike the ethnic cultures of the Germans and Scandinavians, the Irish emphasized inclusion—within limits, of course. Crafted originally as a political strategy, the willingness of the Irish to include outsiders as "honorary Irish," thereby linking them to the benefits and celebration of Hibernian brotherhood, over time became a cultural given. Irish politicians took care to spread the spoils of political patronage across ethnic lines, attended ethnic and religious celebrations of every sort, and emphasized that all St. Paul was welcome to join in Irish activities—all long-established components of local civic culture. When the Sons of Jacob dedicated their new synagogue in 1888, it was only natural that Irish politician Bill Murray would share the speaker's rostrum with Rabbis Cohn and Hess. It was even less surprising thirty years later for the Hibernians to donate their hall for an event sponsored by the local Jewish community. In turn, St. Paulites of every class and ethnic background were cordially invited to attend Irish-Catholic festivities at the Hibernian Hall or the Crusader's Society.[117]

The Irish worked assiduously to position themselves at the center of St. Paul's social world and were highly successful in the endeavor, creating social linkages that brought Germans, Old Stock Americans, and Irish together as the core of the civic compact. The Scandinavians were not wooed so easily. Those who were willing to play by the rules of the civic game were welcomed into the club. As for the rest, stubbornly insisting on their straitlaced principles and penchant for reform, city politics ceded to them the East Side, where they remained largely outside the realm of municipal power.

Though St. Patrick's Day invariably passed without official notice on the Scandinavian East Side, for many St. Paulites the Irish holiday did indeed become a day of city-wide celebration. It was observed with such enthusiasm in 1901 that the archbishop, in the name of Irish respectability, canceled future parades, replacing them with less publicly rowdy indoor merriment at the Hibernian Hall or in individual parishes. Nonetheless, even without the parade, city residents continued to celebrate March 17 enthusiastically as the welcome end to a long winter, a civic day of festivity observed by both "the Irish and their friends." City leaders shared the dais with the archbishop at formal St. Patrick's Day banquets, and ordinary St. Paulites of every stripe marked the day in a variety of ways. For instance, backstairs at the Hill mansion in 1910, the servants, most of whom were either Scandinavian or German, celebrated the day (and the absence of their employers) by all wearing "a little green" and having their fortunes told by a Swedish fortune teller. This seemed not at all peculiar to German maid Celia Tauer; after all, she regularly enjoyed card parties and dances at the Hibernian Hall and, after attending a theatrical entitled "The Wearing of the Green," had proclaimed it a "grand play."[118]

Celia and her friends cheerfully incorporated Irish celebration as part of their calendar of entertainment. St. Paul business and political figures had other, pragmatic reasons to fête their Irish peers. And people at the bottom of the economic hierarchy may have welcomed the holiday as no more than a rare opportunity for public revelry. But, at least for some marginalized people without other networks of support, the Irish must have appeared as powerful potential protectors. Connecting themselves with the Irish may have seemed a means to gain a foothold in the civic community. As a startling example, at the 1909 St. Patrick's Day program in St. Vincent de Paul parish, Chinese-American Catholic Charles Young (one of only forty-five Chinese in the county), was "greeted with thunderous applause" when he took the stage to express his "great pleasure at assisting in [his] humble way in this celebration of the great Irish Apostle, St. Patrick." After offering renditions of "Killarney" and "Come Back to Erin" in Chinese, he was ceremoniously accorded honorary Irish status with the pinning of a green ribbon on his lapel. The benefits this carried for Mr. Young are unrecorded, but with few other avenues into community membership, even this frail link must have seemed a valuable commodity.[119]

Thus, for a wide variety of reasons, the Irish succeeded in creating an ethnic presence that, at least to outsiders, seemed to define the city's public culture. But within the ranks, Irish identity itself was no guarantee of shared interests. Indeed, the Irish could be found as key players on opposite sides of nearly every issue: as officers of the Trades and Labor Assembly; as charter members of the Citizens' Association; as railroad laborers or railroad officials and contractors; as social re-

Fig. 23. "Honorary Irish" Chinese converts pose in front of St. Vincent de Paul Church with their sponsors in 1905. The two African Americans among the sponsors further suggest that the banner of Irish inclusiveness occasionally bridged even racial differences. Courtesy of the Archives of the Archdiocese of Saint Paul and Minneapolis.

formers or as key figures in the liquor trade; as conservative Democratic party bosses, Republican stalwarts, or populist challengers of the status quo. This very diversity of interests was at the heart of Irish power. What all these groups held in common was their Irish Catholicism, a fraternal connection they used to singular advantage.

The bonds of shared ethnicity created instrumental social—and physical— spaces where antagonists might negotiate their differences. These key spaces were, most often, both Irish and Catholic. In the Hibernian Hall, the temperance societies, the Knights of Columbus, and the parish churches, fellow Irish reinforced the cultural link that tenuously united them despite class and political difference. Common Catholicism was important, but the combined identity of Irish and Catholic, with its particularly powerful mythology of shared persecution, was the crucial link, keeping lines of communication open among opposing factions.

Within the ranks of the so-called Irish establishment, individuals often jousted on opposing sides in the political or legal arena, then sociably shared a drink or cigar. In 1907, hewing to principle rather than politics, lawyer Thomas O'Brien went head-to-head with his protégé and friend, Pierce Butler, in a highly publicized railroad regulation case. Though O'Brien often represented the railroads and got his start working for James J. Hill, in this case he opposed the mighty Great Northern and Northern Pacific, with no discernible effect on either his career or his friendship with Butler.[120]

The O'Brien brothers, lawyers John, Christopher, and Thomas, exemplified the broad range of advocacy that might be found within a single family. Though they were firmly entrenched in the civic establishment and held a series of prominent public offices in the course of their careers, the brothers also shared a finely honed sense of social justice and a sister who was married to the son of populist Ignatius Donnelly. With such complicated political leanings, it was not unusual to find the O'Briens arguing opposite sides of a single case, a situation that never diminished their affection for one another.[121]

Even attorney James Manahan, with a well-earned reputation for championing unpopular causes, maintained cordial if wary relations with Irish dealmakers of various persuasions. All these men interacted on a regular basis; they were active in the temperance movement and the Knights of Columbus and frequently mingled at civic affairs, ethnic celebrations, and events supporting Irish causes.[122] Such frequent elbow-rubbing provided opportunities for "reasonable" men to work out their differences in ways that would not unduly rock the civic status quo. Underlying their willingness to compromise was the common understanding that the existing social landscape, whatever its flaws, had created a veritable Irish heaven that required a bit of give-and-take on all sides. As long as the civic project remained foremost in their minds, the claims of Irish brotherhood forgave many other political differences. But, as James Manahan was to learn, there were limits as to how far one could challenge the system.

Manahan, who was not a St. Paul native, once too often ignored the unwritten rules of local politics and let idealism take precedence over protection of local interest. Long a thorn in the side of city politicians and the railroad interests, Manahan breached irrevocably the code of Irish localism in 1911. Representing a group of Methodist reformers, he challenged the city's (primarily Irish) liquor interests, charging the mayor and the chief of police with collusion in illegal alcohol distribution. All this was more than St. Paul's live-and-let-live policy would bear. Manahan soon found himself excluded from the network of Irish insiders. With his law practice shriveling, he moved his office to Minneapolis, where reform politics flourished and where public confrontation was more the order of the day.[123]

His home, nonetheless, remained in St. Paul. Minnie Manahan, unlike her husband, was St. Paul born and raised, the daughter of a prosperous Irish-Catholic innkeeper. Her frame of reference was ineluctably parochial, the comfortable and familiar milieu of Irish St. Paul. Her loyalties, quite predictably, stopped at the city limits. According to Minnie's daughter, "That the cases [Manahan] was trying were of public interest, nay even of national interest, did not concern her in the least. . . . Many a time she regretted that father was not in some other line of work." Minnie was "righteously indignant" at the very idea of leaving St. Paul, which she regarded as "about perfection as a place in which to dwell."[124] As Minnie understood well, though outsiders might derisively label St. Paul as an Irish-Catholic town, within its borders the labels "Irish" and "Catholic" were badges of no small community status.

Indeed, city residents, regardless of class, ethnicity, or religious affiliation, regarded the Catholic Church and its Irish congregants as valued players in the complicated negotiations that kept the city afloat—despite whatever private opinions they may have held about the ubiquitous Irish Catholics. As the city turned more and more to celebrating its insularity and scale as virtues rather than markers of failure in an age of industrial progress, some versions of civic lore even imaginatively incorporated negative Irish stereotypes, turning them on their head to become constitutive elements of the city's charm. In the words of one upper-class matron, the "drive" of Minneapolis could be attributed to "a large population of shrewd, long headed Scandinavians instead of our corresponding immigrant class of soft speaking, darling, shiftless Irish." Undoubtedly, Irish St. Paulites took umbrage at such a characterization and interpreted their role in shaping the character of St. Paul quite differently. But they certainly would have agreed that they were key civic actors. They also quite likely concurred with the lady's broader conclusion—that St. Paul was "satisfied with its size: and had no wish to expand its borders," either geographically or imaginatively.[125]

After their hapless flirtation with the Minneapolis Citizens Alliance, St. Paul businessmen became convinced that the city's special circumstances required local solutions quite different from those in process in their neighboring city, solutions that were more effectively achieved in back rooms through the offices of Irish brokers than through intercity business associations. In fact, as the past had demonstrated, cooperation with Minneapolis seldom brought them any benefit. Accordingly, the local business associations thereafter dedicated themselves to the project of protecting local firms and markets. Taking the official position that "more important to Saint Paul than the securing of new industries . . . is the growth of Saint Paul's present industries," they actively discouraged new enterprises from locating in the city to avoid further fragmentation of their limited market.[126]

The unions took a similarly insular stance, and labor solidarity largely stopped at the city limits. St. Paul unionists most often regarded Minneapolis locals not as allies but as competitors for both jobs and union members. Until 1907, the *Union Advocate* acted ostensibly as the official organ of organized labor in both cities, but Minneapolis union news—admittedly, not very encouraging—was relegated to a separate section in the back pages of the paper. After the launching of the *Minneapolis Labor Review* in 1907, the *Advocate* was freed to energetically feed the fires of civic rivalry, reminding readers of "sneering ejaculations" about "poor old St. Paul . . . frequently heard from our self-esteeming and self-satisfied friends and neighbors in our sister city up the river."[127]

The range of vision from St. Paul was narrow indeed, and local protectionism was a sentiment that ran both broad and deep. As James Manahan learned when he took on the cause of the state's beleaguered farmers against the railroad, class interests in St. Paul were interpreted within a strictly local configuration. Manahan recalled ruefully, "Coming to the Twin Cities with Nebraska ideas, a conflict with the house of Hill became inevitable. Nobody told me that it was treason to the King of Minnesota to criticize his rates and his railroad." Championing the farmers, he learned, would gain him few friends at home. Fellow citizens, including "over-alled mechanics . . . stenographers . . . white collar clerical workers," even the elevator boy in his office building, greeted him with "acrimonious scorn."[128] As anyone in St. Paul could have told him, the railroad was the city's lifeblood. The plight of the farmers in the hinterland was not their concern.

More than class, more than ethnicity, more than religion, insularity had become the defining feature of culture in St. Paul, and local people firmly closed their doors and their minds to events taking place beyond the city limits. The pull of civic loyalty undoubtedly owed much of its force to the fact that it did indeed "deliver the goods." But the quality of life that resulted had its own power to internalize a sense of insularity, an attachment to the "community" of St. Paul, posed in opposition to the world outside its borders.

This fortress mentality is illustrated most vividly in the peculiar system devised to control vice and maintain law and order within the city limits. St. Paul residents had long displayed a high tolerance for its vice economy—alcohol, gambling, and prostitution. City merchants and wholesalers relied on such attractions to entice buyers into the city; the production and consumption of alcohol were key elements of the local economy; and city coffers garnered significant revenues both from licensing fees and from the regular (and expected) payment of fines from saloons, disorderly houses, and individual prostitutes—a practice that, according to one St. Paul lawyer, "took the place of a license." Licensing also was big business. In 1905 alone, St. Paul took in $384,000 from liquor licenses, the single greatest source of municipal income other than property taxes.[129] Moreover, working-class St. Paulites, for a variety of cultural and economic reasons, vehemently opposed attempts at regulation.

Apparently, some number of respectable city businessmen had personal as well as economic reasons to countenance the economy of sin. According to legend, the men of the Minnesota Club were such regular customers of Nina Clifford, St. Paul's most famous madam, that a tunnel was constructed leading directly from the club to Clifford's nearby establishment. Clifford had such powerful connections that, according to one St. Paul reporter of the period, the "three most important people in St. Paul were James J. Hill, Archbishop John Ireland, and Nina Clif-ford."[130] Thus, with all these varied interests and considerations lined up together, Protestant clergymen and reformers had little luck in repeated efforts to clean up the city, and even such a committed foe of sin as the archbishop stepped carefully in opposing the tangled web of interests that supported this underground economy.

Still, though most St. Paulites considered these activities to be relatively be-nign—at least as far as they were concerned—they had to concede that St. Paul's reputation as a wide-open town attracted some decidedly questionable tourists, a problem neatly solved by Chief of Police John J. O'Connor. Well-schooled in the fine art of deal-making by ten years' experience working for the Democratic power broker Patrick Kelly, O'Connor concocted a most ingenious scheme. Immediately after taking office in 1900, aided by his brother Richard, a Democratic Party boss and lieutenant of Jim Hill, the new chief engineered a system of crime control de-signed to keep the illicit aspects of city business from mushrooming out of control without interfering with their freedom of operation. He simply spread the word that criminals of any sort were safe from prosecution in St. Paul as long as they ful-filled three requirements: check in at police headquarters within twelve hours of ar-rival in the city; provide appropriate gratuities to the local police; and "behave themselves" within the city limits. As O'Connor saw his duty, his job was to "keep the streets of St. Paul safe, regardless of the consequences for neighboring cities or states." St. Paul judges apparently agreed, consistently refusing extradition re-quests from other cities.[131]

The "O'Connor System," as it came to be known, was an open secret, and re-spectable St. Paulites commonly endorsed its benefits. The plan operated just as in-tended. Criminals policed one another, and the city was virtually crime-free. Chief O'Connor was almost universally lionized as "vigilant," "keen," and "justly renowned." Indeed, as the police department's official souvenir book boasted in 1904, "Never in the history of St. Paul has human life and the property of citizens been so safe and the virtue of women so assured." When Minneapolis officials com-plained that they were unable to control crime in their city because St. Paul was a "haven for crooks," it may have only increased local satisfaction with the system. Thus, St. Paul placidly took on the role of criminal haven—a system that remained in place for more than thirty years.[132]

To outsiders, then, St. Paul presented a united front of stubborn parochialism. Inside its borders, careful negotiation kept competing demands in relative equilib-rium, a project that required constant tending and usually superseded interest in state or national affairs. However, the fragile balance of the carefully constructed civic compact began to unravel in 1914. The understandings that had negotiated in-ternal differences, Minneapolis dominance, and economic decline were about to come undone by events that seemed utterly removed from the interests of St. Paul. Yet reverberations from a European war would soon shake the city to its core.

Fig. 24. Loyalty Day Parade, September 1917. Courtesy of the Minnesota Historical Society.

II. THE GREAT WAR

Conflict Abroad and Casualties at Home

Chapter 4

RAISING THE FLAG:

The Struggle to Reshape Civic Identity

Even in the best of times, the web of relationships that maintained civic peace required constant tending. With the outbreak of war in Europe in 1914, new tensions signaled treacherous weather ahead for the citizens of St. Paul. International events intruded into its neighborhoods to unleash yet another set of competing loyalties that quickly taxed the mechanisms of civic negotiation to their limits. At first, St. Paulites complacently agreed that the conflagration taking hold a continent away was no concern of theirs. The *Pioneer Press* summed up general opinion that the war was "inexplicable and unpardonable . . . the greatest crime of modern times." Along with most Americans, the overwhelming sentiment in St. Paul was that the United States should remain strictly neutral.[1] However, by the closing months of 1915, U.S. policy had turned hostile toward the German–Austrian alliance. As official rhetoric shifted from an emphasis on neutrality to one of preparedness, public opinion fragmented in multiple ways. Nowhere was this more starkly apparent than in St. Paul.

As anti-German propaganda heated up in the national press, German Americans vocally defended their historic homeland. Not only did they feel compelled to justify Germany's military cause in the face of widespread public condemnation; they also believed their very culture was under attack. As part of the strategy to generate support for the British and French forces, President Wilson had launched a crusade to eliminate "hyphenism" in immigrant Americans. Supposedly, attachment to European roots was a sign of American disloyalty. True patriotism thus required "100 percent Americanism," which, of course, translated to Anglo-Americanism. This domestic agenda, crafted to support Wilson's foreign policy, had profound reverberations in St. Paul. The brunt of the Americanization campaign fell on the city's Germans, but Scandinavians also resented both the slurs on their patriotism and assault on their cultural practices. As for the Irish, with their hatred of all things

British, the prospect of bearing arms to support the Allies was a distinctly distasteful prospect to them as well.[2]

New stresses divided the city along class and ideological as well as ethnic lines. While business interests generally favored the increasingly interventionist government policy, anticipating benefits from the demands of a wartime economy, working people almost universally opposed the war, fearing its costs would fall most heavily on their shoulders.[3] World events increasingly strained carefully nurtured local relationships, and interclass and interethnic connections began to fray. In classic St. Paul fashion, civic leaders sought to divert attention from divisive national and international issues by promoting local commonalities. The vehicle they turned to was a citywide carnival designed to bring the increasingly fractious populace together in a celebration of civic identity.

From 1886 through 1896, when St. Paul was in pursuit of civic grandeur, the city had staged elaborate annual winter carnivals. Two to three weeks of outdoor revelry and the construction of fantastical ice palaces, designed to capture the imagination of a national audience, were evidence of the city's attractions and proof that Minnesota winters were invigorating rather than death-defying.[4] By the mid-nineties, however, ambitions had considerably lowered, and business boosters abandoned the extravagant carnival along with their metropolitan aspirations.

Twenty years later, business leaders revived the tradition. In 1916 and again in 1917, St. Paul again staged fabulous winter festivals but with a different public relations goal in mind. The intention was no longer to attract new investment or residents to the city, though an influx of temporary visitors would be a welcome side effect; this time, the primary purpose was to reunite the increasingly divided citizenry.[5] As far as focusing a national spotlight on the city, even the organizers seemed to agree that drawing attention to Minnesota winters was not an effective public relations ploy. According to Henry Wickham, the Carnival Association's manager, "Many of the businessmen are of the sincere opinion that the word 'ice' used in connection with the Carnival would re-act on the community." Hence, they christened the event the "Outdoor Sports Carnival" and requested that the local and national press refrain from using either the words *ice* or *winter* lest "thousands of people over the country would get an erroneous impression regarding the climate." As one particularly disgruntled Minnesotan claimed, "That damned Carnival has repelled more prospective Minnesota settlers in a week than the Bureau of Immigration can restrict in a year."[6]

The month of January may not have been the most alluring time for showcasing St. Paul's attractions to the outside world, but it was ideally suited for cementing a sense of *local* identity. Minnesotans prided themselves on their ability to triumph over the harsh winter climate, and the Outdoor Sports Carnival would prove that St. Paulites were first among the hardy Minnesotans. It would also provide an array of civic entertainments to bring the wrangling residents of the city together once again.

After agreeing to adopt the theme of "Make It a Hot One" and to banish all mention of winter from publicity for the event, the businessmen's association gave its wholehearted support, spurred on by Louis Hill, son of the old empire builder, the current president of the Great Northern Railway, and the "ringleader, spokesman and chief motivator of the 1916 Carnival and the one that followed in 1917." Hill may have sold the project to his father as a means to increase tourist traffic for the road, but in truth, awash in inherited wealth, the scion of the Great Northern was likely more captivated by the prospect of riding at the head of a grand parade. Unlike the senior Hill, who shunned frivolity in all its forms, Louis's attention to business often took second place to golf, travel, and the pursuit of a general good time. To the genial young Hill, a carnival must have seemed the ideal solution to problems brewing in the city.[7]

By the measures of participation and enthusiasm, the 1916 carnival seemed to accomplish just what its organizers had intended. Thousands of revelers from all across the city took part in the two-week calendar of nonstop entertainment that included harness races; ski jumping, hockey, skating, and curling competitions; pony, dog, and motorcar races; and baseball, tennis, and pushball games—all performed on ice. Most popular of all were the toboggan slides set up throughout the city, where "it was no uncommon sight to see a line of hundreds waiting with toboggans for a turn at the well kept chutes."[8]

At the coronation of the carnival's "Queen of the Snows," the cause of civic unity took center stage. Lest any group in the city feel slighted, the carnival committee democratically crowned all 108 contestants to reign as sovereigns of the celebration. Civic unity also shaped the composition of the three grand parades that wended through the downtown streets during the course of the carnival. In a city notable for its plethora of ethnic associations, not a trace of ethnic character was to be seen among the more than fifty floats or the twenty-two thousand costumed participants. Nor did union workers march as a separate group. Instead, the units were composed either of neighborhood associations or, most predominantly, of business firms, whose colorfully uniformed employers and workers marched together as parts of a single whole. The carnival souvenir book pictorially demonstrates widespread worker participation in this display of business-labor cooperation—from the "boys and girls of the *Daily News*," to the hundreds marching under the banner of West Publishing, to more than two thousand employees of the Northern Pacific Railroad, each group identified by distinctive costume. For those unaffiliated with a participating unit, carnival organizers established the "Carnival Marching Club," with its own colorful and affordable armbands.[9] As a visible attempt to deny the sources of friction in the city, the parade could not have been more plainly articulated for the participants and the estimated two hundred thousand spectators lining the parade route.

The official account of the carnival leaves no doubt that this was the foremost purpose of this celebratory display. The organizers' chronicle repeatedly emphasized "the spirit of good fellowship . . . and cooperation that seemed to be in the air." Moreover, "It was the working young men and young ladies of St. Paul who

actually gave the impetus which carried the big winter fete to such a brilliant conclusion." Lest the magnanimous role of city leaders be forgotten, the organizers reminded citizens that "the carnival was *free*. . . . Whatever of fun and pleasure the
carnival afforded to any one was offered without charge in the best spirit any American city has ever shown":

> Better than all of the advertising and boosting which she received in the eyes of
> the world is the new spirit of civic pride which had its birth in the carnival of 1916.
> Petty jealousies, clung to for years, have been forgotten; bitter, and in some cases,
> harmful business rivalries have been abandoned; small thoughts and deeds are of
> the past; for the Outdoor Sports Carnival has whispered into the ear of Old Saint
> Paul the story of the *big idea*, and the revered old Saint doesn't intend to forget.[10]

Sadly, the "big idea" of fellowship melted away more quickly than the February
snow. In truth, the spirit of civic unity displayed during the carnival was never more
than paper-thin. The city's small businessmen balked at requests to defray the deficit
incurred by the extravaganza, and organizers were forced apply pressure to wring
out the needed funds. Some local business owners grumbled that they had received
no benefit from the event. Even small businesses that had benefited from the carnival demurred when the time came to pay the bill. The proprietor of the Western
Badge and Novelty Company, "official manufacturers of Carnival Badges, Buttons,
Banners, Pennants and Arm Bands," blanched at the request for a hundred-dollar
donation. "If I could subscribe for a small amount I would willingly do so," he wrote,
"but I feel that I cannot subscribe for $100.00 without detriment to my family."[11]

As for the city's working people, they had thoroughly enjoyed the carnival's free entertainments, but that in no way changed their oppositional, if negotiated, relationship with city businessmen. And, after word leaked out that the Carnival Association
carried liability insurance, a delayed flurry of accident claims descended on the organization and the city from working-class carnival participants and their attorneys. In
February, Miss Rose Geiger phoned up Louis Hill directly with her complaint. "She
seemed to think she was entitled to some damages," the irritated Hill informed Carnival Association manager Wickham. He advised Wickham to settle the claim quickly to
keep her from "talking about the matter, until possibly, some claims attorney gets hold
of it and makes it worse." Too late. Claims mounted by the day, with demands ranging
from $1,500 to $18,000 for alleged injuries sustained primarily on the toboggan slides.
The dismayed representative of the carnival's insurance carrier wrote Wickham, "I
am very much surprised to note that these parties know about the insurance cover-
age. . . . Such information is very prejudicial to our interests." None of the claimants
had been hospitalized, and few had even seen a doctor. In the end, to the weary relief
of carnival organizers, the claims were settled for a fraction of the demanded sums.
The tobogganing victims who pocketed the cash may have congratulated themselves
on yet another enjoyment they derived from the carnival courtesy of city businesses.[12]

The following May, James J. Hill expired suddenly, leaving his empire in the hands of his likable but untested heir apparent. The railroad titan's passing marked the closure of St. Paul's glory days and seemed a gloomy portent for the troubled times ahead. It also elevated the junior Hill to a position of even greater influence in the city. Despite the admittedly mixed returns of the 1916 carnival, Louis had considered it an unmitigated success and especially enjoyed his role as grand marshal of the parade. Other businessmen, who bore the brunt of the problems the carnival left in its wake, had less enthusiasm for a repeat performance. But when Hill pressed the case for another carnival, the rest of the business establishment deferred to its most powerful member. Despite an unpaid deficit and an increasingly divided citizenry, the organizers gamely set out to repeat the event in 1917, determined to make the celebration of civic unity even bigger and more elaborate than the year before. Carnival boosters shouldered the task of wresting the needed funds from St. Paul's tight-fisted business owners who, for the most part, fell in line only grudgingly. Those firms that declined to again underwrite the expense of a marching club received a firm reminder from manager Wickham of the greater costs of shirking their civic duty: "Your absence from a list of marching clubs for this year's carnival will be greatly regretted by most of the business men who are sponsors for the carnival."[13]

The organizers, backed by the city's most influential businesses, ultimately had their way. The 1917 carnival was, indeed, "an even hotter one," as its slogan promised. The parades were bigger and more elaborate, and in addition to the events of the previous year, the organizers played up the city's heritage with the construction of a spectacular ice palace, reminiscent of the carnivals in the 1880s, and a dogsled race from Winnipeg to St. Paul, commemorating a trek made by James J. Hill a generation before.[14]

The extravaganza presented an enviable public relations portrait of civic harmony. Once again, the official account declared it "the greatest civic jollification in the world," where "captains of industry and lowly clerks clad alike in rainbow colored carnival habiliments rub shoulders together, marching in close ranks to the stirring rat-tat-tat of the drums or the blare of martial music." "Verily," it was declared, "the Carnival is a great leveler." The *Union Advocate* appeared to agree, lavishly praising the carnival, "conceived, planned, engineered and conducted to glorious triumph by the genius and tireless industry of Louis W. Hill."[15]

The city's working people seemed to relish the carnival as much as they had the previous year. Several unions postponed their scheduled meetings during the course of the festivities. Those that did meet found they could not compete against the civic revels and universally reported dismal attendance. Nor had the inexplicable rash of accidents the previous year dimmed enthusiasm for the toboggan runs or any of the other myriad entertainments. In schools all across the city, carnival fever took over the classrooms. Still, the spirit of civic festivity was a very thin veneer that masked multiple tensions—tensions that erupted to abruptly halt the coronation ceremony of the Queen of the Snows. Only a year earlier, every candidate had been crowned a queen in the name of civic accord; but in 1917, the attempt to choose the carnival sovereign devolved into a near fistfight among the judges on

Fig. 25. Louis Hill at the head of the Carnival Grand Parade, 1916. Photo by Brown's Photo Studios. Courtesy of the Minnesota Historical Society.

the stage of the Capitol Theater, with the result that no queen was chosen at all—an event that went unpublicized but not unnoted.[16]

In the aftermath of the celebration, organizers again encountered hostility from many small proprietors and merchants when they tried to solicit donations to defray the carnival deficit. It seemed that at every door the answer was the same: "Got no benefit & would give nothing." One merchant even threatened to sue the city for loss of business. Small businessmen, saloon keepers, and independent proprietors—the bulk of the city's economy—felt they had already paid the price of civic pride. Not only had they "spent all [they] could afford for buttons and decorating"; for ten days, the carnival had "killed their business," as steady customers abandoned them for the free attractions of the celebration. By the close of the festivities, the consensus among small downtown business establishments was "to hell with the carnival" and its business organizers.[17] The effort to smooth growing class and ethnic frictions had spawned the unintended consequence of creating yet another rift in the civic fabric. This turn of events was most untimely. City business leaders had never before been more in need of allies than in the months when the United States was poised on the brink of war.

The "civic jollification" of the carnival had provided, at most, only a temporary respite from the escalating civic tensions. By 1917, prowar rhetoric had become increasingly strident, both locally and nationally. In January, open debate still had been tolerated in St. Paul, but by late March the tide had turned. Dismayed by the growing antagonism, the *St. Paul Daily News* (the most temperate of the local dailies) tried to moderate the rancor, protesting that "in these stirring days of 1917 it has become 'treason' to hope to avoid the horrors of war."[18] International events, far outside the city limits, had intruded on the carefully constructed framework undergirding both the city's economy and its social landscape.

The German-language daily and weekly papers, *St. Paul Volkszeitung* and *Der Wanderer,* had rallied in vigorous support of Germany in the early years of the war, but by 1917 they no longer dared such open advocacy, pleading instead for American neutrality.[19] The possibility of active support for Germany had become a dead issue even in the German-language press, since there could be little doubt that the United States had already cast its lot with the Allies.

James J. Hill, in his last major financial transaction before his death in 1916, had made that fact abundantly clear. In 1914, Hill had predicted American profit from the European war, declaring, "What we have to sell Europe needs and must buy." But two years later, he worried, "If England cannot buy what we have to sell . . . who else will buy it?" Driven, as always, by economics rather than ideology, Hill teamed up with J. P. Morgan to arrange an enormous, privately subscribed Anglo-French loan.[20]

Hill directed his First National Bank of St. Paul to subscribe heavily to the loan. Though some depositors protested and several German American organizations attempted to organize a boycott against participating banks, the First National had the backing of the business community and weathered the backlash from individual customers without financial damage.[21]

Fig. 26. This 1916 St. Paul Red Cross bazaar featured a candy booth to raise funds for German and Austrian widows. A year later the political climate had made such a humanitarian effort unthinkable. Courtesy of the Minnesota Historical Society.

City businessmen heartily endorsed Hill's economic logic and also perceived advantages to be gained from the war. American intervention could provide a unique means to bolster the local economy without admitting new competitors to the scene. If the city could secure government contracts, dollars would flow into *existing* businesses. Civic boosters had long been divided about encouraging new industry in St. Paul. An influential faction was reluctant to increase the competition in an admittedly limited market. Those who favored economic growth commonly accused the St. Paul Association of Business and Commerce of discouraging new industry "because it would create competition for present St. Paul industries . . . [a] policy that has paralyzed [*sic*] St. Paul and built up Minneapolis long enough."[22] Wartime contracts could provide a solution that suited both camps, and a unified business community awaited the declaration of war with anticipation. The St. Paul Association, ready to serve the cause of democracy, had the foresight to prepare a survey of the city's production capacity. By its calculations, St. Paul was poised to turn out a breathtaking amount of goods, including $3 million worth of clothing, $1.25 million worth of sheet-metal products, $1.75 million in bakery goods, and 36 million pounds of butter.[23] Such visions of unparalleled production—and prosperity—made the "Star Spangled Banner" the most popular tune in the business district.

In most of the city's neighborhoods, the prospect of war had considerably less appeal. In fact, German Americans' shift in favor of neutrality had bolstered an already significant assemblage of noninterventionists. Minnesota congressmen received floods of petitions in protest of the ever more certain prospect of intervention. According to the historian Carl Chrislock, most of the petitions came from "labor groups, German-American societies, and small town leaders."[24] The state's working people almost unanimously opposed intervention, and St. Paul unionists were among the most vocal. Only a day before President Wilson severed diplomatic relations with Germany, the *Union Advocate* reported on a resolution adopted by the St. Paul Trades and Labor Assembly. The Assembly declared its membership to be "unalterably opposed to war," noting that "upon the workers would fall the entire loss both of life and property."[25]

The Trades Assembly spoke from a position of confidence. Union strength in St. Paul had reached an all-time high, with nearly eleven thousand organized workers. The numbers continued to grow, even beginning to encompass unskilled laborers in certain occupations, as well as the city's firefighters and police force. Union officials and employers most often worked out their differences at the negotiating table. The few disputes that had escalated into strikes in 1916 had been resolved quickly with civility, and usually in labor's favor, thanks in part to an increasingly effective labor bloc in the legislature.[26] St. Paul unionists, seemingly secure in the local compact they had negotiated, claimed equal status with business in the civic polity.

The antiwar position of the St. Paul Trades and Labor Assembly was consistent with the official policy of the American Federation of Labor (AFL) and with general working-class sentiment across the country. But, even after the AFL altered its official position in March and pledged its wholehearted service to "safeguard and preserve the republic," St. Paul organized labor continued to lobby aggressively for peace until the day war was declared.[27] In one way, this was a real departure; St. Paul unions usually followed AFL national directives. But on a more substantial level, the local unions' divergence from national policy was entirely consistent with the localistic nature of union consciousness. Most often, the position of the conservative AFL coincided with preferred local modes of negotiation; but when national and local priorities differed, St. Paul unions went their separate way without a backward glance. Close adherence to national policy was more a result of coincidence than policy. In this instance, the commitment to nonintervention ran deep within local union ranks. Somewhat ironically, the parochial independence of the city's unions aligned them for once with their socialist-led and typically more oppositional Minneapolis counterparts—a break with tradition that foreshadowed new labor unity in the months to come.

The strong anti-intervention sentiment of the city's working people also drew them closer to the small local contingent of Socialists. Though most of the city's workers rejected Socialism per se in the voting booth, they were sympathetic to much of its ideology and, notwithstanding the warnings of the Catholic Church and the *Union Advocate*, considered it a legitimate, if misguided, political position. The Trades and Labor Assembly elected Julius Emme, one of St. Paul's most visible Socialists and president of the machinist's union (the only Socialist-dominated union in the city), as chair of its special peace committee. Despite his "radical" politics, Emme was esteemed as one of the Trades Assembly's most active and highly respected members, and as the prospect of intervention heightened, Emme's politics began to align quite closely with those of his fellow trade unionists.[28]

A smaller but still significant segment of St. Paul's middle class also opposed entry into the war. Women, students, and clergymen were particularly prominent in the ranks of peace activists. Students from Macalester College formed a Peace and Neutrality Association, and the Women's Socialist Study Club organized the St. Paul Peace League. The Peace League, which attracted many nonsocialists into its ranks, further legitimated socialism among the city's mainstream elements and briefly created another alliance that crossed class lines. On March 31, nearly a month after diplomatic relations with Germany had been severed, the league sponsored an antiwar rally at the St. Paul Auditorium. More than three thousand people, comprising "all classes of citizens, including a large number of working men and women," enthusiastically demonstrated in the cause of peace. The *Daily News* described the rally as "a patriotic protest."[29]

In the meantime, the St. Paul Association was promoting its own version of patriotism. City businessmen faced some significant handicaps in the pursuit of government contracts. Local opposition to the war presented a major stumbling block. The federal government was unlikely to award war contracts to a city with a reputation for disloyalty. Nor was a disgruntled working class a harbinger of productive efficiency. The key to success, as the businessmen saw it, was to display a climate of unswerving patriotism with as little visible dissent as possible. To promote business profits, they needed to craft a new scenario for civic identity.[30]

On January 23, 1917, as final preparations were being made to launch the winter carnival, a different but not unrelated set of civic preparations was also underway. A group of businessmen and professionals, all members of the St. Paul Association, sponsored a meeting to protest Belgian deportations—a human rights issue that was unlikely to stir up community controversy. Attorney Charles Farnham, one of the organizers, proudly related that it represented the first public voicing of patriotic sentiment in the city and served to counteract the "good many propaganda meetings" orchestrated by "pro-Germans" and pacifists.[31] In the wake of the meeting's positive publicity, the same organizers announced the formation of the Patriotic League of St. Paul by a group of "private citizens," with Farnham as president. The League's stated purpose was to promote "that spirit of true patriotism which calls for readiness and courage in the pending controversy with Germany . . . to defend American rights, American ideals and American honor." Farnham declared that "St. Paul is singularly well organized for this patriotic movement . . . by reason of the large number of energetic and public-spirited men and women who are members of the various carnival marching clubs." The Patriotic League was planning to set the carnival march to a different tune, somehow translating local pride into unified citywide support for the war. Privately, Farnham admitted that the League hoped to "help take the pall off St. Paul."[32]

Publicly, the League focused on positive demonstrations of patriotism. It sponsored numerous rallies and meetings featuring local and national speakers. It also engaged in a vigorous campaign urging businesses and individuals to proudly display the flag. Farnham wrote dozens of letters reminding negligent patriots to keep the banner waving.[33] On the surface, the League's activities seemed fairly superficial and harmless exercises, but the patriotic tunes and parades masked a strategy that was both focused and coercive. The Patriotic League publicly walked a narrow line: if St. Paul was to redeem itself from the "pall" of disloyalty, it was critical that the city display a spontaneous upswelling of patriotism rather than a mere suppression of discontent. Thus, as Farnham explained privately, the League ignored critics who charged that it was "doing nothing but talk." The reality was something quite different, but because "many of the things that we do are of rather a confidential nature," for "political reasons" it was best not to be recognized.[34]

By March, the Patriotic League claimed some seven thousand members, but the numbers were somewhat misleading. Farnham admitted that only half had joined spontaneously, the rest on "suggestion." Though Farnham claimed to use no tactics of "coaxing, argument or anything approximating duress," his correspondence belies that assertion. In fact, the League exerted pressure in numerous ways that were not apparent publicly.[35] Membership subscription lists passed through the city's major businesses from the top down. At the head were boldly scrawled the signatures of the top executives, next the middle managers, and on down the organizational hierarchy. Invariably clustered at the bottom were the names of men who listed their addresses as Frogtown, the YMCA, boarding houses, or the Rondo district. Implicit pressure from employers, whether real or imagined, can be read from the text of the lists themselves.[36]

League tactics were subtle: apply thinly veiled pressure outside as well as within the workplace, often by enlisting neighborhood clergymen or other identified leaders in the cause. The most common approach was to question the loyalty of any individual or group who balked at the invitation to join the organization. When membership applications were slow in arriving from the black community, Farnham expressed his "anxiety" to the African American leaders he had enlisted as the "recruitment committee." "There is no use denying the fact that, tho I don't think it well grounded, there is a pretty wide spreading impression that the colored people of this country are not responsive to patriotic appeal. It is roughly put by some people that, *they* have no flag."[37]

Farnham's carefully worded accusation prompted an indignant reply that black Americans had "no treason, thank God, to atone or explain. . . . No hyphen bridges or qualifies our loyalty"—an unmistakable stab at immigrant St. Paulites who were admitted to the civic community that relegated African Americans to its margins. A stack of signed membership cards accompanied this rejoinder, giving emphatic proof that the slur against the black community was unfounded.[38]

The Patriotic League used similar tactics on pastors of white Protestant congregations. This group was a particularly problematic target, since they answered to no central authority and had a troubling tendency to agitate for peace. When Reverend John Swanson, pastor of the First Swedish Baptist Church, courteously declined to join the League, declaring, "I appreciate your kind invitation but cannot accept it because . . . I am decidedly against this country going into the war," Farnham responded by impugning Swanson's patriotism. But without an economic or racial club to wield, he was unable to sway the peace-loving pastor.[39]

Lutherans proved particularly unmanageable. Splintered internally into four separate ethnic synods, St. Paul's thirty-seven Lutheran churches operated with almost complete autonomy, and local pastors tended to reflect the politics of their neighborhoods. Some congregations expressed what the League considered the proper degree of patriotism, but without an overriding authority to discipline recalcitrant churches, the patriotic organization found it could do little to bring the rest into line. Thus, it came to regard the stubbornly independent Lutheran clergy with general mistrust. Foreign-language congregations were particularly suspect; rife with potentially disloyal immigrants, they merited further "watching." During the course of the war, more Lutheran pastors were charged with disloyalty than any other single group in the country.[40]

Despite their suspicions, the last thing businessmen wanted was to provoke oppositional demonstrations that would stain the patriotic facade they were constructing so carefully. When Farnham received a suggestion from a "concerned citizen" that the League should leaflet a scheduled peace meeting, he rejected the idea out of hand, explaining, "I know that we would resent their doing anything of the sort at one of our meetings and, because of the audiences that we get . . . I should deprecate any disorder of any sort at one of our meetings. So far we have completely escaped it." He confided, however, "I am going to show your letter to a man whom I know will be interested in it, and I think probably he will submit it to the press."[41]

The demand to conform was most effective on the middle class, which the League counted on as its core constituency. The Patriotic League described itself as a community-wide organization spontaneously generated by a group of public-spirited citizens, but in reality it was an arm of the St. Paul Association. Given the climate of opinion in the city, the Association itself considered it impolitic to support the war publicly in early 1917; however, it would later proudly claim credit for activities sponsored by the Patriotic League.[42] The directors and original members of the League all came out of the St. Paul Association, as did the funding for the project. The League drew additional support from elite women's organizations, including the Society of Colonial Dames, Daughters of the American Revolution, and Dames of the Loyal Legion—the wives and daughters of Association members. The men and women involved in this patriotic project were neighbors as well as social equals and business associates. The great majority lived within blocks of one another in the elite neighborhoods of Crocus Hill and Cathedral Hill.[43] In working-class neighborhoods their opinions may have counted for little, but as social and business leaders, they exerted considerable influence among their peers. These same people provided the bulk of financial support to the city's religious and educational institutions. Thus, they were in a position to apply both social and financial leverage on eminent clergy and educators.

The pressure could be fierce. In February, a mild student protest at Presbyterian Macalester College set off a singular explosion of outrage from city elites. Eighty-seven student members of the Macalester College Neutrality and Peace Association petitioned Minnesota's congressmen to take a stand for peace. This action was hardly very threatening, as protests go. Other much more vocal demonstrations in the previous weeks and months had attracted little hostile public reaction. But the students' petition had a larger significance to the image-conscious city leaders. It planted the suspicion that disloyalty was festering within St. Paul's elite institutions and suggested that city was "rotten" at the core. Moreover, the students' action stained the city's patriotism not only locally but also on the national stage, where the dramaturgy of St. Paul loyalty was most important. The state's congressman from Duluth accused the students of "a yellow streaked and coward soul when confronted by duty"—a statement that, unfortunately, was widely quoted in the national press.[44]

Dismayed city leaders reacted swiftly. The Patriotic League joined with local editorialists in denouncing the students. College administrators also frantically disavowed the students' actions, claiming that most of those who signed the letter had been ignorant of its contents. To "vindicate the honor of the school," the college orchestrated patriotic meetings, publicized student enlistments, and circulated a petition in support of government policy. Under pressure, many of the transgressing students retracted their signatures, and as further proof of loyalty, fifteen of the institution's eighteen faculty members telegraphed President Wilson to express their active support for the war to "help overthrow those tyrannous and lawless survivals of a lawless age." Capping off the drama, President Emeritus James Wallace immediately resigned as vice president of the American Peace Society. In a stunning about-face, he declared that "peace as an end in itself becomes a curse" and characterized Germany as "drunk with a materialistic philosophy and a vaulting ambition," which left "general terrorism in command."[45]

Having paid public penance for its transgressions, Macalester was welcomed back into the fold of loyal St. Paulites. The *Pioneer Press* formally commended President Wallace for "one of the most penetrating statements ever written on the ghastly moral degeneracy of peace as an end in itself."[46] The college could once again rest easy; its stature and the financial support that went with it were once again secure. City leaders were equally relieved. The solid front of the loyalty brigade had won the day.

Such coercion was seldom necessary in bringing prominent clergy and educators into the fold. Most accepted invitations to join the Patriotic League with alacrity. The presidents of Methodist Hamline University and the College of St. Thomas solicited memberships from college faculty and staff. St. Thomas, which billed itself as a "Catholic Military College," proudly publicized its War Department ranking as an honor school. Military training was obligatory for all students, and in the course of the war, the college would deliver eleven hundred students and alumni to the armed services.[47]

According to its official publicity, the administration of St. Thomas was "under the control and direction" of Archbishop John Ireland, and to him it owed its military character, along with that of its ancillary secondary school, St. Thomas Military Academy. Ireland's fervent patriotism already was legendary. The former Civil War chaplain, described by one historian as "an imperialist and patriot of the first order," was deeply interested in the emergence of America as a world power.[48] With Ireland at the helm of the archdiocese, official support for the war effort from the Catholic Church was never in doubt.

Religious politics intensified the archbishop's patriotic dedication. Committed to assimilating Catholics into the American mainstream, Ireland had long claimed patriotism to be a particularly notable Catholic virtue. In his view, and that of many in the Catholic hierarchy, the war was a pivotal moment for American Catholicism. It provided an exceptional opportunity to publicly prove Catholics "to be the first patriots of the land" and thereby lay anti-Catholic nativism finally to rest.[49] However, if Catholic ethnics agitated against the war, then the Church itself would be tainted in the process. Thus, Ireland's goals, for his own reasons, paralleled those of the Patriotic League. If St. Paul stood out as a bastion of loyalty, then as a Catholic city it provided proof of Catholic patriotism. Conversely, if it were labeled as a hotbed of sedition, the blame would assuredly reflect most severely on its Catholic population.

The archbishop quickly joined the Patriotic League, as did all his subordinates in

Fig. 27. Archbishop Ireland displayed a proud military demeanor while reviewing St. Thomas cadets in 1915. Photo by Charles P. Gibson. Courtesy of the Minnesota Historical Society.

the chancery. His expressions of patriotism were both fervent and pointed. Immediately upon the declaration of war, he proclaimed:

> All citizens of America should have . . . confidence . . . in the absolute loyalty to America of others of their fellow-citizens. . . . Where today are the Irishmen? Only in far off Ireland. . . . Where today are the Germans? Only in far off Germany: none today on the soil of America. . . . Here are all Americans. It is wonderful this homogeneity of the entire people of America in allegiance to the "Star Spangled Banner."[50]

To his Catholic congregations he mandated, "No reservation of mind, no slackening of earnest act, to be henceforward thought of or allowed."[51]

Most assuredly, Ireland was concerned with protecting his flock from persecution, but he also had a private axe to grind with his German American confreres. For more than three decades, he had been engaged in an intrachurch battle over ethnic nationalism in the American Catholic church. The German faction insisted that German language and culture were an integral part of German Catholicism; if these cultural trappings were allowed to slip away, Catholicism itself would disappear into the sea of American secularism. The Americanizing contingent (primarily Irish), with Ireland as one of its most vocal leaders, insisted that only through Americanization would the church free itself from persecution and truly prosper, an analysis that implicitly privileged the English-speaking Irish Catholics—and Irish clergy—as the model of American Catholicism and its natural leaders.[52]

Though this controversy represented genuine philosophical differences, it also translated into a struggle over real political power. Ireland was vying not only for national position but also for control of his own archdiocese. German Benedictine clergy for years had infringed on the archbishop's authority from their seat of power at St. John's Abbey, seventy miles north of St. Paul. Ireland was painfully aware that the Benedictines often exacted far more loyalty from German American Catholics than did he.[53] In short, Archbishop Ireland was at war with Germany on several fronts and became, thereby, one of the staunchest allies of the city's businessmen. At least at the institutional level, the Catholic Church would wave the flag like an inveterate Yankee.

It is questionable, however, how much weight the archbishop carried among Minnesota's Catholics, even in his home base of St. Paul. German Catholics outside the Twin Cities treated his dictates at best with indifference and, in some cases, with outright hostility. This was especially true in those areas where parishioners were buttressed by German Benedictine pastors. Joseph Busch, bishop of the St. Cloud diocese, complained that in supporting Ireland's position, he was "quite vigorously persecuted in an underhanded and quiet way among the people of his own faith and parish."[54]

In St. Paul, German Catholics displayed no such protest against their archbishop. Perhaps his immediate presence was more commanding in the shadow of the great cathedral. But it is just as likely that the city's Germans simply maintained a pained public silence in the face of their archbishop's apparent complicity in an increasingly public anti-German campaign—a campaign that may have precluded overt protest but was not ideologically persuasive. Certainly, they must have been aggrieved by the *Catholic Bulletin's* frequent articles that extolled the fine showing of British and French Catholic soldiers at the front, with never a word about the virtues of German Catholics on the other side of the trenches.[55] The *Bulletin*, which faithfully reported the patriotic character that infused festivities in the middle-class and heavily Irish parishes of St. Mark and St. Luke, recorded nothing of similar nature in the German parishes.[56]

Perhaps even more telling, St. Luke's was located in fashionable Crocus Hill and St. Mark's in the affluent streetcar suburb of Merriam Park. The working-class Irish parishes of St. Vincent's and St. Mary's reported no patriotic exercises in early 1917. Even among the Irish, the archbishop's model Catholics, his message was viewed and interpreted through the lens of class. The students at St. Vincent's parochial school, sons and daughters of laboring men, imbibed some highly subversive ideas, along with the three R's, from the Irish-born sisters who taught them. The nuns, described by one former student as "very anti-English . . . hostile to the British" and "just anti-government in general," schooled the children in a critique of the war that would have made the archbishop livid. Even as he urged his Catholics to be the "best patriots," the sisters lined up their students to sing "I Didn't Raise My Boy to Be a Soldier" and other "subversive" tunes.[57]

For Irish-born St. Paulites, such as the nuns at St. Vincent's, opposition to the war may have been linked closely to the plight of their homeland. But by 1917, most of the Irish in St. Paul were two or three generations removed from Irish soil. For them, class rather than ethnicity or religion seems to have been the determining factor on the war issue. Grace Holmes, a student at St. Vincent's, later attested that she was profoundly influenced by the Irish nuns, but the lesson the twelve-year-old girl carried with her was a critique based on class rather than on ethnic solidarity. Her youthful interpretation reflected the predominant Irish working-class sentiment in her neighborhood and town.[58]

St. Paul was an anomaly among America's Irish enclaves in 1917. The themes that energized antiwar sentiment among Irish Americans across the country—hatred of British aggression and the concurrent struggle for Irish home rule—never made much of a splash in Minnesota. In St. Paul, the state's Irish stronghold, organized ethnic opposition caused scarcely a ripple in the political stream. No organized Irish protest against the war occurred in the city. In 1916, a petition declaring Irish opposition to "a war driven by English guile and cant" circulated among Irish organizations nationwide Dozens of signatures from well-known Irish enclaves—Boston, New York, Providence, and Butte, Montana—endorsed the petition. But St. Paul, Minnesota, could muster only a single obscure signature. Even Minneapolis made a slightly better showing.[59] Working-class Irish who opposed the war appear to have been less concerned with Irish nationalism than with the possibility of fighting and dying in what they termed a "rich man's war."

The peculiar silence of St. Paul's Irish—as Irish—on the war issue stemmed from two related sources. First, they split along class lines; and second, despite their political differences, they all derived benefits from maintaining the fraternal bonds of Irish brotherhood. Thus, an effort to declare an "Irish position" on the war was neither prudent nor possible. As was almost always the case in St. Paul, some of the most vocal spokesmen on either side of the question were Irish Americans. The socially prominent jurist Pierce Butler and his brother Walter, a wealthy contractor, were directors of the Patriotic League; attorney Thomas O'Brien was president of the St. Paul Association. George Lawson, secretary of the Minnesota Federation of Labor, and James Clancy, president of the Trades and Labor Assembly, acted as spokesmen for organized labor's opposition to the war. Radical William Mahoney, a Socialist trade unionist, and James Manahan, perennial attorney of the downtrodden, also vocally supported the cause of nonintervention.

This variety of evidence confirms how thoroughly the Irish had integrated themselves into the fabric of the city. It also helps to illumine the instrumental quality of Irish ethnicity as it evolved in St. Paul. Unlike the city's Germans, whose preoccupation with specific issues of language and *Kultur* tended to set them apart from the city at large, the Irish used ethnicity as a means to communicate *across* differences. Thus, though James Manahan was politically miles apart from Thomas O'Brien, whose interests were often antithetical to those of James Clancy, they shared the common ground of Irish heritage. Ethnic "brotherhood" provided an arena of civility in which the lines of political negotiation remained open.[60]

To serve this function, ethnicity itself had to appear largely apolitical. In other words, because the city's Irish had varying attitudes toward the war, a publicly enunciated "Irish" position would create internal divisions with the potential to destroy the instrumental cross-class value of ethnic affiliation.[61] Thus, in St. Paul the content of Irish identity evolved into what Werner Sollors has termed a "collective fiction," an almost mythical folklore composed of a vague nostalgia for the homeland, a history of shared discrimination—largely specious in this time and place—and a celebration of Irish culture. The Ancient Order of Hibernians, which in St. Paul emphasized such cultural components of ethnicity, maintained a strong and active membership. In contrast, the Clan na Gael, with its highly politicized agenda, attracted only a tiny fragment of the city's Irish into its organization, with scarcely enough members to function. The choice to shape ethnic identity as apolitical was in itself a deeply political act that reinforced Irish power in the community.[62]

Shared Catholicism also had a certain power to bridge class and ethnic differences, but the "community" of Catholics was riddled with internal divisions that were exacerbated as the country moved toward war. In January, the *Catholic Bulletin* celebrated the election of Thomas O'Brien as president of the St. Paul Association, declaring that his election "reflects credit upon the electors, and at the same time is a source of gratification to citizens of all classes and especially to Catholics."[63] To a point, this was probably true. O'Brien's election reiterated the stature of Catholics in the city, which undeniably benefited the entire group. However, it also acted as a reminder of Irish privilege, particularly at the expense of the city's Germans. Furthermore, the St. Paul Association represented a source of growing friction between working people and the city's business interests. The Irish-Catholic middle class no doubt was gratified by the honor bestowed on one of their own. For other readers of the *Bulletin*, it may have seemed a more dubious honor.

St. Paul unquestionably had become a divided city. By March, the businessmen of the Patriotic League and the St. Paul Association had to acknowledge that, despite their best efforts at generating "spontaneous" patriotism, despite their enlistment of the archbishop and the city's most prominent educators and Protestant clergy, and despite the enthusiastic jingoism of the local press, they had achieved only mixed results. In fact, the city seemed more factionalized than at any time in memory. The Patriotic League was putting enormous energy, time, and money into organizing public displays of patriotism to counteract the city's dubious image. Nonetheless, the troublesome "peace agitators," characterized by the League treasurer as "the same old crowd . . . traveling under a new name," continued to undermine their efforts.[64]

Unsettling letters also regularly arrived at the Patriotic League office and (even worse) appeared in the editorial pages of the daily papers. One writer declared in the *Daily News* that "the American flag is being wallowed in the mire by big business." Another warned the League's secretary: "Don't make the mistake of setting yourselves up as the conscience of the community. . . . My old home community is not represented by the misguided six hundred who belong to the League."[65] A third, employing tried and true St. Paul tactics of community consumerism, addressed himself to the vaudeville theater owner who supplied the space for the noonday rallies:

> I want to remind you . . . that the people that do all the holloring about war are the same people who patronize the Metropolitan and Orpheum [the city's most opulent theaters] and that the people who have to fight in all wars and who cannot afford anything else except a 10 or 15 cent show are the people who patronise your theatre. Shurely if this country gave all her citisens a fair deal should they have to be told when to wear the Flag or when to be Patriotic. I should say, not . . . hoping you will use a little judgement in the future.[66]

Farnham turned the letter over to the U.S. district attorney with his recommendation that "such people need watching."[67] Unfortunately, as the men of the Patriotic League and the St. Paul Association were coming to realize, watching was all they could do. They lacked a mechanism to enforce compliance with their patriotic project, and in any event, attempted coercion might stir up the very displays of opposition that they dreaded.

Technically, as the St. Paul Association later disingenuously claimed, before war was declared, "It did not devolve upon [them] to declare an aggressive attitude toward any of the belligerents engaged in that conflict. . . . It was yet proper that the sympathies and opinions . . . should diverge."[68] This public posture reveals the dilemma that hamstrung the Association and the Patriotic League in the weeks leading up to the war. Despite their high opinion of themselves as civic leaders, the business interests were unable to win over public opinion. If they attempted to impose compliance from within the community, they feared that protests would escalate and further mar the city's image, thwarting their hopes for the war contracts they desired so ardently. Casting about for a means to achieve their ends and at the same time protect themselves from community resentment, the city's businessmen, out of other options, broke with precedent and allied themselves with their Minneapolis rivals in seeking a solution through the power of the state.

On March 31, 1917, the same day that three thousand people gathered in downtown St. Paul in a "patriotic protest" for peace, an extraordinary bill was introduced simultaneously in the Minnesota House and Senate. It called for appropriation of $2 million to fund the creation of a Commission for Public Safety.[69] Believing that a declaration of war was only days away, the Minnesota legislature anticipated—and exceeded—federal requests for state support. No other state or federal commission would be authorized with comparable statutory powers. As it was proposed, the Commission for Public Safety was to be composed of the governor, a commission attorney, and five members appointed at the governor's discretion. In these seven men was vested virtually unlimited authority for the duration of the war to issue and enforce whatever orders "for the public safety and for the protection of life and public property or private property" they deemed necessary—a mandate interpreted to include the right to remove public officials, sanction covert activities, and employ broad police powers, completely free from legislative or judicial oversight. In the heated atmosphere that accompanied the declaration of war, Minnesota legislators rushed to give away their role in state governance, with only a single dissenting vote.[70]

St. Paul business leaders had actively lobbied for establishment of the commission. According to the *Minneapolis Tribune*, "representative business men of Minneapolis and St. Paul crowded the senate chamber" to urge its passage. Charles Farnham proudly asserted that the idea for the commission had originated in the Patriotic League. Though judiciously proposed by a senator from outside the Twin Cities, the bill had indeed been drawn up by Ambrose Tighe, a St. Paul attorney and member of the Patriotic League's executive board.[71] Still, though St. Paul businessmen may well have believed that they were the architects of the commission, as subsequent events were to demonstrate, they were only junior partners in the enterprise. The real power lay in other hands. Once in operation, the Minnesota Commission for Public Safety unswervingly served the agenda of the Minneapolis Civic and Commerce Association and its enforcement arm, the Citizens Alliance. The course of action that it pursued was beyond the scope of anything imagined by the parochial-minded businessmen of St. Paul—one with consequences that far exceeded their designs.[72]

Chapter 5

TAKING AIM:

Enemies of the State

The businessmen of St. Paul and Minneapolis had declared a momentary truce in their rivalry, but the cities were no more "twins" than they had ever been. The business associations of the two cities jointly lobbied to establish the Public Safety Commission, but with quite different goals in mind. St. Paul civic leaders were engaged in a cultural project to rehabilitate the city's tarnished image, which demanded at least the appearance of civic consensus. But in Minneapolis, business interests had a much larger and more specific political end in mind and were not reluctant to use whatever means were necessary to achieve it, regardless of popular opinion.

In ordinary times, Minneapolis leaders made little pretense at intercity cooperation. Privately, they had long ago dismissed their little competitor next door, impatient with its provincial vision and timidity in dealing with organized labor. St. Paul businessmen, though they participated in the Minnesota Employers' Association and the statewide federation of chambers of commerce, most often proved to be cautious and conservative partners. They might willingly lobby legislators on behalf of business interests, but most were reluctant to stir up conflict either with their workers or the community by taking a public stand to rid themselves of union labor.[1] In the estimation of the aggressively antiunion businessmen of Minneapolis, this was no way to run a city.

The men who met for drinks at the Minneapolis Club had no doubt that they *did* know how to run a city, and every economic indicator confirmed their confidence. Minneapolis had outstripped St. Paul in nearly all categories, and in 1917 it had never appeared more prosperous. However, as the city's financial barons were acutely aware, the temporary demand created by the European war masked a looming economic crisis.

As America poised itself to enter the war, the city of Minneapolis faced a number of pressing problems, threatened as it was on one side by dwindling natural resources and, on another, by the political turmoil engendered by a growing range of oppositional movements. Recent political and economic circumstances had mingled to produce a volatile mix with the potential to destroy the city's position as "Queen City of the Northwest." To Minneapolis businessmen, these challenges called for a course of action too ambitious to orchestrate on a municipal level. The impending war propitiously handed them the means to enlist higher powers in their behalf. A commission that would "gather the sovereign powers of the State in a few responsible hands for quick and effective use" could provide the solution to their problems—particularly if the "responsible hands" were linked to those of the Minneapolis business establishment.[2] But to put such an agency in place, they needed statewide cooperation from business interests, especially those in St. Paul. Thus, Minneapolis leaders found themselves in the unusual position of courting cooperation from across the river. As luck would have it, St. Paul businessmen, for their own largely local reasons, were eager to participate. Only after the commission was in place did they ruefully discover that their priorities had no place on its agenda.

The events that unfolded in St. Paul during the war can only be understood within the context of structures of power that operated outside the city. The state government, acting through the Commission of Public Safety, intruded to an unprecedented degree in local affairs, its course of action deeply influenced by the interests of the Minneapolis business establishment. Thus, to untangle the conflicts that ensued in St. Paul, it is first necessary to understand the conditions in Minneapolis that lay behind this domestic wartime campaign.

The twin pillars that had undergirded the Minneapolis economy since its origin—lumbering and grain milling—were both in serious trouble in 1917. The lumber industry was in steep decline, and a revival was impossible. The magnificent forests of northern Minnesota that supplied the Minneapolis mills largely had been cut over by 1915; in 1919, the city's last sawmill would close.[3] Fortunately, the oceans of wheat that blanketed the western prairies seemed an ever-renewable resource to feed the city's flour mills. But a farmers' revolt on the plains of North Dakota was building into a potential disaster for the grain magnates of the Mill City. With lumbering inexorably on the wane, business leaders committed themselves to protecting at all costs the city's position as the flour milling capital of the world.

Milling was only one element of the grain monopoly that fueled the Minneapolis economic engine. A handful of powerful local families had created a vertically integrated agricultural cartel controlled through the Minneapolis Chamber of Commerce—the official grain exchange.[4] Before the turn of the century, the Chamber had been established as a private corporation by act of the legislature, during the administration of John Pillsbury—a name synonymous with flour. Membership in the grain exchange was exclusive and without oversight. Through a series of holding companies and interlocking directorates, its members controlled the entire process of marketing wheat in the region. They owned the line and terminal elevators, the commission houses, and the mills. They unilaterally determined the price of wheat and, moreover, controlled the region's major banks, enforcing their dominance by setting the terms of agricultural credit.[5]

The Chamber of Commerce brooked no incursion on its control of the market. Not only were farmers or independent operators barred from membership; the chamber also refused to handle grain destined for sale outside its domain, thereby thwarting attempts at cooperative enterprises. To the region's farmers, the unparalleled greed of Minneapolis grain interests was responsible for increasing agricultural impoverishment. They also believed that, through its web of economic control and political influence, the Chamber of Commerce virtually ruled the government of neighboring North Dakota, a state almost wholly dependent on wheat production, which provided the largest share of the mountains of grain that poured into Minneapolis elevators.[6]

In 1916, the unthinkable occurred: hard-pressed North Dakota farmers reclaimed their state government. With what historian Robert Morlan has described as a "hymn of hate directed at the Chamber of Commerce," North Dakotans overwhelmingly embraced the banner of the Nonpartisan League, a farmer's organization that had risen from obscurity in only a year. Voters swept the Nonpartisan League candidate for governor into office by a majority of more than four to one and bestowed ninety-eight legislative seats on League-endorsed candidates.[7] This unexpected electoral coup shattered the complacency of the Minneapolis grain trust.

The League's aggressive and well-articulated plan to develop North Dakota "for the benefit of its citizens and to prevent its exploitation for the benefit of outsiders" included a call for a state-run grain grading system, state-owned elevators, and the establishment of a state bank to provide agricultural credit and crop insurance. In effect, farmers were striking at the heart of the Minneapolis profit machine. Furthermore, this democratic "infection" showed every sign of spreading. League organizers were moving into Minnesota, farmers were joining the movement in alarming numbers, and in January 1917, the League showed its confidence by relocating its national headquarters from Fargo to St. Paul.[8] Not surprisingly, Minneapolis businessmen were prepared to go to substantial lengths to wipe the Nonpartisan League off the political map.

Within the city of Minneapolis itself, the Old Stock elites faced another disturbing challenge to their political and economic hegemony. Years of intransigent labor relations dictated by the Citizens Alliance had maintained Minneapolis as an open-shop citadel since 1901. The unwillingness of those in power to consider even moderate reforms had, however, created an unlikely oppositional alliance. Middle-class reformers, AFL unionists, Socialists, and even self-proclaimed radicals of the Industrial Workers of the World (IWW) found common ground.[9] In 1916, two controversies galvanized this alliance. First, the city's police force had helped violently suppress a teamsters' strike, attacking strikers with clubs, blackjacks, and guns.

Second, during controversial negotiations over the city's streetcar franchise, municipal reformers charged that the mayor and city councilmen, who had substantial financial interests in the streetcar company, had "sold out" the public—a claim that proved largely true.[10] The following autumn, fired to action by the combination of antiunion violence and municipal scandal, an improbable coalition of discontented voters elected Socialist trade unionist Thomas Van Lear as mayor, along with two Socialist city councilmen. Minneapolis corporate attorney John McGee, who would later dominate the Public Safety Commission, declared that Van Lear's election made him "sick," a sentiment heartily shared by his fellow members of the Minneapolis Club.[11]

Few of Van Lear's supporters were members of the Socialist Party. Even those who were could be categorized as little more than moderate reformers. Minneapolis-brand socialism posed little threat to the city's capitalist underpinnings. As historian David Nord describes the city's Socialists, "Most of [them] combined a vague socialist millenialism with their day-to-day concerns about street watering and alley grading," operating on the assumption that effective municipal policy would prepare people for a larger socialist vision.[12]

Van Lear had run his campaign on issues of moderate municipal reform, framing the struggle as one between special interests and the public. His most radical plank called for eventual public ownership of city utilities, an issue debated throughout the nation in this period. Furthermore, Van Lear's actual power as mayor was sharply limited by the structure of municipal government, which vested most of the authority in the city council. Nonetheless, the mayor *did* have the power to appoint the chief of police. This position was of signal importance, since the police force was regularly called out to quell labor unrest and protect strikebreakers. As an active trade unionist and former president of the machinists' union, Van Lear could be relied on to neutralize this arm of the antiunion forces.[13] To businessmen committed to the principle of the open shop, the threat was serious. Moreover, Minneapolis elites jealously guarded their position as the city's "natural" leaders, out of the conviction that they had built Minneapolis to its present state of grandeur. The idea of Van Lear as the titular head of the city—a union man as well as a Socialist—seemed a personal affront. Hence the reaction provoked by Van Lear's election had cultural as well as economic underpinnings.[14]

In reality, organized labor was in no position to mount a challenge to the open shop rule of the Citizens Alliance. The teamsters' strike of the previous summer had represented workers' most concerted effort to exert union power in the history of the city. The Minneapolis labor movement had closed ranks behind the teamsters, officially declaring that "the Citizens Alliance had met a foe to be reckoned with." But even twelve hundred strikers supported by union members across the city found themselves no match for organized business, backed by the major banks and the police force. The two-month struggle ended in a crushing defeat, with long-term repercussions: union activists fired, blackballed, or driven from the city, and the union itself reduced to a shell of only 139 members. Workers might express their discontent in the future by voting for a Socialist mayor, but eighteen years would pass before they attempted another major organizing effort.[15] Nonetheless, the cost of maintaining an open-shop city was substantial, and business remained hostile to any form of organized labor, making no distinction between the conservative unionism of the AFL and the revolutionary ideology of the IWW. Thus, when the opportunity arose, it seemed only good business to eradicate them both, once and for all.

The IWW was a visible and lively presence in Minneapolis in 1917. Meetings, lectures, and socials kept the calendar full at both its hall downtown and at locals throughout working-class sections of the city.[16] In 1915, the Agricultural Workers Organization (AWO) of the IWW had established its permanent central office in the city's Bridge Square area, where thousands of seasonal harvest hands and timber workers congregated in search of work. The AWO significantly boosted public perceptions of IWW strength in Minneapolis. During its first year in the city, organizers reported that the union gained more than one hundred new members a week.[17] But of these, most were migrants passing through in search of jobs, and their numbers fluctuated radically according to the season. The settled, card-carrying membership of the IWW probably at no time exceeded more than a few hundred workers.[18]

Thus despite its visibility, the IWW claimed the allegiance of only a small proportion of the city's workers and orchestrated no major labor protest in Minneapolis. Instead, it focused its activities primarily on the iron range and lumber camps of northern Minnesota and the western harvest fields. Nonetheless, IWW activities in the hinterland had an indirect impact on the Minneapolis economy: the city's major capitalists held substantial investments in mining, lumbering, and grain. Consequently, city businessmen kept a vigilant watch on the movement. From 1915 forward, they funded the endeavors of the Northern Information Bureau, a local detective agency that concentrated its efforts on infiltrating the IWW. Financed almost wholly by Minneapolis business retainers, by 1918 the agency's client list included nearly all the major firms in the city.[19] Clearly, city businessmen perceived the IWW as a potential danger even though its involvement in local labor struggles was minimal. The Wobblies, as they were called, publicly and seemingly incessantly stirred up working-class discontent with their harsh critiques of local business practices and of capitalism in general. In Minneapolis, local businessmen damned the IWW as much for its ideas as for its actions.[20]

When the Public Safety Commission geared up for action, it identified suppression of the IWW as its first priority, though the Wobblies posed little actual threat to the war effort. Detailed detective reports supplied the commission with no concrete evidence of subversive IWW activity either in Minneapolis or in the rural regions. The logic behind this campaign was more subtle. The political legitimacy that protected Socialism, trade unionism, and the Nonpartisan League did not extend to the IWW. The syndicalist rhetoric of the Wobblies, often distorted by the local and national press, had set them outside the accepted parameters of protest, even though their organizing tactics were legitimate, and for the most part, their immediate goals were as pragmatic and moderate as those of other union activists. But the commissioners recognized that a campaign against the Wobblies was unlikely to stir public protest.[21]

The Industrial Workers of the World had a public relations problem that was a product of both their own public pronouncements and an already ongoing effort to discredit the organization. The 1914 *Report of the Minnesota Department of Labor* had listed four IWW locals among its roster of Minnesota unions. By 1916, however, the IWW had been expunged from the department's roll of legitimate labor organizations—despite (or perhaps because of) a considerable increase in membership in the interim.[22] The IWW continued to appear in the reports, but in the role of an outside agitator whose disruptive presence could explain away worker protest and delegitimate labor grievances.

Official reports on a bitter miners' strike that shut down the Mesabi Range for four months in the summer of 1916 blamed IWW organizers for instigating the strike and the violence that accompanied it. Strike participants and federal conciliators called in to investigate contradicted that assertion. Nonetheless, the mining companies, the press, and the Minnesota Federation of Labor, along with the state, insisted that the Wobblies had masterminded the protest.[23] The following January, when four thousand unorganized timber workers, scattered in camps across northern Minnesota, walked off their jobs, again officials pointed to the IWW. Wobbly organizers took no part in the strike; still, inflammatory articles declared that the IWW had "opened a reign of terrorism in the woods [with] armed bands of agitators invading the camps and at the point of a gun forcing the woodsmen to leave."[24]

The strike was a failure. The demonization of the IWW, however, was a great success. Journalist Harrison Salisbury, recalling his boyhood in Minneapolis in the teens, remembered the "thrill of fright" he experienced on discovering "IWW" chalked on an alley fence. "Who could have scrawled those dread letters? . . . It must, I realized, have been done by a stableboy or a coachman or someone like that."[25]

As Salisbury's memoir reveals, by 1917 radicalism had become integrated into middle-class suspicions about the working class. Thus, as the Minnesota Commission for Public Safety and the leaders of the Minneapolis Civic and Commerce Association strategized against their enemies, an attack on the IWW assumed an instrumental value that superseded any real danger the organization presented. As America entered the war, a unique opportunity presented itself that gave the sword of patriotism a particularly sharp edge. By exaggerating the subversive threat posed by the IWW, which was already beyond the pale of public opinion, it would require only a bit of manipulation to use real or imagined connections with the Wobblies to discredit other, less suspect movements. The taint of the IWW, for instance, could be brought to bear against Socialists and against the leaders of the Nonpartisan League. The Public Safety Commission acted as the agent to bring this plan to fruition. Within a year, Commissioner John McGee felt free to advise the National

Committee on Military Affairs that "the whole outfit, Red Socialists, I.W.W.s and Nonpartisan League leaders ought to be in interment [sic] camps."[26] As the commission's actions also demonstrated, organized labor was the unidentified fourth subversive element to be subdued.

The propaganda and tactics employed by the Public Safety Commission directed national attention to Minnesota, but the publicity was hardly the sort desired by civic leaders in St. Paul. There, businessmen soon found themselves caught up in a campaign that was significantly more than they had bargained for. None of the commission's identified enemies carried the same threat for St. Paul that they posed in Minneapolis. Certainly, the time was not propitious to move against organized labor. Whatever their private preferences, city businessmen were striving to present St. Paul as willing and able to produce enormous quantities of goods for the war effort. Labor peace was an essential element of this project.

Nor was radicalism a particularly troubling problem in the city. In the absence of a large industrial workforce, the IWW had never been able to establish a beachhead in St. Paul. In reports to the Bureau of Labor in 1914, one of the IWW's two city chapters admitted that it had "not organized a shop or labor local as yet, its work at present being along the lines of educational [sic] and agitation as to what is implied by Industrial Unionism." The other chapter not only had no meeting hall, it also operated without a local secretary. By 1917, the situation had hardly changed. Undercover agents reported that the St. Paul local still waited for a charter and did not have enough members to secure a hall. The secretary of the St. Paul branch was himself an undercover operative.[27] Furthermore, unlike Minneapolis, where ideological differences among Socialists, AFL unionists, and Wobblies often blurred in common cause, the St. Paul Trades and Labor Assembly was unvaryingly hostile to the IWW. The *Union Advocate* regularly published warnings about Wobbly agitation, and even Socialist Julius Emme, the labor assembly's most radical delegate, publicly disassociated the IWW from "the legitimate labor movement."[28]

St. Paul's small Socialist contingent could muster only slightly more support than did the IWW and conveyed no menace to the political status quo. The Irish–Catholic-dominated Democratic Party had a solid cross-class base throughout the city. No Socialist candidate had ever received significant support from city voters. In 1914, trade unionist William Mahoney, running as a Socialist Party candidate, had garnerred a mere 7 percent of the vote in his bid for Congress. The 1916 Socialist candidate made an even poorer showing, with less than 5 percent of the total in his column.[29]

The Catholic Church, of course, had an undeniable influence on local politics. Most of the American church's hierarchy equated socialism with atheism, and many spoke out vehemently against it.[30] Though some Catholic clergy were less dogmatic, John Ireland was not among them. One of the church's leading liberals on most issues, by the turn of the century Ireland had become implacable in his public pronouncements regarding socialism. Not only was it an ideology that threatened both church and country, but also, as he tellingly remarked, "the Social-ist movements in the United States have had for the most part Germans for lead-ers." This linkage between radical politics and German Americans only heightened the stakes in Ireland's long-standing war with members of the German-Catholic hierarchy.[31]

Superficially, St. Paul voting patterns might suggest that the city's Catholics fol-lowed the archbishop's lead on this issue, but the social basis of the city's politics was considerably more complex. Catholic working people did not follow church di-rectives blindly. In fact, the archbishop identified himself as a stalwart Republi-can—a choice that made little impact on either Catholics' loyalty to the Democratic Party or on their personal esteem for the archbishop.[32] Nor were St. Paul Catholics innately conservative. On the contrary, they ignored socialist alternatives because in the Archdiocese of St. Paul the Church itself seemed to incorporate a good part of the socialist agenda.

A political affiliation with "Socialism" might be unacceptable for Catholics, but many of its tenets were approved at least tacitly by the archbishop through the speeches and writings of Father John Ryan. By 1917 Ryan had become a nationally recognized advocate for social justice, championing the same principles he had publicly espoused for thirteen years (1902–15) from his post at the St. Paul Semi-nary. Under the apparently benign gaze of John Ireland, Ryan had become so closely associated with working people's concerns that the Minnesota Federation of Labor explicitly referred to the 1912 minimum wage bill as "the bill of Rev. John A. Ryan."[33]

With Ryan's speeches and writings regularly quoted in the *Union Advocate* and local courts making reference to Catholic social justice doctrine, working people had tangible proof that the Catholic Church effectively backed their needs—a ver-sion of Catholicism that only strengthened their faith and loyalty. For instance, young Grace Holmes, the daughter of a railroad laborer, had internalized a pro-foundly class-based interpretation of her faith; when her father, pushed by eco-nomic necessity, crossed a local picket line, Grace rushed to confession to ask for-giveness both for her father's sin and for hers as well, since she had carried his lunch to him across the picket line, helping to "deprive the laborer of his wages," which in her mind the Catholic church condemned.[34]

With Ryan articulating a social-justice version of Catholicism, the archbishop could concentrate on the moral obligations of family, temperance, patriotic duty, and respect for individual rights (which definitely included property)—all of which cemented his relationship with city leaders. It is important to note, however, that the values the archbishop promoted also were embedded in the belief system of workers as well as the upper class, though interpretations of how to defend those values might differ.[35] Thus, between them, Ireland and Ryan succeeded in broaden-ing the church's teachings to answer a variety of needs encompassing the full range of the political spectrum. The church was a fortification against socialism and a force for change at one and the same time. While radical rhetoric most often demanded that people discard religion in the name of social change, Catholicism as practiced in St. Paul required no such heart-rending choice. Thus, in this Catholic city, Irish-Catholic Democrats set the political tone with the endorsement of the Catholic Church and championed workers' rights. Socialism seemed both unnecessary and irrelevant to most of the working class and, accordingly, remained on the political fringe.[36]

The politics of the Nonpartisan League were no more threatening in St. Paul than those of the Socialists. In fact, city politicians and businessmen were undecided about how the Nonpartisan League would affect them. No doubt, the democratic "prairie fire" sweeping the countryside was somewhat alarming to the Old Guard, but still they speculated that a shake-up of the existing political and economic monopolies might be of some benefit to the city. Minneapolis had so thoroughly monopolized the grain trade that St. Paul literally had nothing to lose. The figures speak for themselves: more than two hundred grain brokers worked out of Minneapolis, fewer than ten in St. Paul; thirty-eight Minneapolis companies operated more than sixty grain elevators that stored in excess of fifty-five million bushels of grain; St. Paul could claim only three. Finally, twenty-eight Minneapolis mills, employing thousands of people, produced nearly fifteen million barrels of flour annually—the greatest output in the world; the output of St. Paul's six small mills, with less than one hundred employees, was not even recorded.[37] Any change to the status quo in this area of enterprise could only work to St. Paul's benefit. City businessmen thus hoped the Nonpartisan League might divert at least some share of the grain trade to St. Paul.

This strategy was not a new one. In 1915 representatives from St. Paul had traveled to Bismarck, North Dakota, to court the business of the American Society of Equity. The Equity, a forerunner of the Nonpartisan League, promoted producers' and consumers' cooperatives and planned to erect cooperative grain elevators, free from Minneapolis control. St. Paul businessmen successfully lobbied the Equity to locate its elevator in their city. Thereafter, the St. Paul Association actively supported the St. Paul Equity Co-operative Exchange and even nominated its president to the Association's board of directors.[38] As was obvious to city businessmen, any foothold they might gain in the grain trade rested on cooperation with farmers' organizations rather than association with the grain trust.

Consequently, St. Paul business enthusiastically promoted itself as the "farmer's friend," emphasizing its difference from Minneapolis. As St. Paul Association secretary, E. M. McMahon strategized, St. Paul should market itself as "the center of co-operative marketing," as opposed to the heartless industrial citadel across the river. The farmer, "dissatisfied with the methods of the [Minneapolis] Chamber of Commerce," would then "determine to make this city his grain and flour, as well as his livestock center." McMahon predicted a bright future from this partnership: "Get the farmer to sell his livestock and agricultural products in Saint Paul, and it will not be very long before he will insist upon buying at both wholesale and retail the goods of Saint Paul houses—farm machinery and other commodities."[39] Transparently, an attack on the Nonpartisan League was not the way to achieve these goals.

The city's politicians also saw potential for gain in this farmers' movement. Democrats held sway in St. Paul, but outside the city limits the party was extremely weak. For years, Republican power brokers had dominated state politics so thoroughly that Minnesota had become virtually a one-party state. Democratic politicians exerted influence at the state level primarily by delivering the swing votes that determined which Republican candidate would be elected. This had worked quite well in securing concessions for St. Paul's interests, but it was a far cry from a strong statewide organization. The city's Democrats, mentally counting up potential NPL votes, contemplated the possibility for a real shift in political power. Because the League was built on the concept of nonpartisan endorsement of candidates rather than as a party organization, an alliance between the Democrats and Nonpartisans could conceivably dethrone Republican control of the statehouse. At the very least, the city's Democrats were withholding judgment for the moment. Local Republicans were equally hungry for this unpredictable bloc of voters, but for them the stakes were a shift in local power. If the Nonpartisan League took hold in St. Paul and politicians played their cards right, Nonpartisan votes cast on the Republican side of the ballot might finally unseat the Democratic monopoly of local politics. In sum, both parties saw some potential political capital in friendly relations with the Nonpartisan League.[40]

Both parties realized that the Nonpartisan League had negative potential as well. The League was striving to effect a farmer-labor coalition, which, if successful, would radically reconfigure the political terrain. But in early 1917 the prospects for this project were not particularly bright, especially in St. Paul. The League had moved its national headquarters to the city in January and had become a very visible presence. Yet, impassioned pleas for farmer-labor unity from NPL leaders seemed to leave organized labor indifferent, even though both groups spoke with a single voice regarding the war. Between January and May, the *Union Advocate* took no notice of Nonpartisan speeches or activities, nor did it promote any sort of farmer-labor alliance.[41]

Within a few short months, all this would drastically change. In the dedicated pursuit of its multiple enemies, the Public Safety Commission managed to catalyze what no grassroots organization had ever been able to accomplish on its own—a viable farmer-labor coalition. As St. Paul civic leaders watched in dismay, the understandings that had held the city together shattered and were remade on different terms. Forming an alliance rare in American politics, farmers and workers ultimately reshaped the terrain of Minnesota politics. But as the members of the Public Safety Commission met for the first time at the state capitol in April 1917, the St. Paul men who had willingly handed them the reins of power had no conception of the social upheaval in store.

A close analysis of the structure and membership of the Minnesota Commission of Public Safety reveals the sources of power that drove its operations. Curiously, from the outset the commission's agenda was directed by aggressive Minneapolis judge John McGee rather than by the governor. McGee was the principal conduit between the Minneapolis Chamber of Commerce and the commission. A corporate attorney who had built his career serving the leading businesses of Minneapolis, McGee reveled in close relations with the powerful men of the Minneapolis Club. As he boasted in a personal letter, "Many people here, in banking, grain, and milling circles, want me to go on the Commission. . . . If I would say to the Governor that I would go on and that I wanted to go on, he would appoint me."[42] This was not an empty boast. Though McGee maintained that he would not lobby in his own behalf, he was well aware that powerful friends would handle that detail for him.

McGee had been deeply involved in shaping the provisions of the commission bill and bragged that it was "most drastic" and had "teeth in it eighteen inches long":

> If the Governor appoints men who have backbone, treason will not be talked of on the streets of this city and the street corner orators, who denounce the government, advocate revolution, denounce the army and advise against enlistments, will be looking through the barbed wire fences of an interment [sic] camp out on the prairie somewhere.[43]

In the estimation of the Minneapolis business establishment, McGee had just the "backbone" for the job, and he accepted the commission's mandate with unmitigated enthusiasm. Once McGee was ensconced, the Public Safety Commission quickly came to define *treason* as synonymous with any opposition to Minneapolis corporate interests.

But what of the governor, the titular head of the commission? The son of Swedish immigrants, a "self-made" man, and an avowed progressive, Governor Joseph Burnquist was expected to hold the reins of the commission in moderate hands. His progressive record was a major factor in limiting opposition toward the original proposal. But the thirty-seven-year-old Burnquist's rise from obscurity to the governor's chair in less than a decade had left this self-made man with many debts.[44]

Working-class Swedes of St. Paul had given Burnquist his entree into politics, electing him as their representative to the state legislature in 1908, only three years after he had passed the Minnesota bar examination. In 1910, they returned him to office.[45] As a Republican and a proponent of county option on the prohibition question, he became the darling of state progressives, who despaired of most St. Paul politicians—Irish, Democrats, Catholics, and unshakably opposed to sumptuary regulation. As a result, he was tapped to run for lieutenant governor in 1912 to provide the party with a progressive cachet and perhaps bring some St. Paul working-class voters along in the process. Without independent means or strong political connections, Burnquist owed his political ascendancy to the imprimatur of Republican power brokers—the state's major capitalists—and he understood full well that his usefulness to the party derived from his ethnic and working-class support. As lieutenant governor, he adeptly avoided controversies that would force him to reveal where his loyalties lay. But when the sitting governor died in 1915 and Burnquist inherited the office, his political debts came due.

Most tellingly, during the 1916 mining and timber strikes Burnquist put the law enforcement powers of the state at the disposal of the embattled companies, a decision that seriously injured his credibility with working-class voters.[46] With the potential erosion of his traditional constituency, Burnquist's political future became even more dependent on the good graces of the state's major businessmen. As the saga of the Public Safety Commission unfolded, it became clear that Burnquist had become no more than a functionary in the employ of powerful backers in Minneapolis. Commissioner and former governor John Lind, the lone voice of moderation on the commission, later recalled, "Poor Burnquist who I think is a good man at heart is weak and was absolutely under McGee's thumb."[47] Thus, the governor's commission appointments were universally applauded by the state's business interests. McGee was foreordained to be chosen, and his fellow commissioners held similar sympathies for the business agenda.

St. Paul businessmen hoped to reward Charles Farnham with a seat on the commission, as payment for his tireless work with the Patriotic League. But commission architects ignored the parochial Farnham in favor of Charles Ames, president of West Publishing, the nation's foremost publisher of law books.[48] As head of one of St. Paul's most prestigious firms, Ames had considerable status among the members of the St. Paul Association; more important, he also shared the objectives of his Minneapolis peers. Unlike most of the city's employers, West Publishing served a national market. With one of the city's largest workforces (it was the single largest employer of women), the company also had thwarted all efforts to organize its employees.[49] Described scathingly by the *Union Advocate* as an "autocratic exponent of democracy," the Yankee Protestant Ames was philosophically much closer to the Minneapolis Civic and Commerce Association than to fellow members of the St. Paul Association.[50] He also circulated socially among Minneapolis elites. This was not a simple cultural affinity. In partnership with his brother-in-law, grain dealer Thomas Winter, Ames had been a part of the Minneapolis grain trust for fifteen years as well as a law-book publisher. He regularly used his West stock as collateral to weather periodic downturns in the grain markets.[51] The Nonpartisan League thus represented an exceptional danger to both his businesses, and Ames gladly accepted the role of point man in the commission's campaign to eradicate the League.

To balance McGee's aggressive posture, John Lind, the popular former governor, was selected to become a second commissioner from Minneapolis. Lind was widely respected throughout the state as a progressive and an advocate of clean government. Moreover, he characterized himself as a "political orphan," refusing permanent allegiance to any party.[52] To Minnesota voters, Lind epitomized virtue and reason. He was indeed his own man; nonetheless, he also was a Minneapolis corporate attorney who numbered the lumber and grain interests among his clients. A close friend of milling magnate William Washburn and a member in good standing of the Minneapolis Civic and Commerce Association, Lind was an outspoken foe of radicalism and gladly took up the challenge to root out the IWW.[53] Later, as the commission's agenda of repression broadened and intensified, he would become a troublesome critic, but for the moment, the aura of progressivism that veiled his affiliations with Minneapolis business made him a crucial public relations asset on the commission.

Governor Burnquist rounded out his appointments with two members from outside the Twin Cities: attorney Charles March, longtime mayor of the small city of Litchfield and loyal Republican Party worker; and Anton Weiss, owner, publisher, and self-proclaimed "master mind" of the pro-business *Duluth Herald*. Though generally in accord with the commission's agenda, March and Weiss proved to serve mainly as window dressing, providing the commission with the appearance of statewide representation. The real work was carried on by the three Twin Cities commissioners and the commission's attorney, Ambrose Tighe.[54]

Tighe, though technically not a member of the commission, was a critical player in this exercise of power politics. As commission attorney, it fell to him to protect its prerogatives from legal or constitutional challenges. As a political progressive and longtime advocate of government regulation, Tighe was well prepared for the task. Also, as a frustrated member of the St. Paul Patriotic League, deeply involved in the city's financial and business dealings, he enthusiastically endorsed state enforcement of the social agenda that had eluded St. Paul's civic leaders.[55]

None of this is to say that an articulated conspiracy to serve Minneapolis business interests existed within the Public Safety Commission. Correspondence between Lind and Tighe, in particular, reveals that they viewed the commission as a vehicle for broad social engineering. In their eyes, it would build the regulatory "machinery to do big things after the war."[56] Over time, they came to be increasingly critical as the commission wielded its powers with autocratic disregard. But by then it was too late to stop the wave of repression they had helped to begin.

As the members of the Public Safety Commission gathered for its initial meeting, they came to the table with a range of practical and philosophical motivations. Still the composition of the commission was carefully crafted to serve a particular constituency of interests. In addition to Tighe, among the six voting members were two more corporate attorneys, a major industrialist, and a governor whose political survival depended on business support. Significantly, no representative of labor or farm interests was asked to serve. In fact, the commission structure all but guaranteed exclusion of any but the most affluent from membership. The position of commissioner was unsalaried, its members serving in a volunteer capacity. Thus, only those whose income did not rely on daily labor could afford to serve. Burnquist used this fact to justify the biased nature of his appointments. Responding to farmers' complaints, the governor disingenuously explained, "No farmer could be found by me who was in a position to give up his work at this time of the year."[57]

With the governor's feeble defense of his appointments, farmers and organized labor acceded to their exclusion with what, in retrospect, may seem remarkably little argument. However, their reaction—or lack thereof—was in large part a matter of timing. By the time the Public Safety Commission was unveiled, America was at war, which virtually closed the social space for dissent. In addition, both labor and farmers envisaged something to be gained by commission intervention. Farmers, concerned about a potential labor shortage, were promised that the commission would ensure them an adequate agricultural labor force. The commission also declared itself the enemy of war profiteering, an abuse that farmers found particularly galling.

As for organized labor, workers' opinion was divided. Railroad workers expected to be outside the commission's purview, anticipating federal takeover of the roads for the duration of the war. Moreover, they looked to government intervention as a blessing, correctly predicting that federal management might well work to their benefit by increasing wages and shortening hours across the board. Indeed, the state's railroad industrialists were notably missing from the ranks of commission supporters. From their perspective, state intervention at any level was nothing less than a curse. Ironically, only the railroad magnates and the IWW seemed to comprehend fully the potential breadth of the Public Safety Commission's powers.

St. Paul unionists, operating in a relatively benign labor-relations climate, believed they could work in partnership with the commission—not an unreasonable presumption. Though they detested Ames, Lind was a reassuring presence, and the other commissioners had no public reputation. Moreover, the common perception was that Burnquist would be the dominant figure. The governor had been somewhat discredited by the 1916 strikes, but his antilabor actions had been confined to the IWW. He had never moved against the "legitimate" unions of the AFL. In addition, St. Paulite George Lawson, secretary of the Minnesota Federation of Labor (MFL), was immediately tapped for a committee appointment, which the commission took care to publicize, describing the labor leader as "almost a member of the Commission." Lawson's apparent influence somewhat reassured the Trades Assembly.[58]

It also appeared plausible to the St. Paul unions that the commission might operate as a neutral arbitrator between business and labor, especially since the legislature seemed increasingly sympathetic on labor issues and the courts had recently made several prolabor rulings.[59] Thus, from the perspective of St. Paul organized labor, the state appeared a neutral force if not an outright ally. Optimistically, labor relied on what in the past had proved an effective negotiating posture, which, as described in the *Advocate* by editor Cornelius Guiney, won them "golden opinions" from the legislature: "They are clear, logical and forcible in expressing their views, yet becomingly modest withal in their attitude. The do not go before a committee and demand what they want but put their wishes forward in a manner that convinces their hearers of the justice and propriety of what they ask for."[60]

The Minneapolis Trades and Labor Assembly, less sanguine about the ultimate triumph of justice and reason, viewed the makeup of the commission with considerable alarm. Led by Socialist Lynn Thompson, it urged the MFL to aggressively protest labor's exclusion. In May, representatives from the state's central labor bodies, the MFL, the Brotherhood of Railway Trainmen, and the Nonpartisan League met in Minneapolis to discuss the problem. Two hours of heated debate, produced an impasse. With the St. Paul Assembly and the trainmen unwilling to challenge the commission, and only a tenuous alliance achieved between farmers and workers, the committee stalled, adopting a wait-and-see attitude.[61]

They didn't have long to wait. Within weeks, the magnitude of the commission's powers became all too clear. George Creel, Woodrow Wilson's Director of Public Information, later described the Minnesota Commission of Public Safety as practicing "a policy of brutal intolerance."[62] People of every economic and social rank across the state came to regret the authority they had invested in "a few responsible hands." But as the Safety Commission swung into action, it was endorsed by a broad array of Minnesotans. The patriotic fervor they displayed was grounded in interest-group politics as much as in love of country. Progressive reformers, St. Paul businessmen, the Catholic archbishop, and even many farmers and organized workers participated either actively or tacitly in the abrogation of civil rights in Minnesota, setting the wheels of the Public Safety Commission in motion.

Chapter 6

THE FIRST VOLLEY:

Policing the Social Order

On April 6, four days before the Public Safety Commission bill passed into law, the United States formally entered the war. Almost magically it seemed, antiwar sentiment evaporated into the air. In the heat of the martial moment, before Minnesota's legislators had time to reevaluate the state of affairs, they handed the Public Safety Commission its desired mandate.[1]

Meanwhile, the civic dilemma that had plagued St. Paul businessmen appeared to resolve itself spontaneously. Spokespersons from every faction affirmed their patriotism. The archbishop ordered Catholics to support the war "without reservation of mind [or] slackening of earnest act," and similar proclamations rang forth from church pulpits of every denomination. The *Union Advocate* urged "Be True Americans Now," and it promised labor's unstinting support. Ethnic organizations adopted stirring loyalty resolutions, and Polish Americans announced their plan to raise a company of Polish volunteers. As the wartime propaganda mill went into high gear, St. Paul's *Tagliche Volkszeitung* anxiously editorialized that the time for criticism was past. No further protest would be heard from the city's Germans.[2] Only the Socialists officially refused to endorse the war, but with a mere five thousand members in Ramsey County they registered a barely audible voice of dissent.[3]

A frenzy of patriotism took over the public life of St. Paul. In just the first ten days of the war, mass enlistment meetings drew thousands of cheering citizens; the newly organized Civilian Auxiliary drilled on the College of St. Thomas parade grounds; the Y.W.C.A. began classes in first-aid training; the Patriotic League organized a women's auxiliary; a local chapter of the Red Cross opened its doors in the First National Bank; and representatives of all the women's organizations met to promote food conservation. As National Guard units and divisions of the naval militia assembled and marched through the streets on an almost daily basis, enthusiasm for the war seemed to sweep over the city.[4]

The Patriotic League's fondest dreams were realized on April 19, officially declared by Governor Burnquist as "Loyalty Day." The Twin Cities strove to outdo one another with flamboyant demonstrations. In St. Paul, schools and businesses closed to encourage the entire city to assemble for mass meetings and a "monster parade" through the business district. The Stars and Stripes waved from every conceivable surface—"from office buildings, from homes, from autos, from horses' bridles." For good measure, the Patriotic League distributed another eight thousand flags to parade marchers. Participants representing the eleven allied nations portrayed an immigrant mosaic that far exceeded the city's actual heterogeneity (but one that notably excluded its predominant German ethnic group). Nonetheless, despite the missing Germans, the visual effect was a stunning display of civic unity, described by the *St. Paul Dispatch* as "an expression of idealism which has not been equaled in the history of the city."[5] The Patriotic League must have been deeply gratified. Perhaps it even crossed the minds of city businessmen that they had been too precipitous in ceding control over local affairs to the state.

Loyalty Day was indeed a testament to national unity and purpose. But the meaning of patriotism was subject to a variety of interpretations and degrees of intensity. The bolts of red, white, and blue that wrapped the city obscured serious resentments and disagreements over how the war should be waged. Despite the demonstrations of unity, many people, perhaps a majority of the city's residents, remained at heart reluctant warriors. Nonetheless, with the stroke of the president's pen, the European war had become America's war, and most agreed that the best hope for peace was to pursue a swift victory on America's terms.

The question remained, who would pay the price—in manpower and in money—to achieve that victory? Working people suspected that they would be forced to shoulder more than their share on both counts, with the wealthy reaping the profits from their struggle. This did not fit their definition of democracy and they were not about to accept such terms in silence. It was in this context that the political struggle would thenceforth be framed—centering on the content and meaning of patriotism itself.

Union labor launched the first salvo with a telegram to Carl Van Dyke, St. Paul's congressman in Washington. Along with four other Minnesotans, Van Dyke had voted against the declaration of war. The Patriotic League predictably called for the congressman's resignation. But the Trades and Labor Assembly responded with a published endorsement of Van Dyke that clearly distinguished working-class conceptions of patriotism from those of the business establishment:

> We the undersigned . . . confidently anticipating and expecting the call that will be made upon us to offer all we have, namely our prospects and our lives in the cause of Our Government, desire to voice our approval and commendation of the stand you have taken in this the great crisis of our Nation, and to disapprove most heartily in the text and sentiment of the note sent you yesterday by the so-called Pa-

triotic League of St. Paul, signed by men without exception financially and physically able to withstand the horrors of war in their respective homes.[6]

Lest labor be accused of disloyalty, a boxed announcement in the next issue of the *Union Advocate* pledged the Minnesota Federation of Labor's "absolute and unconditional loyalty to the government of the United States" and labor's support for the war "forced upon the country against the wishes of its people by the intolerable aggressions of a heartless foreign autocracy."[7]

In labor's recrafted analysis, with the discourse of dissent narrowed considerably in a nation at war, the external menace to American freedoms was no longer a subject of debate. Consequently, class-based differences had to be articulated as a struggle to defend the content of national ideals. Organized labor vowed "unrelenting opposition to all forms of autocracy," including "those of the gilded magnates who seek to exercise industrial despotism in our own land."[8] Patriotism, as defined by labor, demanded equal vigilance against foreign and domestic threats to democratic principles.

For laboring people in St. Paul and across the nation, the vital issues quickly became those of conscription and war financing. The Trades and Labor Assembly immediately called a mass meeting to oppose institution of the draft and to endorse heavy taxation of the wealthy as the fairest and most democratic means to wage the war. In an attempt to gain civic consensus for labor's position, the *Advocate* "earnestly and cordially" invited everyone in St. Paul to attend the meeting, urged union members to bring their nonunion friends, and extended a particular welcome to "the ladies," whose "presence in large numbers is ardently desired." As labor strategists recognized, women, the acknowledged moral center of the community, were particularly critical allies in the struggle for public opinion. Notably, even as the Assembly worked to open a dialogue across class within the local community, it made little effort to effect a coalition with Minneapolis organized labor and extended no invitation for Minneapolitans to participate in the meeting. In time-honored St. Paul fashion, community rather than more broadly conceived class solidarity served as the preferred mode of negotiation.[9]

Labor's leaders declared it "not only their privilege but their duty" to initiate a public debate on critical issues and consciously strove to adapt their traditional negotiating tactics to the new situation by organizing the meeting as inclusively as possible. The program featured a university professor, lawyers, and a venerable Civil War veteran, as well as representatives from both ends of labor's political spectrum. Accompanied by patriotic tunes provided by the musicians' union, the assembled participants adopted a resolution to the president and Congress that opposed military conscription; demanded a graduated income tax to spread the cost of the war equitably among the population; and recommended government appropriation of railroads, factories, mines, and mills—including flour mills—for the duration of the war.[10]

Though the city's businessmen surely blanched at the suggestion of conscription of property (with the possible exception of flour mills), they were less unanimously opposed to other elements of the resolution. In fact, city authorities donated use of the municipal auditorium for the Trades Assembly's meeting, and at least some part of the business community was in sympathy with labor's position on taxation and the draft. A week earlier, the board of directors of the St. Paul Association had passed a surprising resolution of its own: "Be it resolved that in behalf of this association of nearly 5,000 St. Paul business and professional men, we urge upon the government conscription of dollars to be brought about through the imposition of large graduated income taxes, reaching the total absorption of all incomes over $100,000 a year."[11]

On closer examination, the wording of this resolution seems less astonishing. Perhaps the Association had inside information that the financing decisions had already been made in Washington, making this an empty gesture of conciliation designed to uphold the illusion of community solidarity. But it is equally plausible that the sentiments it expressed were genuine. Other than the Hill family, St. Paul claimed few great fortunes. Perhaps some local business interests saw taxation as a means to create a more level playing field in the national market, and particularly between themselves and their Minneapolis rivals. After a "closer study of the problem," no doubt influenced by the most prosperous of its members, the Association considerably modified its recommendations, but throughout the war it endorsed heavy increases in taxation.[12]

The question of manpower conscription was even more complicated, entangled in cultural as well as economic considerations. The martial ideal had captured the imagination of bourgeois America during the Progressive Era. As described by T. Jackson Lears, middle-class Old Stock Americans embraced militarism and romantic idealizations of war as a means of cultural revitalization. In their minds, military courage and discipline exemplified Anglo-Saxon "race traits" that conflated moral and physical courage and privileged them as the natural elites of an increasingly polyglot nation. The rigors of military life also seemed a way to reinvigorate middle-class manliness from the malaise engendered by modern life. The military ideal thus became a means to assert both class and racial superiority—vividly exemplified by the sanctified model of Teddy Roosevelt and his Rough Riders.[13]

Thus, in St. Paul, as in the rest of the nation, middle- and upper-class young men became willing recruits for military adventures. The National Guard had long operated as a sort of upper-class club and included sons of many of the city's first families, including Captain Charles Leslie Ames, son of the future commissioner of public safety. As one St. Paul officer described it in 1905, "Company 'C' today, as always, may be said to carry on its rolls the names of young men of the most desirable class only, and in fact no others can hope to be accepted."[14]

Martial enthusiasm extended beyond the city's Old Stock families. For those without a Yankee pedigree, a military commission conveyed a valued stamp of social status. Jewish attorney Hiram Frankel, Irish politician and future jurist Richard O'Brien, and railroad counsel Frederick McCarthy, a second-generation Irish

American, served as long-time officers of the Guard along with Captain Ames and the scions of other prominent Old Stock families.[15] When wartime needs required the Guard to expand its membership, the Knights of Columbus, encouraged by Archbishop Ireland, jumped at the opportunity to enlist Catholics into the ranks. In the archbishop's estimation, military service both built and exhibited the moral character and patriotic nature of the diocese's Catholics.[16]

Given the status-laden nature of military service, enlistment in the "Great War" became a badge of class honor. Students from local colleges flocked to recruiting stations. As historian David Kennedy has noted, colleges and prep schools throughout the country provided far more than their share of the volunteer army—"the nation's most carefully cultivated youths, the privileged recipients of the finest education, steeped in the values of the genteel tradition, who most believed the archaic doctrines about war's noble and heroic possibilities." Upper-class young men of every political—or apolitical—stripe enthusiastically marched off to participate in what they believed to be the last great adventure. St. Paul native F. Scott Fitzgerald, troubled by status anxieties and filled with romantic notions, left Princeton midway in his senior year to enlist, admitting in a letter to his mother in St. Paul, "I went into this perfectly cold bloodedly. . . . *I just went* and purely for *social reasons*."[17]

It was partly to stanch this flow of privileged youth to the trenches that President Wilson favored conscription, preferring a more expendable class of men for cannon fodder. Wilson, with detailed knowledge of the carnage at the front, had few illusions about the splendid nature of the war.[18] But on the home front, patriotic hyperbole masked the gore with visions of glory, particularly for the upper classes. The very idea of conscription seemed to sully their romantic and decidedly class-driven notions of patriotic sacrifice.

The city's businessmen had pragmatic as well as cultural reasons to oppose conscription. The draft, according to government rationale, would cull the most expendable patriots to bear arms. In Wilson's words, "The volunteer system does not do this. When men choose themselves, they sometimes choose without due regard to their other responsibilities. Men may come from the farms or from the mines or from the factories or centers of business who ought not to come but ought to stand back of the armies in the field."[19] St. Paul businessmen worried that the city's small industrial firms, no different from hundreds of others across the country, might not be deemed "essential" by the powers who would control the draft. In short, they feared the loss of their labor force more than the loss of their sons to the war effort.

Adding to the anxiety in St. Paul, the press was already predicting dire shortages in the agricultural labor force. City employers suspected that their workers would be diverted to the harvest fields. Minneapolis businessmen enjoyed a more protected position. As a milling, lumber, and machine-tool metropolis, the uninterrupted functioning of its industries was assured priority status. Even its garment and textile operations had a productive capacity that privileged them over their small-scale counterparts in the capital city.

St. Paul employers, aware of their more vulnerable position, forecast a local labor shortage that would slow production and drive up wages. The bounteous profits from projected war contracts would then disappear before their eyes. When the St. Paul Association addressed its concerns to the State Employment Commission, it was told that the question of wages "is merely a detail. We believe there is sufficient patriotism on the part of the employer to co-operate with the Commission with reference to the adjustment of wages, and also on the part of the employee a sufficient desire to be of service in this particular irrespective to the size of financial compensation." On the question of diversion of industrial labor to the countryside, the reply was equally unconvincing. The commission was confident that "men will charge up some of their time to a vacation which will put them in physical condition to be of greater service if necessary later on."[20] For employers, schooled in the daily realities of labor relations, these assurances could hardly have been persuasive.

Thus, in the early weeks of the war, for very different reasons, the opinions of the businessmen and working people of St. Paul converged on the two most pressing questions regarding the war. Though labor had vowed to oppose the "gilded magnates" of capital, the *Advocate* made no specific critique of local elites. The plutocrats of Big Business it abhorred apparently did not reside in the relatively modest mansions on Summit Avenue. The businessmen themselves were acutely aware that they were small players in the national wartime economy. As a result, it seemed possible that the city's growing social ruptures might be bridged in the quest for mutual benefit. But, as events would tell, local realities played little part in the decisions that shaped wartime policy. Instead, state and national decisions, beyond the influence of St. Paul, made the city a hapless actor in a much larger game.

Within weeks, the questions of war financing and conscription had been settled. Loan subscription rather than taxation would pay for the great crusade. By the end of April, the first Liberty Loan drive was already underway. Unlike the businessmen of St. Paul, power brokers in Washington had little interest in leveling the playing field among business competitors. On the contrary, government policy from the outset was formulated to preserve the industrial and financial status quo. First among its priorities was protection of the private investment structure on which postwar U.S. trade dominance would be based.[21]

The same set of economic considerations influenced Wilson to endorse conscription, for "its central idea was to disturb the industrial and social structure of the country just as little as possible." The draft resolved several knotty problems for the president: it put an end to the wholesale enlistment of the nation's elite (and, in his estimation, its most valuable) men; it enabled the government to ensure the smooth operation of essential industry; and, an added bonus, it served as a means to Americanize a troublesome immigrant population. Wilson also was swayed by personal political considerations. His nemesis, Teddy Roosevelt, was busy organizing an elite volunteer division, a familiar scenario that might catapult the old warhorse into renewed electoral prominence. But Wilson was able to put a decisive end to that particular political escapade by signing the Selective Service Act.[22]

None of these considerations was affected in the slightest either by mass meetings at the St. Paul Municipal Auditorium or by resolutions passed by the board of directors of the St. Paul Association. However, the decisions made in Washington had profound local reverberations. Not the least of these was the added weaponry they provided for the Public Safety Commission. The commission used real or fabricated fears about draft resistance to justify its campaign of repression; in its role as primary organizer of the Liberty Loan drives, it also coerced bond subscriptions as required evidence of patriotism. In the name of supporting national policy then, the commission gave itself license to police even the most private areas of Minnesotans' lives.[23]

After assessing their options, St. Paul businessmen cast their lot with the Safety Commission, hoping that wholehearted support for commission initiatives would yield them some preferential treatment. The St. Paul Association was particularly eager to volunteer its members for service on the draft board and to take up "the grave task of our business concerns to adapt their plants to produce and distribute the things which will serve the national needs and purposes."[24] In return, the Association looked for assurances that the draft would not impede local business operations. The Association's retail committee drafted a carefully worded letter to the commission. While they did "not wish to work out of harmony" with the war effort, they were compelled to raise critical questions regarding industrial production: "How are employers to secure trained workers to take the place of those called to serve the Government? Will the conscription law be so interpreted that the individual business institution will not be seriously crippled?"[25] Commission secretary John Pardee responded promptly. While making no specific promises, he let it be known that the well-being of loyal businessmen "will be clearly within the field of its consideration"—a powerful incentive to keep the St. Paul Association within the commission fold.[26]

The Association had an additional economic incentive that bound it to the Public Safety Commission. The commission's first official order had been to close down the saloons, pool halls, and movie theaters in the Bridge Square district of Minneapolis, home to "the rough people who do rough work."[27] An even more sweeping order was under consideration—the closing of all saloons and pool halls in the Twin Cities. Such a move would have a far greater impact on the St. Paul economy than on it would on Minneapolis. The liquor trade, along with less sanctioned forms of "vice," was an essential, if unacknowledged, leg of the city's economy. (The only two areas of enterprise in which St. Paul outdistanced Minneapolis were in numbers of breweries and saloons.) The annual renewal of liquor and pool hall licenses alone provided a significant portion of municipal revenues.[28] A further and not insignificant consideration for the city's wholesalers, manufacturers, and jobbers was the continuing desire to promote St. Paul as an entertainment mecca for visiting buyers where, as they advertised, customers would find "diversion and comfort" while they "replenished [their] entire stock from the various houses of the city."[29]

In 1917, however, the reputation of playtime capital had costs as well as benefits for the local economy. City fathers hoped to have nearby Fort Snelling chosen as a major military cantonment, which would have clear economic benefits. Unfortunately, St. Paul's well-known standing as a wide-open town did not set well with military authorities, charged to monitor the morals of the nation's soldiers.[30] Once again, city businessmen took the road of compromise and supported a Safety Commission order that closed all saloons from ten in the evening to eight the following morning, prohibited the serving of women and girls at any time, and banned dancing or cabaret performances anywhere that liquor was served. Though this put a damper on city amusements, the costs might be offset by the economic benefits of a large military presence. As the *Pioneer Press* editorialized, "Certain moral conditions must obtain in this community before it can hope to secure the selection of Fort Snelling as the site of the big military encampment and training ground. . . . Undoubtedly, [the order] will have behind it the support of a large public opinion." But the hundreds of small saloonkeepers and their primarily working-class customers saw little in the order to recommend it. By its vocal support of the measure, the St. Paul Association set off another round of grumbling resentments in the community.[31]

With widespread opposition to the regulations, compliance was difficult to enforce, and drunken soldiers became a common fixture on the local landscape. In September, harried city officials requested a provost guard to "take charge of drunken and disorderly soldiers," to no apparent avail.[32] When the inspector general of the army visited the city in November, he declared, "Conditions worse here than anywhere I know of. . . . If I had my way I would withdraw the soldiers [and] lock the doors on the Snelling barracks." In response, the Public Safety Commission threatened to prohibit all liquor traffic in the Twin Cities. Fearing the total loss of liquor revenues on the one hand and the departure of military troops on the other, civic leaders redoubled their efforts in concert with the Safety Commission to enforce its orders, launching an antivice campaign that further exacerbated frictions in the city.[33]

Other aspects of the commission's agenda were even more difficult for the city's boosters to resolve. With legal mandate in hand, the commissioners had wasted no time in setting up the infrastructure to ferret out their enemies. However, the effusion of patriotism that exploded with the declaration of war, particularly in Minneapolis and St. Paul, created a public relations problem of its own. The commission had been handed wide-ranging powers primarily on the premise that *internal* disloyalty gravely threatened national security. The public displays of patriotism undermined commission claims that Minnesota was riddled with homegrown enemies. To deal with this apparent contradiction, the commission instituted a two-pronged propaganda campaign: First, it labored to establish the belief that pro-German subversives lurked around every corner; as a logical corollary, it then insisted that unstinting support of its policies, self-evidently vital to national security, must serve as the ultimate litmus test of patriotism. To legitimate the extreme measures it intended to pursue, the commission fomented a climate of crisis, charging that Minnesota's immigrant population was overwhelmingly disloyal, especially its Germans and Scandinavians.[34] This official allegation once again cast doubt on the loyalty of the capital city, with its heavy immigrant concentration. Businessmen found themselves in a quandary. Despite their heroically patriotic efforts, the commission seemed intent on establishing that deep disloyalty simmered just beneath the city's public facade. To counter such suspicions, the St. Paul Association redoubled its exertions in support of the war, enmeshing itself ever more closely with the commission's aims and linking the businessmen in the minds of their fellow St. Paulites with its policies of repression.

Though the full range of the Public Safety Commission's activities was not yet apparent in the early months of the war, even in the first days of operation its pronouncements must have given St. Paulites occasion to worry. Commission circulars warned that "anyone who talks and acts against the government in time of war, regardless of the 'Constitutional right of free speech' which has been so sadly abused, is a traitor and deserves the most drastic punishment." According to commissioner John McGee, the state was riddled with a "contemptible [and] disloyal population," overrun with immigrant "vipers."[35]

McGee's vitriolic denunciation drew its energy from a national campaign for "100 percent Americanism" that originated in the White House. Since 1915, Wilson had worked to equate "true Americanism" with support for his preparedness policies and warned that foreign-born "creatures of passion, disloyalty, and anarchy" must be "crushed out."[36] But the nativist sentiments that underlay the movement had much deeper roots. The deluge of new immigrants from southern and eastern Europe who entered the country after 1880 had generated ever-growing fears about the changing face of American society. Before the onset of the European war, however, antiforeign sentiment had been focused on the "new" immigrants, deemed unassimilable and racially inferior to the northern Europeans who composed the first wave of immigration. In fact, before war hysteria enveloped the nation, Germans had been the country's most highly esteemed non-British ethnic group. The war radically changed this configuration as every vestige of German culture became synonymous with aiding and abetting the nation's enemy.[37]

Anti-German crusades became an ugly popular phenomenon all across the nation, but even so, the case of Minnesota stands out. According to the 1910 census, more than 70 percent of the state's population was either foreign-born or of foreign parentage, and 500,000 of these (25 percent of the total population) were of German or Austrian parentage. Thus, the state-sponsored campaign of the Public Safety Commission targeted an enormous segment of the state's population. In widening its sights to include Scandinavians along with Germans, the commission impugned the loyalty of nearly half the state's residents.[38] Only an agency that operated without accountability to voters could adopt such a bold and seemingly self-destructive stance. No other state instituted an agency with comparable independent statutory and enforcement powers. Most other state defense organizations drew their agendas from national directives. Minnesota, in contrast, driven by powerful economic interests, consistently exceeded and sometimes countermanded federal policy—unparalleled in the breadth of its state-sanctioned repression.[39]

The attack on German and Scandinavian Minnesotans could only stain the civic image of St. Paul, where more than one quarter of the city's population was foreign-born in 1910 and a third of those were of Germanic origin. Even these substantial fig-ures seriously underrepresent the German presence in the city, since they do not take into account the second-and third-generation German Americans, who far outnum-bered those of the immigrant generation.[40] The 1905 state census reported 8 percent of St. Paul's population to be German-born, with the adjacent independent munici-palities of South and West St. Paul adding an additional 19 and 21 percent of their populations, respectively. In contrast, Minneapolis was only 3.4 percent German, and Duluth only 2.9 percent. Clearly, anti-German propaganda had civic repercus-sions for St. Paul that were not nearly as severe in the state's other major cities.[41]

The Germans were more than a significant demographic element of St. Paul; they also numbered among the city's most esteemed citizens. Lumber baron Fred-erick Weyerhaeuser headed a long list of socially prominent German businessmen, brewers, merchants, and bankers. Thus, the anti-German campaign struck at the city's civic and business elite as well as its working-class population. The cultural smear was painted with a broad brush that left no German American untouched.

Furthermore, while German St. Paulites maintained a rich, separate associational life, they also made a notable cultural imprint on the city at large. The Schubert Club, St. Paul's oldest musical society, organized by German elites, had become a jewel in the city's cultural crown; the St. Paul Turnverein, a German gymnastic society, played a valued role in civic celebrations and traditionally had welcomed non-Germans as well as Germans among its members. The city's very architecture attested to the Ger-manic influence that was part of its civic life. In the business district, a life-sized, cut-marble statue of "Germania" benevolently observed the city's comings and goings from the top of the Germania Life Insurance Building—a prominent local land-mark.[42] Thus, with elements of German culture identifiably embedded in St. Paul's social and physical landscape, the assault on all things German called the loyalty of the city itself into question. Pressured to expunge all traces of Germanism—music, lan-guage, and even food—the people of St. Paul discarded integral elements of the city's common culture. Long-established German restaurants and beer gardens closed their doors; Wagner, Schumann, and even Schubert disappeared from the programs of the Schubert Club; and German classes dropped from both public and parochial school curriculums. In 1918, Germania herself was ignominiously hauled down from her perch overlooking the business district and the building that had enthroned her rechristened (with unintentional irony) as the Guardian Building.[43] As the former landmark trundled off to the junkyard, St. Paulites bid adieu to a whole set of cultural signifiers that had helped knit diverse elements of the community into a civic whole.

Germans of every class struggled against this outpouring of ethnic antagonism, working even harder than the business boosters to demonstrate their patriotic char-acter. They joined patriotic societies, contributed generously to Red Cross and Lib-erty Loan drives, and made numerous public statements in support of the war. Frederick Weyerhaeuser became the head of finance for the local organization of the

Fig. 28. As part of the frenzy to expunge all traces of German character, the statue of Germania was condemned to the junkyard in 1918. Courtesy of the Minnesota Historical Society.

Patriotic Americans of German Origin and donated $3,000 to the cause; the Sons of Hermann, with four thousand members, held a meeting "to pledge to the nation the loyalty of the Germans of Minnesota"; local Lutheran pastors, in a rare moment of solidarity, published a joint resolution affirming the church's loyalty; and the working-class German parish of St. Agnes described itself as a "huge, seething, melting pot of good American citizenship."[44]

Whatever the city's Germans may have privately thought about the attack on their character and culture, many of them clearly believed that the only way to protect their businesses and their very freedom was to comply in expunging every trace of Germanism from the city. Some people even went so far as to legally change their names—strikingly demonstrated by the case of Robert Auerbach, son of distinguished German-Jewish wholesaler Maurice Auerbach. Though he was raised on Summit Avenue and was serving as a captain in the Home Guard, apparently Auerbach feared that neither his class position nor active service in the Guard was adequate proof of his patriotism. Accordingly, he petitioned to change his surname to his mother's untarnished birth name of Rice, testifying that, for the sake of his children, he "would save them from the odium attached to a German name."[45]

In the climate of fear fostered by commission propaganda, where even city elites felt the chill of persecution, it is not surprising that some German St. Paulites began to turn on one another; neighbors informed on "suspicious" activities of neighbors; Father Alois Kastigar, a German priest from the Assumption parish, even made accusations of disloyalty against eight fellow priests newly arrived in the city.[46] Though such actions were hardly admirable, given the fears that weighed on the German community, they were perhaps understandable. In the polyglot world of St. Paul, where culture and economic interests commingled across ethnic lines, a separatist strategy was simply not feasible.[47] German Americans felt compelled to emphasize their ties to the larger civic community, even at the expense of discarding treasured cultural trappings. The slightest individual act of dissent represented a danger to the entire ethnic group. Thus, to defend their separate interests, they became active participants in crafting the veneer of patriotic civic unity. Beneath the surface, however, the infrastructure of both the ethnic and civic communities had become a house of cards, riddled by private injuries and betrayals.

Nonetheless, for the purposes of "national security," St. Paul's Germans appeared to be model Americans. In a vain search for enemy sympathizers and subversives, the Safety Commission dispatched undercover agents throughout the German areas of the city. Detectives prowled working-class shops and saloons looking for potential troublemakers and draft resisters but heard "nothing mentioned worth reporting." The general opinion of customers at Fraehlingdorf's saloon near the railroad yards, according to its German bartender, was one of resignation. Duty required "everyone to register [for the draft] who is of the right age; there would not be any effort on the part of the Germans he knew to avoid it or attempt to persuade others to do so." The owner of Brandl's meat market expressed similar sentiments: "All thinking Germans feel that the United States comes first and that the

Fig. 29. In 1917, anti-German propaganda affected even these toddlers. Courtesy of the Minnesota Historical Society.

Germans of St. Paul will be found loyal almost to a man." At the end of a long day of spying, agent "C. H." summed up his report, "All the Germans are very careful what they say and there does not seem to be any effort on their part to evade or prevent registration."[48]

A tour of Scandinavian saloons on the East Side the following day was equally unproductive. C. H. trudged up and down Payne Avenue without result. He struck up conversations in Lindell's, Anderson's, Nordstrom's, and Holmberg's saloons and "watched closely for anyone agitating among the men" but had to admit that he found "nothing suspicious in this respect."[49]

In addition, he reported that no socialist or IWW publications were printed in St. Paul, nor could he learn of any socialist literature being circulated in the city. The Swedish-language gazette *Allarm* was owned and published by Carl Ahlteen, a St. Paul Wobbly. But Ahlteen produced the IWW paper in Minneapolis, and not a single copy could be found in the hands of St. Paul's Swedish workingmen. This sort of unproductive report did not bode well for long-term employment prospects in the espionage business. Thus, perhaps in the name of job protection, C. H. qualified his findings with an assessment that, despite all evidence to the contrary, "The Scandinavians and socialists of the working class, especially organized labor, will try and work against registration." With only this weak indictment to show for his day of assiduous spying, he wearily concluded, "At midnight I discontinued."[50]

From its first published statement, the Public Safety Commission had embarked on a propaganda campaign to stir a sense of crisis in the public. To maintain the climate of fear, the commission kept the pallid results of its surveillance operations from public disclosure. Instead, it reemphasized the dangers at hand, though confidential reports from across the state attested that "Minnesota is not going Dutch. The tide of public sentiment is sweeping before it all disloyalty."[51]

Quite clearly, the commission's claims of subversive activity were no more than an unsubstantiated charade. Yet, the less agents turned up, the more the commissioners accelerated both their propaganda and their undercover efforts. Public fears about disloyalty were the necessary underpinning for the calculated campaigns planned against labor and the Nonpartisan League. Many of the state's newspapers, including the *Minneapolis Tribune*, the *Minneapolis Journal*, and the *Saint Paul Dispatch*, also fueled public fears. In April the *St. Paul Daily News*, whose editor strove to maintain some equilibrium, charged the other Twin Cities dailies of printing "with alarming headlines a mass of untrue and inflammatory reports." Two months later, the *Daily News* broke the story of the commission's intelligence bureau; before then, most Minnesotans had little inkling that the state had gone into the business of organized espionage.[52] Even after the story was published, it was months before most average citizens could conceive of the scope of commission surveillance.

Few individuals outside the circle of power realized the breadth and density of the commission's surveillance and enforcement mechanisms, so far did it exceed any previous construction of government power. In late May, the commission formally established a secret service bureau under the supervision of commissioner Charles Ames, but Pinkerton reports dating from April indicate that informal surveillance was in place months before it was officially approved. The new bureau only formally sanctioned and centralized an already existing undercover network. Over the course of the war, agents of the Burns Detective Agency and the Northern Information Bureau, individual private detectives, and deputized "citizen operatives" of the American Protective League all supplemented the covert operations of the Pinkertons and agents employed directly by the commission. Evidence also suggests that McGee maintained a private intelligence network of his own.[53] Arguably, the state harbored more commission spies than subversives.

The commission also established a public surveillance and enforcement system of county directors to carry out its plans on the local level. To ensure the caliber and politics of the appointees, the commission solicited nominations from the Minnesota Bankers Association (MBA). As a letter sent to MBA members explained, "This commission has almost unlimited powers for putting into operation any plans for the general good of any community in the State. . . . What is wanted now is the RIGHT MAN to take up this work."[54] As the letter noted, who was better qualified to choose the "right men" than the state's bankers? In addition to carrying out commission directives, county directors also were expected to report on suspicious local activities. Some directors took these responsibilities on with more enthusiasm than others, depending on local circumstances, and the level of involvement varied considerably from county to county. In the Twin Cities, where undercover detectives roamed the streets continually, the county directors left spying in the hands of professionals. Lucky for them, since other commission demands constituted the equivalent of a full-time job. Ramsey County director Donald Cotton eventually headed no less than nine wartime organizations in addition to his duties as county director. Assuredly, his patriotic endeavor was underwritten by his employer, Illinois Steel, a major beneficiary of war contracts.

Enforcement of wartime orders was another critical matter, and commissioners moved swiftly to mobilize a domestic military force. John McGee claimed oversight of this project—a natural role for the bellicose commissioner who advocated internment camps, firing squads, and the imposition of martial law in Minnesota.[55] By mid-May, McGee was deep into organizing ten battalions of the Home Guard, to replace National Guard units that would be called to the front. Four companies were assigned to St. Paul alone. A volunteer force that answered only to the governor, the Home Guard served in effect as the commission's private army. Major businesses, the Minneapolis Civic and Commerce Association, and the St. Paul Association paid the cost of uniforms and arms, and guardsmen served without pay, thus assuring that they would be drawn overwhelmingly from the business class.[56]

Lest the Home Guard prove inadequate for the mission of domestic protection, the commission also officially endorsed the authority of the Civilian Auxiliaries in St. Paul and Minneapolis, establishing a virtual businessmen's militia. St. Paul organized its auxiliary the day war was declared; two days later, its recruits began drilling on the parade grounds at St. Thomas College. The Minneapolis Auxiliary, of course, had a much longer history. As antilabor enforcement troops, the Civilian Auxiliary had operated for years there to quell strikes and intimidate labor actions. It was so well prepared that McGee was able to purchase seven thousand rounds of Winchester ammunition to arm the Home Guard from the auxiliary's private stock.[57]

It would seem that the commission had created an unbreachable, multileveled organization to support its mission. But all these law-enforcement operatives—from county directors to peace officers—were drawn from the local citizenry, who interpreted their responsibilities through the lens of local circumstance. In Stearns County, with the greatest concentration of Germans in the state, county director Charles Ladner never availed himself of any of the paramilitary options the commission provided. On the contrary, he devoted most of his energies to keeping the commission out of county affairs and defending local people from charges of disloyalty.[58] Minneapolis represented the other extreme. There, every available mechanism was used to suppress dissent, intimidate organized labor, and force radicals to leave town. In addition to the above organizations, the Safety Commission deputized nearly five hundred members of the Minneapolis branch of the American Protective League (APL), with the authority to carry arms and make arrests, as well as engage in covert activities that involved "dictaphones, disguises . . . and hours spent in skillful 'shadowing.' "[59]

In St. Paul, the civilian army operated with less single-minded fervor, or at least with less efficiency. With a history of negotiating problems rather than resorting to force, the businessmen who composed the Guard and the Civilian Auxiliary may have been reluctant to further break down community codes. Perhaps they did not believe the charges of rampant disloyalty in the city or, at least, did not wish to draw attention to them. Or maybe, with little military experience, they were simply inept. At any rate, neither the Home Guard nor the Civilian Auxiliary operated with the dispatch they displayed in Minneapolis. As late as the summer of 1918, Home Guard captain Robert Rice complained of the utter failure his company met in its attempt to police the Payne Avenue saloons. Even at this late date, they had not been issued sidearms. Local saloon patrons simply ignored them as "men deliberately walked out of saloons, passed unarmed guards, walking right away from them." Captain Rice asserted firmly that some of his men "would not participate in another raid of this character."[60]

Ramsey County sheriff John Wagener, a popular figure with organized labor, neglected to commission any special deputies until he was called on the carpet by the Safety Commission in August. Still, when he eventually complied with the commission's orders, his deputies looked similar to the other civilian forces. He recruited more than four hundred men, including "nearly all the members of the St. Paul Rod and Gun Club . . . men who are accustomed to handling fire arms, and many who have volunteered the use of their automobiles." This profile suggests that few, if any, of these deputies were culled from the working class.[61]

Hundreds of middle-class St. Paulites filled the ranks of these various civilian law enforcement organizations, but scant evidence exists that they played any sig-

Fig. 30. Neither passersby nor children appear intimidated by the Home Guard as they patrolled University Avenue in 1917, armed with nightsticks rather than guns. Photo by *Saint Paul Dispatch*. Courtesy of the Minnesota Historical Society.

nificant role in policing the city's social order. St. Paul APL members carried membership cards but not sidearms and dealt primarily in patriotic pronouncements rather than sleuthing operations. Businessmen continued to tread carefully and remained sensitive to community opinion, reflecting their ambivalent relationship with both the city's working people and with the Safety Commission. The businessmen shared some goals of each faction but were entirely aligned with neither. Prominent St. Paul contractor Walter Butler requested military protection for his company's mining investments on the Iron Range; at the same time, though, he asked that his request be kept confidential: "It is well to bear in mind that men engaged as Butler Brothers are in a community for a number of years, do not wish to incurr [*sic*] the displeasure of people engaged in any line of business, and therefore desire that this suggestion to you receive as little advertising as possible."[62] In St. Paul, it was not considered prudent to show one's hand too openly.

State-directed policing and propaganda became a stifling presence in most of Minnesota but were only the tip of the commission iceberg. In truth, secrecy shrouded official operations at every level. The Safety Commission was well aware that few of its activities could bear public scrutiny. Thus, it openly targeted only IWW radicals and German subversives in its initial campaign, but its undercover agents cast a much wider net from the outset. Reports poured in from the Iron Range, where agents chased phantom Wobbly agitators; from German farming districts and rural Nonpartisan strongholds; from Minneapolis, where the Socialist mayor, trade unionists, and IWW radicals were trailed with equal vigor; and from St. Paul, where the only tangible evidence produced were the grumblings of discontented Swedish workingmen. None of the reports upheld the security risks the commission claimed. Agents on the range reported, "Some I.W.W.'s here . . . not causing any trouble at this time," nor were they expected to do so. From St. Cloud, the regional center of the state's most Germanic county: "not the slightest sign of any trouble," "everyone seemed perfectly loyal." Nonpartisan League meetings across the state drew enthusiastic crowds but "nothing said which could in any manner be construed as disloyal or seditious." In Minneapolis, agents infiltrated trade union and IWW meetings, attended socialist gatherings, and frequented working-class saloons but found scant incriminating evidence. Not even the Wobblies who gathered at Flood's Saloon could be caught "contemplating any radical movement."[63] All of this was poor grist for the propaganda mill.

It seems that commission agents had scoured the state in vain to discover a conspiracy worth pursuing. In July, Pinkerton superintendent O. R. Hatfield informed Governor Burnquist that he had withdrawn the twelve agents assigned to German localities because "we felt from the information we obtained there that conditions were such as to not warrant keeping them there any longer."[64] Apparently, Hatfield's conscientious economy did not please the Public Safety Commission. Five days later, in a letter to surveillance chief Thomas Winter, Hatfield outlined a new and expanded agenda for his approval: agents assigned to infiltrate the Minnesota Federation of Labor (MFL) Convention to search out links between the AFL and the IWW; examination of the St. Paul bank account of the Nonpartisan League; and close surveillance of every group that "might have the appearance of being a German organization"—a list that named the pastors of the most prominent Lutheran churches in St. Paul, the German press, and a host of fraternal organizations, including the Catholic Order of Foresters in St. Agnes parish.[65] The Safety Commission swiftly approved this expanded agenda.

In the summer of 1917, though the commission had become a looming public presence, the scope of these investigations had not yet become public. In St. Paul, organized labor continued to hope that it could work with the commissioners to promote labor's interests. The Trades and Labor Assembly supported the commission-endorsed Labor's Loyal Legion, a patriotic organization of the state's workers, and MFL secretary George Lawson held a position on the Ramsey County Commission's advisory council. The Trades and Labor Assembly consistently stressed labor's commitment to the war effort and renounced any connection to radicalism, a policy that served to distance St. Paul workers from their more oppositional Minneapolis counterparts. To the *Union Advocate's* editor, Cornelius Guiney, moderation was the key to union security. "Organized workers are assailed and imperiled from within their own ranks by men and women . . . who create the impression that the whole body of labor is hostile to the policies and decrees of the government." Whether "misguided zealots" or "rank traitors," they had no place in the legitimate labor movement.[66]

No doubt, Guiney would have been surprised to discover that he himself was under investigation, along with the "misguided zealots" and "rank traitors" he condemned. In June and July, even as the Trades and Labor Assembly repeatedly vowed unstinting support for the war and promoted Liberty Bond sales, commission spies infiltrated union meetings and monitored the MFL convention in July. They spread out to investigate labor leadership throughout the state, including St. Paul. Guiney came under scrutiny, as did Socialist Julius Emme and other union officials. After shadowing the suspects and interrogating neighbors, agents produced universally disappointing results. The *Union Advocate* appeared to be "a conservative Labor paper" with "no radical articles," and Guiney's neighbors "all speak very highly of him." Even Emme's reputation survived intact, despite numerous attempts to uncover incriminating evidence on his activities.[67]

Undaunted, agents continued to search the city for evidence of treason. The scope of surveillance spread from ordinary working people to the middle class. By midsummer, nerves were on edge in St. Paul as word began to spread of neighbors and co-workers under investigation. Conversations became more guarded, and people with nothing to hide began looking over their shoulders. The city's small contingent of Socialists and Wobblies, composed primarily of "Jews, Germans and . . . Scandinavians," held halfhearted meetings in local parks, but more often than not, agents described the gatherings as resembling family picnics more than political meetings. Fear had become a palpable companion at these outings. While the city sweltered in the July sun, rhetoric cooled down considerably as the price of free speech grew increasingly dear.[68]

These ominous signs notwithstanding, both organized workers and employers in St. Paul believed they could maintain the internal equilibrium of their working relationship apart from the struggles going on around them. Surely, the city had proved its patriotism. Registration for the draft had proceeded on June 5 "without a sign of trouble," as more than twenty-two thousand men reported as required. If not enthusiastic, the boys of St. Paul seemed at least resigned. As one young man remarked, "We won't kick, Captain, although we know it is a ticket to the graveyard." Each group of departing recruits received a rousing civic send-off. A typical scenario might include an inspiring speech by Archbishop Ireland and an escort to the train depot by the Great Northern Marching Band, a detachment of St. Thomas Cadets, and members of the Winter Carnival Queens club.[69]

The first Liberty Loan drive had been another testament to the city's patriotism. With the St. Paul Association, the Knights of Columbus, and the Trades and Labor Assembly all vigorously promoting the purchase of bonds, "the campaign proceeded to a triumphant close," and the city nearly doubled its quota, with a total subscription

Fig. 31. Draftees, waiting to board the train to Camp Dodge, Iowa, in 1917, display an attitude of grim resignation rather than the patriotic enthusiasm that characterized the business establishment. Courtesy of the Minnesota Historical Society.

of more than $11 million. Civic leaders were particularly pleased with the results, since the state as a whole fell nearly $2 million short of its goal. Minneapolis had exceeded its quota by only 37 percent—well short of St. Paul's showing.[70] By this measure at least, St. Paul had proved its detractors wrong. As further evidence, the St. Paul Association could point to more than a dozen separate wartime endeavors that it had organized, staffed, and funded—and the list continued to grow.[71] With the city seemingly united behind the war effort, employers and workers hoped to return to business as usual.

Not that they were unaffected by the intrigues swirling around them. The St. Paul Association worked closely with the Safety Commission in hopes of promoting the city's business interests. It organized and administered the Civilian Auxiliary, and contributed the bulk of its membership. The Association also provided men and financing for the Home Guard. But at the same time, city leaders tried to keep up the appearance of harmonious relations with its working people. In May, the city council raised the pay of skilled city workers a minimum of 10 percent to bring them up to union scale. The Trades Assembly reported also that several unions had been granted wage increases, describing the negotiations as "harmonious and pleasant throughout. . . . The best feeling prevails between employers and employees."[72]

"Good feelings" notwithstanding, disturbing whispers about the Safety Commission's activities were beginning to leak out of the capitol, edging the Trades and Labor Assembly toward cautious cooperation with the Nonpartisan League and the railroad brotherhoods. Both organizations received invitations to attend the MFL convention in July. Also, in June the Assembly nominated Julius Emme "by acclamation" to a seat on the its executive board, a public affirmation that labor retained an independent voice. Still, the Assembly endeavored to identify its interests with the patriotic cause, thereby enlisting state and federal support for labor issues. When St. Paul's nonunionized American Hoist and Derrick Company won a $3 million government contract, the Assembly launched both a formal protest and a public relations campaign impugning owner Oliver Crosby's patriotism. The *Union Advocate* also editorialized that Safety Commissioner Charles Ames had a patriotic duty to implement the eight-hour day for his workers, since shorter hours had proved to have a positive effect on efficiency and profitability. Though "this would not make [Ames] any more humane or careful of the lives and welfare of his employees for their sakes," as one of the commissioners he had a special obligation to support wartime efficiency.[73]

In the summer of 1917, alliances in St. Paul were indeed complicated and unstable, but union workers, assessing their gains in recent months, were overall a confident group. Union membership was growing daily. In May alone, the Trades and Labor Assembly reported five new unions, including the city's firemen and police force. Most negotiations were settled amicably, and even the few strikes that occurred had been resolved without a serious breakdown of civility. The summer was filled with picnics, steamboat excursions, and dances that celebrated union culture. Collective confidence was high.[74]

In St. Paul, where residents put such great store in the social meaning and accountability of place, public demonstrations always played an important role in defining the contours of community. This was never more important than in the unstable months of 1917, when conflicting interests pulled loyalties first one way and then another. As Labor Day approached, workers seized the opportunity to demonstrate union strength and also reaffirm labor's place in the larger polity. For weeks, the *Advocate* drummed up support for the parade, declaring, "It is now up to the unions in the city to make the celebration all it should be in magnitude, high character, and impressiveness. . . . a public display of the strength, solidarity and spirit of the labor movement."[75]

In 1917, labor would visibly claim its place in the city twice over, since the same week marked the dedication of an impressive new union hall located in the center of the business district. No longer would individual unions meet in scattered locations across the city. As the *Advocate's* editor noted, the new hall had symbolic as well as practical importance—a testament in bricks and mortar to labor's unity and to its place in the life of the city.[76]

The city's business and professional men joined with labor in using these public occasions to reaffirm civic understandings and relationships destabilized by the war. Most businesses and all banks closed in honor of the holiday, and post offices remained open for only one hour in the morning. The Labor Day edition of the *Advocate*, swelled to three times its normal size, was stuffed with dozens of advertisements, congratulatory messages, and expressions of support for the union movement from local professionals, banks, and businesses of every size. The *Advocate*, in turn, was "deeply and sincerely thankful to its friends in business circles, in official positions and in other walks of life for the generous measure in which they have encouraged and supported its present Labor day edition."[77]

The paper also overflowed with profiles of local politicians sympathetic to labor's interests, with special emphasis on either their own or family ties to the labor movement. Not surprisingly, neither the governor nor any member of the Public Safety Commission received notice—nor did they appear in the parade. The only high-ranking state official to be honored was Secretary of State Julius Schmall, who declined to ride at the head of the parade with the other dignitaries, preferring instead to march with his fellow members of the Typographical Union.[78]

The integrated role of labor in the city could be read in the ranks of the parade itself. Naturally, in this turbulent year patriotism was the most evident theme, with flags waving everywhere and "enough patriotic music to send a whole army to victory." All union men who had enlisted were urged to march in uniform, and the First Minnesota infantry led the first division of the parade, bearing banners urging enlistment. The unionized police and firemen marched in dignified cadence in a place of honor near the marshal, representing the fusion of community service and union consciousness. Eight automobiles followed closely behind, carrying the mayor, city commissioners, representatives of the Assembly's Labor Day committee, and other invited dignitaries. Then came the real heart of the parade. As the columns wended their way along the route, they were an impressive sight to the people who filled the sidewalks to watch them pass. More than eight thousand union members, representing twenty-seven of the city's unions and accompanied by half a dozen bands, marched in dignified precision. Dignity was indeed the order of the day. This was serious business, and the committee had emphasized that "proper decorum and regularity" must be maintained.[79]

The parade was declared an unqualified success. Two days later, the grand opening ball and card party at the new trade union hall provided yet another opportunity for celebration and congratulation. "The crowd was large, the spirits of the company were high, the feet of old and young were jubilant." The ball was "a palpable triumph from every point of view, even the financial receipts exceeding the most sanguine expectations."[80] In assessing the week's events, St. Paul union members could assure themselves that labor was riding high, at least within the city limits, where it really mattered. No one could have predicted that within the month the turbulent currents that swirled below the surface of the city would become a tidal wave, and the social edifice they had so carefully constructed would all come crashing down.

Chapter 7

THE WAR OF ST. PAUL AND THE END OF THE CIVIC COMPACT

Throughout the summer of 1917, the pattern of repression accelerated, but organized labor seemed to sleep through the warning alarms. Violent attacks on the IWW, sanctioned and even organized by the Public Safety Commission, conveyed no threat to St. Paul's "legitimate" AFL unionists. Nor did witch-hunts against German immigrants alarm the loyal labor movement.[1] Not even news of the Safety Commission's intelligence network pierced union's confidence.

Organized farmers had a much clearer grasp of the forces aligned against them. Before the declaration of war, Nonpartisan League leaders had been unanimous isolationists. But U.S. intervention demanded a nimble rhetorical adjustment. Thereafter, the League critiqued the conduct of the war—specifically, manpower conscription and business profiteering—but was careful not to criticize the cause itself. This tactical maneuver reflected organizers' acute sense of danger rather than a change in ideology. To Arthur Townley, the League's president and organizing genius, the war was primarily "an annoying interruption of the progress of League programs"; those programs were organized around domestic economic issues, not foreign policy. The important thing, Townley stressed to organizers, "was to get [the farmers] into the organization first and educate them afterwards." If that required flag waving, then League principles would be framed in patriotic terms.[2] As evidence of surveillance and intimidation mounted, lecturers turned up the volume of patriotic rhetoric, always careful to couch their critiques of the grain trust and war profiteering as a defense of treasured democratic principles.

But the Public Safety Commission was not so easily distracted from its mission. Under its direction, local officials and law enforcement officers, commission county directors, and undercover agents assiduously transcribed every NPL meeting, combing the speeches for indications of disloyalty. If the content yielded no incriminating evidence, agents of the Safety Commission claimed to find disloyal intent in the *manner* of delivery. While one accuser, for example, conceded that Arthur Townley "made some patriotic references," he reported that "every patriotic statement that was made by him was attended by a sneer and a snarl." Though even in wartime Minnesota purported sarcasm was not yet grounds enough for prosecution, First Amendment rights carried increasingly less protection, and all negative characterizations were filed as part of a growing cumulative case against the League. When the state successfully prosecuted Townley for sedition the following year, it claimed that his declarations of patriotism were merely a cover for seditious sentiments, conveyed through "suppressions, implications, insinuations, sneers and innuendoes."[3]

Desperate to enlist the support of organized labor to his cause, the harried Townley had moved the League's national headquarters to St. Paul partly to achieve that end.[4] In September, conditions seemed ripe for him to make a move. Two months earlier, the government had fixed the price of wheat for the duration of the war, netting Midwestern farmers about $1.85 a bushel, when it had been bringing between $2.50 and $3.00 in the western markets. Though this created hardship for the farmers, it was a boon to the milling trust and opened the door for commodities profiteering.[5] At the same time, the cost of living was escalating rapidly, outpacing wage increases and creating economic hardship for the state's working people and farmers alike.[6] The twin issues of war profiteering and inflation provided a common rallying point to bring farmers and workers together at last. With the weight of the Public Safety Commission pressing in on his organization, Townley called a Conference of Producers and Consumers to discuss the high cost of living.

At first, the Trades and Labor Assembly had its doubts about the convention. In the estimation of many of its officers, St. Paul labor was better served by maintaining community goodwill, and "radical" demonstrations that might endanger established relationships should be avoided. The Assembly and the Saint Paul Association recently had sponsored a joint loyalty rally in the city, with Samuel Gompers as the featured speaker. The event appeared to solidify the amicable local understandings between business and labor. Furthermore, labor's energetic support for the war effort seemed to impress the Safety Commission. The governor had just appointed H. W. Libby, a union man from southern Minnesota, as commission secretary, which, to labor leaders, was a positive sign. In fact, the Assembly, over the protest of Socialist union leader Julius Emme, had voted 47 to 21 to send a formal letter of appreciation to Governor Burnquist for the appointment.[7]

With some trepidation, Assembly members eventually agreed to send ten delegates to the conference. George Lawson, secretary of the MFL, was chosen to speak on behalf of St. Paul workers.[8] The more cautious officers of the Assembly knew they could rely on Lawson, who was trying to work with the Safety Commission, to keep them from becoming embroiled in any proposals that might be deemed radical.

St. Paul labor's rank and file demonstrated considerably more enthusiasm than did than the officers of the Assembly. More than four thousand people attended the first day's program, and on each successive day, attendance grew. The Nonpartisan League made the most of this opportunity to broaden its political base with spirited calls for farmer-labor unity. By the second day of the conference even the most cautious union members had become caught up in the groundswell of a new and unprecedented political coalition as representatives from every farmer organization, all the railroad brotherhoods, and labor organizations from Iowa, Wisconsin, and Illinois, as well as Minnesota, converged on St. Paul.[9]

The St. Paul Trades and Labor Assembly, traditionally wary of alliances forged outside the city, was notable for its absence from key committees, but judging from press reports, the local rank and file, who enthusiastically filled the auditorium, was well ahead of its elected officials. By conference end, union officers belatedly had scrambled to get aboard the popular bandwagon. The Public Safety Commission noted the burgeoning support for the Nonpartisan League with dismay. Attendees enthusiastically endorsed the "common interests of labor and the tillers of the soil"; the mayors of St. Paul and Minneapolis spoke in support of working people's issues, and national figures, among them Congresswoman Jeanette Rankin of Montana and Senators William Borah of Idaho and Asle Gronna of North Dakota, added their strong endorsements. "Kaiser Burnquist," as speakers labeled the Minnesota governor, was conspicuously absent. Perhaps the most unsettling names on the speakers' roster were the scattering of middle-class merchants and businessmen from St. Paul—evidence that a cross-class alliance might be coalescing. John Baer, the Nonpartisan-endorsed congressman from North Dakota, captured the spirit of the convention, describing "an army of voters moving on the trenches of wealth, irresistible as a prairie fire and as formidable as a front of bayonets."[10]

By the third and final day of the conference, such calls to arms had generated a fever pitch of enthusiasm. When Judge Eli Torrance of Minneapolis took the podium, the audience was "deaf to [his] patriotic appeal." As vividly recounted by the *Dispatch*:

> Where five minutes before the audience had yelled hoarsely and stamped their feet in enthusiasm . . . they applauded but stiffly and spasmodically at the appeal of Judge Torrance. . . . [His] words, "My God! Men, the safety of our nation is more important than mere questions of sale and barter," brought a cold response, mainly from Twin Cities citizens who were present.[11]

It appeared that a new era in popular politics was about to begin. No one in the St. Paul auditorium that afternoon could have guessed that within hours the Nonpartisan League would sustain what would be an ultimately fatal blow.

The capstone of the conference was to be a speech at the final session by Wisconsin senator Robert LaFollette, the war's most prominent critic. Eight thousand spectators overflowed the auditorium, and an equal number gathered outside. LaFollette's speech on the topic of war financing was a huge success with the audience. The few critics who tried to heckle the senator were silenced by a surge of hostility from LaFollette's countless supporters. As the conference ended, the aura of solidarity exceeded all that the League had hoped to accomplish. Cornelius Guiney put the *Union Advocate* to bed that night with a glowing account of the "illuminating and entertaining event." It was, he claimed, "a strong demonstration of the devotion of our people to the government and their determination to hold every form of selfishness and disloyalty . . . to strictest accountability." In addition, the conference augured "the closest possible affiliation between organized farmers and organized labor."[12] Arthur Townley and other League strategists believed they were on the verge of realizing their dream of a farmer-labor coalition.[13]

Morning found a new reality that reflected a nightmare rather than a dream. To the shock of those who had heard the senator's address, headlines in the local papers scorchingly denounced LaFollette as a traitor and discredited the entire conference in the process. Press reports ignored the substance of the speech, seizing instead on a brief remark made in response to a heckler—that the sinking of the *Lusitania* had not been adequate cause for the United States to declare war. Such sentiments, declared the *Minneapolis Journal*, were "more disloyal, more treasonable, than the utterances that have landed lesser pro-Germans in Prison." The *Pioneer Press,* not to be outdone, called for LaFollette's immediate arrest on crimes of sedition and treason.[14] Through the Associated Press wire service, selectively chosen excerpts of LaFollette's speech painted both the senator and his enthusiastic audience with the brush of disloyalty, exposing the "shame" of St. Paul and Minnesota on the front page of newspapers across the country. The conference had become a debacle of major proportions.

Interestingly, LaFollette's stance on the war declaration was scarcely news. He had led the opposition debate on the floor of the Senate with precisely the same argument. Why, then, should reiteration of a familiar, even if unpopular, political stance elicit such an explosion of journalistic outrage? An editorial in the *Minneapolis Journal* provides a clue: "This has torn the mask from the Nonpartisan League and revealed what it really is."[15]

Indeed, after a flurry of denunciations of LaFollette, including a demand by the Minnesota Public Safety Commission that he be expelled from the Senate, the real object of attack quickly became clear. The Safety Commission finally had the weapon to obliterate the Nonpartisan League. LaFollette was a traitor and the League, personified by its president Arthur Townley, was guilty by association. As Charles Ames jubilantly confided to fellow commissioner John Lind, though "every effort was made to give [the conference] a patriotic aspect, this was made difficult by their 'unfortunate' selection of speakers, and the notorious speech of LaFollette spoiled the effect altogether."[16] At last the gloves could come off in dealing with the Nonpartisan League, and for the duration of the war the League faced relentless pressure from the commission and increasingly harsh attacks by the press. Association with the League itself became tantamount to treason.[17]

The immediate effect of the LaFollette incident was to fracture the nascent cross-class coalition that seemed about to emerge from the conference. This polar-

ization was especially apparent in St. Paul, where the problem of civic identity recaptured center stage. The city had been embarrassed in the national press, and
once again its loyalty was in question. All the efforts to prove its patriotism gone for
naught. The *Pioneer Press* insisted that "the people of St. Paul had no part . . . in
the sedition gathering at the auditorium." They had been "hoodwinked" by Townley and the Nonpartisan League. The Minneapolis editorial slant was slightly
different; "Robert M. LaFollette, fugleman of sedition, *was permitted last night in
St. Paul . . .* [to go] to the extreme limit of anti-Americanism and pro-German-
ism. . . . Has not the time come to put an end to this sort of thing?" Minneapolis, it
went without saying, would never have permitted such a travesty.[18]

Understandably, St. Paulites who had participated in the conference blamed the
Nonpartisan League for their unpleasant predicament. Independent merchants
might protest the high cost of commodities, but the cost of association with a "trea-
sonous" organization was considerably higher; they quickly joined with the St.
Paul Association in civic damage control. The Association organized a "monster patriotic rally" featuring Teddy Roosevelt himself to "redeem [St. Paul] from any
stain that might have been cast upon it." According to the *Pioneer Press*, nearly the
entire city participated in the demonstration, including six thousand "workers of
St. Paul," who marched in a mile-long parade "between lines of cheering citizens
numbering at least 75,000."[19]

Even allowing for journalistic hyperbole, attendance at the demonstration was
impressive. Assuredly, many of the participants who marched in the contingent
from Labor's Loyal Legion had enthusiastically applauded Senator LaFollette only
days earlier. This apparent about-face was driven by more than self-interest. Nor
was it a case of simple patriotism. For this moment at least, St. Paulites had closed
ranks to defend their city's honor, which was under attack from every side. The defensive posture so familiar to city residents generated a heightened *local* loyalty that
linked them momentarily against all outsiders—whether Nonpartisan Leaguers,
Minneapolis businessmen, or the national press. This demonstration was more
about place than nation. As Roosevelt resoundingly declared that "St. Paul is absolutely American through and through and from top to bottom," the crowd
cheered wildly at their common vindication.[20]

The St. Paul farmer-labor coalition might have died an infant death in the ruins
of the Producers and Consumers Conference but for another set of events that was
unfolding, largely unnoticed, amid the hoopla surrounding the conference and its
aftermath. A brewing labor dispute would prove to be unlike any St. Paul had previously seen. By the time it was over, the social text of the city would be fractured
along multiple fault lines; long-standing modes of negotiation would be destroyed
and refashioned. Powerful forces, untrammeled by local constraints, were about to
breach the city limits.

Readers of the *Daily News* may easily have missed the harbinger of trouble that appeared among the letters to the editor in the Labor Day edition. But the letter, ti-

tled "Street Car Man Protest," laid out a challenge that was rapidly gathering steam:

> Editor, Daily News: This is to let the public know how patriotic the street railway company is. Every drafted man was out the time lost taking the physical examination. They work their men all the way from 10 to 20 hours during fair week and on special occasions, and only give them straight time; and if one kicks about putting in such long hours he is discharged. If they were not such a bunch of "rubes" they would insist on their rights and get a day off once in a while. Let it soak in, boys.
> ORGANIZE[21]

Apparently, the writer was not alone in his grievances. Only days later, employee representatives from all the car barns met with company officials of the Twin City Rapid Transit Company (TCRT). Claiming that it was impossible "to give our wives and children a somewhat decent existence" at their present wages and protesting unfair working conditions, they hoped to negotiate a three-cent raise and some improvement in the terms of employment. The company turned them down flat—a message that "soaked in" immediately. On September 20, the day of the LaFollette speech, frustrated workers took their case to officials of the St. Paul Trades and Labor Assembly to enlist its assistance in organizing a union. The Assembly, newly settled in its impressive headquarters, buoyed by its show of strength on Labor Day, and flush with recent negotiating successes, confidently offered its help. As added incentive, here was an opportunity to show the union boys across the river the clout of a real labor movement. What the Assembly failed to consider was that it was taking on a Minneapolis rather than a St. Paul employer, and one backed with all the might of the Minneapolis Citizens Alliance at that.[22]

The TCRT, one of the giants of Minneapolis organized capital, owned the exclusive franchise for all the car lines in both cities. Horace Lowry, the company president, was a dedicated open-shop employer and stalwart member of both the Minneapolis Civic and Commerce Association and the Citizens Alliance. Though he had been involved in management of the TCRT for more than a decade, he had assumed the presidency of his father's company only in 1916 and already had weathered an attack from public-ownership advocates in Minneapolis. He was not about to have his authority challenged a second time—certainly not by his employees.[23]

Labor's grievances against the TCRT went back a long way. The company's often-claimed commitment to the "public good" had seldom extended to its workers. Founder Tom Lowry had built his transportation monopoly on a shaky foundation of land speculation, gobbling up real estate that increased in value only after his streetcar lines connected his holdings to the city center. Scrambling to expand as quickly as possible, he was often short of cash and, as he candidly admitted when he cut wages in 1889, "The only way to increase the profits was to reduce the men's wages," a strategy that he turned to repeatedly over the years. Onerous working conditions combined with inadequate wages had had created a long-standing list of labor grievances against the TCRT.[24]

The St. Paul Trades and Labor Assembly also had more recent pressing reasons to challenge the TCRT. In 1907, the company had moved its manufacturing shops to St. Paul's Midway area, where it built all the cars for its lines. Suddenly, the Minneapolis employer became one of the area's principal manufacturers, employing more than five hundred employees in skilled trades—all of them nonunion workers. This represented a serious threat to other closed-shop agreements in the trades. Two years later, Horace Lowry, as president of the Arcade Investment Company, developed a block of land in downtown St. Paul long held by his father. Acting as his own general contractor, he erected the Lowry Hotel and Lowry Professional Building, and the Field-Schlick department store, again with nonunion labor. The Lowry name emblazoned in the midst of this union city, along with the ubiquitous streetcars, was a constant irritant to the city's organized workers.[25]

Thus, a welter of festering grievances with the TCRT caused self-interest and worker solidarity to converge, and the Trades and Labor Assembly vowed to assist the carmen's organizing campaign with all the resources it could muster. It would need them. This was an organizing campaign that required an unprecedented degree of cooperation between Minneapolis and St. Paul workers. Historically, alliances between locals in the two cities had been hampered by intercity competition for members' affiliation, as well as by widely disparate relations between labor and business. A dozen trades had established joint Twin Cities locals by 1917, but their membership numbered only 1,166, a mere 3.5 percent of the total Twin Cities union membership.[26] Moreover, the joint locals all dealt with multiple employers on both sides of the river and had scant success in negotiating the closed-shop contracts in Minneapolis that were common practice in St. Paul. In short, the joint Twin Cities labor movement had an ephemeral foundation on which to base its streetcar campaign.

This organizing effort would be uncharted territory for a second reason. It was the first time Twin Cities labor tested its resolve against a single employer who operated in both cities. St. Paul organized labor had no experience in confronting the power that undergirded the open shop in Minneapolis. The civic framework that had traditionally mediated labor relations in St. Paul carried no weight in this struggle. To the contrary: the TCRT and the Citizens Alliance welcomed the challenge to show weak-kneed St. Paul employers what Minneapolis-style organized business could accomplish. Thus, the impending confrontation represented a face-off between Minneapolis business and St. Paul organized labor.

The company swung into action almost immediately. On September 20, the carmen formally invited the Amalgamated Association of Street and Electric Railway Workers of America (AASERE) to send in an organizer. Less than a week later, thanks to company spies on its payroll, the TCRT had identified and fired twenty men involved in the organizing effort. Then, in a tactical maneuver designed to halt the organizing effort, Horace Lowry granted the requested pay raise and improvements in working conditions. At the same time, he fired another thirty-seven men active in the union effort, sending a pointed message that no union presence would be brooked in the TCRT.[27]

The carmen were undeterred. Temporary bread and butter concessions, as they knew, were unprotected gains without organized representation. Thus, with the full support of both cities' labor bodies and the arrival of a national organizer from the AASERE, they disdained Lowry's offer and signed union cards instead. Membership swelled quickly to more than one thousand workers, who demanded the reinstatement of the fired carmen and recognition of their union.[28]

Lowry and his friends in the Minneapolis Citizens Alliance were prepared for the men to refuse his offer and plotted out their strikebreaking stratagem with methodical efficiency. Hennepin County sheriff, Otto Langum, immediately invested the six-hundred-man Minneapolis Civilian Auxiliary with the power to bear arms and make arrests, and warned it to prepare for immediate mobilization. The Auxiliary prepared itself for possible disturbances by stepping up its training maneuvers, drawing up a "war map" of the city at its headquarters in the courthouse, and posting assignments for each individual unit. None of this was new ground for the businessmen's private army.[29]

Curiously, the forces of law and order in St. Paul made no similar preparations. They seemed to expect a settlement by the state board of arbitration, indicating that Lowry had not made them privy to the scope of his union-busting plans. Despite the impending crisis, the Civilian Auxiliary made no tactical plans, nor did the chief of police issue an alert to his officers. In the midst of a major labor dispute, St. Paul's mayor and two of the city councilmen blithely went off to Chicago to attend the World Series.[30]

The Trades and Labor Assembly also seemed to expect an arbitrated settlement. After all, the only real issue to be resolved was the right of labor to organize. The country was at war and the government had shown exceptional sympathy toward organized labor, taking the position that national interest required every effort to avoid work stoppages. Also, as the *Daily News* editorialized, "A transportation strike involves much more than a strike in any ordinary industrial establishment. The public is a direct third party to the situation, with a greater interest at stake than either the company or its employees." The *News* reflected widespread local sentiment in its plea to "keep the peace, the industrial peace of this community." The retail grocers had formally petitioned the Assembly to do all in its power to avoid a strike that would have "disastrous" consequences for local businesses. Even the state, with its patriotic posturing, seemed a potential ally. From the perspective of St. Paul unionists, workers held both the patriotic and the civic high ground. As insurance, they continued to vigorously distance themselves from any connection with radicalism.[31]

As the city's workers approached a struggle that relied heavily on community support, St. Paul's labor press went to great lengths to protect labor's position as a respectable and respected member of the polity. The logic of the strategy is self-evident. At the same time that the Safety Commission was hunting down the IWW, it disingenuously displayed increasing cordiality to the city's AFL labor representatives. The city's union leaders therefore thought themselves well positioned to negotiate on the carmen's behalf. In letters sent to the board of arbitration, the Safety Commission, and to Lowry himself, the union "invok[ed] their aid in the endeavor to effect a harmonious and satisfactory adjustment of all the difficulties involved in this critical situation." Their Minneapolis counterparts likely thought they were daft but agreed to delay a strike call until the board of arbitration could act.[32]

St. Paul unionists had no way of knowing that attempts at negotiation were pointless. Lowry and the governor had been conferring for days, in secret. The streetcar magnate ignored union attempts to negotiate and refused to reinstate the fired workers or meet with the board of arbitration. Nor did the commission make any effort to exercise its broad powers to avert the crisis. As was rapidly becoming clear, neither the company nor the state had any desire to avert the impending strike.[33]

On Saturday, October 6, the carmen walked out. By five A.M. the Minneapolis Civilian Auxiliary was out in full force patrolling the streets of Minneapolis, As the strike gathered momentum throughout the day, strikers and sympathizers, intimidated by the armed patrols, confined themselves to heckling the deputies and "Thomas Lowry's scabs." Earlier in the day, at the Minneapolis headquarters of the Yellow Taxicab Company, where workers were also on strike, armed strikebreakers had shot and stabbed two protesters while police stood by—a powerful reminder of the cost of activism in the Mill City. [34]

Workers looking for a safer space to protest may have taken themselves to St. Paul, where law enforcement had taken no special precautions and people went about their business more or less as usual throughout the day. But as evening came on, downtown streets began to fill with milling pedestrians and signs of trouble were unmistakable. At 6:30 P.M. the sound of shattering glass set off a melee, as protesters began pelting rocks at streetcars passing by. Within hours, the situation had escalated into a full-scale riot, like nothing St. Paul had ever seen. Crowds numbering in the hundreds gathered near car barns up and down the line, and pandemonium descended on the business district. While striking workers tried to persuade motormen and conductors to abandon their cars and join the strike, hundreds of unidentified rioters smashed car windows, cut trolley ropes, pulled cars from the tracks, and manhandled the operators. By midnight, the TCRT was forced to shut down operations until morning.[35]

A close reading of the night's events as they played out downtown reveals the complicated social text of the city in mid-1917. The *Pioneer Press,* which generally favored conservative business interests, portrayed the event as an exercise of unparalleled violence: "Conductors and motormen were stoned from cars and ran to save themselves as the anger of the throngs vented itself on the property of the Twin Cities Rapid Transit Company." The *Daily News,* on the other hand, which addressed a more diverse audience, had a different slant. Though it chronicled the demolition fully, the paper also emphasized that damage was confined only to TCRT property and gave prominent notice to union claims that "the men guilty of the disorders are not strikers, but strike sympathizers and others of a class seeking such opportunities to make a demonstration."[36]

Who were these rioters? Notwithstanding union disclaimers, a number certainly were carmen—and their wives, who were equally invested in the outcome of the strike. The *Pioneer Press* described women and boys in their teens alongside the men, "shouting 'scab,' 'yellow,' and similar epithets at car crews, shaking fists and even plunging bare hands through the car windows."[37] But the magnitude of the fracas strongly suggests that it was not confined to strikers and their families. Instead, the carmen's cause gave a wide range of people an opportunity to express pent-up discontent.

The citizens of St. Paul had long begrudged Tom Lowry the profits he had siphoned from the city through his lucrative streetcar monopoly. The union's call for community support stressed that "the company owes much to the residents . . . in return for the favors they have granted it." The claim that "a vast majority of the people of St. Paul and Minneapolis sympathize with the street car men" was probably particularly accurate in St. Paul.[38] Even more broadly, however, since the Safety Commission seemingly had taken control of the city, all sorts of people had a variety of festering grievances and almost no outlet to express them: young men required to register for the draft; German and Scandinavian ethnics; saloonkeepers forced to curtail their businesses; opponents of the war pressured into silence; and a general population faced with wartime shortages, an escalating cost of living, and a repressive regime that forbade even the expression of their opinions. The list of possible grievances was almost endless. Notably, uniformed enlisted men from nearby Fort Snelling enthusiastically joined the fray. Although they probably had little interest in the streetcar conflict, they may have had their own reasons to smash windows. The milling crowd opened up a social space for diffuse protest, legitimated by the grievances of the streetcar men and protected by anonymity from state retaliation.[39] The mayhem that overtook St. Paul conceivably had multiple sources only coincidentally related to the specific issues of the carmen.[40]

The riot may have been a protest against forced consensus, but in many ways, it was also a community protest rather than a drama of internal conflict. The crowd smashed hundreds of windows but only those of the offending streetcars. The surrounding stores, automobiles, and lampposts remained untouched. The enemy was an outsider, and in that respect, the protest took on some elements of a community celebration. Popcorn wagons and peanut stands did a booming business; according to the *Daily News*, "The only thing missing in the downtown crowds was the balloon man." Along with the damage reports, the *News* ran a series of whimsical human interest vignettes captioned, "Sighs, laughs and frazzled raiment mark noisy evening of strike rioting." In this account at least, the fracas sounded more like a carnival than a violent confrontation. Though at center this was a labor protest and not a carnival, exuberance mingled with anger. The social portrait that emerged in St. Paul looked quite different from that in Minneapolis, where a civilian army held its fellow citizens at bay. Streetcar passengers, children, college students, even middle-class matrons appeared unfazed by the chaos. At worst, it was a mild irritation and, for some, a source of considerable amusement.[41]

In Minneapolis, Hennepin County sheriff Otto Langum posted guards at the bridges linking the cities to prevent the contagion from spreading. But the forces of law and order were conspicuously absent in St. Paul, where police and sheriff's deputies made only perfunctory efforts to intervene. Ramsey County sheriff John Wagener, who had been elected with the strong support of organized labor, was not eager to use force against his constituents, though it was claimed he had 450 deputies at his disposal. The members of the Civilian Auxiliary, who might have approached the task more diligently, were at home for the evening—as was the entire day shift of the St. Paul police force.

St. Paul's unionized policemen were decidedly reluctant to put down a protest of fellow unionists, many of whom were also relatives, neighbors, and friends. Press reports claimed that police were "powerless to stop the destruction," but in fact they simply chose not to employ the powers available to them. In nearly every instance, the police managed to "arrive on the scene after the cars had been stopped, the crews pulled off, and the windows smashed." When they were on hand, they simply "stood around."[42]

In the Sunday morning postmortem, the unionists were jubilant, the businessmen in a panic, and the St. Paul chief of police largely unruffled. Nothing quite like the evening's events had ever before been witnessed in the city, though St. Paul had long practiced a selective enforcement of law and order. City leaders had given Chief John O'Connor a free hand for fifteen years, ignoring or tacitly endorsing his questionable practices. The chief was routinely lionized for his "uncanny" ability to ferret out criminals and keep the peace within the city limits. Thus, when he was questioned about police inefficiency following the riot, he blithely defended himself with the claim that he had placed thirty officers on a single streetcar, to ensure it would get through the city. His motive appears somewhat suspect, however, since only forty officers were on duty that evening. As three fourths of his men sped off to the outskirts of the city, only ten were left to maintain order in the riot zone.[43]

The *Pioneer Press* tried to lay the blame on IWW agitators. Chief O'Connor, preferring to cite outsiders rather than city residents as the source of the trouble, agreed that Wobblies were behind the problem (though he offered no evidence to back his claims). As Horace Lowry struggled to maintain car service, the strike gained momentum by the hour, with more than one thousand men now counted in the strikers' ranks.[44]

Sunday evening, two thousand angry protesters who had again gathered downtown were temporarily held in check by patrols from Fort Snelling, deployed ostensibly to control the "many soldiers . . . taking part in the riots." Meanwhile, one hundred members of the Civilian Auxiliary bedded down in the St. Paul armory, waiting for a call to action that never came. According to the fort commandant, his patrols "had a moral effect on the crowds." More accurately, the deployment of federal troops temporarily suppressed expressions of protest, but the moral effect was one of widespread indignation at military interference in local affairs—with "all the aspects of military police as they paced back and forth with rifle and bayonet." The following day, James Clancy, president of the Trades and Labor Assembly, protested to the city council that "the sight of armed men and soldiers patrolling the streets . . . is something that gets men on their uppers. It is not conducive to the preservation of peace in St. Paul."[45]

The council agreed. The military usurpation of local authority and the widespread community support for the strikers led it to express sympathy for the carmen's cause, put responsibility for the riots on "hoodlums" rather than the strikers, and intimate that it might revoke the TCRT's franchise to operate in the city.[46]

This was not at all what Horace Lowry had hoped to achieve. He had misjudged the local culture and seriously underestimated the weakness of his position as an outsider in this parochial city. Clearly, the deployment of troops was a tactical mistake. By some invisible authority, they were recalled to the fort. Thwarted in his efforts to keep the cars running, Lowry was forced to close down the St. Paul lines by nine P.M. Sunday; on Monday, service limped along with less than a third of the cars in operation. In Minneapolis, meanwhile, "The strike situation was reported quiet. . . . No rioting and the street car service was said to be normal."[47]

The Public Safety Commission had remained uncharacteristically aloof from a situation that had clear potential to disrupt the war effort. Nor was the governor anywhere to be found on Saturday evening, as the capital city erupted in protest, though he had kept in close contact with Lowry in the days preceding the strike. The commission it seems, was confident that the TCRT, with the network of deputies and civilian forces the commission had helped to put in place, would break the organizing effort without official state intervention and the political repercussions that were sure to follow. By Monday morning, the governor was compelled to reassess the situation.

Labor representatives urged the governor and the Safety Commission to intervene. What was more important from the commission's perspective was that St. Paul businessmen were alarmed. Transportation into downtown was nearly at a standstill, hundreds of workers were forced to walk to work, and shoppers stayed at home. Even more distressing to the business leaders, the Trades and Labor Assembly was threatening a general strike in support of the carmen that would have serious repercussions for the local economy. The business agent for the carpenters' union reported to its members that he had received "many calls from contractors on big jobs" urging him to try to get a settlement to "prevent a threatened general strike, which they thought would be very disastrous to the community." Furthermore, Monday marked the kick-off of the second Liberty Loan campaign and, as labor spokesman James Clancy pointedly noted, "It would not look well for St. Paul if the opportunity to purchase a large amount of bonds was lost because of a sympathetic strike."[48] Most compellingly, St. Paul labor's unprecedented militancy, buttressed by widespread community discontent, might force the TCRT to capitulate. Moreover, a victory against the powerful streetcar company might encourage St. Paul unionists to broaden their horizons to other open-shop holdouts in the city. Oliver Crosby, president of American Hoist and Derrick, a nonunion firm, led a delegation of the St. Paul Association to demand the restoration of civic order.[49] Very likely, Commissioner Charles Ames, a fellow open shop employer, supported the initiative.[50]

By Tuesday afternoon, after yet another night of intermittent rioting, the Safety Commission and the TCRT had worked out a deceptively evenhanded agreement to end the strike. The commission ordered the strikers back to work; in return, the company agreed not to discriminate against union members and to submit the cases of the fifty-seven discharged employees for individual review by the commission. Horace Lowry, in an abrupt about-face, expressed his "satisfaction" and stated that "we must obey cheerfully and patriotically the order issued."[51]

Lowry's good cheer should have been a warning of what was to come, but the elated union men turned a sympathy demonstration scheduled for that evening into a victory parade. More than ten thousand workers and sympathizers participated in "one of the biggest parades and mass meetings ever held by labor in the Northwest." Chief O'Connor guaranteed that he would have the situation "well in hand," and union representatives pledged to "do all in their power to keep order downtown." As insurance, in the armory a battalion of the St. Paul Home Guard was at the ready. Nonetheless, as the meeting broke up after a heartfelt rendition of the "Star Spangled Banner," despite precautions, promises, and pleas from speakers to leave the meeting peacefully, the crowd, estimated at four thousand people, "ran wild" according to the *Pioneer Press*, "creating a reign of terror." For four hours the mayhem continued, with rioters "attacking street cars and taking from policemen the prisoners they had made." Unaccountably, once again, the Home Guard received no orders from the governor to move and remained in the armory throughout the night. Perhaps the governor feared that local guardsmen, when put to the test of loyalty, might not have proved any more willing to quell a community disturbance than were local police or deputies.[52]

The final night of rioting, after the carmen had declared victory, is a testament to the welter of grievances that simmered beneath the suffocating mandate for patriotic consensus. A very different sort of oppositional consensus appeared to be forming in St. Paul. The reluctance of local authorities to intervene suggests that city officials, politicians, and businessmen understood the tenuous position they were in. Interestingly, the *Daily News* relegated the riot to page two, and though it admitted that "the violence and disorder exceeded that of last Saturday," it emphasized repeatedly that the rioting was "the work of rowdies" and that no strikers were involved.[53] A companion editorial pressed the point and put the blame squarely on the company:

Two lessons may well be learned from this strike: First, that conciliation and arbitration should be resorted to BEFORE a strike, thus averting much trouble. An arbitration in the office is worth several riots in the street. Second, that lawlessness and disorder during a strike are not due to the strikers themselves, but to hoodlum elements which use such an opportunity to break loose.[54]

The rioters may have been rowdies rather than strikers, but they represented an ethnic cross-section of the city. Of thirty men arrested during the strike, seven had recognizable Scandinavian surnames, seven Irish, five Yankee, and four German; French, Scottish, and Polish names filled out the roster. Only two could be tied to the IWW. The Wobblies were committed to jail for trial; the others were let off with fines or, in the case of assault charges, a few days in the workhouse. The sitting judge, J. W. Fineout, echoed the *Daily News*: "Not a striking carman or a member of organized labor has been arrested. The rioting has been caused by a rowdy element that had no interest in the strike."[55]

Labor spokesmen also worked to calm the troubled civic waters. Immediately following the arbitration order, the Trades and Labor Assembly praised the Safety Commission, "the highest authority in the state," for taking hold of the situation "with firm hands" and compelling the company "to yield to justice, reason and common sense for the good of the whole people and all their interests." Union leaders in St. Paul breathed a collective sigh of relief and optimistically expected their world to return to its established order, a world defined by place as well as class. An item featured in the *Advocate* on October 12 indicates how little had changed:

"Poor old St. Paul!" is one of the sneering ejaculations frequently heard from our self-esteeming and self-satisfied friends and neighbors in our sister city up the river. But look! "Poor old St. Paul" subscribed $17,597,500 to the new Liberty Loan in three days, while Minneapolis, in the same period, subscribed only $5,677,800, with all its boasted superiority in wealth, enterprise and public spirit, and its established superiority of nearly 100,000 population.[56]

So much for solidarity. It seems that civic pride and community allegiances were far from dead.

St. Paul leaders congratulated themselves that the civic compact had been repaired, but neither the Safety Commission nor Minneapolis businessmen intended St. Paul's peculiar political terrain to deter them. Events following the settlement made the nature of their partnership abundantly clear. Within twenty-four hours, union activists began to recognize that the war was not yet over. Men reporting back to work in both cities complained of attempts to "freeze them out." They also encountered prominently placed notices from Lowry asserting that the settlement "carried with it no recognition of the union and the company will in the future as in the past deal only with men as individuals or with the newly elected co-operative committee" (the TCRT's hastily established company union). Thomas Shine, international vice president of the streetcarmen's union, declared that the notice was "like waving a red flag before a bull."[57]

The TCRT's intention was to break the union, notwithstanding Lowry's "cheerful" compliance with the Safety Commission's directive. Though the company agreed to rehire thirty-two of the fifty-seven fired workers, the setback was only temporary. Its "co-operative committee," designed to siphon off union membership, was constructed as a classic company union, with Lowry as its "constitutionally declared president . . . with final arbitration power." More ominously, workers in the barns observed the armoring of cars, hardly a sign of amicable settlement.[58]

The union immediately brought its complaints to the Safety Commission, which equivocated publicly but worked behind the scenes with the TCRT. The commission collaborated with the company in its union-busting schemes, as is evidenced by correspondence between Thomas Winter, head of the commission's surveillance bureau, and a company official. Winter recommended intelligence operative B. J. Randolph as ideal for the TCRT's "needs." Randolph, a self-described "fast and experienced gunman" who was "chain lightning with a pistol," had proved his mettle on a commission assignment in northern Minnesota. In recommending Randolph to the TCRT, Winter stated, "He needs a bath . . . but for mixing with the lower classes Randolph is O.K. . . . I am mistaken if you can get a better man for certain lines of work."[59] What that sort of work might entail was left unspoken.

Tensions escalated when the company issued buttons to identify members of the company union. The AASERE responded by issuing buttons of its own to identify legitimate union men. Those wearing the yellow union button quickly discovered that it singled them out for discrimination, verbal and even physical abuse. Nevertheless, public opinion was clearly in their favor. Passengers who encountered carmen wearing the blue company union button "in some cases would throw their nickel on the floor and in some instances spit on it before giving it to the conductor or throwing it on the floor."[60]

Unaware of the depth of commission complicity with the TCRT and backed by community support, the union appealed for redress to the Safety Commission. Numerous other Twin Cities unions also formally petitioned the governor to help the carmen.[61] In response to public outcry, the commission appointed a three-man advisory committee to investigate what had come to be called the "button war." The choice of appointees guaranteed the outcome before deliberations had even begun. Two Twin Cities businessmen, both alleged to be stockholders in the TCRT, and Samuel Kerfoot, president of Hamline University (an institution endowed by Thomas Lowry and whose president of the board of trustees was also a director of the Minneapolis Citizens Alliance), composed a report that delighted Horace Lowry. "In discretionary cases where the evidence was evenly balanced," they felt compelled to "resolve doubts in favor of the company." Indeed. They recommended the "total disuse and abandonment of buttons" and the outlawing of union activity on the company's property, stations, and cars. In effect, their recommendations would end the carmen's organizing drive.[62]

The Safety Commission endorsed these recommendations, giving them the force of law. More tellingly, it used the opportunity to enact a statewide "status quo" resolution. Commission spokesman John McGee, with his eye on breaking the unions, stated, "This is not a convenient time for agitation about abstract principles like Unionism or non-Unionism or the closed shop and the open shop. The great thing now is to have the work done." With a single stroke, the commission outlawed all strikes and organizing efforts throughout the state for the duration of the war. Not even the most conservative union member could accept such a devastating mandate. The carmen voted to defy the button order.[63]

Elated Minneapolis businessmen were unconcerned that the status quo order also applied to employers, since they had maintained the open shop almost universally throughout the city. They inundated the governor with congratulatory telegrams on his "wisdom and integrity" and prepared the Civilian Auxiliary for another expected union protest. Disgusted by the apparent ineptitude of St. Paul law enforcement in the October riots, they sent Minneapolis Auxiliary officer Edward Karow to train the St. Paul forces in riot-control techniques.[64]

Ramsey County sheriff John Wagener quickly sent Karow packing back to Minneapolis. St. Paul could handle its own affairs, he assured local authorities, then proceeded to ignore the situation. Surprisingly, Charles Ames backed Wagener's claim—the first sign that the St. Paul commissioner sensed the danger of a frontal attack on organized labor in his home town.[65] Perhaps Ames, attuned to the St. Paul labor movement, recognized an unfamiliar militancy among the unions as well as an enhanced solidarity. Though the organized crafts continued to keep their distance from the IWW, their attitude had perceptibly changed. By the end of October the *Advocate* proclaimed in boldface type, "BAD BOSSES HAVE CREATED THE IWW." Radicalism, it ominously warned, was the natural result of employers' "unreasonable hostility to unionism." Another troubling sign was the wholehearted support of the railroad brotherhoods for the striking carmen. A permanent alliance between the brotherhoods and the craft unions would add considerable muscle to the movement. The Minneapolis-conceived union busting strategy appeared to be backfiring. Instead of breaking the union movement, it might well lead the craft unions to expand their sights, most notably, to West Publishing itself. As the president of the city's largest unorganized workforce, Ames was already under constant attack in the union press. Conceivably, with backing from the organized trades, his workers might revolt.[66]

Moreover, Ames was distressingly aware that labor was moving closer to the Nonpartisan League which had donated $5,000 to the strike fund and strongly supported the workers' struggle. Ames was determined to destroy the League and Arthur Townley in particular, considering him "a dangerous man to be intrusted [*sic*] with such political leadership as he desires to secure." Most certainly, Townley was dangerous to the grain trust in which Ames was so deeply invested. With an insider's understanding of the social foundations of the labor movement in St. Paul and the business community's ambivalent assessment of the League, Ames was less confident than his Minneapolis peers that these oppositional movements would crumble under a two-pronged attack. He may have feared that a secondary campaign against organized labor would obstruct his primary objective of destroying the League.[67]

Ames also may have been influenced by his colleagues in the St. Paul Association to restore peace in the city. The threatened general sympathy strike would bring business to a standstill. Even those enterprises without union workers, such as West, would be hamstrung with so many essential functions of commerce controlled by organized labor. Last and definitely not the least of businessmen's worries, the street violence indicated an ominous breakdown of the social fabric and, into the bargain, was bad publicity for the "patriotic city." With the second Liberty Loan campaign just underway, the corps of elites who had dedicated so much effort to reconstructing the city's image could not afford to have the loan campaign sabotaged by embittered workers. Undoubtedly, Ames was under considerable local pressure to hold the Safety Commission and Horace Lowry in check.

A contemporary chronicle of the war cryptically noted that "back of them all [the patriotic enterprises] was the St. Paul Association, always a prime mover in the great war-time undertakings, and back of that, presumably, certain seldom named individuals, the sort of men who can manipulate the springs of public action without official position or publicity." The man best situated to "manipulate the springs of public action" and bring Horace Lowry into line was Louis Hill. Only Hill had the economic and political might to challenge the Minneapolis combine behind the Safety Commission. The streetcar workers, with a lucid understanding of where the power lay in St. Paul, petitioned Hill to intervene with the TCRT, as a company stockholder and as one deeply invested in the success of the Liberty Loan campaign and its effect on St. Paul's image.[68]

Under other circumstances, the heir to the Great Northern might have become involved in the dispute, but a local streetcar strike was small change in comparison to his present problems. Hill's attention was focused on the imminent likelihood that the government would seize control of the nation's rail system. Moreover, unlike his father, Louis was less dedicated to the day-to-day business of running a financial and railroad empire, let alone the gritty dynamics of labor relations. Instead, he preferred to travel or devote his energies to more lighthearted civic projects like the Winter Carnival or the Liberty Loan campaign. When in residence in St. Paul, Hill spent most of his time at North Oaks, his farm on the outskirts of the city, insulating himself from tiresome interactions with the city's small businessmen and certainly from its workers.[69] To the frustration of businessmen and workers alike, Hill remained aloof from the conflict, depriving St. Paul citizens of their most powerful potential advocate. Without the backing of Louis Hill, Charles Ames could only slightly influence the drama that was playing out in the city.

The TCRT, with the private endorsement of the Safety Commission, moved aggressively against the union carmen and intentionally pushed the situation toward a crisis. In what could only be interpreted as a declaration of all-out war, Lowry immediately locked out employees who continued to wear the union button and fired the president of the St. Paul local on a charge of "disobedience." Making it clear that he had no intention of rehiring union workers, Lowry advertised for replacements in the rural papers. When labor representatives attempted to protest his actions, they found themselves cooling their heels day after day in the governor's waiting room while company officials had free access to the governor and the commission. In a clear indication of how the deck was stacked, Safety Commissioner John McGee proposed to give union organizer Thomas Shine "twenty-four hours to get out of the state." Though the commission failed to pass McGee's proposal, the *Advocate* labeled the resolution "an insult to the whole manhood and citizenship of Minnesota."[70]

Therein lay the crux of the conflict for St. Paul union members. More than wages and hours were at issue, more than the right of a single union to organize. The *manner* in which they were treated was an affront to the dignity of workers, their position in the community, their citizenship, and their very identity. It was a question of respect. If city officials and local businessmen did not support them, then all the understandings constructed over decades were at an end.

City officials saw their working-class constituency eroding by the day. At a city council meeting in late November, fifteen hundred workingmen greeted the entrance of the mayor and councilmen in stony silence, then erupted in a "tremendous outburst of applause" for public works commissioner Oscar Keller, who alone had vigorously supported the striking workers against the TCRT. Speaking before the gathering, Keller declared what everyone in the room had come to realize: "The whole line of action had been arranged in advance by the street car company and the safety commission. . . . The minds of the commissioners were already made up." The commission's actions were "a direct challenge to every man, union and nonunion in St. Paul." What the councilman didn't say was that St. Paul elected officials had scarcely more influence than the city's union members. Though the mayor and councilmen unanimously voted to "compel the company to fulfill its obligations," in reality, without assistance from the state, there was little they could do.[71]

As the struggle wore on, it attracted increasing attention from national players with a stake in its outcome. The canny Samuel Gompers stepped in to announce that St. Paul had been chosen to host the 1918 National Convention of the AFL the following June—a coup for local boosters. The convention would be by far the largest ever captured by the city: nearly one thousand participants to occupy the city's hotels, dine in its restaurants, shop in its stores for a full two weeks—not to mention the national exposure. This appealing prospect gave local businessmen further incentive to end the strike and reestablish harmonious relations with the city's unions. The convention carried with it both a carrot and a stick: as interpreted by *Advocate* editor Cornelius Guiney, it was "a high compliment to our city" for its "public spirit, entire loyalty and sterling trade unionism of our people" — a compliment that clearly counterposed St. Paul against Minneapolis and one that could be rescinded if St. Paul businessmen turned against the city's unions.[72]

Still, local interests found themselves stymied as the Safety Commission continued to demonstrate that it answered to no authority but its own. Not even the president of the United States could bring it to heel. Woodrow Wilson, alarmed at the prospect of a general strike at a major transportation artery, appointed a federal mediator to intervene. The unions thankfully agreed, but Lowry refused to negotiate.[73] With the law of the state on his side, Lowry had no intention of giving ground. Governor Burnquist, answerable to Minneapolis business interests, was compelled to follow suit. In a wire to the labor secretary, he declared, "Interference at this time will simply result in an attempt to defy a duly constituted authority of Minnesota."[74]

The Safety Commission's open defiance of the president undermined whatever validity remained of its claims to patriotic purpose. Nonetheless, the commission retained the power ceded to it by the legislature—power enough, it seemed, to defy the federal government, let alone the local officials and businessmen of St. Paul. The *Union Advocate* was outraged; "HAS OUR GOVERNOR GONE MAD?" a headline read. In labor's estimation, Burnquist had shown himself "utterly unfit" for his office by trampling the arbitration offer "in the mire under his imperial feet." It was clear to the labor unions at last that no mediating authority would negotiate in their behalf.[75] Already near the boiling point, tensions in the city exploded.

On December 2, following a labor rally in a downtown park, several thousand frustrated working people vented their anger against the streetcar company by smashing windows, tearing up tracks, and attacking nonunion carmen. Superficially, the riot was a recurrence of the October melees, but the atmosphere in the biting December wind was noticeably different from the carnivalesque events of the autumn. Streetcar employees, out of work for over a month, had little cause for celebration; the city's working people who believed themselves betrayed by ineffectual local officials as well as state authorities, were in a serious mood. James Manahan, counsel for the Nonpartisan League and a speaker at the rally, recalled the "tense crowd of toilers." "These men are in earnest," he remembered thinking. "It means more than sympathy for the streetcar union. Each man is fighting for himself."[76]

The mayhem ran unchecked for four hours. Once again, the local police proved either unable or unwilling to restore order. Rather than protect TCRT property or its nonunion employees, they advised the fleeing carmen to remove the company numbers from their hats to avoid detection by the crowd. Sheriff Wagener ignored the company's demands to protect its property. Governor Burnquist finally resorted to calling out the local battalion of the Home Guard, but by the time it arrived on the scene, the rioters had largely dispersed. The damage was considerable: fifty disabled cars, forty injured men, countless tracks torn up, and car service completely suspended for the night.[77]

In Minneapolis, all had remained quiet. The Civilian Auxiliary, called out in force by Sheriff Langum, patrolled the streets, routed any "potential troublemak-

Fig. 32. Striking streetcar men attempted to claim the patriotic high ground in their struggle against the Twin City Rapid Transit Company, accusing both the company and the Public Safety Commission of undermining the war effort by refusing to negotiate. Courtesy of the Minnesota Historical Society.

ers," and "prodded people coming out of downtown union meetings." Outfitted in crisp, new uniforms, armed with .30 caliber rifles as well as riot sticks—and trained to use them—the businessmen's army followed its deployment plan to the letter. Streetcar bells clanged eerily in the bitter afternoon chill as the cars crisscrossed the city, unmolested on the empty streets.[78]

The renewed violence dismayed union leaders, who feared that public opinion might turn against them. Lowry and the Safety Commission had repeatedly accused the movement of disloyalty, claiming it was led by "I.W.W. agitators, pro-Germans, and toughs," who were in cahoots with the "deeply disloyal" Nonpartisan League. In the aftermath of the latest riot, union spokesmen once again insisted that organized workers took no part in the disorder. To federal officials, they repeatedly stressed that "the union men and women of St. Paul and Minneapolis . . . are intensely patriotic" and that they were fighting for "the rights of free citizen-

Fig. 33. Tension is apparent in the faces of listeners at the December 1917 strike rally in Rice Park. Courtesy of the Minnesota Historical Society.

ship" and democracy." Therein lay the justice of their claims. They feared, with reason, that the powers aligned against them would use the riot to as an excuse to step up their attack.[79]

Though speakers at the rally had urged listeners to leave peacefully, something ignited the simmering anger, and union leaders were suspicious that the explosion was not spontaneous. The *Advocate* reported:

> To many disinterested persons it looks as if the rioting was a grand stand play arranged in advance by the street car company and its friends to bolster up their failing cause, and some have even gone so far as to suspect that the company or some of its backers may have hired the rioters to make a disturbance and force the [Home] Guards into action.[80]

At the very least, Lowry had provided an inviting target by turning off the power to the St. Paul lines just as the meeting was breaking up, *before* the rioting commenced, "leaving its cars standing empty and dark on the tracks." Though the unions could not prove their suspicions, the *Advocate* claimed that Lowry had declared that "all he needed was to get the Home Guards out, as the company had $2,000,000 to spare to beat the unions and would spend that sum if necessary."[81]

If this was Lowry's strategy, it was stunningly successful. The Safety Commission, in consultation with the Minneapolis Civic and Commerce Association, took charge, for St. Paul law enforcement was either too inept or intransigent to handle the situation. Suspicious of where the local Home Guard's loyalties lay, the governor called out units from Austin, Red Wing, Mankato, Winona, Duluth, Faribault, Crookston, and Morris. More than four thousand merchant and businessmen civilian soldiers enthusiastically boarded trains to put down what was called by the Guard "the War of St. Paul."[82]

It was war indeed. By Monday morning, the city was under virtual martial law. The governor suspended Sheriff Wagener, elected by the citizens of Ramsey County, for dereliction of duty, and the commission moved swiftly against prominent labor supporters who had spoken at the rally preceding the riot. James Manahan, city commissioner Oscar Keller, and St. Paul state representative Thomas McGrath were arrested and indicted for "inciting a riot and sedition." Authorities refused to consider 180 witnesses prepared to testify that the speakers had urged the crowd to leave the meeting peacefully. No inquiry was made into the TCRT's possible role in the episode.[83]

These draconian—and legally questionable—measures may have restored order for the moment, but they did nothing to cool tempers in a city teetering on the verge of a general strike. Working people defended their champions by calling on the claims of local loyalty and self-government against an autocratic and unconstitutional state authority. The St. Paul Association, desperate to put an end to the turmoil in the streets, had made a grave tactical error by urging the governor to suspend Wagener. Working people responded with a petition bearing twenty thousand signatures demanding his reinstatement, declaring that Wagener "was suspended without cause at the request of some twenty-one business representatives under the cloak of the St. Paul Association. . . . He was born and reared in St. Paul, has faithfully filled many public offices, and has always been a law-abiding citizen; the man appointed to fill his place is practically unknown to the people of St. Paul." In local parlance, the suspension of the popular and well-known local sheriff in favor of an "outsider" was an affront in itself, but the new sheriff quickly provided other concrete reasons for union supporters to demand his dismissal. No sooner did he assume office than he threatened to "start a reign of terror that would never be forgotten if there should be any rioting" and predicted there would be "many funerals in union homes."[84]

The civic compact seemed irreparably broken. Class loyalties now defined the political terrain. When the cases of Manahan, Keller, and McGrath came to trial, Ramsey County judge Frederick Dickson, elected by the people of St. Paul and faced with sixteen hundred witnesses eager to testify on the defendants' behalf, dismissed the charges out of hand. In Dickson's opinion, Manahan was guilty only of sympathy for union labor, which, in St. Paul at least, was "a good thing." His worst offense, the judge wryly observed, was in calling the Safety Commission a bunch of "pinheads," an estimation with which the judge seemed to concur. The Nonpartisan League, the Farmers' Equity Co-operative Exchange, and local politicians joined with Twin Cities unionists to honor labor's vindicated heroes with a victory banquet at the Ryan Hotel. The evening's speeches celebrated the "triumph of justice over venom" and decried the Safety Commission's disloyalty to the war effort and abuse of its powers.[85] The *Dispatch*, pro-business to the core, expressed a different opinion of the verdict, declaring the dismissal a gross miscarriage of justice, "merely an admission that the influences which operate for harm in such a case are so subtle that it is extremely difficult to enforce the spirit of the law, and at the same time, adhere to its letter."[86]

Judging from the subsequent careers of the defendants, the voters of St. Paul agreed with Judge Dickson rather than with the *Dispatch*. McGrath won reelection to the House in 1918; Keller was elected to Congress in a special election in 1919; and Manahan retained an untarnished reputation as a defender of the common people. With political positions hardening, the mediating structures of community had come unglued, and local politicians and hopefuls found it increasingly difficult to straddle the class divide. Mayor Vivan Irvin, dismayed to find himself stripped of most of his powers, endorsed the union cause. Irvin, a wholesale grocer and a Republican into the bargain—precarious credentials in the present climate—declared himself "a business man, not, however, a business man who is opposed to organized labor." "You people . . . are fighting for your rights," and the mayor, for one, offered his full support.[87]

As the city became increasingly polarized, complex factors determined where loyalties would lie. This was not a simple case of business versus labor. Instead, it was a much more fractured story, one in which several levels of coercion operated to complicate the social dynamics. Organized businessmen wavered, giving support to one side and then the other, partly because the ground was shifting beneath their feet, and partly because they were divided among themselves. Certain influential members of the St. Paul Association clearly supported the commission and urged the governor to suspend Sheriff Wagener—in what proved to be a major tactical error. The Association also initially opposed federal intervention in the streetcar dispute, affirming its "absolute confidence" in the Safety Commission to handle the matter.[88] But allegiances were not as simple as they might seem.

St. Paul businessmen were bound to the Safety Commission in multiple ways that made them helpless to stop it from destroying either the image or the working relationships of the city. The commission controlled fuel and labor allocations, transportation priorities, and virtually every aspect of commerce in the city. It also had the demonstrated power to supersede local government. And as it had shown repeatedly, it could at will assume authority in a myriad of unspecified areas.

In its quest to advance local interests, the St. Paul Association had gone into partnership with the commission, an arrangement that was proving increasingly costly. The array of wartime committees and events the organization was expected to manage and finance was seemingly endless, along with responsibility for the Liberty Loan drives and the recruitment and outfitting of the Home Guard.[89] The man-hours required to meet the demands were staggering, as were the out-of-pocket costs to Association members. The businessmen discovered early on that they had boxed themselves into a corner. It was simply impossible to refuse a commission "request" without calling one's loyalty into question, with the attendant consequences.

Only the railroad executives dared to question or refuse a commission request. With the roads under federal management, the Safety Commission had no club to wield against railroad officials. Moreover, the Hill family remained the most powerful financial interest in the state. Thus, the Safety Commission's correspondence with the Great Northern and Northern Pacific bore an almost obsequious tone, offering "hearty thanks" and apologies for the "good deal of trouble" its requests might cause company officers. The railroads' insulated position also allowed Great Northern president W. P. Kenney, to refuse a request for funds to outfit Home Guard troops.[90]

Other businessmen did not have similar latitude. For example, when St. Paul Association secretary E. M. McMahon asked reimbursement for a printing bill "done by the Association at [commission] request (or order if you wish)," he was informed that the "civic bodies" in Minneapolis and in Duluth had covered such expenses as a patriotic contribution. Thus, it had been presumed that "you would rather take care of it in your office." The unspoken implications were clear. The Association paid the bill, and McMahon apologetically promised, "I shall try to see to it in the future that no bills are sent to the Commission which should properly be taken care of here."[91]

As the months rolled on, bill piled upon bill, and Association coffers and enthusiasms were equally depleted. But the commission was too powerful to deny. This is not to suggest that city businessmen were covert union allies. On the contrary, they were no more enamored of organized labor than were their counterparts in any other city. City leaders were genuinely outraged and frightened by the riots, the destruction of private property, and the disruption of business. All things being equal, they probably would have preferred that the unions disappear into the Mississippi River. But they were also faced with national publicity of the worst sort, armed soldiers patrolling the streets, the imminent prospect of a city-wide sympathy strike and, along with it, the possible loss of the biggest convention St. Paul had ever hosted. A negotiated peace with reasonable labor unions had served them well for more than two decades and was certainly preferable to the present state of affairs. According to the *Union Advocate*, "Some of the most prominent and broad-minded men in the Association" privately urged the governor to accept federal mediation "as the easiest and most graceful way out of the difficulty," but they were overruled by others "whose narrow vision was more in line with [the governor's] own."[92]

Independent contractors, retailers, and other smaller businessmen, dependent on working-class patronage or taxed to the limit by patriotic mandates, were most sympathetic to labor's struggle. The major businessmen—those who were recipients of war contracts and dependent on the commission's good will to keep their operations running—understandably were most reluctant to incur its enmity. Thus, divided in its own ranks, the St. Paul Association was unable to resolve a situation that had spun out of local control. With every move, however, the businessmen were drawn further into the commission's orbit. Yet, neither obedient complicity with the state nor an appeal to federal authority seemed likely to extricate them from the mess they were in.

Perhaps moral authority would have more command. In St. Paul, the preeminent figure in this arena was indisputably Archbishop John Ireland. Though Ireland regularly involved himself in every aspect of city life, he had remained uncharacteristically aloof from the present labor conflict. Ireland's reluctance to involve himself may well have stemmed from his own troubled history with the TCRT. His disastrous partnership with Tom Lowry in the 1890s had nearly bankrupted the archdiocese and caused the archbishop great personal humiliation. As the ultimate cost, it had made him financially subject to the oversight of James J. Hill—a circumstance that, no doubt, rankled still. In sum, the archbishop's association with the TCRT had bequeathed an assortment of very unpleasant consequences. All of this must have left Ireland with few friendly feelings for the streetcar monopoly. A quarter century had passed, and Jim Hill was in his grave. Still, in St. Paul, where the past was never far from mind, John Ireland had no desire to rekindle memories of his follies with the TCRT. As an old man in failing health, he may have hoped his battles were behind him. But with the return of rioting in December, he felt driven to act.

The *Catholic Bulletin*, official voice of the archdiocese, had remained silent on the strike throughout the autumn as Catholic workers took their cause to the streets. But after the December riot, the *Bulletin* issued an unusually stern rebuke and warning, which the archbishop surely had authorized. After prefacing its proclamation with the disclaimer that "we have nothing to do" with the controversy itself, the *Bulletin* proceeded to denounce the "open violence and attack upon citizens and property such as characterized the actions of the St. Paul hoodlums last Sunday." The "abominable scenes of destruction" destroyed the reputation of St. Paul, which, "as represented by its better element, has presented to the nation a rare example of steadfast loyalty and devotion to law and order." Even worse, such disgraceful conduct stained the reputation of the city's Catholics. As the *Bulletin* declared, "The corruption of the good is the rottenest kind of corruption." "Every Catholic," it warned, "who engages in or contributes to such unlawful violence is guilty of mortal sin."[93]

The *Bulletin* saved its most damning assessments for "certain cheap politicians" who inflamed the minds of the workingmen. The Catholic "cup of shame" was filled to overflowing to "witness the disgusting servility, the cowardly sacrifice of duty presented by certain public officials . . . [who] grasped the opportunity to curry favor with the worst elements of the city." Though the culprits went unnamed, it was common knowledge that Manahan, McGrath, and Keller were Catholics all, as were Chief O'Connor and Sheriff Wagener. Then came the heart of the diatribe: "It is precisely such action on the part of prominent men, who are Catholics, that often draws the fire which our enemies are ever willing to level against the Church."[94]

No doubt this rebuke was generated in part by pressure from prominent businessmen, Catholic and non-Catholic alike. But it also sprang from deeper roots in the philosophy that had guided Ireland for more than thirty years. The church affirmed its value to society as "the great prop of social order." Certainly, this had proven true in St. Paul since its days as a frontier village. If prominent Catholics as well as working-class congregants defied Church authority, the stature of the institution itself was in danger.

In the present atmosphere of suspicion, the church was in a particularly vulnerable position. Though no local institution worked harder to prove its patriotic mettle, still the Catholic Church was home to the majority of the city's Germans. For some patriots at least, egged on by Safety Commission propaganda, anti-German and anti-Catholic prejudice mingled in a volatile combination. In November, the rectory of German St. Agnes parish was blown to bits in an explosion that rocked the surrounding Frogtown neighborhood. When apprehended, the bomber declared his "hatred of the Catholic Church." The *Catholic Bulletin* reassured its readers that "the police believe that the man is demented." Perhaps so; nonetheless, for the archbishop, placed under protective guard after the incident, it was an acute reminder that the church still had its enemies. Despite his personal distaste for the streetcar company, the archbishop could not afford to have the church put at risk by unruly Catholic workers who might alienate its influential allies.[95]

How this played out in the individual parishes is open to speculation. Though no records remain, local pastors in working-class neighborhoods may have had more sympathetic words for their embattled parishioners. On the other hand, the narrow escape of St. Agnes's pastor may have caused them to consider their words carefully. But whatever sentiments they expressed within parish boundaries, no public statements of support were forthcoming. John Ireland ran a tight ship. The priests who served the city parishes had nearly all been groomed in the St. Paul Seminary, acculturated from boyhood to the archbishop's authority. Thus, Ireland's priests seldom raised their voices in public opposition to ecclesiastical policy.[96]

Very likely, working-class parishioners were less tractable than the parish priests. Though Catholicism ran deep, the content of workers' faith was interpreted within the social context of their lives. When the archbishop aligned himself so clearly with the St. Paul Association and the Safety Commission, his class bias was painfully apparent to Catholic working people. The *Bulletin,* perhaps fearing a class-inspired backlash, pulled out all the stops to maintain the Church's authority. "Any Catholic," it thundered, "who takes part in an unlawful attack upon citizens or property and suffers death as a result of such participation will be deprived the right of a Christian burial."[97] This was a drastic warning, calculated to give even the most militant Catholic pause. Though it is impossible to gauge the internal effect of this dire pronouncement, some working-class churchgoers undoubtedly took the warning to heart; others, feeling betrayed by their church as well as their community, may have responded with empty pews at Sunday Mass. Rioting did not recur, but workers showed no lessening of resolve or belief in the moral authority of their cause. Above all, this episode demonstrated to them that the Catholic Church as well as the local business community had irrevocably, if reluctantly, crossed the class divide.

Undisturbed by the polarization of local St. Paul politics, the governor and Safety Commission spokesman John McGee used the December riot to buttress their case against federal intervention. In light of the recent riot, McGee argued, "reopening of the decision . . . would be an incentive to further riots and agitation." The commission tenaciously held to its claim that "the Street Car controversy . . . was stirred up for political purposes by agents of the Nonpartisan League." McGee and Ames had repeatedly characterized the League as far more dangerous than the IWW—an assessment that was essentially correct, though not for the reasons that they proffered.[98]

The commission presented a unified public face, yet privately, dissension among its members was growing. McGee was becoming bolder and more fanatical; Burnquist echoed the position of his Minneapolis supporters. Lind and Ames, however, had increasing reservations about the commission's excesses, each for his own reasons. But, as they were about to discover, not even the lofty title of Commissioner gave them license to question the course that had been set.

The commission's general lack of "business efficiency" and common sense was a growing irritant to business-minded Charles Ames. Most specifically, Lowry's campaign against the union was exacting too high a price. The imminent general strike would cost Ames and his fellow members of the St. Paul Association dearly.[99] Even more worrisome to the commissioner, every day that the conflict dragged on, labor moved closer to the Nonpartisan League. To Ames's frustration, the commission seemed blind to the dangers of this alliance, even though the national press had noted the warning signs. *Survey* magazine observed, "Of seeming unimportance in itself, this [general] strike . . . is of national significance because of its implications and the possibility of the amalgamation of the labor and agrarian groups into a powerful political machine."[100]

While in Washington on private business, Ames urged the governor to allow him to discuss mediation with the secretary of war. Burnquist categorically refused, but Ames, convinced of the folly of the commission's stance, disregarded the order and met with federal officials on his own authority. To Ames's shock and chagrin, when

Burnquist learned of the meeting, he fired off a telegram dismissing Ames from the commission. Since the governor seldom made a move without McGee's approval, it may be assumed that McGee was behind this measure, settling what may have been a longer, ongoing argument with Ames over management of the situation in St. Paul.[101]

McGee turned his sights on Commissioner Lind the following day. Lind had shown no qualms about hunting down and eradicating "radicals" but repeatedly expressed reservations about other commission targets. He had built a valued reputation as "a friend to labor," a stance that was anathema to McGee. Moreover, he had embarrassed McGee publicly by scoffing at his claim that the state was riddled with German subversives.[102] As the months passed and McGee's power grew, so did Lind's aversion to his crude tactics of repression. Priding himself as Minnesota's foremost statesman, Lind also felt personally compromised by McGee's open contempt for President Wilson and his cabinet. The final straw came on December 5 when McGee, infuriated by Thomas Van Lear's public criticism of the commission, proposed to remove both the Minneapolis mayor and his chief of police from office. Lind blocked the action as both imprudent and illegal, enraging McGee, who then let loose a verbal barrage of abuse aimed at his fellow commissioner. According to Lind, McGee called him "everything vile you can think of before the committee— with the governor in the chair." This personal affront apparently moved the high-minded Lind more than any of the larger injustices he had tacitly permitted despite his qualms. He walked out of the chamber and never returned.[103]

As Lind and McGee were going head to head at the capitol building, only blocks away an estimated fifteen thousand persons gathered at the auditorium to demand federal intervention in the streetcar controversy. Pointedly, workers left their jobs to attend the "protest convention." Trades and Labor Assembly president James Clancy warned that though this was not a formal general strike, if the federal government did not act, "the issue will be placed in the hands of the rank and file of union labor." Lest his meaning be unclear, he continued, "I hope federal arbitration comes quickly. It may be difficult to restrain the men if the convention reconvenes."[104]

In Washington, smarting with humiliation at his dismissal, Charles Ames must have taken cold comfort from reports of the meeting. His worst fears were confirmed. James Manahan, sympathetic "representative of the organized farmers of the Northwest" and now the favorite of the labor movement as well, reiterated the sentiments that had caused his arrest three days earlier. Other Nonpartisans also joined labor leaders at the podium to express their support for labor's cause. Several speakers excoriated Horace Lowry, "the czar of the Twin Cities Rapid Transit Company," and "the union haters" of the Public Safety Commission. The mayors of both cities added words of sympathy. The audience cheered as a union organizer proclaimed that the men and women of the union movement had no need for the IWW to agitate them to action. "The persons in the present movement have five Ws in their title, which is: 'We Won't Work, Will We, Until This Trouble is Settled?' " If federal mediators did not arrive within the week, the strike would be on. To cap off the show of solidarity, the gathered protesters appointed a committee of labor leaders and Nonpartisan representatives to discuss the formation of a "permanent organization." The dreaded farmer-labor alliance was at hand.[105]

Secretary of War Newton Baker, alarmed about the effect a general strike would have on the war effort, pressed the commission to accept a special mediation committee. McGee, however, imperiously informed him that "the trouble is practically over now and will not be serious unless interference from Washington should revive it." Burnquist, in turn, offered assurance that he had the problem in hand and that soon all would be resolved. To prove his sensitivity to the situation, he disingenuously claimed to have dismissed Ames because he was "obnoxious to Union labor"; as another conciliatory gesture, the governor pointed out, he had appointed commission secretary and lifelong union man Henry Libby to replace Ames. Appearances were never more deceiving. For the first and probably only time in his career, Ames had earned favorable comment in the union press for his actions in Washington. As for Libby, the commission secretary had already proved himself a company rather than a union man—a "Pecksniffian self-seeker and obsequious lick-spittle of official power," in the words of the *Union Advocate*. His brothers in the Winona machinists' lodge celebrated Libby's new position by expelling him from the union by a vote of fifty-nine to two. In short, no hope of reconciliation was on the horizon, and as the clock ticked toward the appointed hour, the unions and the state squared off for another battle.[106]

At ten A.M. on December 13, the strike commenced. By noon, ten thousand Twin Cities workers had left their jobs. Union leaders anticipated the number to rise to thirty thousand by day's end. At last, with a general strike underway, the government stepped in with a promise to dispatch the president's Mediation Commission immediately to the Twin Cities. Telegram from Washington in hand, MFL president E. G. Hall called off the strike less than four hours after it had begun. Notably, not a single case of violence had been reported. Buoyed by the promise of federal help, union leaders signed a pledge to forego any further sympathy strikes. That was a fatal miscalculation.[107]

"Glory hallelujah!" declared the *Advocate*. "Democracy and personal liberty still live in the United States." Union supporters heaved a collective sigh of relief. Though they had maintained a united front, no one had been happy about the prospect of a strike, especially with Christmas approaching. The locked-out carmen, now in desperate economic straits, wanted only to return to their jobs in peace. The other unions, which for months had generously supported the carmen's relief fund, were facing the winter season, always notoriously slow for the building trades. Their finances would be stretched, even without the burden of a sympathy strike. The railroad shopmen maintained their new solidarity with fellow local unionists, but they only reluctantly agreed to strike, noting that "neither the railroad shopmen nor organized labor in general had any grievance against the railroads." In all, the organized workers of the Twin Cities had been pushed into a strike that no one wanted, and they readily welcomed President Wilson's efforts on their behalf.[108]

The victory celebration was sadly premature. As the subsequent months of negotiations proved, the federal government had only been stalling for time, with neither the power nor the will to enforce compliance with its recommendations. Working people's initial enthusiasm gave way to deep disillusionment as Lowry and the Safety Commission defied the Mediation Board's recommendations for what, in real terms, was an extremely small compromise. Specific union demands had shrunk to very modest proportions: the right to belong to a union and wear a union button without fear of discrimination, and the reinstatement of men fired for union membership. Had Lowry capitulated, these concessions would not have compromised the open shop either in the TCRT or in Minneapolis. But Lowry and the Safety Commission had a more ambitious agenda: to break the union movement across the board.[109]

The open-shop businessmen of Minneapolis and the Safety Commission knew what was hidden from the ordinary citizens on the street: federal officials had no power to counteract the Safety Commission's authority. Even in wartime, the Wilson administration had relied on what historian David Kennedy described as the substitution of "aroused passion for political authority . . . persuasion, propaganda, and the purposeful fueling of patriotic fires . . . [rather than] unilateral exercises of government power." The regime of repression that weighed so heavily on Minnesotans, though it was driven by specific local circumstances, was made possible by the policies of a weak national state.[110]

That weakness became glaringly apparent as the months passed. Secretary of Labor William Wilson arrived in St. Paul, as promised, and declaimed on democracy and justice to an appreciative audience of more than eight thousand working people.[111] But even as they joined in singing the national anthem and gave three rousing cheers for the United States, Horace Lowry and the Safety Commission put the mediators on notice that they would not be bound by their decision. When the president's commission published its findings in February, recommending that the company should rescind the button order, rehire the fired carmen, and not discriminate against union members, Lowry ignored them. Compliance, he declared, "would be imposing a gross in-justice" on those loyal employees who had provided a "public service" throughout the controversy. Commissioner McGee, who by now had superseded the governor as commission spokesman, was blunt. In his estimation, the president's commission was composed of "union labor men and socialists." Furthermore, he added, "There is no power on earth that can budge me one inch from following the path of duty as I see it." Apparently, he was correct.[112]

As the discussions dragged on and the unions waited in vain for relief, their grievances disappeared into official limbo. Since they had pledged to forego any further sympathy strikes, they had become no more than observers to their fate. The ineffectual mediators cooled working-class faith in a government that seemed unable to act in their behalf. To workers, this was yet another level of betrayal, and patriotic enthusiasm was ebbing fast.

The troubles in St. Paul were part of a much larger pattern that deeply distressed President Wilson and his advisers. The war required maximum efficiency and uninterrupted production at whatever price. Yet, in 1917 the Labor Department recorded 4,450 strikes—more than in any single previous year. Clearly, the government had to take a more forceful hand. Thus, in March 1918, the National War Labor Board (NWLB) was instituted to assuage labor militancy and control employers like Lowry who, according to a frustrated member of the mediation commission, had "put [himself] squarely on record in opposition to the war policies of our government." Though the NWLB granted unions little real power, at the very least it guaranteed their right to exist. That alone was enough to stir the Safety Commission to action.[113]

Intending to forestall NWLB interference, Governor Burnquist reconvened the moribund state board of arbitration. The streetcar men, trapped in the morass of state and federal bureaucracy, submitted their grievances once more to the state. Spring gave way to summer, and still they had no resolution. When the board finally awarded the union a partial victory in June, ordering the company to rehire "desirable" men at their previous wage rate and level of seniority while conveniently sidestepping the question of union membership, Lowry again refused to comply. The Safety Commission, with no pretense of impartiality, calmly ignored Lowry's defiance of state authority.[114]

The carmen's case had been shuffled from the state arbitration board to the Safety Commission to the president's Mediation Commission and back to the arbitration board. Facing another blind alley, the weary union men saw no alternative but to appeal to the federal government once again. The NWLB took the case under advisement, where it languished for the duration of the war. On November 22, 1918, immediately following the armistice, the board ruled that it had no jurisdiction and returned the case to the state. The Great War had ended, and with it ended the government's incentive to advocate for workers' rights. So also ended the "War of St. Paul." The open shop had won the day.

In the final months of the Great War, the people of St. Paul were well schooled in the uses and abuses of power. Once Lind and Ames had departed from the Public Safety Commission, John McGee wielded undisputed authority. His fanaticism gained national attention when he testified before the Senate Military Committee in April 1918. Announcing that the U.S. attorney "lacks a fighting stomach," he recommended that civil courts be replaced by military courts martial, since "you can't depend on juries." The civil courts, he said, were infected with "chicken-hearted judges . . . incompetent, inefficient, lazy, cowardly prosecuting attorneys and seditious and disloyal elements in the population from which juries are drawn." Furthermore, he advised the stunned senators, "Where we made a mistake was in not establishing a firing squad in the first days of the war. Now we should get busy and have that firing squad working overtime." Tellingly, he noted, "If we had throughout the state judges like those in Hennepin County [Minneapolis] . . . the situation . . . would be very much improved."[115]

The senators sat speechless, but at home in Minnesota, where the mantle of repression pressed on every aspect of daily life, none of this news was surprising. Minnesotans knew from experience that no mechanism existed, either at the state or federal level—let alone by local authority—to bring the Safety Commission under control. As grossly understated by commission attorney Ambrose Tighe, "The ruthlessness of the Commission's procedure shows if further evidence was required, how dangerous it is to vest even good men with arbitrary power."[116]

The "good men" of the Safety Commission, with their increasingly draconian mandates, alienated an ever greater number of the state's citizens. Faced with an accompanying decline in patriotic enthusiasm, the commission, under McGee's direction, simply tightened the screws. In St. Paul, where wholesale discontent had found an outlet in the streetcar riots, the commission brought in military and paramilitary forces to maintain support for the war effort as well as to break the carmen's union.

Authorities had used charges of draft evasion sporadically throughout the war to harass immigrants and working people, but by March 1918, in Minneapolis they had refined the tactic with regular, large-scale "slacker roundups," orchestrated by the Safety Commission and carried out by the American Protective League (APL). Apparently, the St. Paul APL lacked the fighting spirit of the Minneapolis chapter, which temporarily protected St. Paul working people from such organized harassment. But in May, a "work-or-fight" order issued by the National Selective Service Board proved a boon for Safety Commission aims. The order moved unemployed men to the top of the draft lists, making unemployed workers (including the locked-out carmen) legitimate quarries to be hunted down along with draft evaders. With a federal mandate, the commission could call on the Department of Justice to bolster laggard local forces. In July, Justice Department officers led two battalions of the Home Guard and local APL members in a citywide sweep. They scoured hotels, saloons, poolrooms, parks, theaters, the YMCA, and the railroad stations—anywhere working-class men might congregate. Fifteen hundred men were transported to the armory for questioning and fifty-one deposited in the county jail to be either inducted or incarcerated. To working-class St. Paulites, the city itself seemed to be under siege.[117]

For the organized businessmen, hoping yet to repair the civic compact, the raids must have been equally unwelcome intrusions. The patriotic enterprise had become a millstone of enormous proportions. The railroads, extricating themselves from onerous "public-spirited" financial obligations, withdrew from membership in the St. Paul Association, depriving the organization of $4,000 in annual dues. Other businessmen, however, could not free themselves from patriotic arm twisting so easily. Nonetheless, they had increasing reason to question the role they were asked to play. Their association with the commission was deeply alienating to the city's working people; moreover, the anticipated war contracts had materialized only for a few of the city's largest enterprises. Smaller manufacturers who lacked the productive capacity to be considered essential industries—the majority of those in St. Paul—instead found their operations curtailed. In response to a nationwide fuel crisis, they were ordered to reduce operations rather than gear up for the war effort. St. Paul's meager flour mills received a directive to operate no more than two days a week. Yet, the booming Minneapolis industrial complex appeared to be swimming in wartime profits. An undercurrent of dissatisfaction was surfacing in Association meetings, and by the spring of 1918, members had begun to refuse expenditure approval for some commission "requests."[118]

Faced with an increasingly hostile public, McGee and Burnquist relied ever more openly on coercion. Prospects were not good for the third Liberty Loan campaign, launched in April. Though the St. Paul Association once again marshaled its members to run the operation, given the clear signs of discontent, the commission dared not trust even the business community to back the loan drive wholeheartedly. Thus, a committee of bankers was appointed to estimate the "proper share" for men "of some means," who were then informed of their expected contribution. Over the objection of local Liberty Loan workers, who argued that "those most able to subscribe would be incensed by such high-handed methods," the plan was put into action. Prospects who balked at forced subscription might receive the following letter:

> It has been reported to Liberty Loan Headquarters that you refused to buy any Liberty Bonds. The report coming from authentic sources leads us to believe that you are apparently able to do so. Before reporting this to Washington, the Committee desires to be fair with you and if you have any statements to make, you may do so by calling Liberty Loan Headquarters.[119]

If middle-class people were becoming reluctant patriots, voluntary contributions were even more difficult to wring from workers in the embattled city. The ailing archbishop did his best to stir Catholic loyalties, composing an episcopal letter to be read in parish pulpits. "A Catholic community without the record of having subscribed its full quota of this loan would be a dishonor to the Catholic Church. . . . Let there be no such community in the Archdiocese of St. Paul," he pleaded.[120] But in the wake of the intracommunity battles, neither the archbishop nor the business leaders of the loan drive carried much persuasive power in working-class neighborhoods.

Undaunted by the poor voluntary showing, the Safety Commission initiated raids to ferret out loan "slackers" as well as draft evaders. Deputized loan workers stopped working people and immigrants on the street, demanding proof of Liberty Bond purchase. Anyone who could not provide the proof was presumed to be an enemy alien or, at the very least, disloyal. The only way to escape further investigation was to purchase a bond.[121] By the fourth campaign, the Safety Commission went even farther, issuing subpoena forms to its county agents for use in compelling "delinquents to appear to answer all necessary questions." As a testament to the power of the politics of fear, every Liberty Loan campaign ultimately exceeded its subscription goal in St. Paul.[122]

In the sanguine assessment of one contemporary chronicle, "If actual resentment was felt here and there it found little public expression." But public silence was a poor measure of private opinion under the Safety Commission's regime. In September, F. W. Premer, a manager for the prestigious St. Paul Fire and Marine Insurance Company, discovered that no criticism was so petty as to go unnoticed. Premer was accosted at his office in front of fifty employees by a Safety Commission agent, who accused him of singing German songs in his home and "belittling the Red Cross." The outraged manager complained of his treatment to the Bureau of Investigation and the U.S. attorney but found that neither authority had the power to reprimand the Safety Commission—a lesson assuredly not lost on his fellow businessmen.[123]

With McGee at the helm of the commission, even men of influence in the city knew they were unprotected from accusations of disloyalty. Samuel Dittenhofer, owner of the Golden Rule Department Store, treasurer of the St. Paul Association, and chairman of the St. Paul chapter of the Red Cross, generously gave time and money to Association projects in support of the war effort. He had turned over his show windows for patriotic displays and donated space in the store for recruiting stations and a Red Cross booth. Still, he was powerless to object when a detail of Marines carried out a slacker raid in his establishment, harassing his customers and demanding proof that they had purchased Liberty Bonds.[124]

By mid-1918, it was clear to city businessmen and politicians, as well to its working people, that they no longer had a voice in the direction of their city. In light of the power that could be brought to bear against them, they made only weak attempts to repair the social damage and bided their time, waiting for the commission's mandate to expire with the armistice. Meanwhile, the unions gamely struggled on, though their hopes were fading. Holding fast to the claims of civic accountability, they chided local officials. Streetcar service, they maintained, had become deplorable. Moreover, the cars, operated by ill-trained strike breakers recruited from the countryside, frequently jumped the tracks, barreling into nearby buildings and unwary pedestrians. Why, the Trades and Labor Assembly asked, did the city council "hesitate and dodge" rather than protect "the rights, the comfort, the convenience and the general welfare of the citizens and taxpayers of St. Paul?" Why, indeed. The unpalatable truth, as the council ruefully had come to learn, was that without intervention by the state, the council was powerless to intervene.[125]

As the war ground to an end at home, St. Paulites surveyed the social wreckage of their city and feared the world would never be the same, certainly not the world they had constructed within the closed confines of St. Paul. While the carmen's case wound on through the waning months of the war, city leaders had time to reflect on the course they had taken. Lured by visions of profit and prestige, they had made their city a pawn in a game where they were only marginal players. To their regret, they had learned that St. Paul was expendable in this larger scheme.

Ironically, however, though the "War of St. Paul" had mercilessly battered the city, it also had an impact that far outweighed the outcome of a single labor dispute in an unimportant mid-sized city. The very qualities that caused Minneapolis power brokers to dismiss St. Paul as a parochial backwater were the essential catalyst that would eventually change the political landscape of the state, humbling the Minneapolis business establishment in the process. In Minneapolis, where social conflict was a daily fact of life, powerful business interests did not hesitate to use whatever methods were necessary to maintain the established order. The wartime campaign of repression was merely an opportune extension of previous practices. But in St. Paul, where economic survival depended on cooperation, civil society did not adjust easily to the new order imposed from outside the city. When the streetcar controversy erupted, it was St. Paul, home of "conservative" unionism, that provided the social space for protest, rather than Minneapolis, where worker discontent and radicalism were closely monitored and forcibly suppressed. St. Paul was unprepared to deal with open conflict in the streets, psychologically as well as militarily. But, at the same time, workers were culturally armed to act by the sense of entitlement and outrage they derived from rights embedded in a long-standing civic compact.

The riots that shook St. Paul, and the rallies, demonstrations, and trials that followed, created a public drama with rare political potential. Not only did they bring together the powerful railroad brotherhoods and the AFL unions in an unprecedented alliance; they also served to transform Minneapolis and St. Paul unionists from rivals to allies. Most important, they created a public forum for the Nonpartisan League to demonstrate its support and thereby bring workers into its camp. With generous cash contributions and particularly with the indictment of James Manahan for his support of the carmen, the League had fused the interests of farmers and labor. As Trades and Labor President James Clancy noted, "We in the city didn't know what the Nonpartisan League was until we held a banquet . . . for Messrs. Manahan, Keller and McGrath, in celebration of their release from the indictment brought against them for observing the right of free speech in Rice Park."[126]

As the Public Safety Commission continued its pursuit of the League throughout the course of the war, branding Townley and his associates as traitors on the flimsiest of charges, the parallels with its attack on the unions became only too apparent.[127] Domestic battles on the homefront reformulated working-class definitions of loyalty and patriotism. Trade union leader William Mahoney, who became a founder of the Farmer-Labor Party, described the window of political opportunity that had opened. Before the streetcar strike, he explained, "Organized labor in general felt some scruples against aligning itself with the League on account of the taint of disloyalty that the politicians and newspapers had fastened on it." During the strike, however, St. Paul unionists found that while traditional avenues of mediation crumbled—the Democratic politicians who ran city hall, local business connections, and even the Catholic Church—the League had proved their staunchest ally. "This fact," according to Mahoney, "made it easy to induce co-operation, although it involved a departure from organized labor's traditional course; it meant the launching of an independent political course."[128]

Within the city, the Safety Commission's machinations had undone decades of work to nurture cross-class relationships. Even the anti-German campaign, which in large part had been a mask to hide the commission's true agenda, had unanticipated results. Between 1910 and 1920, nearly seven thousand residents of German birth and fifteen hundred of Austrian birth disappeared from the census rolls, declines of 49 and 38 percent, respectively from 1910 census figures. Though some attrition was due to death, a report sponsored by the St. Paul City Planning Board admitted that most of the decline was undoubtedly due to the hostile wartime climate. Quite likely, however, the drastic drop in numbers reflected a reinvention of cultural self-identity more than actual outmigration.[129] In other words, many German St. Paulites, who had once proudly embraced their ethnic distinctiveness, now either concealed or discarded their German heritage, partly as a conscious choice and partly because the social organization of their lives had been radically transformed. Forced to abandon many of the ethnic associations and cultural practices, including language, that had defined the German ethnic community, the separate world of the German working class had come undone. With the *Tagliche Volkszeitung* driven into bankruptcy by the commission's harassment, the teaching of German banned from the St. Paul school curriculum, German teachers dismissed from their posts, and German saloons and beer gardens forced out of business, the ethnic fabric that had supported German separatism unraveled.[130]

This pattern was repeated in cities across the country. The distinctive culture of *Deutschtum* that had bonded Germans together across class emerged from the war as only a weak shadow of its former robust self. One scholar of German ethnicity has argued that "the German-Americans, as German Americans, did not emerge from the war at all. The war had so enhanced the distance between the German and the American that no hyphen could stretch from the one to the other." Though such a characterization ignores the countless enclaves of rural German Americans who maintained their cultural practices for at least another generation, it does capture the typical urban cultural transformation.[131]

In St. Paul, with its substantial German population, this cultural shift had a significant impact on the political geography of the city. Stripped of the ethnic trappings that had held the enclave together, the Eighth and Tenth Wards, the heart of the German community, showed a radical decrease in German-born residents between 1910 and 1920 as upwardly mobile Germans relocated to the ethnically heterogeneous and prosperous Tenth and Eleventh Wards at the western edge of the city—"spacious and well supplied with park and recreation areas, in contrast to the older districts of the city."[132] As a result, interclass loyalties weakened, and working-class Germans moved both culturally and politically closer to other workers in the city, especially to the well-positioned Irish labor and political leaders. With German ethnicity erased from the cultural landscape, the vacuum was quickly filled by the vigorous presence of the ubiquitous Irish. Postwar St. Paul looked more than ever like an "Irish town," as German culture vanished from the scene.

St. Paul's trials in the war changed more than the local or even the state landscape. The streetcar controversy and the campaign against the Nonpartisan League were important parts of a cumulative national crisis that would drive a restructuring of federal powers. Federal policy that had traditionally ceded authority for domestic order to the states had proved woefully inadequate during the war.[133] The Wilson administration, bound by the states' rights tradition of the Democratic Party, was helpless to bring intransigent employers like Horace Lowry into line. Moreover, Minnesota authorities, intent on destroying the Nonpartisan League, had flagrantly ignored pleas from Washington to halt their crusade. The president had consistently courted Townley's support, and George Creel, Wilson's director of public information, had stated unequivocally, "Despite attacks, I believe intensely in the loyalty of the Nonpartisan League. I have done all in my power to defend it from unfair assaults."[134] Nonetheless, as in the case of the streetcar controversy, federal officials found their power distressingly limited. The lessons learned during the war prompted Washington policymakers to begin centralizing power at the federal level. The events in Minnesota thus had a catalytic effect on the development of the modern state. As part of a larger national crisis in governance, they had helped lay the foundation that would later support the New Deal.

People in St. Paul had been buffeted by bewildering political winds, but they also had been historical actors of some magnitude, though they only vaguely understood this larger role, if they noted it at all. They continued to play out their daily lives on a local stage. The more significant forces these local conflicts had helped to set in motion absorbed St. Paul citizens far less than the shattered social compact at home. The task before them, as they saw it, was to sort out the broken threads of the social web that had held their community together. Somehow, they hoped to find a way to put their immediate world in order.

Fig. 34. Selby Avenue, 1929. Courtesy of the Minnesota Historical Society.

III. FROM BATTLE ZONE TO "HOLY CITY"

New Alliances, Old Loyalties, and the Power of Place

Chapter 8

VYING FOR POWER:

The Showdown between Business and Labor

Not a shot had been fired on American soil, yet the Great War left St. Paul a city in social ruins. In the minds of working people, business and political leaders had betrayed the civic compact, damaging old relationships seemingly beyond repair. As for city leaders, they appeared to be in command of a rudderless ship. Pushed and pulled by state and national forces beyond their control, local leaders could conceive of no plan to reestablish the old relationships on which they had depended. To add to the confusion, St. Paul's two towering figures of economic and cultural authority had gone to their graves. The death of James J. Hill in 1916 had created a climate of economic uncertainty assuaged only slightly by the succession of his son Louis, known better to the public for leading a carnival than a railroad. The spectacle of Louis, in full regalia, riding at the head of the Winter Carnival's grand parade, was no substitute for the comforting persona of the gruff, rumpled, and decidedly businesslike old empire builder.

The loss of the anchoring presence of Jim Hill endowed added importance to the stabilizing role of John Ireland. Thus, the death of the archbishop in September 1918 was even more socially unsettling than that of Hill two years earlier. Though the eighty-year-old Ireland, in faltering health for more than a year, had failed to mediate the streetcar controversy, he had seemed to rally as the fight dragged on, offering hope to both sides that they might yet effect a truce everyone could live with. The *Catholic Bulletin*, pleading for "industrial concord" and insisting that "the Church is the Best Friend of Working Classes," published numerous articles extolling the social-justice teachings of Father John Ryan, well remembered and loved by St. Paul working people from his years at the St. Paul Seminary. The *Bulletin* also regularly invoked the social justice doctrines of *Rerum Novarum*, the papal encyclical that had been Ryan's first inspiration. At the same time, Ireland continued to condemn "mob violence" and the destruction of property.[1]

Unfortunately, the aged archbishop could exert little influence on either the Safety Commission or on Horace Lowry and thus was confined to strategies of local damage control. The St. Paul Democratic-Catholic political bloc was clearly coming apart, as workers lost faith in both political and religious leaders. The archbishop gamely took up the challenge, overturning the *Bulletin*'s editorial policy of avoiding political commentary.[2] Accordingly, in the early months of 1918, the paper turned out a flurry of pieces condemning socialism. To the question, "Can a Catholic Be a Socialist," the paper's answer was, "a most emphatic No!" The *Bulletin* took an even more active political stance in a series of thundering attacks on Charles Lindbergh, the Nonpartisan League candidate for governor, whom it accused (with some justification) of anti-Catholic bias.[3]

The efforts of the archbishop and the *Bulletin* were a qualified success. Lindbergh was defeated in the statewide gubernatorial primary, his supposed Nonpartisan League disloyalty supplemented by charges of anti-Catholicism. In heavily Catholic St. Paul, however, where the issue of loyalty had been used as a club against working people, Lindbergh lost by just the thinnest of margins. Only his alleged anti-Catholicism kept him from winning the primary. Nonetheless, Lindbergh's near-victory in the seat of the archdiocese suggests that for many Catholics, injuries of class had trumped religious solidarity. As the *Daily News* remarked, "The great mass of the Lindbergh vote . . . voiced an emphatic PROTEST against real wrongs as well as fancied grievances."[4]

Clearly, the events of the war had damaged old archbishop's credibility with working-class Catholics. Still, he remained one of the few figures of stability in a social world where all the rules seemed to have changed. For fifty years, he had been an emblem of both authority and protection. His death in September seemed to mark the ending of an era, and the city came to a virtual standstill to mark his passing. For three days, thousands of mourners stood in line to pay their respects. The state supreme court suspended hearings in order to attend the services, classes were canceled in city schools, and flags flew at half mast throughout St. Paul.[5]

Condolences and testimonials flooded in from national and international dignitaries extolling Ireland's statesmanly accomplishments. But local leaders mourned a different sort of loss. Mayor Larry Hodgson described him as "distinctly a citizen of St. Paul, known and loved personally by thousands, and honored and esteemed by our citizenship without regard to class or creed . . . best of all . . . a kindly, neighborly associate with his fellow men." The St. Paul Association echoed these sentiments: "Though his influence for good was world-wide, to his fellow citizens of St. Paul he always appeared the kindly clergyman they had known from boyhood." The eulogy of the *Union Advocate* was a bit more tempered, describing the departed prelate as a "controversialist," who nonetheless "was always strongly sympathetic and deeply and sincerely interested in the welfare of those around him." From any perspective in the factionalized city, the mediating presence of the archbishop would be sorely missed—as plaintively captured in the *St. Paul Dis-*

Fig. 35. Mourners overflowed the cathedral for the funeral of Archbishop Ireland in September 1918. Photo by *Catholic Bulletin*. Courtesy of the Archives of the Archdiocese of Saint Paul and Minneapolis.

patch: "Who will fill . . . the large place occupied by Archbishop Ireland? The time seems to be no more when any one man may in all things be all."[6]

Times had changed indeed—nowhere more obviously than in the reconfiguration of local politics. In 1918, for the first time in St. Paul memory, the Trades and Labor Assembly had entered into the arena of independent labor politics. Declaring that organized labor had received "nothing but broken promises and bad faith from men it had helped to put in public office," the Assembly endorsed three independent trade union candidates to run for city council.[7] The Democrats naturally were dismayed at the defection of much of their traditional constituency. But the labor slate indicated more than a mere political split. It marked a much larger cultural chasm as well. The traditional negotiating language of community and common civic responsibility that had mediated labor negotiations in the past was discarded for a political rhetoric grounded squarely in class. "Big business" and "the privileged class," in the wake of the streetcar struggle, had become "the foes . . . and the oppressors of the working people." The formerly conciliatory *Advocate* urged union voters, "Arise in your strength! Assert your manhood! Hurl your enemies and oppressors from their entrenchments."[8]

Despite such bellicose pronouncements, union leaders were not ready to tackle formal establishment of a labor party; they were hesitant to break completely with former allies until the political waters had been tested. Nor were they prepared to formally align themselves with the city's small Socialist contingent. By a large majority, the Trades Assembly voted against endorsing Socialist mayoral candidate Julius Emme, though he was an officer in the organization. Instead, labor threw its support to popular Democratic journalist Laurence Hodgson, who had amassed a strong record of support for working-class issues. Labor also endorsed the reelection of Republican councilman Oscar Keller, workers' most reliable elected ally in the streetcar strike. Picking and choosing its candidates without regard for party affiliation, labor began sorting friends from enemies in ways that transcended old party loyalties.[9]

The three labor candidates sailed through the primary election. Then, after a contentious campaign that only exacerbated class tensions, one of the three, James Clancy, president of the Trades and Labor Assembly, became the first union man elected to the city council, with the other two labor candidates defeated only narrowly. Not content to rest on their laurels, the newly politicized St. Paul unions set their sights on the upcoming state elections.[10]

The battle line that labor drew allied workers with the state's farmers in support for the gubernatorial bid of Charles Lindbergh, the Nonpartisan League candidate. The labor press, stressing the common interests of workers and farmers, took a new interest in farm issues. As framed by the *Advocate*, farmers, like working people, were fighting for the right to organize. They faced a common enemy in Big Business. The only difference was one of "circumstance and the form of organization." When Lindbergh was eliminated in the primary, done in by accusations of disloyalty and anti-Catholicism, the Trades Assembly's campaign committee turned to independent David Evans, a political neophyte, rather than the Democratic candidate, declaring that "both of the [party-backed] candidates were distinctly plutocratic candidates." Though the Farmer-Labor coalition would not establish itself as a party until 1921, Evans campaigned with the informal designation as the farmer-labor candidate.[11]

When the dust had settled, despite the political liabilities he had acquired in the course of the war, Joseph Burnquist—mantled in patriotic rhetoric, supported by the Republican machine, and the beneficiary of a disorganized and fragmented opposition—narrowly won reelection to the governor's seat. Nonetheless, the results in St. Paul held an ominous portent for the established parties. In the state's Democratic stronghold, the defection of labor enabled Burnquist to outpoll the Democratic candidate by seventy-nine votes in the county-wide returns; however, the combined Democratic and Farmer-Labor votes had repudiated Burnquist by nearly a two-to-one margin. More tellingly, the obscure and ill-financed Farmer-Laborite Evans won the city proper with the solid support of organized labor. The split in Democratic ranks had broken the party's dominance in the city.[12]

Despite little time to organize and less experience in independent political action, St. Paul's labor bloc also had returned two union-backed candidates to the state legislature and elected three new union legislators. In addition, it had helped to carry Fred Tillman, a member of the Brotherhood of Locomotive Firemen and

Enginemen, to the critically important position of Railroad and Warehouse Commissioner. Though labor-endorsed candidates officially ran under the banner of the established parties, the Labor Campaign Committee considered that only a temporary convention. As committee chairman William Mahoney assured the Trades and Labor Assembly, "We have laid the foundation for a powerful political force in St. Paul . . . to give organized labor a controlling influence in the government of the city."[13]

As chairman of the Labor Campaign Committee, William Mahoney quickly vaulted from political obscurity to become the most important figure to emerge from labor's initial foray into independent politics. Mahoney had arrived in St. Paul in 1905, a young Irish firebrand with pressmen's credentials, a law degree, and a fully developed socialist critique of capitalism. Settling into the local pressmen's union and the politically marginal Socialist Party, Mahoney had no faith in the local compact between business and labor. At meetings of the Trades and Labor Assembly, he was an irritating voice of dissent, insisting to anyone who would listen that "the capitalist, or employing class, have economic interests that are opposed to the interests of those who depend upon their own labor for a living." For years his critique fell on deaf ears. In 1914, Mahoney made a futile run for Congress as a Socialist and, in the process, was schooled in the contours and limits of labor solidarity in St. Paul. Flaying the Democratic Party for its stance on national issues, Mahoney had failed to realize that St. Paul's version of the Democratic Party was a distinctly local operation, where national issues resonated only when they impinged on the status quo. When he attempted to present a campaign speech to his union brothers in the Trades and Labor Assembly, Mahoney was shouted down by supporters of Carl Van Dyke, a candidate with both Democratic and union credentials. Undaunted, the young radical declared, "I will not trim; I will not compromise." Principles intact, Mahoney was trounced by Van Dyke, garnering only slightly more than two thousand votes, or 7 percent of the total cast.[14]

After his disastrous campaign, the disenchanted Socialist virtually disappeared from the public eye. But when the opportune moment presented itself in 1918, Mahoney enthusiastically jumped back into the fray, his rhetoric undimmed. At last, the changing political climate had created a forum where he could be heard. Mahoney's name began to crop up regularly in the *Union Advocate*, where for years it had been most notable for its absence. Labor candidates arriving to address union meetings were invariably accompanied by "William Mahoney, member of the labor campaign committee." By the close of the campaign, he had been elevated to committee chairman.[15]

Though Mahoney's political principles were unchanged, he judiciously shed his association with the Socialist Party, insisting that he had quit the party for patriotic reasons when war was declared. Even while a member, so he claimed, he had never considered it to be "of any practical political significance"; rather, it was "an educational movement." Besides, he noted, "The term 'socialism' is a vague and indefinite one" that covers "a great range and diversity of ideas and beliefs . . . which have no connections with . . . political views." This disclaimer was more than a bit disingenuous. As Mahoney admitted years later, in the spring of 1918 he and the other "labor Socialists" had strategized to link the various strands of organized labor with the Nonpartisan League. Mahoney was the chief architect of the plan. He had worked out a deal with George Lawson, one of the old-line Federation of Labor leaders, and together they crafted a permanent political organization to promote labor's interests and bring the trade unions closer to the farmer organization. Whereas during the 1918 campaign Lawson had declared that organized labor had not the "slightest use" for any of the Socialist labor candidates, by 1919, according to Mahoney, the Socialist Party had the state federation of labor "in its palm." In the four years since his electoral defeat, Mahoney had clearly become more adept at negotiating the parameters of St. Paul politics.[16]

Mahoney used every means to realize his vision of labor politics. In 1919, when James Clancy was elected to the city council, by acclamation Mahoney succeeded him as president of the Trades and Labor Assembly, a turn of events that the *St. Paul Dispatch* and the *Pioneer Press* reported with some alarm. From his new position of power, Mahoney negotiated the Assembly's purchase of the *Union Advocate* from Cornelius Guiney, the paper's owner for more than twenty years. Mahoney squeezed the old labor editor out, giving him the "alternative of selling the *Advocate* to the Trades and Labor Assembly or having a rival labor paper established." The sale effected, Mahoney installed himself as "editor, manager, bookkeeper, solicitor, and in fact everything but actual printer." As Mahoney recalled, "Along with this change came new and progressive ideas, and the old conservatism that so long characterized the labor movement of St. Paul was supplanted by new concepts of labor's place in the political and economic world."[17]

That same year, Mahoney and former Minneapolis mayor Thomas Van Lear, another "ex-Socialist," began to lay the infrastructural groundwork for the Farmer-Labor Party. Thanks to what an admirer termed a "long and eloquent plea" delivered by Mahoney at the 1919 MFL convention in July, delegates voted to establish the Working People's Nonpartisan Political League (WPNPL), whereupon Mahoney immediately produced a constitution, a platform and a declaration of principles that he and Van Lear had worked out in advance. Though the WPNPL remained structurally separate from the rural-based Nonpartisan League, the intent was to eventually meld the two organizations into a third party of farmers and workers. Paid organizers, both men and women, fanned out across the state, selling the organization to unions and to women's groups, who with the imminent passage of the Nineteenth Amendment had become a promising source of newly enfranchised voters. By the end of the year members were flocking into the organization at the rate of some three thousand per month.[18]

Even as the organization developed a statewide focus, Mahoney continued to look after local interests. He used his influence to funnel attractive financial perks back into the ranks of the St. Paul labor movement, leveraging extra "city campaign" funds and allocating an extra fifty cents per membership to be returned to the local assembly treasury. A new day was dawning in Minnesota politics, but in St. Paul, the political landscape had not been entirely transformed.[19]

One aspect of St. Paul labor politics, however, had changed noticeably. Suddenly, women had become central rather than peripheral figures in labor's calculations. While the city counted 13,558 union members in 1918, only 580 of those were women, nearly all in the fur or garment trades—a constituency that had received minimal attention from the Trades Assembly. However, with the passage of the suffrage amendment and labor's new preoccupation with electoral politics, the incorporation of women into labor strategies assumed new importance—as voters and workers, as well as moral arbiters of community norms.[20] The WPNPL declared as a founding principle that it supported the complete equality of women with men, a position that Mahoney had taken in his 1914 congressional campaign. On the local front, the *Union Advocate* made a noteworthy shift in its editorial policy. Throughout most of the war, it had agonized over the dangers of women filling men's jobs; by September 1918, however, it espoused equality in pay for men and women.[21]

Women workers responded with measurable enthusiasm to labor's new attention. By 1920, St. Paul unions counted at least two thousand female members, an increase of 350 percent that was all the more remarkable in a city with limited employment opportunities for women. Garment workers, waitresses, and clerks seized the opportunity to organize. The wives of working men organized as well, establishing Housewives' Union No. 1 to "organize their purchasing power" in support of union solidarity. The Housewives' Union formalized the consumer tactics that had long been embedded in the civic compact, endorsing certain products and places of business and urging the boycott of others—a strategy closely noted by the city's merchants and manufacturers. Demonstrating a willingness to jump into the electoral arena as well as the traditional women's milieu of consumer politics, housewives affiliated their organization with the WPNPL. With the addition of all these varied new constituents, the meaning and active membership of "union" had considerably broadened.[22]

The largest surge in women's labor activism came from a single source—the organization of the city's teachers, which alone increased women's presence in the unions by 128 percent.[23] This new partnership between teachers and organized labor presented the potential for a particularly powerful cultural realignment that union leaders recognized and worked to foster. City schools had long been low on the list of St. Paul priorities. With most of its Catholic children attending parochial school and the children of the elite in private institutions, public education ranked far below street maintenance in allocation of public funds. In 1917, St. Paul ranked twenty-two out of twenty-five comparable cities in its school expenditures, while its best showing was in street maintenance—an ordering of priorities that may not have been unrelated to labor's leverage in city politics. City teachers were notoriously underpaid and in 1918, they rose in protest when the commissioner of education attempted to establish a "merit system" that would leave teacher salaries entirely to his discretion.[24]

When three hundred educators voted to affiliate with the American Federation of Teachers, the education commissioner responded with wholesale dismissals for "incompetence," which propelled the teachers into the Trades and Labor Assembly, where they were welcomed.[25] For the increasingly militant Assembly, the teachers' predicament spelled opportunity. Not only did the new union augment organized labor's presence in the city; not only was it composed almost exclusively of women; but most important, these were women with middle-class credentials who had been injured by the city's supposed civic leaders. With old linkages between labor and the middle class crumbling, the alliance of middle-class, female teachers with the labor movement was an invaluable means to reinforce labor's respectability in the realm of public opinion.

The Trades Assembly threw its full support behind the teachers' cause, excoriating the "despotic and obstinate administration of the school system" and accusing the commissioner of "wholesale importations of outside teachers to take the places of our home instructors." Calling on the traditional rhetoric of community, the *Advocate* condemned the replacement of "faithful, experienced teachers. . . . *The teacher whose home interests are here is the one who will give the best service to the schools.*"[26] Thus, even in the midst of labor's new militancy, the old claims of community obligation framed a contest with changed and somewhat confusing configurations.

With this breakdown of the social ordering, city businessmen and politicians found their authority challenged from seemingly every angle. At the 1918 Labor Day parade, the city's teachers, firemen, and police marched with twenty thousand fellow trade unionists, including the railroad unions (making their first-ever appearance in the parade).[27] Worker solidarity seemed about to overwhelm the old precarious balance between business and labor. Indeed, with labor's new interest in independent politics, the unions had begun to reach out in multiple directions to expand their constituency. Teachers, women telephone operators, unskilled labor, and the packinghouse workers of neighboring South St. Paul—all were sheltered under the umbrella of the Trades and Labor Assembly.[28] By 1920, St. Paul reported ninety-six unions with a total membership of nearly twenty-seven thousand—a 266 percent increase from prewar levels.[29]

With the strength of numbers and the breakdown of the civic compact, workers turned increasingly to direct action rather than negotiation. The experiences of the past eighteen months had convinced them that civic mutuality had lost its persuasive power. Economically pressed by the soaring cost of living and the consequent decline in real wages, and with the multiple grievances of the streetcar strike and Safety Commission harassment to spur them on, they perceived few common interests with city employers. Thus, St. Paul, that model of labor harmony, began to experience an unprecedented wave of strikes.

In November, even as the nation celebrated the end of the war, it was clear that another sort of war was brewing in St. Paul. That month alone, garment workers, ice-wagon drivers, and telephone workers—including more than four hundred women operators who had organized in October—walked off the job. From the following January to June of 1920, no less than twenty strikes involving more than seven thousand workers rattled the local economy. Even the city breweries, traditionally among the unions' most favored employers, were struck by the coopers' union. Most unsettling to city employers was a new solidarity between skilled and unskilled workers. When the building laborers struck for an eight-hour day and a ten-cent increase in the hourly wage, the Builders' Exchange ignored the demands of these easily replaceable common laborers, as, indeed, they always had. After three weeks without a settlement, however, in a sharp break with precedent, the skilled trades walked off the job in sympathy. Bricklayers, plasterers, teamsters, team owners, plumbers, tile setters, structural iron workers, sheet-metal workers, electrical workers, painters, and hoisting engineers—in all, 1,250 workers—stood shoulder-to-shoulder with their unskilled brethren. Within a week, the builders conceded defeat.[30]

The disorganized employers were no match for this show of union solidarity, and nearly every strike was resolved to labor's advantage. The resulting working-class ebullience prompted even unorganized workers to protest. By the end of 1919, the contagion of worker militancy seemed unstoppable, part of a growing national phenomenon. Industrial strife bombarded employers across the country, undergirded in their minds by communism, syndicalism, and other assorted forms of radicalism. As historian Melvyn Dubofsky summed up the state of the nation: "The year 1919 was like no other in history. Industrial conflict reached unprecedented levels as more than 3,000 strikes involved over 4 million workers. Even police walked out. Race riots and bombings proliferated. Two American Communist parties appeared. The world had been turned upside down."[31] When placed in such a national perspective, the conflicts that erupted in St. Paul were relatively tame, and its fledgling labor politics the mildest sort of radicalism. However, local conflicts were not experienced in relative terms. This break from long-standing practice seemed an upheaval of earth-shaking proportion to the employers of St. Paul. News from other cities only heightened businessmen's fears that the situation would deteriorate.

Some in St. Paul looked to Minneapolis as a model to contain this escalating problem. There, the Citizens Alliance, with the aid of the Civic and Commerce Association and the newly organized American Committee of Minneapolis, never wavered in its campaign against organized labor. Lockouts, surveillance, blacklisting, and the dismissal of union employees continued as standard practice. The three organizations together had crafted an impressive machine to put down strikes, control the press, and enforce a unified employing class. Thus, the 1918–19 strike wave in Minneapolis resulted in only small and scattered victories for labor.[32]

As early as January 1918, a group of St. Paul executives met with members of the Minneapolis Citizens Alliance at the Minnesota Club. Their purpose was to discuss organizing a St. Paul version of the Minneapolis organization. But proponents of the scheme were soon hamstrung by fellow St. Paul businessmen. According to historian William Millikan, too many of the city's leading businessmen remained "bitterly opposed to a public campaign for the open shop in their city."[33]

Ironically, the wartime experiences that had created such solidarity among working people caused deep divisions within the business community in the waning months of the war. The members of the St. Paul Association continued to be harried by demands of the Safety Commission, while the profits of patriotism had not met expectations, with only a few of the city's largest concerns reaping the promised returns. Association members grumbled over assessments that brought them little benefit, and the luster of patriotism had dulled. The city's most respected German citizens had borne the insults of suspected disloyalty, which further fragmented the business class. Moreover, the rivalry with Minneapolis was far from dead. In fact, the war had only increased the old antagonisms. Responsibility for the ongoing streetcar dispute, which had turned the city into a war zone, was laid at the door of Horace Lowry and his associates in the Minneapolis Civic and Commerce Association.[34]

Before the leadership of the St. Paul Association could craft a unified plan to deal with labor militancy in the city, they realized they had to put their own house in order. Thus, in 1918, rather than taking up the cause of the open shop, they set about the project of expanding their membership and creating good fellowship among their disaffected ranks. In his inaugural address to Association members, newly elected president C. H. Bigelow repeatedly stressed the "democratic" nature of the organization: "No particular class of citizens should be represented by the President of the Association." Yet, "if the truth were known," he confided, his chief interest was "in the huge predominating class of the non-organized employed," whom he had "the greatest affection for." These were small businessmen, independent proprietors, white-collar workers (precisely those who, in the wake of the 1917 Winter Carnival, had suggested the St. Paul Association should "go to hell"). To bring them on board, the Association instituted a sliding membership scale based on income and attempted to reshape the elite St. Paul Athletic Club, underwritten by the Association, as a cosmopolitan and yet "democratically affordable" club—a social milieu "where all citizens may meet and mingle and, by better understanding of each other's problems and points of view, mold a public opinion which will ward off all extreme and radical influences on our city."[35]

Following the unionization of city teachers and with the extension of the vote to women on the horizon, the Association also took a new interest in incorporating women into the organization. In appreciation of the "splendid work" of city women in the war effort, the board of directors reinterpreted the Association's bylaws to make women eligible for membership. The ten dollar membership fee would be payable quarterly, "so as to make it possible for the largest number of women . . . to secure all the advantages of the St. Paul Association."[36]

Yet, even as the Association competed with labor for the loyalties of the pivotal group of "middling" St. Paulites, publicly it maintained the appearance of reasonable sympathy for local labor issues, careful to craft its policies in language "to which [labor] could not reasonably take exception." Essentially, while the businessmen marshaled their forces to take on labor, they tried to employ a strategy of local containment through a public facade of moderation and compromise.[37]

In private, however, a group of key business leaders agreed that they were in a crisis. As if the evidence of local labor troubles was not enough, the nationally promulgated Red Scare of 1919 had them seeing dangerous radicals lurking around every corner—though there was scant evidence of subversive activity in St. Paul.[38] Fears stirred up by press propaganda were augmented by covert reports funneled from Minneapolis Citizens Alliance operatives and especially from private detective Luke Boyce. Boyce's operation, the Northern Information Bureau, devoted itself exclusively to the surveillance of radical activities, especially in Minneapolis. Though Boyce shared his confidential reports with Military Intelligence, the Department of Justice, and selected Minnesota congressmen, his primary audience were the private businesses who kept him on an annual retainer. Thus, as an entrepreneur whose stock in trade was radicalism, it was to Boyce's advantage to paint as lurid a picture of impending revolution as possible. Yet, despite his agents' best efforts, he was unable to unearth substantive evidence of radical activities in St. Paul. Still, as Boyce assured his business clients, the contagion so apparent in Minneapolis showed definite signs of spreading.[39]

This message resonated with the leadership of the St. Paul Association. In November 1919, the Association's president called an emergency secret meeting of its present and past board of directors. The purpose was to "decide on certain policies" that would be "unwise" to explain in detail through a letter."[40] The problem to be addressed was the threat of radicalism and their "failure to convince a considerable portion of clear-thinking men as to the constructive community service which [we] are anxious to render." To the frustration of these business leaders, the majority of employers refused to heed the warning signs. At most, they gave only "half-hearted support" and were not "sufficiently interested to organize," hoping instead to return to the live-and-let-live plan that had operated before the war.[41]

Most St. Paul workers demonstrated an equal reluctance to embrace radical solutions to their problems. Luke Boyce and his agents had been unable to come up with a shred of subversive activity despite their unstinting efforts; union labor had refused to endorse Socialist Julius Emme in his run for mayor, though he was an officer of the Trades Assembly; the farmer-labor alliance was still extremely shaky, with significant resistance to establishing a third party; and the NPL and WPNPL continued to operate as separate entities. The intercity labor pact stood on only slightly firmer ground.[42]

Though St. Paul and Minneapolis workers were allied in the WPNPL, it is important to recognize that the cultural content of their politics had been formed in quite different ways. In Minneapolis, where employers had been battling with organized labor for nearly two decades, workers had no illusions that they could reach a peaceful détente with business. In St. Paul, on the other hand, labor politics emerged from a long tradition of union power. Workers there intended to expand union influence and improve their position, but they had little desire to overturn the system entirely. The majority of those who had been part of the old civic compact—both labor and business—only gradually were towed into the wake of the increasingly polarized leadership contingents. But with the pact of community loyalty broken and traditional lines of communication dissolved by the war, local solutions were much more difficult to negotiate than in the past.

In February 1920, the city's teamsters, buoyed by labor's victories, came up with an offensive that jolted city businessmen into united action. The teamsters announced that they would henceforth refuse to haul materials or goods to or from any operation deemed unfair to union labor or to work for anyone else who supported these unfair employers. Business interests reacted with predictable alarm. As they informed the public, the teamsters were as vital to the economy as the railroads—each providing critical transportation links. "Through the control of the teaming industry of a city," they warned, "it is possible to enforce the closed shop domination in practically every industry in a community. Once the unions have complete control of the teaming industry, other industries dependent upon teaming or trucking can be forced to unionize."[43]

It is probable that the teamsters devised this plan on their own; the *Advocate* was strangely silent on the matter, quite likely judging such a direct challenge to city business to be premature. It certainly went against the grain of the customary practice of framing labor issues in terms of the "public good." And it left labor far too exposed to criticism at a politically crucial moment. With a full slate of labor candidates proposed for the upcoming city election, strategists were focusing on expanding their constituency. The teamsters' threat to shut down the local economy seemed to work at cross-purposes to that goal. Though the union tried to win over the public by differentiating individual needs from those of business, their assurances nonetheless made it clear, perhaps unintentionally, that the teamsters held the upper hand. "If any householder has sickness in his house and is out of coal," they promised, "we will investigate, and if the coal is actually needed, we will see that it is hauled,"—a high-handed statement that was unlikely to win them many sympathetic allies.[44]

To the contrary, the teamsters had unwittingly accomplished what the men of the St. Paul Association had been unable to achieve for the past two years. They had generated the sense of urgency that finally moved city businessmen to support employer action against the unions. In this way, the Citizens Alliance of Saint Paul was inaugurated. As the Alliance newsletter admitted, "For seventeen years the business men of Minneapolis had . . . endeavored to get the St. Paul business men to form a similar organization," but not until the teamsters had driven home "the menace of the closed shop" were businessmen "sufficiently interested to organize."[45]

It can only be imagined what William Mahoney had to say in private conversation. The tactic had seriously injured labor's chances at the polls. In January, the Trades Assembly was confident enough to endorse Socialist Julius Emme for councilman and to nominate Mahoney (drafted by unanimous acclamation) as its candidate for mayor. The assembly also launched a careful press campaign to assure the public that "there is no danger that Bolshevism will ever submerge organized labor." But the teamsters had undermined labor's position with its broader civic constituency. Opponents dusted off old accusations of radicalism against Mahoney as well as Emme. The Republican *Pioneer Press* combed the paper's files for past evidence of Mahoney's radical politics. Despite his present disavowal of socialism, the *Press* reminded readers, only six years earlier, Mahoney had run for Congress under the Socialist banner, declaring then that "he was not the labor man, but a Socialist candidate." Moreover, the paper's political reporter claimed, "The socialists have grabbed control of the St. Paul Trades and Labor Assembly"—a coup by a "cunning lot" that supposedly had the majority of the city's "conservative" union men up in arms.[46]

Socialism never had been particularly popular in Catholic St. Paul, but confined to the political margins, neither had it registered any notable sense of public alarm. However, in the highly charged atmosphere that spring of 1920, suddenly it appeared more sinister. Even a past association became politically deadly. The campaign thus became framed as a contest between Americanism and Bolshevism. Broadsides prepared by the Democratic Party urgently declared, "Your vote is needed to help save St. Paul from Socialism. . . . If you believe in the Church, in the home, in the school, and in the orderly administration of government, be sure and vote right."[47]

Feeding the sense of urgency, both the *Pioneer Press* and the *Dispatch* daily featured news of radical activities, culling their evidence from across the country. When a national roundup of "Reds" ensnared sixteen radicals in St. Paul, even the usually temperate *Daily News* made the most of the sensational event, though it noted that fourteen of the sixteen arrested were Russian aliens, "outsiders" rather than established members of the community. Ludicrously, the *News* reported that, according to Department of Justice agent T. E. Campbell, "Minneapolis and St. Paul were headquarters of the Communist party in the Northwest, if not in the entire United States."[48]

A group of Republican businessmen added organized fuel to the fire. The same individuals who were lobbying for a St. Paul Citizens Alliance also contributed liberally to the Minnesota Sound Government Association (SGA), formed in January 1920 with the stated purpose to counter "certain sinister influences . . . at work to overthrow the present form of government . . . fostered by socialistic leadership both within and without the State." Its unstated purpose, however, was to destroy the nascent third-party movement in Minnesota. During the St. Paul electoral campaign, the SGA churned out reams of propaganda aimed at stirring public fears about radicalism.[49]

Despite the concerted counteroffensive of the Democrats and Republicans, the labor slate swept intact through the primary, leading all other contenders by substantial margins. As the results came in, the enormous crowd assembled at labor's campaign headquarters displayed an "enthusiasm that bordered on the hysterical."

UNION VOTERS, IT IS YOUR DUTY TO ELECT THESE CANDIDATES FOR OUR CITY'S WELFARE

Fig. 36. The Trades and Labor Assembly challenged the political establishment by proposing a full labor slate for municipal offices in 1920. Solid working-class support swept all five candidates easily through the primary. *Minnesota Union Advocate*, 23 April 1920.

The predicted split in labor's ranks between its radical leaders and the supposedly conservative rank and file proved merely a hopeful figment of political forecasters' imaginations. With gross understatement, the *Press* acknowledged that "the huge vote cast for the entire Council labor ticket was a surprise."[50]

Labor's impressive turnout in the primary jolted complacent St. Paulites, made increasingly uneasy by the teamsters' actions and press portrayals of labor's leaders as dangerous radicals. As a result, both Emme and Mahoney went down to defeat in the general election, Mahoney overwhelmingly outpolled by the popular Democratic mayor, Larry Hodgson. Assuredly, this was only a slight setback for labor politics; the three labor candidates untainted by radicalism won election to the council, evidence that general support in the community for labor had not eroded significantly. However, it served as a strong reminder that acceptable political dissent in St. Paul was confined within narrow parameters. For Mahoney's personal political aspirations, his defeat was a bitter blow. He claimed the "fix was in" between the Democratic machine ruled by Richard O'Connor and his brother John, the powerful chief of police: "The first obligation of the O'Connor politicians is to the interests back of the 'machine' whether they be the criminals on St. Peter St. or the big business interests." His charge was not without merit. But what he failed to ac-knowledge was that, voter manipulation aside, political positions that played well in Minneapolis or in the rural areas faced a different test with St. Paul voters. Protec-tion of local interests remained the paramount concern.[51]

While Mahoney, immersed in his own defeat, saw the election as a failure, to city businessmen it represented an alarming victory for labor that only increased their commitment to put down union power. Three of the city commission posts, includ-ing public safety, were now in the hands of union men. Moreover, Mayor Hodgson, who had always displayed a strong sympathy for labor, was but the lesser of two evils. Accordingly, the newly organized Citizens Alliance launched an all-out as-sault on organized labor, with the unified backing of city business interests. By the end of the year, it had won open-shop contests with the cooks and waiters, journey-men plumbers, mill workers, electricians, plasterers, building laborers, and tailors. Labor found itself suddenly on the defensive.[52]

Despite these business victories, the real heart of St. Paul union power lay in the building trades, where the closed shop was nearly universal. Most of the union con-tracts there did not expire until spring of 1921, and the Citizens Alliance used the intervening time to prime its weapons. Construction projects delayed by the war had generated a postwar building boom, which in turn created a shortage of skilled workers in the construction trades—as high as 47 percent in some occupations. The builders, realizing that this labor shortage gave the trades considerable negoti-ating leverage, laid out a plan to circumvent the unions. The Alliance organized trade schools for bricklayers, plasterers, metal lathers, plumbers, and various other trades. It also established a Free Employment Bureau, whose stated lofty goal was to make it possible "for all good mechanics to get work without paying dues or trib-ute to anyone for the right to work." Teaming up with their counterparts in Min-neapolis and Duluth, the Citizens Alliance then formed the Minnesota Building Employers' Association, which agreed to cut wages 20 percent across the board, ef-fective immediately, or at the earliest expiration of present contracts. To court the public's endorsement of their actions, the Alliance had opinion pieces inserted in the local papers that placed the blame for a current housing shortage and the con-current high cost of housing on inordinately "high labor demands." Piously be-moaning the fact that these unfortunate conditions had their most serious impact on the poor, leading them to "crack-brained and unscrupulous agitation," the Al-liance used circuitous reasoning to blame working people themselves for their plight. By the time union contracts came up for renegotiation in May, labor faced a formidably armed foe. Within months, St. Paul went from a model of closed-shop unionism to an almost entirely open-shop city—which the Citizens Alliance then touted as "St. Paul's greatest industrial asset."[53]

The unions did not go down without a struggle. The Trades Assembly launched its own public relations campaign to counter the antiunion propaganda of the Citi-zens Alliance. The *Advocate* also frantically urged "workers of all crafts and classes . . . to stay away from St. Paul," to no avail. As the employers put their plan into action with imported and newly trained workers, strikes broke out, one after another, in all the building trades—sometimes as many as six or seven at one time. Fights broke out on the picket lines, as union workers desperately attempted to stem the flow of scabs into the construction sites. Four bombings accelerated the rising levels of violence—workers and employers each blaming the other for the crimes.[54] The contours of these confrontations, it must be noted, were very different from the streetcar riots in 1917, which were directed solely at the property of the TCRT, owned by Minneapolis outsider, Horace Lowry. These contests, in contrast, pitted St. Paulites against one another, fracturing internal social relations more deeply than ever before.

Working-class neighborhoods rallied behind the strikers. During the sheet-metal workers' strike, the entire West Side neighborhood erupted into a near riot, with the tacit approval of local police. Indeed, in the polarized city, the Citizens Alliance found little support from official sources. As the organization's history bitterly noted, the unionized police force either stood by, or "in flagrant instances, the members of the police force were found assisting the strikers and the pickets." Moreover, the elected city safety commissioner was a union man. Nor were the courts much help; judges displayed a disturbing tendency to dismiss charges against arrested protesters, accepting what the Alliance termed the "perjured testimony" of strikers brought before the bench.[55]

Nonetheless, though the unions determined to "fight to the last ditch," the business offensive triumphed. Backed by a statewide federation of employers, it had the means to outlast the striking workers. As Citizens Alliance president E. H. Davidson astutely noted, two things were "absolutely essential to the success of the Open Shop Movement. One is influence and the other is money and both are based on a large membership."[56] With the substantial resources of Minneapolis and Duluth to back them up, they had money and influence in abundance; the unions, even with the support of local police, elected officials, sympathetic judges, and popular opinion, were no match.

These were heady days for the Citizens Alliance. In 1921, the second-largest building year in St. Paul history, two thirds of the construction projects were contracted on an open-shop basis. By 1922, the building trade unions were completely defeated. The Alliance capped off its campaign with an assault on the printing trades, the last bulwark of union power, more than six hundred members strong. In conjunction with Minneapolis and Duluth printers, St. Paul employers declared for the open shop and locked out employees who refused to give up their union cards. Ignoring union requests for arbitration, they imported strikebreakers and set up hired guards who protected scabs and beat up picketers. After a two-month battle, union workers were forced to concede defeat. When the pressmen and typographers applied for their old jobs back under the new terms dictated by the printers, the companies played their final card. C. H. Bigelow, president of St. Paul's largest printing concern, spoke for his fellow printers, informing the state industrial commission that he did not run an open shop (defined as at least 50 percent nonunion employees); he ran a nonunion shop. As he candidly admitted, "I would discharge any employee should I learn that he was a member of a union"—a statement that only two years earlier would have been unthinkable in St. Paul.[57]

For all practical purposes, labor relations in St. Paul now seemed indistinguishable from those long in force in Minneapolis. However, a close examination suggests a cultural bifurcation beneath the surface of employer unanimity. The arrogant confidence displayed by the printers was the exception to the rule. Unlike Minneapolis, in St. Paul the union movement had long been a popular and powerful part of the civic fabric, and public opinion was far from united behind the Citizens Alliance. Nor was official sanction of its actions universally forthcoming. Though the organization had the backing of the city's financial institutions, its most prestigious firms, and the railroads, the St. Paul Citizens Alliance never came close to reaching its goal of 100 percent participation by local businesses, most of which were heavily dependent on local patronage.[58] With the volatile politics simultaneously at play in the city and public opinion leaning toward the unions, the Alliance realized it could not long enforce its dictates without an intensive public relations campaign.

Thus, the Citizens Alliance waged a propaganda battle with the unions over the open shop. The unions branded the members of the Alliance as "unscrupulous agitators and fomenters of industrial discontent" who were destroying the sanctity of working-class homes; furthermore, the employers were responsible for an influx of disreputable transients into the city who were forcing respectable "old-time residents" to leave town. Perhaps labor's most effective argument was its warning to small businesses that reduced wages for workers meant comparably reduced buying power. As labor framed the contest, calling on traditional St. Paul economic logic, the open-shop employers were hurting local business as well as union labor.[59]

The Citizens Alliance responded in kind, reiterating its charge that "labor's radical leaders" were responsible for depressing the building industry, thereby causing a housing shortage and consequent high rents in the city. According to the Alliance, labor's greed had forfeited its right to public sympathy; it had fomented mob violence and, even worse, was driving business out of the city. To prove its benign intentions, the organization policed its members' wage practices carefully; any employer who undercut the agreed-upon scale was brought into line by pressure from the Alliance, backed by the city's banking interests. According to Alliance propaganda, far from hurting small businesses, the organization had been formed only as a last resort, a public service "for the protection of the city's interests." By "uprooting the tree of class consciousness" the Alliance aimed to reestablish harmony among the city's warring factions.[60]

Nothing could have been more unlikely in the embattled city. Class had become the defining identity in St. Paul. The elites who directed the Citizens Alliance had set themselves up against a broad range of St. Paul citizens, shattering the power of civic identity and place-based loyalty in the process. Temporarily buttressed by Alliance counterparts in Minneapolis and Duluth, they held fast for the moment, but

Minneapolis business interests, always a fickle partner in the past, would prove a poor model in the battle for St. Paul's future.

Meanwhile, the defeat of union labor paradoxically had generated a boon for labor politics. The heyday of St. Paul's Citizens Alliance between 1920 and 1925 produced more than an open shop. It swelled the ranks of the nascent Farmer-Labor Party. It also created a political climate that nudged the party's politics significantly leftward. In 1920, farmer-laborism had been a loose coalition of workers, farmers, and disaffected political progressives. Its candidates, according to political scientist Millard Gieske, "seemed to be progressive political moderates, generally more content with economic and regulatory reform than with limited socialism." In his run for mayor, William Mahoney had gone to great lengths to stress his moderate position and disavow his connection with the Socialist Party. By 1923, such tortuous self-justifications were no longer necessary—either for the party or for Mahoney personally. He seized the moment with vigor.[61]

Outraged by the business attack on labor and yet elated at the opportunity to finally put his political vision into action, Mahoney worked tirelessly to turn the Farmer-Labor Party into a disciplined organization with the political clout to transform society. Though in 1922 the FLP had captured the state legislature, a senate seat, and half the congressional delegation, Mahoney considered it a diffuse protest movement without an infrastructure or coherent platform, what he termed merely "a miserable shell and a delusion." The first step necessary to solidify the party as a political power was to formally unite the Nonpartisan League and the WPNPL into a farmer-labor federation that would act as the operational and policymaking nerve center of the party. Mahoney, from his position of power in the Trades Assembly and the WPNPL, had the muscle to drive the plan through, despite internal opposition derived from growing anxieties about Communist infiltration. The political vision behind this "permanent and reliable political agency" was unmistakably Mahoney's: "We favor a strict militant movement. . . . The struggle of the masses against predatory special interests is no holiday affair." Under Mahoney's leadership, the party's trajectory shifted appreciably leftward. As he assessed the situation, St. Paul workers at last were politically primed to align themselves with the rest of the state in a class-based assault on the forces of power. As was soon to be proven, however, the euphoria of the political moment had led Mahoney's judgment seriously astray.[62]

Chapter 9

HARD TIMES IN THE "HOLY CITY":

Old Alliances and New Deals

In 1924, the social fabric of St. Paul appeared transformed. Both in the realm of electoral politics and labor relations, the city bore a striking resemblance to Minneapolis, apparently dragged into the realities of twentieth-century corporate and industrial America at last. However, cultural forms and customs operate in complex ways beneath the surface of what is narrowly defined as politics. As internalized components of identity, they are not easily or abruptly shed. Moreover, in St. Paul, the old networks of communication and mediation had bestowed real power on those who tended these linkages and real benefits for those who had been part of the resulting civic compact. Thus, for a range of cultural and pragmatic reasons, people across the city, from all rungs of the social and economic ladder, labored under great odds to keep the lines of mediation and the culture of civic insularity from collapsing entirely. That project was serendipitously aided by economic and political circumstances completely beyond their control.

The city's postwar building boom, artificially induced by the halt of construction during the war, proved to be of short duration. Even at the height of demand in 1920, local development lagged behind other cities, hampered by what the *Pioneer Press* decried as "particularly conservative" local investors. As the paper tartly observed, Minneapolis, only "a single streetcar fare" away, was the major beneficiary of such shortsighted policy.[1] But by 1921, both cities were heading into an economic downturn. Minnesota, like all the farm states, found its economy faltering nearly a decade before the national financial collapse. In 1921, the state was in the midst of a farm crisis that had profound reverberations for St. Paul manufacturers, wholesalers, and retailers, dependent on the regional market. Adding to their woes, the return of the railroads to private management had boosted transportation costs for goods moving in and out of the city, and mail-order firms such as Montgomery

Ward and Sears, Roebuck increasingly competed with local merchants for scarce consumer dollars. Returning servicemen boosted unemployment levels to new highs, compounding the economic stress. And with the passage of the Eighteenth Amendment in 1919, the spigots were turned off in city breweries and in the hundreds of saloons that were so important a part of the local economy.[2]

It is not surprising, then, that business squared off against organized labor—an historically common response to economic hard times. Nor is it surprising that working people turned to a vision of a more humane, cooperative commonwealth. What is most instructive about the case of St. Paul is that a counter-strategy also operated in the midst of this polarizing political climate. St. Paul was no stranger to economic stress. Its culture had been shaped within a similar context, exacerbated in the present circumstances but familiar none the less. Even as political and labor positions hardened, other less visible forces were at work to resolve the present crisis through more traditional means.

The Catholic Church was in an unusually difficult position. In 1919, John Ireland's successor, Archbishop Austin Dowling, had arrived in St. Paul to inherit a daunting array of problems—restive parishioners, whispers of radicalism, an oppressive debt load from Ireland's building projects, and not least wearing, continued dependence on the good will of the heirs and associates of James J. Hill.

That the authority of at least some of the parish pastors was slipping is evident from an item that appeared in the *Catholic Bulletin* not long after Ireland's death. "Be loyal to your pastor," it commanded. "His work is to administer to your soul, not to please you. . . . Be regular in attendance to church services. . . . Bear your fair share of the financial burdens of the parish. . . . Show constant respect and deference to those set over you in the Lord." The same issue condemned "cowardly whelp[s] who send anonymous letters of complaint" about the paper's editorial policy. Clearly, some portion of the city's Catholics were showing signs of rebellion.[3]

The *Catholic Bulletin*'s condemnation of the streetcar strikers had generated resentment among working-class Catholics. Perhaps attuned to the repercussions from that intervention, the *Bulletin* treated a telephone operators' strike the following November in a considerably more judicious manner, editorializing: "There is nothing better for the working man or woman than a labor union: it is a necessity and a bulwark of Labor. A strike also, when conducted properly, has its excellent features. All sane people approve of both unions and strikes when they obey the law of reason." Even though the *Bulletin* claimed to have "no opinion in the matter of the strike itself or its good or bad reasons," it seemed "too bad" that the operators had chosen to strike during the influenza epidemic. "Now, whether they win or lose, the operators seem to have rather alienated the good will of the people at large." The gentle tone of this rebuke emphasized the church's role as a concerned advocate rather than an opponent of workers' interests.[4]

Class was not the only basis for Catholic disaffection. As the new archbishop set about putting his diocese in order, he had many inherited fences to mend. Ireland's commitment to Americanization and his concomitant privileging of Irish Catholics had created a fallout among the city's other ethnic Catholics. The war years had been particularly difficult for the church, which had been attacked for fostering "foreignism" in its schools and parishes rather than American values. To defend against such charges, Archbishop Ireland had banned any language but English from the schools and the pulpit. Dowling was left to undo the resentment this generated among ethnic parishioners. Accordingly, in 1922 he decreed that at Sunday High Mass, the most important service of the day, in the national parishes the sermon must be preached in the national language. "Any modification of this rule," he warned, "will not be permitted unless after agreement with me in writing."[5]

Dowling worked assiduously to make the church more widely representative of its Catholics, decreeing that for all important occasions, celebrants on the altar should reflect the church's ethnic diversity. As one of Dowling's clerics assessed it, inclusiveness was the archbishop's most memorable quality. On taking charge of the archdiocese, Dowling had declared, "I'm an American; I'm not an Irishman" (though indeed he was an Irish American). In contrast, the priest recalled, "With [Archbishop] Ireland you must get the idea that [the church] was all completely Irish."[6]

Ireland's aggressive Americanization efforts had produced another unintended consequence that added to his successor's problems. As the newer immigrants became familiar with American ways, they began to acquire the tools and the confidence to agitate in their own behalf. Ireland's army of Irish clerics did not meet their satisfaction. Moreover, the Czechs were no more happy with a Polish priest than an Irish one; they wanted priests of their own ethnic background. Nor was the presence of an ethnic pastor always enough to keep immigrant Catholics happy with parish operations. The members of Italian St. Ambrose parish refused to pay their pastor's salary because the newly established parish did not provide them "sufficient service" comparable to what had been available at Irish St. Mary's, where they had formerly worshipped. The harassed archbishop plaintively wrote, "It seems to me a strange thing that when I send them a good Italian priest they should make so many difficulties."[7]

At heart, Dowling was a conciliator, both in internal church affairs and as an emissary to the larger community. He cautioned his priests to avoid "abuse, exaggeration or personalities in our exposition of . . . Christian living." Even when taking a stand against marriage between Catholics and non-Catholics, it must be done "in such a way as to give no offense." His ventures into politics were similarly gentle, countering radical critiques of society with a message of optimism. "Democracy is not bankrupt," he promised. "It still has the heart and power and the means to right wrongs. Let us renew our faith in the government that has brought us safely thus far." Stepping back from Ireland's leap into politics in 1918, Dowling considered that "it would be unwise . . . to point out that Catholic influence had affected the policy of either party."[8]

The archbishop faced problems of finances as well as faith. Catholic parishes

Fig. 37. The First Communion celebration at Italian St. Ambrose parish in 1925 comfortably blended Catholic, Italian, and American iconography, demonstrating that the process of Americanization was well under way in the city's ethnic parishes. Courtesy of the Minnesota Historical Society.

were expected to be self-sustaining. While the archbishop set clerical salaries, parish coffers provided the funds and also bore the expense of maintaining the parish plant. In addition, the archdiocese counted on parish contributions to support diocesan endeavors. If contributions fell off, the archdiocese felt the pinch. The combination of a soaring cost of living, disgruntled parishioners, and postwar pleas for European relief strained diocesan resources nearly to the breaking point. The archbishop reluctantly raised pastoral salaries in 1919, acknowledging that "it is manifestly impossible for the priest to support the parochial house on the allowance provided some years ago." Anticipating an unfavorable reaction from the parishes, he warned the pastors, "I need not caution you so to present this matter to your people as not to provoke unfavorable comment."[9]

Inundated by requests to support an array of European relief agencies as well as the home missions that served Indians and "our neglected Negro brethren," Dowling did his best to encourage local Catholics to give generously to the various causes in addition to supporting parish and diocesan needs. However, St. Paul Catholics, absorbed in their own battles, resented the demands on their increasingly scarce resources. Through his efforts to reestablish amity among the city's Catholics, Dowling was attuned to this groundswell of discontent. When yet another plea for funds arrived at his door, his reply was curt: "Prefer you not to undertake any campaign at present in this diocese. Times are hard and parochial and diocesan burdens excessive."[10]

The archbishop's burdens were certainly excessive. As he tried to mediate between working-class parishioners and city elites, the commonalties of Catholicism were all but obscured by class differences. Dowling was acutely aware that his strapped diocese was dependent on the support of both factions. Weekly parish contributions alone were not enough to keep the mammoth institutional structure running. A single gift of $100,000 from wealthy contractor Timothy Foley outmatched the sum of a hundred collection plates. Many of the city's most substantial Catholics had joined the Citizens Alliance. Quite clearly, the archbishop dared not take an oppositional stand to the city's business interests. Moreover, Dowling had inherited a dependent relationship with the heirs of James J. Hill, important benefactors he could not afford to alienate. Writing to Hill's daughter Clara, the archbishop thus was compelled to assure her, "I feel it an honor to be in any way, however slight, of service to you."[11]

Still, though Dowling attempted to maintain a neutral position in the public contest between business and labor, behind the scenes he took initiatives to shore up labor's crumbling position, saving the *Union Advocate* from bankruptcy in 1923. In the optimistic days of 1920, when the Trades Assembly had taken over control of the paper, it had set up its own printing plant, making the production of the paper a truly independent enterprise—and also taking on a considerable load of debt. Two years later, confronted by the onslaught of the Citizens Alliance, the paper was in dire straits. As editor William Mahoney recalled, the new unions "soon went to pieces and the membership of the old unions began to decline." Circulation and revenues slid as advertisers disappeared from the paper's pages—some as a deliberate maneuver, others intimidated by the Citizens Alliance. The *Advocate*, shunned by former advertisers and "overwhelmingly in debt," limped along, on the verge of shutting down. At the darkest moment, the Catholic Church stepped in to avert imminent disaster: with the approval—and probably at the instigation—of the archbishop, the *Catholic Bulletin,* awarded its printing contract to the *Advocate,* "in the face of terrific opposition from the Citizens Alliance." According to Mahoney, the contract with the *Bulletin,* which had more than twenty-five thousand subscribers, saved the *Advocate* from closing and "marked the turning point in the independent and profit-producing career of the *Minnesota Union Advocate.*"[12]

Thus, Austin Dowling, while never the forceful presence John Ireland had been, worked behind the scenes—advising his clergy, mediating parish conflicts, balancing support for working-class grievances against the demands of powerful business leaders. Though not entirely successful, the archbishop succeeded in minimizing the damage to the church as he steered it through the treacherous waters of the early twenties. Wedded to the content of their faith, Catholics would only reluctantly repudiate the institutions so important to their identity. Still, without the flexibility that characterized Dowling's stewardship, it is quite probable that common Catholic identity would have lost its potential power altogether. As it was, when conditions in the city began to change, the church was positioned once again to assume a central role as mediator.

These were unhappy days for the Irish brotherhood as well as for the Catholic Church. The Irish had emerged from the war as the unchallenged emblematic ethnic group of St. Paul, with most traces of German culture driven underground by wartime persecution. Though claims of Irish fraternity had always masked a range of political and class positions, the cross-class meeting ground of common ethnicity had weathered the war largely because the ethnic leadership had promoted no official political position on the war. Thus, displays of Hibernian culture and solidarity flourished as the status of German ethnicity withered. As a result, at war's end, Irish fraternalism had scarcely been bruised by internal dissension. In the winter of 1920, St. Paul declared an official "Irish Week," to be devoted to raising funds in support of an independent Ireland. The steering committee for the week-long event represented the full political spectrum, and more than a thousand men and women volunteered to canvass the city for the Irish cause. Clearly, ethnicity retained its power as a unifying force.[13]

Two years later, the teaming up of this disparate group—even in the cause of Ireland—no longer was remotely possible. A newly oppositional political climate had undermined the power the Irish derived as civic brokers. The Democrats were in full retreat, as increasing numbers of their constituents defected to the Farmer-Labor camp. Attempts to lure the Farmer-Laborites back into the Democratic fold met an intensely hostile reaction from Irish FLP leader William Mahoney. In fact, the specter of fusion caused Mahoney to redouble his efforts to shore up the Farmer-Labor infrastructure.[14] Irish businessmen who, in the past, had nurtured their ethnic ties with Irish working people, especially union officials, now sided with the Citizens Alliance. Self-made Irishmen like Joe Shiely, the son of a teamster, embraced the open shop. Wealthy contractors Walter and William Butler, who had helped to found the local bricklayers' union and were blacklisted for their efforts, joined the assault on the building trades. Their brother Pierce, a corporate attorney, backed business interests to the hilt. On the other side, labor leaders Mahoney, James Clancy, and even moderate George Lawson repudiated these fellow Irishmen.[15]

Despite this political bifurcation, the Irish remained key actors in St. Paul. But they had divided into separate camps of influence where ethnic ties solidified internal solidarity but had little power to broker settlements, between opposing sides. When the Irish turned their negotiating skills to creating partisan unity, ironically they increased rather than deflected the potential for militant civic conflict.

Inside the separate camps, Irish connections continued to operate in familiar ways. Though political insurgent Mahoney feared Democratic incursions into

Fig. 38. By the close of World War I, the Irish had secured their place as the emblematic ethnic group in St. Paul. In 1919, the officers of the Ladies Auxiliary of the Ancient Order of Hibernians proudly displayed their status with the trappings of ethnic sisterhood. Courtesy of the Minnesota Historical Society.

Farmer-Labor ranks, he continued to work with George Lawson, the much more conservative secretary of the MFL. Even more important was his ongoing relationship with NPL activist James Manahan, whose commitment to nonpartisan politics differed from Mahoney's party-based strategy for social change. Despite their differences, Mahoney convinced Manahan to use his considerable influence with the farmers of the Nonpartisan League effect a formal merger with the WPNPL. In bringing suspicious farmers and conservative craft unionists into alliance with the left-led wing of the labor faction, these Irish St. Paulites played critical roles, no doubt drawing on years of past association.[16]

Across the class divide, moderate Irish Democrats like the O'Brien brothers worked closely with their more militantly antiunion brethren, coalescing a bloc of "Irish power" that shared influence in the Citizens Alliance with its Republican

Protestant leaders. Over cigars at the Minnesota Club, on the links of the Town and Country Club, and in the meeting rooms of the Citizens Alliance and the St. Paul Association, the Irish elite worked in concert with their Protestant peers to break organized labor's hold on the city and thwart the infant Farmer-Labor Party.[17]

The mythic elements of Irish identity nonetheless maintained their hold, deeply internalized, with long-established cultural value. As one St. Paulite explained, being Irish made him feel "special."[18] But the unifying power of Irishness had been severely circumscribed, giving way to a factionalism that belatedly focused on international as well as local politics. The struggles in postwar Ireland at last had captured the attention of Hibernian sons and daughters in St. Paul—who, according to one disgruntled partisan, had "badly muddled" and failed to financially support efforts to "circumvent English propaganda" during the war. But as attention shifted from the home town to the homeland, bitter debate over the fate of the Irish Republic only further fragmented the local Irish community. Although relief for suffering Ireland continued to elicit Irish support from all quarters, it flowed through politically distinct channels rather than community-wide social events. The St. Paul chapter of the Ancient Order of Hibernians persistently lobbied legislators in Washington, and construction magnate E. T. Foley served as Minnesota chair of the American Commission on Irish Independence, while other more militant Irish men and women pledged clandestine allegiance to the Clan na Gael. In short, the fractious world of Irish politics mirrored and exacerbated local tensions. The social world of Irish St. Paul had split—seemingly irrevocably—down the middle.[19]

The single tenuous thread that held the Irish together across class and political difference was their affiliation with the Catholic church. The character traits attributed to "Irish" and "Catholic" remained interchangeable in the minds of Protestants, whether for good or for ill. Thus, lumped together by these cultural markers, the varied members of the Irish "community" maintained superficial bonds, tended by the conciliatory efforts of the archbishop, despite deep rifts in the ethnic fabric. When circumstances changed, these links of common identity would be resurrected once again to play an important role in the life of the city.

In 1924, the policy of live and let live that had characterized St. Paul business, labor, and politics seemed consigned to history. But politics and culture intertwine as the sum of multiple variables. In St. Paul, several factors came together by mid-decade to halt internal polarization and spur citizens to revive the place-based politics, grounded in the civic insularity, that had sustained the city in the past. When that shift occurred, the Catholic Church and the Irish brotherhood resumed familiar roles of community mediation, though in somewhat altered form.

Times were hard by 1924. The depressed economy discouraged both working people and small businessmen. To William Mahoney, however, the dismal economic circumstances held real promise for advancing his agenda to move Farmer-Labor politics leftward, toward the establishment of a cooperative commonwealth based on public ownership and state regulation. More than simply a boon for the fortunes of the state party, circumstances seemed ripe for the formation of a national party as well. Backed by the Minneapolis trade unions, which long ago had been forced by business into more daring politics than those of the capital city, Mahoney laid the plans for a national presidential nominating convention to be held in St. Paul. The FLP would nominate Robert LaFollette, the political hero of the state's working people and farmers.[20]

When the Communist Party (CP) also endorsed LaFollette and pressed for an invitation to attend the convention, Mahoney agreed. Overriding opposition from other FLP strategists, he declared his conviction that "the time had come for a great coalition movement among all progressives." Almost immediately, the strategy backfired. Though Mahoney offered repeated assurances that "there was no fear of the Communists dominating [the convention]," both Farmer-Labor leaders and current FLP officeholders were dismayed. The local press made the most of the party's alleged radical affiliations; AFL president Samuel Gompers denounced the convention; and, even worse, Mahoney found himself red-baited from within the party itself, most notably by party co-founder Thomas Van Lear. As a final blow, Robert LaFollette, the party's intended presidential nominee, refused to attend the Communist-tainted convention, accusing Mahoney of collaborating with the Communists "to deceive the public." Thus Mahoney found himself discredited by the respected LaFollette as well as by the leadership of his party.[21]

The convention was a disaster. Mahoney had thought he could control the Communists. Instead, according to former CP member Benjamin Gitlow, he "fell into the snares of the Communists and could not extricate himself." The CP moved "heaven and hell" to get delegates to St. Paul, even chartering a special train from Chicago. More than a thousand Communists from all parts of the country converged on the convention. Suddenly radicalism, that nebulous threat, was front and center in downtown St. Paul.[22] Though the CP was formally limited to ten delegates, it had surreptitiously stacked the trade union delegations and proceeded to overwhelm the Farmer-Laborites, who then began to bolt. As one anguished farmer shouted from the floor, "This is not a farmer-labor convention; it isn't a convention composed of representative farmers and workers. . . . You must have every communist in the United States in this room. . . . The laborers are not here—only the communist members of their organizations." In truth, only a quarter of the expected four thousand delegates had registered their credentials; the majority were unwilling to participate in the compromised convention. With radicals clearly in the majority, FLP regulars, including the delegate from the St. Paul Trades Assembly, began to exit in protest despite Mahoney's frantic efforts to hold the convention together. The Communists then took charge, dictating both the platform and the nominating process.[23] To complete the debacle, after reducing the FLP to total disarray, three weeks later the Communists withdrew endorsement from the nominees they had forced on the convention in favor of Workers' Party candidates William Z. Foster and Benjamin Gitlow.[24]

The local papers reported the proceedings in excruciating detail. Friendly reporters at the *Daily News* did their best to craft a sympathetic portrayal, describing Mahoney as a tragic figure, "the quiet mannered, little gray-haired man, who dreamed this whole dream of organizing the discontented midwest." Tricked by the duplicitous Communists, "his hopes verge on despair—and all because of his faith in mankind." The *Pioneer Press* put a different slant on the story. It described Mahoney as "failing miserably" and "ignominiously defeated" but also accused him and the other Farmer-Labor leaders of collusion with the radicals. According to the paper, "They had been warned fully of the nefarious plans of the reds." Obviously then, they approved of the "red-stained planks." The lesson to be learned, the *Press* editorialized, was that the Farmer-Labor Party was clad in a "red-stained dress," and "William Mahoney [was] finally disclosed in his true color."[25]

In either interpretation, the events, spelled an enormous setback for Farmer-Labor aspirations. Mahoney's flirtation with the Communists dashed the reelection hopes of present FLP officeholders and swept the Republican ticket into office, in a humiliating if temporary repudiation of the FLP. Though the party would recoup, several important consequences evolved from the 1924 convention that were not as immediately apparent. In the words of political scientist Millard Gieske, William Mahoney had learned the "bitterest and most lasting political lesson of his life." From that point on, Mahoney became not only an adamant anticommunist but a confirmed moderate. Defeated as a Socialist in 1914 and 1920, the events of 1924 finally convinced him that his political vision could be secured only in incremental steps. In 1925, he led the charge to ban Communists from membership in the Farmer-Labor Federation. He would not stray far from the middle of the road again. Nor would St. Paul Farmer-Laborism. For the remaining life of the party, the St. Paul faction acted as a consistent drag on leftward movement in the party's politics. The faction also worked increasingly with local Democrats—a relationship that was cemented during the 1928 presidential campaign of Irish-Catholic Democrat Al Smith. When the two parties merged in 1944, St. Paul politicians from both parties played key roles in permanently domesticating farmer-labor populism in Minnesota.[26]

St. Paul businessmen discovered that they, too, had reaped some undesirable consequences from the Communist "invasion." The businessmen knew they had little to fear from radicalism in the city, thanks to regular reports from undercover agents in the Northern Information Bureau and the Citizens Alliance. Nonetheless, they had encouraged the press to make the most of supposed Farmer-Labor radicalism, and screaming headlines about "uncontrolled" Communists suggested that St. Paul had become a veritable Moscow on the Mississippi. The papers' readers, without access to inside information, were genuinely alarmed—exactly as the Alliance had hoped. But rather than turning public opinion against labor, this perceived threat to civic peace was laid at the businessmen's door. Ordinary citizens seem to have shared the opinion of "red hunter" Luke Boyce. Boyce warned the clients of his Northern Information Bureau that Alliance "methods of agitation and oppression were very rapidly converting conservative [union leaders] into becoming radicals of the fighting type."[27] In the assessment of many St. Paulites, the appearance of radicalism in the city was due directly to the intransigent business practices of the Citizens Alliance.

Assessing the tenor of public opinion in 1924, the editor of the *Pioneer Press* confided to his publisher, "We have deliberately refrained from discussing the work of the Citizens Alliance in order to keep the inevitable controversy over its activities as quiet as possible. For us to carry on a publicity campaign in behalf of the Alliance would not only stiffen the opposition but would breed violent acrimony both against the Alliance and against us."[28] Since the *Press* was ardently pro-business and most working-class people preferred the more populist *Daily News*, the editor's concern suggests that dislike for the Alliance extended well beyond the working class. The Citizens Alliance, despite its success in establishing the open shop in the city, had never been able to gain widespread public approval for its efforts. Small businessmen declined to join the organization, likely influenced by union claims that reduced working-class wages meant reduced buying power. The alleged emergence of radicalism in the city only increased already existing antipathy for Alliance methods.

The Alliance was incensed that local citizens were less grateful than they ought to be for its civic services. The organization's history, commissioned in 1925, conveyed a decidedly defensive, even petulant, tone. "The public suffers through ignorance" of the problems businessmen faced, it complained. "It should be constantly borne in mind that this action [organization of the Alliance] was not taken until the overt acts of the local labor leaders forced it. . . . Our citizens, resting safely in their homes, failed to realize how near our city had verged on absolute anarchy while someone else went out and fought their battles and made their security possible." The publication liberally interspersed its narrative with carefully selected supporting quotes from Archbishop Ireland and Cardinal Gibbons. (It did not include, however, the more recent quote from the *Catholic Bulletin*—that "all sane people approve of both unions and strikes when they obey the law of reason.")[29]

All this suggests that the Citizens Alliance was not popular force in the city. Nor, within its ranks, was all running smoothly. The Town and Country Club may have appeared to working people as the fortress of a unified business class, but inside the clubhouse, St. Paul's civic elite were less than wholeheartedly in accord. In the early twenties, in the midst of the business campaign against labor, more than a hundred of the club's members from the wealthiest old Protestant families split off to form their own exclusive club south of the city. This defection, "damned by a lot of [the club's] members," suggests that the Old Stock partnership with St. Paul's Irish and German Catholic elites was a shaky one, characterized by both cultural and ideological rifts. Thereafter, the Town and Country Club coalesced as a primarily Catholic bastion, affectionately referred to by its members as the home of the Irish mafia, the core of influential middle-class business and professional leaders who were most engaged in the day-to-day business of running the city.[30]

Though a causal connection cannot be made between this schism and the trajectory of the Citizens Alliance, by the mid-twenties the organization had taken on a distinctly conciliatory cast, particularly in the building trades, which were dominated by Catholic construction firms. This may have stemmed partially from an inadequate supply of skilled nonunion workers; or perhaps the working-class origins of most of the builders held them more accountable to their employees. Public opinion certainly played a role. At least in part, however, it seems certain that the Catholic Church was behind this shift in the war between business and labor.

In the depressed economy of the twenties, the church had become a critically important source of business for local contractors. Despite financial hard times, the archbishop authorized construction or expansion of numerous parish schools during this period. More important, between 1919 and 1926, contracts were let to build the impressive—and costly—churches of St. Mark and St. Luke, as well as the equally imposing chapel of the College of St. Catherine, a new Catholic orphanage, and a chancery and new residence for the archbishop. Most significantly, in 1921 the archdiocese launched the Archbishop Ireland Educational Fund, an extraordinarily ambitious building campaign with a fund-raising goal of $5 million. Over the decade, the bulk of that not-insignificant sum was poured into the St. Paul construction industry through various projects, most notably the construction of Cretin High School, a minor seminary at the College of St. Thomas, and a $3 million project to build the preparatory seminary of Nazareth Hall.[31]

Thus, the Catholic church came to play a critical role in a triangular relationship with business and labor in the city building trades. It was the single largest source of construction in the hard-pressed city, one connected, moreover, to city elites. The Ireland Fund's board of directors included Pierce Butler (of the Butler Brothers construction family), Edward Foley (of Foley construction), and Michael Waldorf (of Waldorf Paper Products)—not to mention directors of the city's three largest banks. The two largest single contributors to the fund were Mary Hill and construction magnate Timothy Foley, each of whom donated a half-million dollars to the cause.[32]

Foley's gift highlights one aspect of the complicated and symbiotic relationship between the church and Catholic elites. While the gift was specifically earmarked for the endowment of the College of St. Thomas and thus not directly tied to the construction projects, Foley Brothers Construction received the contract for the $3.75 million seminary project at Nazareth Hall. Lest the Butler brothers feel slighted, they received the contract for St. Luke's Church, projects at St. Thomas and St. Catherine's Colleges, and the building of parish schools. In turn, these major contractors subcontracted with dozens of smaller city firms and suppliers.[33]

The relationship between the building campaign and city working people was no less complicated. Another million dollars in pledges had come from the parishes of St. Paul—pledges unlikely to be fulfilled if the church was seen as a partner of the Citizens Alliance. If the pledges went unkept, the building projects would remain on the drawing board, and the contractors would lose these critical contracts.[34] At the same time, during the first thrust of the Alliance offensive, financially strapped union members could not afford to hold out for a closed shop. The church projects, which would not dare refuse to employ union workers, offered them a temporary solution, to pressing financial problems.

Given the complicated interdependencies between the Catholic Church, business, and labor, the open shop operated quite differently in St. Paul than in Minneapolis, where no such considerations were in play. Contracts for church projects required particularly delicate negotiation. For instance, in 1923 Foley Brothers won a major multiyear contract to renovate St. Paul's Union Depot (owned by the railroads). Every subcontract for the project contained the following clause:

> It is agreed and understood by the parties hereto that the Contractor is conducting the construction work on the St. Paul Union Depot on an "Open Shop" basis, and the subcontractor agrees to perform his work hereunder on such basis.[35]

In contrast, not a single contract for Foley's multiple archdiocesan projects contained a similar clause, stating simply that "all work to be done in first class workmanlike manner, and to be satisfactory to the owner, architects and contractor." It appears that when the Catholic Church was the owner, the terms of "satisfaction" differed from the desires of the Citizens Alliance. Thus, though the projects might ostensibly be classified as open shop, Foley closed its eyes to labor relations negotiated in the small firms that supplied the numerous craftsmen who worked on the jobs.[36]

At most, the city's open-shop church builders appear to have adhered to the minimum employment ratios set out by the Alliance in its propaganda pieces—up to 50 percent of the jobs could go to union workers. The builders also pledged to uphold the city-wide wage scale. Certainly, the building tradesmen were not content with this state of affairs. Wages were considerably lower than the old union scale, but it was understood that the present economy would not support wartime wage levels. Furthermore, the lockouts and blacklisting in common practice in Minneapolis must have made the St. Paul situation a somewhat preferable compromise.[37]

Also helping to ease the friction were the priests and nuns on hand at the building sites, who sometimes acted as watchdogs over labor practices. At the College of St. Catherine, President Sister Antonia McHugh, grounded in the social encyclicals and the rights of labor, kept an eye on workers' well-being during construction of the college chapel. When they worked overtime to meet impending deadlines, she provided meals for the men and gave them boxes of cigars in appreciation. Builder Walter Butler declared he was "much pleased with doing this chapel"; as "a place to worship God," it was an act of religious piety (as well as a lucrative project). The many Catholic workmen on the job may have held similarly complex sentiments—proud to put their skills to work in the name of their faith, especially when that faith protected their rights as workers on the job, thanks to Sister Antonia. The Citizens Alliance touted the beautiful church as a testament to open-shop efficiency, but the labor amity that characterized its construction had considerably more complicated underpinnings.[38]

By mid-decade, labor relations in the building trades had become a curious hybrid, taking their cue from the success of the archdiocesan projects. Though most contractors claimed to maintain an open shop in theory, they often negotiated wages and working conditions with union representatives who spoke for fully 50 percent of workers on the job. Contractors also began to regularly subcontract with union shops in the skilled trades, a practice that Citizens Alliance manager William MacMahon deplored. All of this suggests that the unions were making a comeback in the skilled trades and that, if the 50 percent nonunion rule was maintained at all, the nonunion percentage was increasingly likely to be made up of unskilled laborers.[39] Evidently, the Catholic building campaign played a significant role in this shift in labor relations. The interdependency between the local building industry, dominated by Irish Catholics, the Catholic working class, and the institutional church mediated the conflict generated by the open-shop campaign. This Catholic coalition also may have caused the schism between Catholic and Protestant elites, at the Town and Country Club—a split that seriously undermined business solidarity.

St. Paul businessmen, especially in the construction industry, simply could not afford to maintain an all-out offensive against organized labor. Local building permits had peaked in 1923, with a value of $36 million. Thereafter began a slow decline. By 1928, even the Citizens Alliance admitted that business was undeniably "dull," a condition that "some people blamed on the Citizens Alliance." Still, with the infusion of the Catholic building campaign, St. Paul's per capita building expenditures outpaced those of either Minneapolis or Duluth.[40] With the health of the building industry increasingly dependent on the Catholic Church and the contributions of working-class parishioners, self-preservation demanded a mediated stance with organized labor.

The purse strings of the archdiocese were tied in complicated ways to the content of Catholic doctrine. Using the church's leverage as an employer to speak out on behalf of working people, the archbishop took an increasingly active stand for social justice, most often speaking through Reverend Jeremiah Harrington, a student of John Ryan and his successor as professor of moral theology at the seminary. Much as Archbishop Ireland had tacitly sanctioned Ryan's role as labor advocate, Archbishop Dowling gave Harrington similarly free rein.

Harrington maintained close ties with the embattled forces of organized labor. In 1926, he teamed up with the MFL to organize workers' rights rallies in St. Paul, Minneapolis, and Duluth. A man who minced few words when it came to social justice, Harrington stood staunchly at labor's side. In an address given at the 1925 MFL convention, he invoked the philosophy of "working class development and high destiny in the world" that infused the moral theology of "our own Dr. John A. Ryan." Echoing the religious imagery of populist William Jennings Bryan, the priest gave notice to "the capitalistic plutocrats of the industrial and commercial world that the Catholic Church will not stand supinely by while capital is placing a crown of thorns on the bowed head of labor, while crucifying broken humanity on a cross of industrial gold." The following year, he published *Catholicism, Capitalism, or Communism,* an argument for the "Catholic Way" of distributism—a system based on social justice that would redistribute wealth more equitably—as the answer to the country's woes. The influence of the Catholic Church, he maintained, would ultimately force the abandonment of capitalism, since "the spirit of the Catholic church and the spirit of Capitalism cannot permanently co-exist together."[41]

These were strong public statements, but the church also set up its commitment to social justice as a bulwark against the dangers of radicalism that had generated a climate of public fear. Reiterating a familiar refrain, Archbishop Dowling argued that the church offered the best defense against radicalism. Whether or not the local business community agreed with his argument, for practical reasons at least, it acceded to his logic.[42] Thus, in St. Paul, the seat of the archdiocese, where the Catholic Church had the economic clout as well as the moral authority to put its doctrines into action, it recaptured its place as the central mediator of civic tensions.

By 1925, even as the Citizens Alliance published the history of its great success in establishing the open shop, it faced internal defections as well as public distaste. Moreover, to maintain the open shop, the organization found itself in a most peculiar position: It had to court the city's working people as well as its employers. Again and again, manager MacMahon stressed that "Open Shop employers never have, and do not now, bar union men from employment on open shop jobs." Moreover, their policy was to give preference to St. Paul residents. The Minneapolis Alliance made similar claims, which in that city were patently false. In St. Paul, however, it appears that the rhetoric represented actual policy. Given the tenor of public opinion, the Alliance had little choice. By 1929, the organization had taken on a notably conciliatory tone, claiming that its differences had never been with local unions, who "often have very little voice in the policies of their organizations." Rather, the city's labor troubles were due to the interference of "international officers [who] have no interest in local affairs and are only interested in seeing that the demands of their international unions are met." Local business agents, the Alliance charged, were forced by these "outsiders" into positions that harmed the well-being of local interests, both business and labor. Backed into a corner, the Citizens Alliance resorted to the familiar rallying cry that St. Paul was imperiled by forces operating outside its borders.[43]

Committed to demonstrate the benign intentions of the Citizens Alliance, MacMahon increasingly found himself in the odd position of labor advocate. When complaints came in that an employer was undercutting the established scale, MacMahon rushed to the worksite to "insure the payment of a wage more in accordance with American principles of justice and fair play." With recalcitrant employers, he enlisted the help of local lenders to insist that a minimum-wage clause be inserted into the contracts. Though the Alliance bragged that the city had been free from strikes or lockouts for several years, MacMahon acknowledged that only his constant efforts at mediation kept "the kettle . . . from boiling over." Predictably, agitation was most common in the building trades.[44]

In St. Paul, it had become apparent that the only way to justify the open shop was to embrace the principles of progressive industrial relations with a vengeance. That meant delivering higher wages, better working conditions, and shorter hours—in short, eliminating the causes for workers' protest. In a letter to city employers, MacMahon urged them to:

> find and eliminate the causes of strikes and labor turmoil. . . . Industrial controversies cannot be eliminated by paternalism on the part of management; it cannot be abolished by patronizing overlordships; but it can be obliterated by thorough and complete understanding by management and workers of their mutual problems, their mutual aims, and their mutual responsibilities for the success of the enterprise and their own well-being.[45]

This strategy of labor management echoed almost exactly the terms of the old civic compact. In the changed industrial climate, MacMahon was recommending a return to personalized relationships and an emphasis on mutual benefits: "Mr. Employer, tell your fellow workers about your and their business. Tell them personally if possible. . . . not patronizingly, but with sincere appreciation of their interest in *their*, and incidentally *your* business. It is *their* business, too, you know. It is where they make their living, just as you do. . . . Mr. Employer, it is up to you."[46]

Of the employers who took his strategies to heart, to MacMahon's chagrin more than a few turned to the familiar mechanism of the unions to negotiate their peace with labor. Some businessmen, in fact, found employers' associations far more coercive than labor organizations. When interviewed by a representative of the Citizens Alliance, the owner of Stoltz Dry Cleaners "was loath to state just how many of his people were union members," declaring that he had no complaints about the union people. He was, however, highly dissatisfied with the tactics of the Twin City Dry Cleaners Association and no longer wished to be a member of that organization. Similar disaffection was apparent among the members of the Building Employers Association. In 1929, despite a 5 percent increase in wages agreed upon by the Building Employers Association, union membership was on the rise, and contractors increasingly ignored even the appearance of maintaining an open shop.[47]

Gradually, as the twenties rolled on, individual businesses made their peace with organized labor in a variety of ways, working out pacts that served the interests of both sides in each particular case. For example, the Purity Baking Company (owned by the Foley construction family) made an agreement with the bakery drivers' union to eliminate independent jobbers who sold baked goods to the local grocery stores. Known as "bobtailers," these independents owned their own trucks and had specified territories. The bobtailers bought the products from the company at wholesale, marked them up a few cents and sold them to the retailers. According to one former bobtailer, both the union and the company "were very happy to sign a contract." The company gained control of the routes and absorbed the excess markup, and the union added the former independents to its membership rolls, in a reorganization that profited both the company and the union.[48]

The case of the bakery drivers represents only one variant in an array of inventive, locally specific, and sometimes indirect routes by which the unions gradually recouped the losses of the early twenties. The local specificity of these arrangements worked against solidarity either between Twin Cities unions or Twin Cities employers. While the unstinting opposition of Minneapolis business to organized labor served to increase militancy in both the beleaguered unions and the Minneapolis Farmer-Labor Party, circumstances in St. Paul set politics and labor on a different trajectory. According to Mock Larson, a member of the St. Paul teamsters in the 1920s–1930s, "Minneapolis and St. Paul . . . were really enemies. They didn't cooperate with each other and they didn't get along with each other." Minneapolis unionists, out of necessity, "had to be rough," but their style wasn't "comfortable" to union men in St. Paul. "In St. Paul most of the people were in favor of unions"—both blue-collar people and the middle class. "Minneapolis was really a foreign place. . . . St. Paul was home."[49]

It is noteworthy that Mock Larson, Swedish through and through, raised in the Scandinavian enclave of the city's East Side, only rarely visited Minneapolis, the center of Minnesota Scandinavian culture. "It wasn't the thing to do." Ethnic affiliation had no power to override hometown loyalties. As he explained, "You didn't go to Minneapolis and spend your money. Keep it home because if you go to Minneapolis and spend it, it will be gone. It won't turn over eight times like it will in St. Paul. . . . People really felt that they should spend their money at home and not somewhere else."[50]

As for the Citizens Alliance, by the close of the decade its influence was scarcely felt. In 1931, when R. N. Cardozo & Bro., the city's largest furniture merchant, requested bids for a multistory new building, it rejected the two lowest bids from open-shop contractors in favor of a firm "approved by the business agents as 'Fair to Organized Labor.' " The Citizens Alliance decried Cardozo's choice as neither "fair, right, [n]or reasonable," without effect. Though the Alliance professed to find it "difficult to understand why any merchant should so arbitrarily limit employment on his building project to the small minority represented by the unions," most St. Paulites understood quite well the familiar social pact between the company and its customers.[51]

By the 1930s, according to A. W. Lindeke, a prominent businessman, St. Paul had perfected a "method for the handling of controversial labor matters, which . . . was and is unique in this field." As he described it to *Fortune* magazine:

> The method—an employer's contract by which the employers in a given industry agree to and are legally bound by a contract to pay no less than a certain minimum wage, to work no more than certain maximum schedules or hours, to follow other provisions covering collective bargaining, handling of complaints and violations,

and a procedure of arbitration. These employers' contracts or agreements are arrived at after conferences with representatives of labor, and while the provisions are
accepted by labor, labor is not a party to the contract.[52]

Employers in other cities might have found the circumlocutions of Lindeke's explanation and the tortuous contours of St. Paul labor relations bewildering, but it
all made perfect sense to those who had struggled to reestablish the working relationships of the city. Despite the internal turmoil of the twenties, St. Paul
parochialism reemerged alive and well at the end of the decade. The local solutions
crafted to deal with the city's economic and social problems drew on familiar mechanisms based on long-standing cultural traditions and economic circumstances.
The restructured civic pact only intensified old tendencies toward insularity.

The Catholic Church, in helping to navigate these troubled times, reaped increased prestige, and its Irish Catholic members gladly resumed their roles as nego-
tiators of the civic peace. In the process, the claims of ethnic brotherhood mended
the rifts within the Irish community. But renewed manifestations of ethnic identity
took on a more subtle, less overtly institutionalized character. By the mid-twenties,
identifiably Irish organizations had all but disappeared in the city—their utility as a
meeting ground greatly diminished by internal arguments over Irish politics. In
1920, the Minnesota order of the AOH (headquartered in St. Paul) had ranked
among the top ten states in membership, but only four years later, its rolls were
sadly depleted; by 1924 St. Paul counted just over one thousand members, only
thirty-nine more than Minneapolis. Two years later, St. Paul president T. J. Doyle
reported the utter failure of a recent membership drive, confiding to his counterpart in Minneapolis, "I am getting a little skeptical about our Dear Old Order,
though I would not say so to any but you."[53]

By 1927, the Clan na Gael, though it maintained a presence in Minneapolis, had
suffered an ignominious dissolution in St. Paul. Though the head of the order
pleaded with Minneapolis leaders not to "lose sight of the possibility of reorganiz-
ing St. Paul," they were unable to "arouse former members . . . to any action that
would possibly make them the least bit active."[54] Apparently, Irish St. Paulites had
determined that dabbling in the politics of Ireland carried local costs that outweighed their interest in the old homeland.

This strange inversion of Irish organizational activity evolved quite naturally
from the relative stature of the group in the two cities. In Minneapolis, where
Irish residents perceived themselves still as victims of social snobbery and discrimination, the protective shield of ethnic organizations maintained a tenacious
hold among the city's Irish.[55] Ethnic discrimination at home also nurtured the
empathetic bond with injuries visited on ancestral Ireland. But in St. Paul, the situation was something entirely different. By the mid-twenties, the social status of
the Irish had been fully secured, buttressed by their function as civic mediators.
Many of the city's most prominent Old Stock families had at least one Irish
branch grafted onto the family tree. With Irish Catholics integrated into every so-

cial, commercial, and political institution, even working-class Irish were unlikely to experience any sort of ethnic discrimination. Students of assimilation theory might describe this as a stage of "structural assimilation." As succinctly captured by Philip Gleason, the evidence of structural assimilation—intermarriage and entry into membership in the social clubs and institutional organizations of the host society—depended not on "how one acted but of who one interacted with." In the estimation of a number of social theorists, when a group achieved such a degree of social integration, the withering of ethnic consciousness was likely to follow.[56]

At first glance, St. Paul's Irish may have seemed well on their way down this assimilative path, but social reality seldom conforms to the neat progression of theoretical models that elide the particularities of place. The integration of the Irish into the power structure of St. Paul enhanced rather than diminished the grip of ethnic identification, despite the fading importance of ethnic institutions. If anything, an Irish surname had become an asset rather than a liability, a defining emblem of civic membership and status. With increasing frequency, folks who traced even a modicum of Irish ancestry in a multiethnic heritage portrayed themselves as Irish through and through. Even the haughtiest of Old Stock St. Paulites, while they may have held themselves aloof, acknowledged that the mythical components of Irish identity had infused themselves into the fabric of St. Paul's civic culture.[57]

Therein lay the key. The Irish in St. Paul no longer had need for the protection of ethnic institutions. But neither had they been invisibly assimilated into the "mainstream" culture of St. Paul. Instead, civic culture had accommodated itself to the Irish, comfortably settling into a public self-identification of the city as an "Irish town"—a description that utilized "Irish" as descriptive shorthand for an entire system based on internal compromise, with Irish brokers at the fulcrum of its equilibrium.[58] But the content of Irish identity that emerged from the struggles of the war and its aftermath had itself been transformed in the process. The temporary intrusion of factionalism over the political fate of Ireland had added to the local conflicts—a brew that threatened the benefits and underpinnings that made St. Paul such a heaven for its Irish. Thus, local considerations and the requirements of Irish brokerism doomed international political consciousness to a very short tenure. By mid-decade, as the city struggled to resurrect its old ways of coping with internal tensions, homeland politics slipped quietly from sight. The claims of Irish brotherhood rejuvenated themselves informally within the venues of larger institutions— the Town and Country Club, Knights of Columbus, Trades and Labor Assembly, and City Council, to name just a few—rather than through ethnic institutions.

The reinvigorated Irish identity that emerged at the end of the twenties eschewed divisive ethnic politics for the commonalities of cultural trappings, situated in some mythical past, disconnected from the present-day politics of Ireland. It was, in effect, a "new social form." In *Beyond the Melting Pot*, Nathan Glazer and Daniel Patrick Moynihan described this process as a dialectical interaction between group heritage and American conditions, but the ethnic identity that evolved in St. Paul derived at least as much from local contingency as from the group's place in the national consciousness.[59] The Ireland of their imagination was thereafter quite specifically and exclusively defined by and situated within the geographic confines of the city of St. Paul.

The Catholic Church and its Irish had played essential roles in preserving the city's cross-class insularity and eventually resurrecting the terms of the civic compact. But another element had also operated, even in the most bitter days of civic strife, to keep St. Paul's fortress mentality alive.

In his history of the founding of St. Paul published in 1875, historian J. Fletcher Williams had exclaimed, "What Saint Paul Owes to Whiskey!"—an epigram no less pertinent in 1930 than in 1875.[60] Perhaps the single issue on which the citizens of St. Paul were in nearly unanimous agreement in 1920 was their opposition to the recently passed Eighteenth Amendment—a bill initiated, ironically, by rural Minnesota congressman Andrew Volstead. The amendment prohibiting the production and sale of alcohol had dealt the city's economy a potentially crippling blow. The trade in liquor and beer, from the prosperous turreted breweries to the hundreds of saloons scattered across town, was the source of critical income and jobs, and the consumption of alcohol was an integral part of the immigrant city's cultural fabric. St. Paul residents responded to this economic and cultural assault in predictable fashion: they ignored the law. Though prohibition was routinely flouted in cities and towns all across the nation, St. Paul was particularly well prepared to take its insurgency to an extreme.

Public antagonism toward prohibition was widespread. One teetotaling Irishman took up drinking on principle, declaring "He wasn't going to let any goddamn Swede tell him when he could have a drink."[61] Such strong antagonism toward the law, supported by the long-standing collusion between police and criminals that had made the "O'Connor System" an effective, if peculiar, method of law enforcement, turned a potential economic disaster into the most thriving sector of the city's economy. In short order, St. Paul attained dubious distinction as one of the bootlegging capitals of America.

In one way or another, almost everyone in the city seemed to profit from this arrangement. At the level of home production, moonshining became a standard part of the housekeeping routine. Chief of Police Michael Gebhart, who succeeded John O'Connor in 1920, complacently estimated that at least 75 percent of city residents were either distilling whiskey or making wine or beer by 1922. In most cases, the spirits were intended for personal use and created a new locus of social interaction at the neighborhood level. Italian immigrant Salvatore Vruno regularly treated his Irish and Jewish neighbors with liberal draughts of his homemade wine. His son vividly recalled the men "laughing and carrying on" in the garage behind his father's house. Many other entrepreneurial St. Paulites created a small-scale cottage industry out of moonshining to supplement inadequate incomes.[62]

A significant number of local folks entered into the illegal production and distri-

Fig. 39. Two young St. Paul moonshiners, caught tending their father's still in 1921, appear completely unfazed as they pose for the cameraman of the *Daily News*. Photo by *Saint Paul Daily News*. Courtesy of the Minnesota Historical Society.

bution of alcohol on a small commercial scale. Neighborhood speakeasies did a booming business. As everyone knew, operations like the Produce Café near the city market were saloons in everything but name. There was nothing surreptitious about the nature of the café, which sponsored regular beer-drinking contests among its working class–patrons. With legal beer and whiskey suppliers ostensibly shut down, the needs of such saloons created a profitable niche in the economy for basement and backyard operations that produced wine, whiskey, brandy, and beer.[63]

All this was small change, however, in comparison to the organized production and distribution network that developed in the city. As a major railroad center, with Canada as its northern neighbor, St. Paul was particularly well situated to become a key distribution point for alcoholic contraband. By the mid-twenties, prohibition agents claimed to intercept more than two thousand quarts of liquor a week at the Minnesota-Canada border. City vice bosses had lost no time turning the new law into a profitable industry. The chain of command spread from local neighborhoods to national bootlegging rings. Local entrepreneurs, such as Abe Gleeman, established something of a family economy. Operating out of his family's West Side basement, with the help of his father, brother Irving, and neighbor Morris Zuken, Abe bottled barrels of alcohol, loaded them up in the family car, and delivered them to speakeasies and individual middle-class residences, where home delivery by the local bootlegger was as expected as a visit from the milkman or the grocer. According to Gleeman, in one two-month period alone, he purchased $20,000 in alcohol from the local syndicate to bottle for resale.[64]

Abe's brother Bennie leapt into the bootlegging industry on a grander scale as part of the local syndicate that supplied the small operators who delivered the booze. The syndicate greased its operation by setting aside 14 percent of its profits—more than $3,000 a month—for "protection from those in charge of law enforcement." Atop this pyramid was liquor czar Leon Gleckman, who connected local operations to a national bootlegging network. In 1926, when federal investigators broke a major ring operating out of Cleveland, a startling 41 of the 112 people indicted in the case lived in St. Paul.[65] The commerce in illegal alcohol, dominated by Jewish entrepreneurs, only added to the money-laundering, fencing, and gambling operations already overseen in the city by Irish crime boss Danny Hogan, cementing an Irish-Jewish interethnic alliance and enhancing the cachet of St. Paul for criminals from all over the country. According to one local resident, "It was pretty hard to get caught in St. Paul because the only people that were going to arrest anybody were the Feds. And when they came to town, the police tipped off everybody." The city was rapidly becoming a nationally infamous haven for gangsters.[66]

But in St. Paul, neither gambling nor bootlegging were considered "real" crimes. Moreover, the vice economy provided all sorts of jobs and income throughout the city. According to crime chronicler Paul Maccabee, bribes flowed to police detectives, aldermen, grand jury members, judges, and even federal prosecutors. Trucking concerns and warehousers worked in tandem with the bootleggers, getting their share of the spoils. And rumors abounded that the local breweries were in cahoots as well. Some entrepreneurs, like the Gleeman brothers, made substantial amounts of money in the bootlegging trade, and many more, primarily Irish and Jewish working-class folks, found that city bootleggers paid wages that far outpaced what they could earn from legitimate city employers. The syndicate paid $12.50 a day for loading and unloading trucks, while Northern States Power Company paid only a dollar a day for ten backbreaking hours of ditch digging.[67]

To "respectable" St. Paul, this illicit culture seemed glamorous and daring. Middle and upper-class citizens flocked to shady nightclubs like the Hollyhocks Club, where they could drink and gamble alongside gangster celebrities. The Green Lantern Saloon, acknowledged headquarters of the criminal element, had a decidedly mixed clientele, according to owner Harry Sawyer: "All walks of life. State senators, attorneys, bootleggers, business men, lawyers . . . policemen . . . newspapermen . . . printers." As one woman recalled, the aura of danger was a powerful lure. She had insisted that her boyfriend take her to the Green Lantern: "All the gangsters hung around there, and I wanted to see it." In the dreary twenties, the well-heeled and stylishly turned out gangsters exuded a "wicked glamour" that lent them an aura more akin to movie stars than criminals.[68]

Many working people viewed the gangsters less as celebrities than as benefactors, outlaw folk heroes who liberally dispensed jobs and favors during hard times. The Gleeman brothers, who ran the Produce Cafe as part of their operations, lent money freely to their Italian immigrant customers. When Bennie Gleeman was sent to jail (in a rare conviction that required two retrials to make it stick), he "sold" his nearly new Oakland automobile to Sam Vruno, to be paid for whenever he was able. "They as much as give it to him is what they did," recalled Sam's son. "Bennie couldn't use it because he was going to jail and he wanted Pop to have it."[69]

Amid the labor and political conflicts, the vice economy created a neutral zone where a peculiar sort of cross-class socialization flourished. Former teamster Mock Larson recalled that in the twenties, he regularly played poker above the Noodle House on West Seventh Street with gangsters, police detectives, and the treasurer of the Schmidt Brewery. When the game was over, they would all pile into a car and head to the Hollyhocks nightclub for a midnight snack. According to Larson, "That's the way St. Paul was in those days. All friendly." Though Mock remembered that all sorts of people hobnobbed in the speakeasies, he never socialized with his poker partners on other occasions—nor did he share the tales of his adventures with his strait-laced Swedish-American parents.[70]

Inevitably, as more and more criminals from outside the city found their way to St. Paul, this "benign" arrangement began to unravel. Gangland shootings became an increasingly common occurrence that disturbed the civic peace. But until two prominent local businessmen were kidnapped in separate incidents in 1933–34, most citizens countenanced the illegal activities that created jobs and funneled money into the city. The only public manifestations of crime in St. Paul were bootlegging and gambling, which to most citizens seemed no crime at all. Local people chose to ignore evidence that the city had become a haven for bank robbers as well as bootleggers. In 1932, 21 percent of all bank robberies committed in the United States occurred in Minnesota—but not a single bank was robbed in the capital city. Small towns in neighboring Wisconsin, Iowa, and the Dakotas also reported more than their share of bank heists. Newspaper accounts of the crimes frequently noted that the robbers were "last seen heading for St. Paul."[71]

None of this bothered local people in the least. The gangsters themselves acted as informal enforcers of law and order inside the city limits. As crime reporter Bill Greer recalled, he often heard stories about petty felons who were "[taught] some manners" when they plied their trade in St. Paul. As he shrewdly observed, "It was a safer town to live in for most people when you had the criminals making sure there was no crime." Gangsters and residents alike referred to St. Paul with perverse local pride as the "holy city"—an odd sort of sanctuary centered in the Green Lantern Saloon rather than in the cathedral on the hill.[72]

As the twenties drew to a close, St. Paul returned to its insular, prewar world view and mode of operation. With a sinking economy that neither class politics nor a business offensive had managed to turn around, city residents resumed the traditional internal arrangements that pitted St. Paul, imaginatively and geographically, against the world. St. Paul problems were met with St. Paul solutions, mediated by the Catholic Church, a thriving vice economy, and local politics, that fused the Democratic and Farmer-Labor Parties in all but name. The Irish reclaimed their role as critical brokers in all these arenas, reviving a somewhat altered version of the old civic compact, which spread the benefits of compromise throughout the city. Meanwhile, across the river the war between business and labor continued unabated, moving Minneapolis ever closer to an inevitable conflagration.

In 1930, the skylines of St. Paul and Minneapolis each were punctuated by an impressive new landmark—the $5 million, thirty-two-story Foshay Tower in Minneapolis and an equally costly, magnificently embellished Art Deco city hall–county courthouse in St. Paul. The stories behind these building projects illustrate the profound differences that characterized the two cities as America settled into the Great Depression.

The Foshay Tower, the tallest building in the Northwest at that time, was built as headquarters for the far-flung utilities empire of Wilbur Foshay, a *nouveau riche* newcomer to Minneapolis financial circles. It also was built entirely with union labor. Foshay's unusual decision to break with the policy of the Minneapolis business establishment resulted from a complicated mix of business philosophy, public relations strategy, and personal pique. The utilities magnate had long been of the opinion that well-paid and satisfied employees not only turned in the best performance but also encouraged the public to invest in Foshay securities. For both these reasons, Foshay considered it good business to hire union labor. His calculation paid off well. The tower was completed on schedule in 1929, without labor troubles of any kind. According to a public broadcast delivered by Foshay, "The union men who constructed the Tower had not only cooperated wholeheartedly in their work . . . they had produced an honest dollar's worth of labor for each dollar paid them."[73]

Foshay's progressive labor practices netted him more than a well-built skyscraper. For ordinary people across the country, they situated the Foshay Companies as a good industrial citizen—publicity that Foshay expected to boost purchases of company stock. In the loosely structured securities market of the twenties, Foshay's holding companies were entirely dependent on continuous sales of stock—"ten or fifteen dollars from each of thousands of John Does"—to keep the multi-tiered structure solvent. The capital for construction of the tower itself had been raised by the issue of special stock packages designated to underwrite construction costs.[74]

Neither Foshay's business practices nor his public relations endeavors sat well with the Minneapolis business establishment. The upstart Foshay, who in just twelve years had parlayed $6,000 in capital into utilities holdings in twelve states and five countries, was unable to buy his way into the closed circle of Minneapolis society, though he supported a range of civic projects and purchased homes in prestigious Kenwood and on Lake Minnetonka. The union-built tower may have been revenge for his social snub. The magnificent structure rising in the middle of the business district overshadowed the Rand Tower and the Northwestern Bank Building, both under construction at the same time. While the Foshay Tower proceeded right on schedule, these two open-shop projects were plagued by constant labor disputes. Moreover, the construction and dedication of the tower received extensive coverage in the national press. A three-day dedication extravaganza, capped off by an original march composed and directed by John Philip Sousa, celebrated union labor as well as Wilbur Foshay—an unmitigated affront to the civic leaders who worked so tirelessly to maintain Minneapolis as the "open-shop capital of America."[75]

Foshay's day in the sun proved exceedingly brief. He never had the opportunity to settle into his lavish offices on the tower's twenty-eighth floor. Northwest Bancorporation, Minneapolis's preeminent financial institution, long a major force behind the Citizens Alliance, had recently completed the absorption of several smaller banks that had extended credit to Wilbur Foshay. When the stock market crashed in October, Northwest called in the loans. The $25 million utilities empire found itself $300,000 short. Denied short-term credit from the Minneapolis banking establishment, the Foshay Companies collapsed into bankruptcy. The company's receiver, a director of Northwest, then called in the common stock, leaving Foshay personally destitute as well as financially ruined. He never recovered. Whether intended or not, the city read a larger moral in this personal tragedy: employment of union labor in Minneapolis carried an exceedingly steep price.[76]

Contrast this with the saga of the City Hall that went up in St. Paul at approximately the same time. In 1929, William MacMahon of the Citizens Alliance declared, "St. Paul stands at the threshold of better days,"—a prophecy that unfortunately proved a decade premature. In terms of the local construction industry, however, his projection was quite sound. City voters, by a margin of more than 70 percent, had recently approved a $15 million bond issue to fund a five-year program of civic improvements, including a $4 million combined city hall and county courthouse. The St. Paul Association had opposed similar bond issues in 1927, but a year later, with the local economy sinking, it backed the bond proposal fully. To counteract the "dull building years," that were battering local businesses—St. Paul crafted a policy that prefigured the strategy that would underlay the New Deal's Works Progress Administration (WPA) four years later. It would use municipal funds to artificially boost the local economy—generating jobs and thereby increasing local buying power.[77]

The City Hall project provided a much-needed economic infusion; but it also was designed to symbolize the capital city's progressivism and civic pride. With that purpose in mind, the planning commission selected the ultramodern, Art Deco design of Chicago architects Holabird and Root as an appropriate representation to "take proper cognizance of [St. Paul's] future."[78] Ironically, this monument to modernism was constructed wholly within the parochial terms of the civic compact derived from the city's past.

Though a Chicago firm won the primary contract, in the opinion of St. Paul citizens, the overriding purpose of the project was to benefit *local* interests. Accordingly, the contract for the building's interior design was awarded to St. Paul architects Thomas Ellerbe & Company.[79] To demonstrate that labor had not been left out, the planning commission pledged to employ only St. Paul labor and, though the Citizens Alliance lobbied for the virtues of the open shop, Foley Brothers, which worked increasingly with local unions, won the job of general contractor. The old system of spreading the wealth within the city limits was up and running.[80]

The underlying logic of the project was tellingly revealed following the stock market crash in October. The cost of materials plunged and the building could have come in far under its allocated budget, but instead the planning commission authorized Ellerbe to elaborate its interior designs, creating "decorative details of unparalleled opulence." Imported woods and marbles from all over the world arrived in St. Paul to be cut, finished, and installed by skilled—and unionized—local craftsmen. Door handles, light fixtures, mailboxes, stair railings—every embellishment was crafted locally with labor-intensive, luxurious detail. All of this meant more jobs for St. Paul craftsmen. Building laborers also received a share of the surplus funds—a 12.5 percent pay raise across the board. When the building was completed on schedule in 1932, most city residents must have agreed that the museum-quality edifice was in every way a fitting representation of St. Paul's civic identity.[81]

The first occupant of the lavish offices in the new City Hall was none other than newly-elected mayor William Mahoney. The veteran Socialist/Farmer-Laborite had finally attained the office for which he had yearned so long. Mahoney's political principles were essentially unchanged, but political savvy and new economic circumstances won him the people's endorsement at last. No longer could he be painted as a dangerous radical: His repudiation of the Communists was a matter of public record; he had personally engineered their expulsion from the Farmer-Labor Association. He also had mended fences with the city's Democratic politicians. Larry Hodgson, Mahoney's opponent in the 1920 mayoral race, warmly endorsed the labor editor's campaign. Mahoney and Hodgson, whom Mahoney had once considered part of the "vile political ring" that ruled St. Paul, were now the closest of friends. As Hodgson wrote to Mahoney, "I feel so truly close to you that I think of you as a friend that would stand by me in any personal calamity. . . . I am proud to have been associated with your campaign."[82]

The confrontational attacks on plutocracy and special interests that had characterized Mahoney's politicking in his younger days were notably absent from his 1932 campaign. Instead, he emphasized the need for the community to pull together to save their imperiled city, pledging an administration that would protect the interests of "every member of society." Immediately on taking office, the new mayor put his promises of inclusive government into action. In a letter sent to every church, fraternal society, neighborhood organization, union, club, and business organization—from the Ramsey County Medical Association to the Knights of Columbus to the Ladies' Sunshine Club to the Hod Carriers and Common Laborers Union—the mayor asked for the names of volunteers who would be willing to serve on civic committees. In the letter Mahoney declared, "I want to take the people of Saint Paul into the government and share in its activities and responsibilities. Let us develop a complete democracy wherein everyone feels his power and duty."[83]

Cynics might dismiss this initiative as no more than a political maneuver, but it bears noting that the broadly participatory municipal government that Mahoney was promoting was consistent with his life-long political agenda, implemented incrementally in terms that localistic St. Paulites would understand and endorse. At any rate, the lists of volunteers that poured into the mayor's office testify that a good number of St. Paul citizens believed in the sincerity of the effort and responded to the invitation with enthusiasm. In the words of one correspondent, "It is high time for a new deal in public affairs. It is cause for gratitude that your administration promises a change and we can only wish you Godspeed and promise you such humble assistance as it may be in our power to try." Working people, in particular, took seriously the invitation to participate in the public life of the city. As Max Keller of the Federal Employees Union wrote, "Sorry to say that I cannot serve personally because my job demands me to work nights and like often meetings & etc. are held at night time and I could not attend. I understand your idea and my dear Mr. Mahoney you deserve credit for your undertaking."[84] The Citizens Alliance had less enthusiasm for the city's new labor mayor. As a "civic organization," it too received the invitation to participate in the "complete democracy" of the new administration, which elicited a strained response from the Alliance general manager: The organization always fulfilled its civic duties to work for the "public welfare," and its members had always given generously of their time to work for the "common good"—a claim that must have amused the mayor.[85]

He could afford to be amused. The influence of the Citizens Alliance was fading fast. As Mahoney tackled the city's economic problems, even businessmen began to be impressed. No less a civic leader than Homer Clark, who had succeeded Charles Ames as president of West Publishing, confided to a friend in 1933, "St. Paul has a Labor Mayor, Mr. William Mahoney, and strange to say, after seeing him in action for nearly a year, people like Mr. Prince [president of the Merchants National Bank] and myself are glad that he beat the conservative candidate."[86]

The businessmen had good reason to applaud the mayor. St. Paul was in dire financial straits. Burdened with the bond debt it had incurred to fund municipal improvements, the city could not have been in a worse position when it was hit by the full force of the Depression. Delinquent property taxes had become so endemic that the city was unable to meet its payroll in 1933. Mahoney worked out a municipal bailout with the local banks, contingent on the willingness of city employees to accept 85 percent of their wages due, with the rest to be paid as funds became available. Mahoney's credibility with St. Paul working people uniquely positioned him to convince the employees to accept the deal. City workers may have been further persuaded to compromise on wages because Mahoney also was working to bring down inflated utility rates. Making good on his campaign promise to protect the people from unfair corporate practices, the mayor had established a committee to explore municipal takeover of the local power company. Furthermore, he remained committed to creating jobs for the unemployed as a substitute for relief, giving citizens an opportunity to earn an "honorable living"; this policy, he declared, would enrich the community and save the destitute from degradation. In a time when relief still carried with it a powerful stigma, this route was preferred by the unemployed as well as by the general population.[87]

Mahoney may have no longer been a militant, but neither had he devolved simply into a deal maker. Rather, he had rechanneled his vision of a more just society into a form that was politically palatable in St. Paul. Reform, as the mayor had come to understand, must be framed in locally chauvinistic as well as idealistic terms. Along with his other initiatives, he had committed his administration to "free the city from underworld influence"—a goal that met with wide approval after the repeal of Prohibition in 1933. With the demise of bootlegging, the benefits of the "Holy City" no longer outweighed St. Paul's growing reputation as a "mecca for criminals." The resumption of legal production of alcohol and licensing revenues from more than one thousand "beer parlors" in the city made the loss of the illicit revenues considerably less painful. Moreover, according to one contemporary analysis, "The national attention focused on St. Paul by the blatant activities of nonresident gangsters interfered seriously with its own rather quiet activities . . . slot machines, graft, and other non-violent enterprises." The glamour of the gangster era had dimmed significantly as criminals began to ignore the rules of the O'Connor system that had kept the city free from crime. Gunfire occasionally invaded quiet neighborhoods as gangsters settled grudges with one another; furthermore, nationally publicized shootouts between the FBI and notorious criminals like John Dillinger and the Barker gang further blackened St. Paul's civic reputation, as did widely quoted accusations by J. Edgar Hoover that city police were working hand in glove with the criminals. The final straw was the kidnapping in 1933 of William Hamm, heir to the Hamm's brewing fortune, followed seven months later by the abduction of a fellow brewing heir, Edward Bremer.[88]

The increase in crime at home and the intense national publicity that went with it unified local citizens in their determination to clean up the city. But, paradoxically, St. Paul's unsavory reputation also heightened its culture of civic defensiveness. It was one thing for local business leaders to raise a $100,000 war chest to finance a campaign against corruption—that was an internal matter. It was quite another for the U.S. attorney general to label St. Paul as a "poison spot of crime." Thus, even as Mahoney launched a campaign to reform the police department, he insisted publicly that the city had no crime problem. A grand jury investigation concurred, "quietly whitewashing everybody concerned." The day after the grand jury's findings were published, John Dillinger shot his way out of a St. Paul apartment, in a dramatic rebuttal of the city's public relations claims.[89] But as blatantly as the evidence belied official pronouncements, to many local people it seemed no contradiction at all. Quietly ousting the criminal element was taking care of city business; denying its existence was standing up for the hometown—a distinction that the mayor had come to understand quite well.

Still, William Mahoney was defeated in his bid for reelection in 1934, a victim of his success. The municipal ownership plan that the old socialist had first advocated in 1914 and again in 1920 was about to be realized at last. Engineering and feasibility studies had been completed. All that remained to put St. Paul in the utilities business was passage of an amendment to the city charter, which appeared almost certain to be voted into law. In the final weeks before the election, Northern States Power Company orchestrated a desperate campaign against the mayor, blaming him for the city's financial troubles and for the crime wave that had overwhelmed the city during his administration.[90]

Indisputably, Mahoney had inherited the first problem, but he was indeed unintentionally responsible for the second—though not because of personal corruption, as accused by his opponent. To the contrary, when Mahoney had declared his war on crime, he had broken the pact that kept the city internally crime-free. In 1932, Mahoney's new police chief, Tom Dahill, had announced, "Gangsters and would-be gangsters are not wanted here and we intend to do everything in our power to drive them out." Though the chief proved as good as his word, the deep-seated corruption in the St. Paul police department took time to root out. In the meantime, the criminals launched a counteroffensive, reasoning that "if Dahill could violate the O'Connor agreement to leave crooks alone, [it] was time to violate O'Connor's prohibition against major crimes in St. Paul." Thus, the immediate result of Mahoney's anticrime crusade was an unparalleled crime wave. His opponents used this as evidence that the mayor was in league with the city's criminal element.[91]

St. Paul voters, immersed in an economic panic that was far beyond the mayor's control and deeply alarmed by the escalating violence in the city, were swayed by the attacks against the labor mayor. As former mayor Hodgson wrote his "dear old pal" Mahoney, "I am sure you were the honest choice of the people. The last three days of the campaign a bunch of crooked money and a lot of political conniving raised havoc. . . . But we fought an honest battle. . . . I feel as you do, that common sense can always obtain its wishes peacefully. But when poisoned newspapers mislead the people what can we do?"[92]

Though Hodgson regarded the defeat as "the enthronement of . . . the Northern States Power Company" and a great "setback for Liberalism," it did not presage renewed conflict in the city. The record of Mark Gehan, Mahoney's successor, and an Irish-Catholic Democrat, demonstrates how firmly the culture of compromise had been reinstated in St. Paul. The power company retained ownership of its electrical plant, but the barely averted municipal coup caused the company to reduce its rates and quietly accept a $125,000 increase in property taxes. Mayor Gehan continued Mahoney's initiative to provide jobs for city residents, taking advantage of newly available federal programs to win seven thousand WPA jobs and an additional $900,000 in relief for the suffering city. Aided by the FBI, he also was able to take credit for the campaign Mahoney had begun against crime in St. Paul, somewhat rehabilitating the city's reputation. And finally, he fulfilled the former mayor's pledge to pay city workers the remainder of the salaries they had deferred during the crisis of 1933. Though Mahoney's defeat had prompted Larry Hodgson to wonder "if the great monied concerns can ever be dethroned except by Revolution," no revolution was in the making in St. Paul. Rather, the agenda of Gehan's "pro-business" administration largely carried out the program of the labor mayor—a pattern that remained intact throughout the decade. The series of Irish-Catholics who traded office between 1932 and 1942, whether Democrats or Farmer-Laborites, were indistinguishable in their strategies to keep the city operating.[93]

The Great Depression marked one of the most volatile moments in the nation's history—a time when the future of both capitalism and the American political system were in doubt. Yet, the upsurge of discontent that swept across the country made only minimal waves in St. Paul. Mahoney's attempt at municipal ownership was the last trace of radicalism to surface in city politics. St. Paul had fought its battles a decade earlier and come to its own conclusions. For most residents, neither the alliances they had made outside the city nor reliance on the state or federal government had proved a substitute for local solutions brokered through local institutions. That belief would continue to inform their politics for years to come.

EPILOGUE:

Political Change and the Power of Place

In the spring of 1934, the ongoing strife between business and labor in Minneapolis culminated in a momentous truckers' strike, a skillfully organized labor offensive that catapulted the city into a state of virtual civil war.[1] The nation watched as the city's working people battled police and deputized businessmen in the streets—a struggle that finally broke the hold of the Citizens Alliance, leaving Minneapolis, in the estimation of *Fortune* magazine, with "the clearest Left-Right alignment of any city in the land."[2]

Across the river, in "the capital of the most radical U.S. state," business went on as usual. In May, St. Paul teamsters, in the midst of their own disputes, had initially agreed to join the pending strike, but at the eleventh hour, they had reached a separate agreement with city employers. When the Minneapolis teamsters staged a second strike in July, St. Paul union men again promised support, then withdrew it at the last minute. Ultimately, the city boundaries had proved unbreachable.[3]

The truckers' strike set off a decade of labor protest in Minneapolis that finally defeated the open shop and, in the process, strengthened the left politics of the Farmer-Labor Party. In the meantime, St. Paul remained relatively free from labor troubles—and decidedly removed from the struggle taking place in its sister city. In the estimation of St. Paul teamster Mock Larson and most of his contemporaries, "Minneapolis was really a foreign place."[4]

When a correspondent from *Fortune* arrived in the Twin Cities in 1936 to assess the situation, he described Minneapolis as brought to the verge of revolution, electrified by employer arrogance and industrial ferment. In contrast, to the journalist's New York eye, St. Paul seemed sunk in complacency and consigned to oblivion. As described in what he titled an "epitaph for a city," St. Paul appeared "cramped, hilly, stagnant," with narrow streets and small buildings, few new industries, and "the atmosphere of a city grown old." Its people had "less breeziness, less cordiality" than those in Minneapolis. According to *Fortune*, St. Paul was a dying, commercial backwater. It had "no labor troubles" because it had "unionized years ago in a nice A. F. of L. way, about the time the city stopped growing."[5]

This outsider's snapshot portrait of St. Paul obscured the complicated social processes that underlay the pact between labor and business—understandings that continued to be negotiated on a daily basis in the city. Moreover, the economic and social landscape that seemed to him so contrary to twentieth-century ideals of progress and growth fundamentally undergirded the relationships St. Paulites most valued. What *Fortune* labeled "an unmistakable inferiority complex" was far more complicated. St. Paul parochialism sprang from economic and cultural sources that alienated the city not only from Minneapolis (in what the correspondent assessed as "more than conventional intercity rivalry") but from the rest of the state as well. This "Irish-Catholic town" self-consciously defined itself as an island of exceptionalism.[6]

However, neither inherent qualities of Catholic conservatism nor an Irish predisposition for deal making could account for the choices made by St. Paul workers, as contemporaries and historians have been wont to claim. After all, the three Dunne brothers who led the Minneapolis strikes were born and raised as Irish Catholics, as were strike activists (and St. Paul natives) Grace and Dorothy Holmes.[7] Rather, both the politics of Catholicism and the contours of Irish identity were shaped within the particular economic and social milieu of the city. They were fundamentally influenced by—and left their impression on—the social geography in which they were embedded. The culture of St. Paul, as of any other locale, was the product of its historical relationship to place.

Of course, this culture continued to be a process as well as a product. The settlements in place in 1934 were not inviolable. Internal tensions continued to require constant negotiation. But the city never again experienced economic and social disruptions comparable to those it endured from 1917 to 1925. The depression of the 1930s only exacerbated already existing local economic woes. Each time that traditional, insular strategies successfully resolved municipal problems, their cultural legitimacy was reinforced, enhancing their power to negotiate the next round of difficulties. For the next thirty years, St. Paul's economy remained in relative equilibrium—neither exceptionally robust nor in further decline. As a result, the mechanisms crafted to protect its weak economic structure in the early twentieth century proved their worth again and again.

Despite the intense localism that characterized the cultural politics of the city, St. Paul residents did not isolate themselves from the transformations taking place in state and national politics—an impossible task even if they had desired to do so. City voters enthusiastically embraced Farmer-Laborism at the state level and consistently favored left-liberal and reformist policies in state and national matters from the 1930s onward. City officials energetically pursued state and federal funds for municipal improvement and aid. But, as a study published by the Massachusetts Institute of Technology in the 1950s concluded, local politics had different contours. St. Paulites made a sharp distinction between politics writ large and those that most immediately influenced their daily lives.[8]

The MIT study, completed in 1959, provides an instructive portrait of the ways that cultural persistence reinforced itself in the face of social and political change. Demographically, geographically, and economically the city had altered very little in the intervening decades. The population had reached 300,000—an all-time high attributable to the baby boom rather than in-migration—but only 2.5 percent was nonwhite, with a black population described as "predominantly middle class." Seventy-three percent of residents claimed a religious affiliation: 40 percent identified themselves as Catholic, 29 percent as Protestant, and 4 percent Jewish. The city showed exceptional residential persistence: approximately 70 percent of people owned their own homes in 1959.[9]

Not only did people remain in the city; they tended to stay in the same neighborhoods for generations, anchored by the city's forty-four parishes. Real estate ads prominently featured the parish in which residential properties were located and Catholics commonly used the mental map of parish affiliation to situate one another within the social order.[10] While some working-class neighborhoods continued to exhibit a somewhat recognizably ethnic character, middle-income neighborhoods were ethnically and occupationally mixed, as they had been for decades. Summit Avenue was still the most prestigious address in town. At the other end of the social spectrum, problems of poverty remained largely unaddressed by municipal authorities, left to the ministrations of private agencies and individual philanthropy, aided by the increasing availability of state and federal funds. Minneapolis also continued to serve as a convenient catch basin for the city's social problems. As the MIT study observed, "St. Paul does not have a skid-row; it uses the ample Minneapolis one." By the standard of eastern cities, the city was strikingly free of slums. Thus, the relatively small scale of St. Paul's poverty problem allowed it to remain invisible to the public eye.[11]

Economically, the city neither grew nor declined substantially. The business community upheld its long-demonstrated priority to protect the functioning of the existing economy and showed "no interest . . . in attracting new business." Union priorities, concerned with job protection, differed little from those of business; thus, business launched no further organized assaults on union labor, leaving the Trades and Labor Assembly an open field to strengthen its local political power. When the Farmer-Labor Party merged with the Democratic Party in 1944, the separate strands of ethnoreligious and labor politics formally united in the Democratic-Farmer-Labor Party (DFL) to turn the city government into an unchallenged "stronghold of labor."[12]

Though city elections were nominally nonpartisan, candidates blazoned the all-important "DFL-Labor Endorsed" signifier—an almost sure-fire guarantee for election. The city's sixty-five thousand union members (and their families and friends) carried formidable clout. By 1959, the labor-based culture of DFL politics infused much of the middle class as well. Descendants of immigrant workers, long established in the city, composed the bulk of the business and professional class. Their interests might no longer be tied materially to those of the unions, but they had learned their allegiances at their father's knee, and "union" remained a sacred word in many middle-class households.[13]

The building trades continued to predominate in the leadership of the Trades and Labor Assembly, and they steered an unerringly "moderate" course. As described by political scientist Alan Altshuler:

> The hereditary aristocrats of labor in St. Paul—all Catholics of course—have so much in common that differences between the younger, more activist and the older, conservative leaders are moderated. All come from the same parishes and neighborhoods. The older leaders have a paternal feeling for the younger ones, and they, in turn, respect the experience of their elders. The younger leaders have put new vigor in the labor movement. At the same time, the older leaders have dampened impetuous and aggressive action.[14]

The localistic interests of labor fit quite neatly with those of business. The large proportion of homeowners created city-wide opposition to high property taxes; both business and labor dedicated themselves to protecting the local economy; and the regime of the Public Safety Commission had left an enduring distaste for state intrusion into municipal affairs. In sum, both business and labor dedicated themselves to the overall goal of protecting the status quo.[15]

Thus, business seldom roused itself in any organized way to oppose the labor-dominated Democratic Farmer Labor Party. The Republican party was so weak in the city that conservative candidates ran for city office as "independents" and avoided mention of Republican endorsement, unlike the DFL-backed candidates. In truth, the range of difference between conservative and liberal candidates often was so slight as to practically eliminate issue-based politics from St. Paul elections. Instead, campaigns revolved on personalities and local pedigrees rather than substantive political divergence.[16]

In the assessment of the MIT study "being Catholic is almost essential for political success in St. Paul . . . [and] among the Catholics, the Irish predominate." Indeed, Catholic influence remained ubiquitous. Campaigns often devolved into debates over the moral fitness of candidates, and the intellectuals of the St. Paul DFL were primarily professors from the College of St. Thomas. (It was from this milieu that Minnesota senator Eugene McCarthy came to power.)[17] Moreover, the church continued as a critical private provider of social services, most notably by educating more than a third of the city's children in its parochial schools. Though it remained "scrupulously detached" from overt meddling in politics, its influence was nonetheless deep and undeniable.[18]

Most of the city's labor leaders were Catholics, and the church and union hall shared their allegiances equally. The fusion of religious and labor principles owed much of its durability to the efforts of Father Francis Gilligan, who had arrived as a young priest in the city in 1928. Gilligan, the orphaned son of textile workers and a native of Fall River, Massachusetts, had honed his social justice sensibilities as a student of John Ryan at Catholic University. Throughout his long life in St. Paul, Gilligan worked tirelessly to foster lines of communication between the church and the unions. In the thirties, he established traveling Catholic "labor schools" as a bulwark against Communist infiltration of local unions. Taking his labor school from parish to parish, he strove to educate workers in the social-justice principles of Catholic unionism. Pragmatic schooling in labor law and parliamentary procedure augmented ideological lessons, arming Catholic workers to influence both political and union decision making. The "labor priest" also became a regular attendee at the weekly meeting of the city's union business agents, each week bringing in tow a different Catholic cleric, ostensibly to offer an opening invocation for the meeting. His underlying purpose, however, was more to educate the priests than the workers. As he confided years later, some middle-class Catholics (including certain unen-lightened priests) had an unfortunate tendency, especially in the thirties, to confuse unionism with Communism. To counter such misperceptions, as part of his labor ministry Gilligan endeavored to educate the middle class (and the succession of archbishops under whom he served) on the importance and social value of unions. Thus, the social-justice principles that John Ryan had first espoused at the St. Paul Seminary some thirty years earlier came full circle, carried forward by Francis Gilligan in St. Paul's union culture of the thirties and forties.[19]

Irish influence was more difficult to trace in tangible ways. Though St. Paulites themselves tended to agree with outside assessments that theirs was an "Irish town," this was a product of image more than substance, as indeed it had always been. A succession of Irish mayors held office throughout the 1950s, but the ethnic composition of the city council was considerably more diverse. Of the six council members in 1959, two had Swedish surnames and two German. Only one, Eliza-beth DeCourcy, was Irish, a member of the prestigious O'Brien family and sister of a priest. The final council seat belonged to Jewish Milton Rosen, re-elected by St. Paul voters for a tenure that stretched from 1930 through the sixties. The popular Rosen received the ultimate accolade from the city's Irish in the 1970s, honored in the annual St. Patrick's Day parade. Thus, the perception of Irish dominance, at least among elected officials, endured as a cultural emblem more than as fact.[20]

This apparent diversity, however, masks a more subtle operation of cultural pol-itics that retained the indelible imprint of years of Irish-Catholic brokering and ide-ology. Voters endorsed candidates of differing ethnic backgrounds, but only when those candidates met the standards of traditional St. Paul politics, a mode of oper-ation and set of priorities that were identified as typically "Irish"—the ineluctably parochial system of give-and-take that had underlain the civic compact for sixty years.

Thus, in many ways, in 1959 the city held fast to the political culture it had reestablished in the 1930s. In other ways, changing circumstances demanded a rethinking of the parameters of the civic compact. The most striking change was the reversal of public tolerance for vice. The benefits of corruption no longer outweighed the costs. The city's public vilification as a criminal haven had wounded local pride; more important, felons also increasingly had plied their trade within the city limits. Finally, with new access to federal and state subsidies to buttress the local economy, the St. Paul could afford to shed its old reliance on vice revenues. Though outside support was not adequate to foster substantial economic growth, it was sufficient, if the city was fiscally conservative, to keep the economy running—a modest goal that satisfied the desires of the majority of St. Paul residents.

After finally dissolving its pact with crime, the city had cleaned house with a will. By the 1950s, according to a disinterested analyst, there was "no organized crime, vice, or corruption in the city." Municipal jobs, including those of laborers and temporary workers, were subject to a strict civil service code, eliminating patronage, which helped to foster a climate of "clean" municipal politics. Nor were the unions tainted by any trace of scandal, either internally or in the person of political hacks. Labor prided itself on its good citizenship, taking the lead in an array of civic and charitable projects.[21] By the 1950s, most of the previously marginalized ethnic groups (with the notable exception of African Americans) had forged their way into politics and business, broadening the range of civic identity and muting ethnic divisiveness. All in all, St. Paulites congratulated themselves on the success of the pact they had made.

Hometown pride notwithstanding, the city had a decidedly shabby air in 1959, especially in comparison with bustling Minneapolis. The downtown was devoid of new construction; schools were aging and inadequate; the sprawling homes in Crocus Hill and even the mansions on Summit Avenue showed evidence of wear and tear. Though it managed to maintain the status quo, the city had scant resources for infrastructural maintenance, let alone municipal improvements. Voters consistently rejected municipal bonding initiatives. The passage of the $15 million bond issue in 1929 had nearly bankrupted the city—a mistake voters would not soon repeat. They did not approve another major bond issue in the ensuing thirty years.

St. Paul's threadbare appearance began to make a dramatic turnaround by the 1970s, thanks to expanding state and federal incentives. Government subsidies injected the funds for education, urban renewal, and social services that local government could not or would not spare. This economic boon was warmly welcomed in the city and reinforced the bifurcated nature of St. Paul politics. Voters wholeheartedly embraced liberalism in state and national politics, fitting their ideology of social justice neatly into the pattern described as "Minnesota progressivism." But the paradoxical value of such liberalism was that it sustained local insularity. City politics retained a distinctively parochial and conservative character. In short, the changing nature of the state enabled the city to adhere to old ways of operating within the civic compact.[22]

By the 1990s, St. Paul no longer appeared a shabby, conservative backwater. The national press increasingly touted the city for its quality of life, clean government, good schools, and vibrant "community"—all of which reinforced the old claims of civic loyalty and the parochial outlook it carried. Suddenly, quality of life had become a capital resource. In 1989, *Newsweek* declared St. Paul one of "America's best places to live and work." Never the beneficiary of industrial progress, the city was spared the subsequent upheavals of deindustrialization in the postindustrial age. New, "clean" industries began to favor St. Paul for its hometown amenities. With its historic buildings refurbished, Summit Avenue the last showpiece of Victorian America, and "cozy" tree-lined urban neighborhoods, St. Paul found its reputation rehabilitated as the late twentieth-century version of a model city.[23]

Still, though companies might regard the city's quality of life as a locational asset, new arrivals in St. Paul have often found themselves relegated to the cultural periphery. Though local people are described as unfailingly polite, newcomers discover the depth of their disconnectedness when asked the ritual introductory questions, "Where did you go to school?" or "What parish are you from?" Even transplanted Minneapolitans, lacking the essential locators to situate themselves in the social landscape, find it difficult to shake the feeling that they are perpetual outsiders. As much as the city has changed, at its core it has remained something of a cultural island, wedded to the insider-outsider mentality passed from generation to generation.[24]

Civic defensiveness comes to the fore at the slightest provocation. When Minnesota's iconoclastic governor recently joked on national television that drunken Irishmen had laid out St. Paul's incomprehensible street system, his remarks evoked a storm of protest for the conflated ethnic and civic slur. His admission that he preferred his hometown of Minneapolis added fuel to injured sensibilities.[25]

St. Paulites' intense sense of alienation from Minneapolis is only slightly diminished, though residents do partake of its recreational and cultural amenities. In 1936, *Fortune* advised that the most important thing to know about the Twin Cities is that "they hate each other." In 1999, despite numerous institutional forms of metropolitan planning and cooperation, the assessment retains some accuracy—at least on the St. Paul side of the river. A recent issue of *The Economist* noted that "the cities will co-operate under pressure, but most of the time they simply don't bother, any more than a typical St. Paulite would bother to go to downtown Minneapolis and get lost." Although the *Minneapolis Tribune* consistently attempts to foster intercity cooperation (and expanded readership), St. Paul residents remain suspicious of Minneapolis motives. The *St. Paul Pioneer Press* energetically feeds the old rivalries—an editorial policy that appears to reflect more than shape public opinion. A typical statement by St. Paul mayor Norm Coleman hearkened back to traditional city affirmations that smaller is better: "In St. Paul, our future is our sense of history. We take the old and make it new. In Minneapolis, they just make it new." This characterization eerily echoes an argument made against urban development in 1927: "[St. Paul] is satisfied with its size, it loves its wooded boulevards curving about its sightly river. . . . If [development] goes on, we'll get bigger and bigger, and then . . . we might as well be living in Minneapolis."[26]

The predominant attitude in St. Paul regarding growth remains cautious, especially now that its small-scale virtues have assumed a national currency. In a 1997 survey of Twin Cities residents, 91 percent of St. Paulites rated the quality of life in their city as good or excellent; 68 percent felt a strong sense of rivalry with Minneapolis; and 97 percent stated that, all things being equal, they would not consider moving to their sister city. Even more telling, fully 48 percent of those surveyed declared that no amount of money or other incentives would induce them to make such a move.[27]

A distinctive cultural imprint endures, even at the end of the twentieth century, though both its roots and rationale have long been obscured. The names of James J. Hill and John Ireland are ensconced both in St. Paul's built environment and its civic memory, and the gangster era has been transformed into the stuff of romantic legend. But few present-day St. Paulites are familiar with the history of DFL politics, rooted in the vanished Farmer-Labor Party. Fewer know of labor's struggles with the Citizens Alliance, and most would find the excesses of the Public Safety Commission an inconceivable departure from their understanding of Minnesota progressivism. Even the rivalry with Minneapolis endures simply as a cultural given, its economic and political roots understood only vaguely.

The city's historical memory is selective and truncated. But the cultural residue of these events continues to have an inchoate power to inform life and politics in the city. In an era when organized labor has been in retreat throughout much of the country, it remains a powerful political actor in St. Paul, due as much to traditional loyalties as to its material importance to the city. Class, religion, even a selective sense of ethnic character—all continue to be shaped by a history of meanings embedded in place. These meanings, lyrically captured in a recent study on place-based consciousness, "may not be visible at any given moment but . . . quickly come to the surface as events change. Rather than a reservoir, stagnant and bounded, history is more like a complex system of underground rivers and springs, creating its own subterranean pressures."[28] The city's history has many facets. The social construction of "St. Paul" takes on a variety of meanings across its terrain— shaped by lived experience in neighborhoods, churches, schools, and all the variegated strands that make up an urban entity. What I have termed *civic identity* is both the container and the sum of all these meanings, the common denominator that grounds the multiple pieces in place—both literally and figuratively.

"If there were a great upheaval of the hills upon which St. Paul is built and the entire city slid into the Mississippi and disappeared, it would hardly make a ripple in the economic life of the United States of America"—so *Fortune* dismissed the city in 1936.[29] In fact, this assessment was largely true. But to some 230,000 people who called the city home, St. Paul was the center of the universe. More pointedly, any one of hundreds of other towns and cities across America could be individually dismissed as economically irrelevant in the larger scheme of things. But it was in just such singly unimportant towns and cities that most Americans lived out their lives. The internal workings of these small and mid-sized local venues are centrally important to understanding the larger fabric of American politics and culture.

In its efforts to craft a civic community, St. Paul was no more unique than any other city or town. It is exceptional only in that its rivalry with Minneapolis made the internal dynamics that underlay the construction of civic identity more starkly apparent. Similar contests over the obligations and meaning of place occurred in chambers of commerce, in union halls, in churches, and on city streets throughout the nation, with widely varying impact on local culture, politics and society. Whether the result was a deeply divided citizenry, an intense parochialism, or something in between, the struggle over civic identity had a real meaning in the way people interacted in the everyday world of their lives. Moreover, it affected their relationship with the larger world outside their immediate community. The twists and turns of national politics cannot be understood without taking into account the predominantly local issues that most immediately inform political choice.

Both the postmodern emphasis on identity and the focus on late twentieth-century cultural politics suffer from a lack of attention to the importance of place as a critical part of the formative process. The saga of St. Paul serves as a cautionary tale. The contours of ethnic identities can only be mapped within the economic and social contexts in which people experienced their place in the world. Nor can we situate the role of religion in public life if we deny its contingent relationship to the power structures and politics in place-specific locales. Finally, the concept of class is historically comprehensible only if we differentiate between a category objectively defined by economic and employment criteria and the subjective content of class identity as experienced in daily life. Working-class political choices emerge not from the triumph of either class or cultural identity but rather from a complex culture of class forged within a set of local circumstances.

Moving from an interior to a macro-political perspective, the case of St. Paul demonstrates the interactive, if unequal, relationship between local politics—broadly defined to include ethnicity, religion, and class—and the state. The outrages of the Public Safety Commission broke down historical barriers that had divided farmers from workers and Twin Cities unionists from one another. The resulting alliance generated the birth of the Farmer-Labor Party, which came to make a lasting impact on both state and national politics. However, the particular economic and social terrain of St. Paul politics made its own peculiar—and lasting—impression. Local considerations and the enduring ties between St. Paul Farmer-Laborites and the Democratic Party pulled the FLP to the right and helped to effect the DFL merger. Furthermore, the distinctive political culture of St. Paul produced a particular variant of "Minnesota progressivism." While Hubert Humphrey emerged from the political culture of Minneapolis, the social-justice element of St. Paul politics went to Washington with Eugene McCarthy, where in 1968 he became a rallying figure for the movement to end the war in Vietnam. Parochial politics thus can be seen to reverberate far beyond local boundaries.

As the other side of this exchange, local contours are shaped for good or ill by larger national and international forces, clearly evident in the powerful impact the world war exerted on the internal politics of St. Paul. In the ensuing decades, the growing interventionist role of the federal government increasingly influenced local calculations. St. Paul became the coincident beneficiary of federal initiatives designed to combat the more pressing urban problems facing other cities. From the New Deal agencies of the 1930s to the urban renewal efforts of the 1970s, federal funds provided the critical infusion that kept the economy and municipal structure intact. This was an ideal partnership for a city that had long ago eschewed growth for maintenance of the status quo.

The political economy of St. Paul evolved from its continuing dependence on commerce rather than industry, small businesses rather than large corporations. Consequently, its problems—and solutions—bore little resemblance to those of Chicago, New York, or Detroit. Studies of such major urban centers have noted a perceptible transformation in politics and social relations that accompanied the shift to large-scale industry, a key marker in the periodization of urban history. But St. Paul and Minneapolis offer a spatial perspective on the contours of urban culture that complicates the temporal model. The economy of the metropolitan area that comprises the Twin Cities was bifurcated from the cities' origins. Their distinctive economic configurations deeply influenced the place-based social relations that molded their cultural terrain. St. Paul prided itself on its difference from Minneapolis, its self-identified absorption with community and neighborhood—virtues that, in the late twentieth century, seem to have trumped the long-standing urban quest for development and "progress."[30] But it is important to note that Minneapolis, with its more elastic labor market, relieved St. Paul of many potential "social problems"—the poor, the unemployed, and until very recently the bulk of minority in-migration. It is questionable whether St. Paul could have sustained the community identity it so prized without the safety valve of Minneapolis next door.

This raises a final point about the endurance of culture in the midst of social and political change. The understandings that developed in the city's formative period were challenged and renegotiated again and again. As was apparent following the streetcar strike of 1917, when the civic compact failed, loyalties and alliances soon crumbled and were reformulated on different terms. However, each time that customary modes of negotiation proved their worth, the outcome reinforced long-standing traditions of civic insularity and accountability. Neither a bastion of great wealth nor one of widespread poverty, St. Paul was a city characterized by a settled working class and moderately prosperous professionals and businesses who shared power out of mutual necessity. State and federal initiatives assisted the city to maintain the illusion of itself as an island of stability in a sea of change. Thus, loyalty to Minnesota progressivism—and the Democratic Party—were grounded in a desire to defend existing local culture and custom.

The political choices that upheld these values derived from structural contingencies that were specific to St. Paul. But the underlying values that informed those choices do not represent an anomaly. To the contrary. Much of the architecture of insurgent politics throughout history has sprung from similarly "conservative" goals of protecting a valued way of life—from the struggles against land enclosure, to the Luddite movement, to the Farmers' Alliance, to much of the history of American labor. All these celebrated movements for change were rooted in the politics of place.[31]

Of course, place-based cultural defensiveness also has a darker side, with the capacity to nurture a catalogue of evils—nativism, racism, fascism, ethnic cleansing—as critics of localism often have rightly noted. The point here is not to make a value judgment on the manifestations of place-based consciousness but rather to emphasize the compelling power of local priorities to shape the political landscape—for good or ill—throughout history. Rather than dismiss St. Paul as an anachronistic case of local conservatism, its politics should be understood as a variant of much more widely held cultural values that are put to use in a variety of ways in any given historical moment and place. As summed up by historian Arif Dirlik, "The question of place is not one to be resolved at the level of theory; not only because difference is nearly impossible to theorize, but also because to theorize is to abolish difference, and to appropriate it to an academic discourse that has its own priorities, which do not coincide with the priorities of everyday life."[32]

The political lesson is evident. The priorities of everyday life lie at the heart of political choice. We cannot understand the past, nor can we effectively use it to make a better future unless we take place-based consciousness seriously—in all its cultural complexity. In a recent article reinterpreting the meaning and uses of nostalgia, Jackson Lears emphasized the political power embedded in place-based history, the many instances when "loving memories of the past could spark rebellion against the present in the service of future generations."[33] This reminder is particularly timely today, with national policy-making increasingly divorced from the realm of everyday life and political apathy a growing infection. In the search to reverse this trend, a reconnection between local and national concerns seems imperative. But to accomplish this end, policy makers must first understand the logic of local communities to extract the common ties that can bring people together despite a welter of differences.[34] History provides a vital key. The politics of place is a powerful force that can either cause people to close their minds to social change or, if taken fully into account, can become a compelling wellspring for political action.

Abbreviations

Newspapers, Magazines, and Journals

CB	*Catholic Bulletin*
DM	*Daily Minnesotian*
DN	*Saint Paul Daily News*
Disp.	*Saint Paul Dispatch*
JAEH	*Journal of American Ethnic History*
JAH	*Journal of American History*
JUH	*Journal of Urban History*
JWH	*Journal of Womens' History*
MD	*Minnesota Democrat*
MH	*Minnesota History*
MJ	*Minneapolis Journal*
MP	*Minnesota Pioneer*
MVHR	*Mississippi River Valley Historical Review*
NC	*Northwestern Chronicle*
P&D	*Saint Paul Pioneer and Democrat*
PP	*Saint Paul Pioneer Press*
RCH	*Ramsey County History*
Trib.	*Minneapolis Tribune*
UA	*Minnesota Union Advocate*

Archives and Manuscript Collections

AASPM	Archives of the Archdiocese of Saint Paul and Minneapolis, St. Paul, Minn.
AD	Austin Dowling Papers
CA	Citizens Alliance Papers
CASP	Citizens Association of Saint Paul Records

CF   Celia Forstner and Family Papers
CRW   Charles Rumford Walker Papers
CTAU   Catholic Total Abstinence Union Papers
CWA   Charles W. and Mary Leslie Ames and Family Papers
D-PP   Saint Paul Dispatch-Pioneer Press Papers
DC   Davidson Company Records
DRC   Donald R. Cotton Papers
FAB   Fred A. Bill and Family Papers
FBIC   Foley Brothers Inc. Company Records
HDF   Hiram D. Frankel Papers
JI   John Ireland Papers
JJH   James J. Hill Papers
JJHRL   James J. Hill Reference Library, St. Paul, Minn.
JM   James Manahan and Family Papers
JNL   John and Norman Lind Papers
JRJ   James R. and Margaret Weyerhaeuser Jewett Papers
MBP   Michael Boyle Papers
MCO'D   Michael C. O'Donnell and Family Papers
MCPS   Minnesota Commission of Public Safety Papers
MHS   Minnesota Historical Society, St. Paul, Minn.
MMHD   Mary Mehegan Hill Diaries
NIB   Northern Information Bureau Records
PLSP   Patriotic League of Saint Paul Papers
RL   Richard Leekley Papers
SPOSCA   St. Paul Outdoor Sports Carnival Association Records
SPWCA   St. Paul Winter Carnival Association Papers
SSP   Saint Paul Seminary Papers
T&C   Town and Country Club Records
TLA   Saint Paul Trades and Labor Assembly Records
WF   Weyerhaeuser Family Papers
WL   Wilson Library, University of Minnesota, Minneapolis, Minn.
WHM   William H. MacMahon Papers
WM   William Mahoney Papers

Frequently Cited Reports and Documents

BOL   *Biennial Reports of the Bureau of Labor of the State of Minnesota*
DOL   *Biennial Reports of the Department of Labor of the State of Minnesota*
LID   Labor and Industry Department Records, State of Minnesota

Other Abbreviations

B   Box
F   Folder
LB   Letterbook
mss.d.   Manuscript draft

Notes

Introduction

1. The best account of the 1934 truckers' strike remains Charles Rumford Walker, *American City: A Rank-and-File History* (New York, 1937); quote appears on 117. See also Philip A. Korth, *The Minneapolis Teamsters Strike of 1934* (East Lansing, Mich., 1995). For a participant account, see Farrell Dobbs, *Teamster Rebellion* (New York, 1972).

2. Across the spectrum of political persuasion, scholars consistently identify the events in Minneapolis, along with strikes in Toledo and San Francisco, as key events of 1934. See, for example, Alan Dawley, *Struggles for Justice: Social Responsibility and the Liberal State* (Cambridge, Mass., 1991), 372–76; Harvey Klehr, *The Heyday of American Communism: The Depression Decade* (New York, 1984), 125–28; and American Social History Project, *Who Built America? Working People and the Nation's Economy, Politics, Culture, and Society*, 2 vols. (New York, 1992), 2: 361–66.

3. For examples of contemporary analysis, see "Revolt in the Northwest," *Fortune*, April 1936, 112–19, 178–97; and Walker, *American City*. Historical accounts of the strike accord St. Paul no more than a line or two in the narrative, but several scholars have suggested to me in conversation that the Catholic Church may have been behind workers' indifference, an assertion quite in keeping with Marc Karson's often-cited analysis of the relationship between the Catholic Church and the labor movement. Karson, *American Labor Unions and Politics, 1900–1918* (Carbondale, Ill., 1958), 212–84.

4. Recent work in the fields of psychology and psychiatry has taken new interest in the central importance of spatial identity, positioning place as "a core element of identity formation." Mindy Thompson Fullilove, "Psychiatric Implications of Displacement: Contributions from the Psychology of Place," *American Journal of Psychiatry* 153 (December 1996): 1520.

5. Alan Pred, "Structuration, Biography Formation, and Knowledge: Observations on Port Growth during the Late Mercantile Period," *Environment and Planning D: Society and Space* 2 (1984): 251.

6. Charles Tilly, "What Good Is Urban History?" *JUH* 22 (September 1996): 713.

7. Ibid., 711.

8. Thomas Bender challenged this analysis more than twenty years ago in his compelling re examination of the scholarship on community and social change; nonetheless, urban studies of the Gilded Age and the twentieth century continue, by and large, to rest on the interpretive framework of linear community decline delineated in the work of Robert Wiebe. See Thomas Bender, *Community and Social Change in America* (Brunswick, N.J., 1978; rpt., Baltimore, 1978);

and Robert H. Wiebe, *The Search for Order, 1877–1920* (New York, 1967). The classic work on the resilience of community in the nineteenth-century city remains Herbert G. Gutman, "Class, Status, and Community Power in Nineteenth-Century American Industrial Cities," in *Work, Culture and Society in Industrializing America* (New York, 1977), 234–60.

9. In crafting a definition of regionalism, Patricia Nelson Limerick notes that "while geography plays a role in their definition, regions are much more the creations of human thought and behavior than they are the products of nature." Limerick, "Region and Reason," in *All Over the Map: Rethinking American Regions*, ed. Edward L. Ayers, Patricia Nelson Limerick, Stephen Nissenbaum, and Peter S. Onuf (Baltimore, 1996), 96.

10. On the self-conscious construction of nationalism, see Benedict Anderson, *Imagined Communities: Reflections on the Origin and Spread of Nationalism*, rev. and expt. (London, 1991). On the contractual and mythic elements of nationalism, see Geoff Eley and Ronald Grigor Suny, introduction to *Becoming National*, ed. Geoff Eley and Ronald Grigor Suny (New York, 1996), 4–5.

11. I intentionally exclude race from this discussion, since racial difference almost universally precluded membership in the so-called civic community, and racial boundaries, whether de jure or de facto, were seldom, if ever, bridged in a meaningful way by white civic leaders. This is not to say that people of color did not attempt to participate in the civic project. In the Twin Cities, however, nearly 99% of the populations were of white, European stock, making it a simple task to exclude others from their imagined communities.

12. A similar interactive relationship between regional and national identity is delineated by Edward Ayers and Peter Onuf in the introduction to *All Over the Map*, ed. Ayers et al., 8–9.

13. Limerick, "Region and Reason," 93.

14. My analysis counters that of scholars who argue that place-based loyalties subsume other differences, creating a culture of consensus. For an example of that argument, see Alexander von Hoffman, *Local Attachments: The Making of an American Urban Neighborhood, 1850 to 1920* (Baltimore, 1994). Rather, the language of community formed a set of rhetorical codes, described by Werner Sollors as "a common language within which dissent can take place." The existence of this vocabulary in no way assures consensus, but it does make a dialogue possible. Werner Sollors, *Beyond Ethnicity: Consent and Descent in American Culture* (New York, 1996), 59.

15. David A. Gerber, *The Making of an American Pluralism: Buffalo, New York, 1825–60* (Urbana, Ill., 1989); Michael Kazin, *Barons of Labor: The San Francisco Building Trades and Union Power in the Progressive Era* (Urbana, Ill., 1989).

16. David M. Emmons, *The Butte Irish: Class and Ethnicity in an American Mining Town, 1875–1925* (Urbana, Ill., 1990); Kathleen Neils Conzen, *Immigrant Milwaukee, 1836–1860: Accommodation and Community in a Frontier City* (Cambridge, 1976); Timothy Meagher, ed., *From Paddy to Studs: Irish-American Communities in the Turn of the Century Era, 1880–1920* (New York, 1986).

17. The lack of attention to the interactive relationship between the Catholic Church and local communities is exceptionally notable, probably due to scholars' reliance on official proclamations that emanated from higher authorities outside the communities. But the dialectic between church and society operated in a similar manner in every denomination, as compellingly demonstrated in Jonathan D. Sarna, " 'A Sort of Paradise for the Hebrews': The Lofty Vision of Cincinnati Jews," in *Ethnic Diversity and Civic Identity: Patterns of Conflict and Cohesion in Cincinnati since 1820*, ed. Henry D. Shapiro and Jonathan D. Sarna (Urbana, Ill., 1992), 131–64.

18. See also the case of Cincinnati. James H. Campbell, "New Parochialism: Change and Conflict in the Archdiocese of Cincinnati, 1878–1925," ibid., 94–130.

19. Paula M. Kane, *Separatism and Subculture: Boston Catholicism, 1900–1920* (Chapel Hill, N.C., 1994).

20. In countless cities, such intercity rivalries were common conventions that fostered civic loyalty (though St. Paul and Minneapolis took their antipathy to an extreme degree). As Werner Sollors observes, the "strategy of outsiderism and self-exoticization" is one of the most common and potent characteristics of group identity in general: "In America, casting oneself as an outsider may in fact be considered a dominant cultural trait." Sollors, *Beyond Ethnicity*, 31.

21. Tilly, "What Good Is Urban History?" 716.

Chapter 1: The Economy of Culture

1. Charles W. Johnson, *Another Tale of Two Cities: Minneapolis and St. Paul Compared* (Minneapolis, 1890), 14–15; William Watts Folwell, *A History of Minnesota*, 4 vols. (St. Paul, 1926), 3:479–89.

2. Johnson, *Another Tale*, 17–21.

3. Ibid., 6–7.

4. Jocelyn A. Wills, "Tangled Webs: Entrepreneurial Dreams, Imperial Designs, and the Evolution of Nineteenth-Century Urban Elites, St. Paul–Minneapolis, Minnesota, 1849–1883" (Ph.D. diss., Texas A&M University, 1998), 262–63; Charles W. Johnson, *A Tale of Two Cities: Minneapolis and St. Paul Compared* (Minneapolis, 1885), 6.

5. Wills, "Tangled Webs," 264; Johnson, *Tale of Two Cities*. In 1880, the population of St. Paul officially stood at 41,473 and that of Minneapolis at 46,887—an 8.8% advantage for Minneapolis. St. Paul had not begun to stagnate, however; both cities continued to grow at remarkable rates. In 1885, St. Paul claimed 111,397 residents and Minneapolis 129,200—increases of 169% and 175%, respectively. Thus, to optimistic St. Paul number crunchers, the race by no means seemed lost. Department of the Interior, Census Office, *Statistics of the Population of the United States at the Tenth Census, 1880* (Washington, 1883), 226, 229.

6. Johnson, *Tale of Two Cities*, 6–7; T. M. Newson, *Pen Pictures of St. Paul Minnesota and Biographical Sketches of Old Settlers* (St. Paul, 1886), 2.

7. Johnson, *Tale of Two Cities*, 88.

8. Ibid., 7.

9. Ibid., 93–94.

10. *Trib.*, 28 March 1890, quoted in Lucile M. Kane, *The Falls of St. Anthony: The Waterfall That Built Minneapolis* (St. Paul, 1987), 153.

11. *PP*, 22 June 1890; Johnson, *Another Tale*, 25–27; *Disp.*, 11 July 1890.

12. *PP*, 10 August 1890; Johnson, *Another Tale*, 8–9, 44, 46–58.

13. Johnson, *Another Tale*, 91.

14. The final tally for the 1890 census accorded Minneapolis a population of 164,738; 133,156 for St. Paul. By 1920, Minneapolis had increased to 380,582 and St. Paul to 234,698. From 1920 forward, St. Paul has fluctuated very little, with a 1992 population of 265,266. Bureau of the Census, *County and City Data Book, 1994: A Statistical Abstract Supplement* (Washington, 1994), 758.

15. Folwell, *History of Minnesota* 1: 160; Newson, *Pen Pictures*, 55–56.

16. Arthur J. Russell, *MP*, 6 February 1851, reproduced in Theodore C. Blegen and Philip D. Jordan, eds., *With Various Voices: Recordings of North Star Life* (St. Paul, 1949), 217.

17. Testimony from *Sale of the Fort Snelling Reservation*, quoted in Folwell, *History of Minnesota*, 1: 220–21.

18. J. Fletcher Williams, *A History of the City of Saint Paul and the County of Ramsey, Minnesota* (St. Paul, 1876), 79–83; Newson, *Pen Pictures*, 25. On the Selkirk colony and the flight of its settlers south, see Folwell, *History of Minnesota*, 1: 213–19.

19. For first-person reminiscences of the fledgling settlement, see Williams, *History of the City of St. Paul*, and Newson, *Pen Pictures*.

20. Marriage between white men and Native American women was accepted across class in this fluid society, including among the agents of the American Fur Company who became the town's civic leaders. Women were in short supply on the frontier; moreover, an alliance with native tribes smoothed business negotiations between traders and native peoples. Henry Sibley, who became the acknowledged leading citizen of St. Paul, had informally "married" a Dakota woman. Though he later shed the extralegal arrangement and formally married a more "appropriate" spouse, he publicly acknowledged and cared for the daughter produced by the alliance. I am indebted to Rhoda Gilman for clarification of Sibley's first "marriage." See also Wills, "Tangled Webs," 34. For a penetrating analysis of the unfixed nature of racial identity in Minnesota's early period and the subsequent and speedy hardening of racial categorization, see Bruce M. White, "The Power of Whiteness or, the Life and Times of Joseph Rolette Jr.," *MH* 56 (winter 1998–99): 179–97.

21. Newson, *Pen Pictures*, 9–12.

22. On the complicated organization of the American Fur Company, see Rhoda R. Gilman, "Last Days of the Upper Mississippi Fur Trade," in *People and Pelts: Selected Papers of the Second American Fur Trade Conference*, ed. Malvina Bolus (Winnipeg, 1972), 103–35. On Sibley, see Roger G. Kennedy, *Men on the Moving Frontier* (Palo Alto, Calif., 1969), 41, 47; the Sibley quote is on p. 47.

23. For biographical sketches of Sibley, Rice, and Flandrau, see Folwell, *History of Minnesota*, vol. 1.

24. Newson, *Pen Pictures*, 128–38, 406–8, 432–37.

25. Before 1849, when Congress carved out Minnesota Territory, St. Paul was governed as part of Wisconsin Territory. The seat of formal government and source of law enforcement was located at Madison, Wisconsin, some 250 miles to the southeast.

26. Newson, *Pen Pictures*, 49–73; Williams, *History of the City of St. Paul*, 153–76.

27. Ibid. Most of these early entrepreneurs also had either direct or indirect connection to the American Fur Company. See Wills, "Tangled Webs," 35–39.

28. Daniel Fisher letter, 1852, reproduced in *Bring Warm Clothes: Letters and Photos from Minnesota's Past*, ed. Peg Meier (St. Paul, 1981), 54; Williams, *History of the City of St. Paul*, 173–74, 304–8, 325, 360; Albro Martin, *James J. Hill & the Opening of the Northwest* (New York, 1976; rpt., St. Paul, 1991), 64–68; Newson, *Pen Pictures*, 502; *Minnesotian Weekly*, 22 October 1853.

29. "A Stranger Sketches St. Paul," *MP*, 6 February 1851.

30. St. Paul's population grew from 1,083 in 1850 to 4,716 in 1855. By 1860, it would reach 10,401. Williams, *History of the City of St. Paul*, 467.

31. Letters of Elizabeth Kingsley Fuller, 1853, reproduced in *With Various Voices*, ed. Blegen and Jordan, 249–50; Grace Flandrau, "Saint Paul: The Untamable Twin," in *The Taming of the Frontier*, ed. Duncan Aikman (New York, 1925), 142.

32. Matilda Rice, "The Fourth of July in the 1850s," *Disp.*, 27 June 1895.

33. On the distinction between the cultural meanings embedded in faith and institutional practice, see Robert Anthony Orsi, *The Madonna of 115th Street: Faith and Community in Italian Harlem, 1880–1950* (New York, 1985).

34. James Michael Reardon, *The Catholic Church in the Diocese of St. Paul: From Earliest Origin to Centennial Achievement* (St. Paul, 1952), 39–47; quotes are from letters of Lucien Galtier, reproduced in the text.

35. Ibid. Since these numbers far exceed the recorded population of the settlement in 1844, Galtier must have counted transient worshippers as well as all Catholics in the much larger territory for which he was responsible.

36. Newson, *Pen Pictures*, 73; Reardon, *Catholic Church*, 43–49, 72–74; Sister Helen Angela Hurley, *On Good Ground: The Story of the Sisters of St. Joseph in St. Paul* (Minneapolis, 1951), 15.

37. On the Irish character of the Catholic Church, see James S. Olson, *Catholic Immigrants in America* (Chicago, 1987), 25; on nativism, John Higham, *Strangers in the Land: Patterns of American Nativism, 1860–1925*, 2d ed. (Rutgers, N.J., 1969); on the background and character of the French missionaries, M. M. Hoffmann, *The Church Founders of the Northwest* (Milwaukee, 1937).

38. Reardon, *Catholic Church*, 62, 72–77. Though Cretin had seven priests at his disposal, they served the entire diocese, which in 1851 covered 166,000 square miles of wilderness—all of present-day Minnesota and the Dakotas as far west as the Missouri River. Still, two or three priests always were in residence in St. Paul, the major population center.

39. Sarah P. Rubinstein, "The French Canadians and French," in *They Chose Minnesota: A Survey of the State's Ethnic Groups*, ed. June Drenning Holmquist (St. Paul, 1981), 37–40, 45–46.

40. "Proceedings, Constitution, and By-Laws of the Catholic Temperance Society of St. Paul," membership lists, and minutes of meetings, Catholic Temperance Society F, B1, CTAU papers, AASPM.

41. Hoffmann, *Church Founders*, 329–36; *MP*, 26 January 1855.

42. *MP*, 29 July 1852; *MD*, 12 February 1855.

43. The 1885 city directory records 5 church-sponsored homes for orphans, the aged, and the poor (4 of them Catholic); 3 church-run hospitals (1 Catholic); 10 "benevolent and charitable societies" (9 Catholic); 25 private schools and academies (19 Catholic); and an industrial school for

"wayward" boys, run by the Sisters of the Good Shepherd. Only Hamline College, chartered by the Methodists in 1854, was yet in operation, with Presbyterian Macalester College about to open its doors. The unlettered state of St. Paul's early Catholic residents made postsecondary education a lower priority for the diocese. By 1905, however, the upward mobility of the Catholic population had cleared the way for establishment of the College of St. Thomas (for men) and the College of St. Catherine's (for women), as well as the St. Paul Seminary and two more private secondary schools. *R. L. Polk & Co.'s St. Paul City Directory* (St. Paul, 1884–85); Reardon, *Catholic Church*, 653–60.

44. Cretin to Lyons, Propagation of the Faith Society, 22 February 1854, quoted in Hoff-mann, *Church Founders*, 337; *MP*, 29 July 1852.

45. *NC*, 20 April and 29 June 1867; Lyman Palmer, quoted in Hurley, *On Good Ground*, 66. No firm numbers exist for parochial school enrollment in this period. Estimates fluctuate wildly in the pages of the *Northwestern Chronicle*, the city's Catholic newspaper. In 1868 the *Chronicle* claimed that St. Paul's parochial schools enrolled 3,200 children, while only 1,000 were enrolled in the public schools—an improbable increase from the 900 claimed a year earlier. Still, it seems likely that at least half the city's school population attended parochial schools. *NC*, 5 September 1868.

46. Daniel Fisher to Arthur J. Donnelly, St. Michael's Church, New York, 1852, quoted in Hoffmann, *Church Founders*, 330.

47. Newson's vivid pioneering chronicle contains numerous biographical entries of original French Canadian settlers who sold their land for far less than its value. Only one French Canadian, Louis Robert, appears to have amassed any significant wealth in St. Paul's boom years. A veteran of the fur trade, Robert was one of the town's original proprietors and became active in politics. According to Newson, he controlled the French vote and, together with William Murray, who controlled the Irish vote, he was a power in Democratic politics in the city. When Robert died in 1874, he left an estate of $500,000.
More typical of the early Canadian landholders was the fate of Charles Bazille, who "had so much land he did not know what to do with it, and placing no value upon it, gave it away almost indiscriminately, so that in his declining years he was poor." Or witness the case of Vital Guerin, another original landholder. Guerin's property was valued in 1849 at $150,000. Generous to a fault, he helped many of "his poor countrymen" and donated land for the courthouse, the capitol building, and several Protestant churches, as well as the land for the Catholic church. By the end of his life, however, "his property was taken from him and he became poor." Newson, *Pen Pictures*, 41–44, 16–19; see also Wills, "Tangled Webs," 73–74.

48. The 1880 census records 1,472 persons of Canadian birth living in St. Paul, or 3.5 percent of the population. Even this figure is greatly misleading, however, because the census makes no distinction between Anglo and French Canadians. The city continued to draw Anglo-Canadian migrants at the same time that it lost its French population. Rubinstein, "French Canadians," 45; *Twelfth U.S. Census, Population, 1900* (Washington, 1901), 458, 800.

49. Williams, *History of the City of Saint Paul*, 354, 365, 376–77.

50. Ibid., 380.

51. Ibid., 380–81, 369–70; Henry Rice to Franklin Steele, 27 May 1861 (emphasis in the original), quoted in Wills, "Tangled Webs," 129.

52. Marion Daniel Shutter, ed., *History of Minneapolis: Gateway to the Northwest*, 3 vols. (Chicago, 1923), 1: 78–82; Kane, *Falls of St. Anthony*, 33.

53. Kane, *Falls of St. Anthony*, 31–37.

54. Ibid., 37; William C. Edgar, *The Medal of Gold: A Story of Industrial Achievement* (Minneapolis, 1925), 1–9.

55. Gaillard Hunt, *Israel, Elihu and Cadwallader Washburn: A Chapter in American Biography* (New York, 1925).

56. Kane, *Falls of St. Anthony*, 88.

57. Ibid., 49–52.

58. Ibid., 12–29, 60; on Steele's downfall, see Wills, "Tangled Webs," 117–18, 129.

59. Wills, "Tangled Webs," 120; for a demographic breakdown of Old Stock residents in St. Paul and Minneapolis, see John G. Rice, "The Old-Stock Americans," in *They Chose Minnesota*, 55–72.

60. For a roster of the city's early residents in which scarcely more than half a dozen non-

Anglo names are listed, see John H. Stevens, *Personal Recollections of Minnesota and Its People and Early History of Minneapolis* (1890) and p. 306 for the establishment of the New England Society; on "New England of the West," see Kane, *Falls of St. Anthony,* 39; on the importance of Maine organizations, see Sharon A. Boswell and Lorraine McConaghy, *Raise Hell and Sell Newspapers: Alden J. Blethen & the Seattle Times* (Pullman, Wash., 1996), 42.

61. Kane, *Falls of St. Anthony,* 38, 53; Arthur J. Russell, "The Man Who Named Minneapolis" (1925), in *With Various Voices,* ed. Blegen and Jordan, 220–21; Stevens, *Personal Recollections,* 310.

62. Wills, "Tangled Webs," 206.

Chapter 2: Money, Status, and Power

1. T. M. Newson, *Pen Pictures of St. Paul, Minnesota* (St. Paul, 1886), 698; J. Fletcher Williams, *A History of the City of St. Paul, and of the County of Ramsey, Minnesota* (St. Paul, 1876), 385.

2. William Watts Folwell, *A History of Minnesota,* 4 vols. (St. Paul, 1926), 2: 37–58.

3. Jocelyn A. Wills, "Tangled Webs: Entrepreneurial Dreams, Imperial Designs, and the Evolution of Nineteenth-Century Urban Elites, St. Paul–Minneapolis, Minnesota, 1849–1883" (Ph.D diss., Texas A & M University, 1998), 106–8.

4. Merrill E. Jarchow, *Amherst Wilder and His Enduring Legacy to Saint Paul* (St. Paul, 1981), 12–133; Wills, "Tangled Webs," 129–32. As Wills notes, "The Civil War, as an exogenous factor in the region's growth, stimulated investment in Minnesota and other resource-rich areas far removed from battle, but linked closely enough with the northern war effort to supply it with timber, grain, solders, and other supplies." Wartime demands also inflated the prices of these necessary products. Wills, "Tangled Webs," 131. On the importance of the "Indian business"—which included both receipt and administration of federal contracts and the cash infusion of Indian annuities—for Minnesota's fledgling economy, see Bruce M. White, "The Power of Whiteness or, the Life and Times of Joseph Rolette, Jr.," *MH* 56 (winter 1998–99): 185–87.

5. Wilder's correspondence lays out in detail his strategies to acquire homestead lands through the use of covert agents—an example of the sort of entrepreneurial opportunism that played itself out repeatedly across the frontier following the passage of the Homestead Act. See Jarchow, *Amherst Wilder,* 67–70; on Wilder's friends and business partners, see 54–78, 96, 116.

6. Calvin F. Schmid, *Social Saga of Two Cities: An Ecological and Statistical Study of Social Trends in Minneapolis and St. Paul* (Minneapolis, 1937), 14, 19; on elite involvement in municipal improvements and civic causes, see Wills, "Tangled Webs."

7. On the development of Minneapolis industry, see Lucile M. Kane, *The Falls of St. Anthony: The Waterfall That Built Minneapolis* (St. Paul, 1987), 81–113. In Chicago, the transformation from a mercantile to an industrial economy in the 1860s carried with it a notable shift in the relations between business and labor. According to historian Richard Schneirov, this change was "at the core of a larger social transformation" because profits became dependent on the "process of labor rather than speculative and mercantile activities." Richard Schneirov, *Labor and Urban Politics: Class Conflict and the Origins of Modern Liberalism in Chicago, 1864–97* (Urbana, Ill., 1998), 22. In St. Paul and Minneapolis, these two forms of wealth creation remained bifurcated and created quite different social relations in the two cities.

8. James K. Benson, *Irish and German Families and the Economic Development of Midwestern Cities, 1860–1895* (New York, 1990), 29.

9. John Bodnar, *The Transplanted: A History of Urban Immigrants in America* (Bloomington, Ind., 1985), 6–8, 13–16, 26–27; Walter D. Kamphoefner, Wolfgang Helbich, and Ulrike Sommer, eds., *News from the Land of Freedom* (Ithaca, N.Y., 1988), 17–18.

10. Hildegard Binder Johnson, "The Germans," in *They Chose Minnesota: A Survey of the State's Ethnic Groups,* ed. June Drenning Holmquist (St. Paul, 1981), 153, 169–73. Similarly, Kathleen Conzen notes that in Milwaukee during the 1850s–1860s, the public image of the Germans was "generally one of industry and thrift, tempered with an intellectual and cultural aura that was the marvel of the city's native born." Kathleen Neils Conzen, *Immigrant Milwaukee, 1836–1860: Accommodation and Community in a Frontier City* (Cambridge, Mass., 1976), 124.

11. Benson, *Irish and German Families*, 286–89; LaVern J. Rippley, "German-American Banking in Minnesota," in *A Heritage Fulfilled: German Americans*, ed. Clarence Glasrud (Moorhead, Minn., 1984), 97–98, 108.

12. *R. L. Polk & Co. St. Paul City Directory* (St. Paul, 1875, 1885, 1896); Albert Nelson Marquis, *The Book of Minnesotans: A Biographical Dictionary of Leading Living Men of the State of Minnesota*, vol. 1 (Chicago, 1907). Such German/American partnerships were enormously important factors for occupational and income upward mobility in the first-generation immigrant group. As Conzen meticulously maps in her study of Milwaukee, Germans in that city made much slower progress up the economic ladder than they did in St. Paul. Despite relative advantages of skill, capital, and numbers over other immigrant groups, Germans had a difficult time moving into the more prosperous echelons of commerce and industry, which were dominated by American-born entrepreneurs. Conzen, *Immigrant Milwaukee*, 85–125.

13. *Davison's Minneapolis City Directory* (Minneapolis, 1896).

14. "Revolt in the Northwest," *Fortune*, April 1936, 116; Carey McWilliams, "Minneapolis: The Curious Twin," *Common Ground* (autumn 1946): 61–65.

15. W. Gunther Plaut, *The Jews in Minnesota: The First Seventy-five Years* (New York, 1959), 39, 47; Marilyn J. Chiat, "Work and Faith and Minnesota's Jewish Merchants," *RCH* 28 (spring 1993): 4–5.

16. Plaut, *Jews in Minnesota*, 280–81.

17. Chiat, "Work and Faith," 4–5, 9; Hyman Berman, "Political Antisemitism in Minnesota during the Great Depression," *Jewish Social Studies* 38 (1976): 247; Laura E. Weber, "Gentiles Preferred: Minneapolis Jews and Employment, 1920–1950," *MH* 57 (spring 1991); Plaut, *Jews in Minnesota*, 273–75, 280–81.

18. Chiat, "Work and Faith," 4; Plaut, *Jews in Minnesota*, 287–89.

19. *DM*, 5 June 1857.

20. Benson, *Irish and German Families*, 286–89.

21. Sister Helen Angela Hurley, *On Good Ground: The Story of the Sisters of St. Joseph in St. Paul* (Minneapolis, 1951), 36.

22. Ann Regan, "The Irish," in *They Chose Minnesota*, 142; Newson, *Pen Pictures*, 149–50; on city election returns, see Williams, *History of the City of St. Paul*.

23. On Irish machine politics, see Steven P. Erie, *Rainbow's End: Irish-Americans and the Dilemmas of Urban Machine Politics, 1840–1985* (Berkeley, Calif., 1988).

24. Historian Kerby Miller notes that by 1880 Irish Americans were primarily native born. Kerby Miller, "Class, Culture, and Immigrant Group Identity in the United States: The Case of Irish-American Ethnicity," in *Immigration Reconsidered: History, Sociology, and Politics*, ed. Virginia Yans McLaughlin (New York, 1990), 115. Statistical evidence is not available for St. Paul, but an instructive anecdotal portrait emerges from nineteenth-century histories of the city. Among the numerous Irish who merited mention, none arrived in St. Paul directly from Ireland. See Newson, *Pen Pictures*; Williams, *History of the City of St. Paul*; and Regan, "The Irish," 130–32.

25. A similar political and social pattern developed among the Irish in San Francisco. There, however, the Irish constituted the largest group of foreign-born, whereas in St. Paul by 1890 the Irish ranked a distant third behind German and Scandinavian-born ethnics. See Timothy Sarbaugh, "Exiles of Confidence: The Irish-American Community of San Francisco, 1880–1920," in *From Paddy to Studs: Irish-American Communities in the Turn of the Century Era, 1880–1920*, ed. Timothy J. Meagher (New York, 1986), 161–79.

26. Regan, "The Irish," 142; St. Paul City Directory, 1885, 1896.

27. Regan, "The Irish," 142.

28. *U.S. Census*, vol. 2: *Population, 1910* (Washington, 1913), 994, 1014.

29. In 1910, the Irish labor radical Con Lehane, making a tour of American cities to promote support for Irish nationalism, included St. Paul as a key Irish-American stronghold along with Boston, New York, Chicago, Seattle, and Butte, Montana. David M. Emmons, *The Butte Irish: Class and Ethnicity in an American Mining Town, 1875–1925* (Urbana, Ill., 1990), 358.

30. Clara Hill Lindley, *James J. and Mary T. Hill: An Unfinished Chronicle by Their Daughter* (New York, 1948), 46–51, 54, 83.

31. Albro Martin, *James J. Hill & the Opening of the Northwest* (New York, 1976; rpt., St. Paul, 1991), 26–58.

32. Matthew Josephson, *The Robber Barons: The Great American Capitalists, 1861–1901* (New York, 1934); on mismanagement of the Northern Pacific, see 165–70; for Hill's quote, see 245.

33. Martin, *James J. Hill*, 114–45, 330.

34. Ibid., 463–64; Wills, "Tangled Webs," 246–50.

35. Martin, *James J. Hill*, 511; "A Hundred Years with Minnesota Irish," in *Souvenir of the Diamond Anniversary of the Ancient Order of Hibernians* (St. Paul, 1959), 66.

36. Lindley, *James J. and Mary T. Hill*, 1–6, 9–11.

37. This is not particularly surprising, given the timing of the Hill family's emigration from Ireland. As Kerby Miller notes, "During most of the eighteenth century, and even well into the nineteenth . . . differences in political power, social status, and wealth did not *necessarily* translate into bitter antagonism between Protestants and Catholics." Evidence indicates only mild anti-Catholicism in the east Ulster agricultural district that had been home to the Hill family. Kerby A. Miller, *Emigrants and Exiles: Ireland and the Irish Exodus to North America* (New York, 1985), 42, 190.

38. Martin, *James J. Hill*; Marquis, *Book of Minnesotans*; and Horace Samuel Merrill, *Bourbon Democracy of the Middle West, 1865–1896* (Baton Rouge, La., 1953), 174–78. Mary Hill's diaries also provide evidence of the long-standing nature of these friendships. The diaries are held in the James J. Hill Reference Library (JJHRL), St. Paul.

39. Thomas D. O'Brien, *There Were Four of Us, or Was It Five* (St. Paul, 1936), 96, 102.

40. On the railroad contracting practices, see Josephson, *Robber Barons*. On Huntington's Southern Pacific, see William Deverell, *Railroad Crossing: Californians and the Railroad, 1850–1910* (Berkeley, Calif., 1994).

41. *Seventy Years: The Foley Saga* (Los Angeles, 1945), 3–24; Martin R. Haley, *Building for the Future: The Story of the Walter Butler Companies* (St. Paul, 1956), n.p.

42. Benson, *Irish and German Families*, 267–68, 282, 298; Martin, *James J. Hill*, 347; "The Shiely Story," privately reprinted from *American Builders* (1952), courtesy of Teresa Shiely Diebel.

43. Joseph L. Shiely, speech given on the occasion of his fiftieth wedding anniversary, courtesy of Teresa Shiely Diebel; "The Shiely Story."

44. John McCarthy to Captain Fred Bill, 21 May 1922, B1, FAB, MHS; "Milton and McCarthy Family History," comp. and ed. Patricia Willie Brady and Sister Mary Paula McCarthy, n.d.

45. Merrill, *Bourbon Democracy*, 3; Horace Samuel Merrill, "Ignatius Donnelly, James J. Hill, and Cleveland Administration Patronage," *MVHR* 39 (December 1952): 505–18.

46. Ignatius Donnelly, quoted in Martin Ridge, *Ignatius Donnelly: Portrait of a Politician* (St. Paul, 1962), 223, 261.

47. Regan, "The Irish," 143; Merrill, *Bourbon Democracy*, 174–79.

48. Similar political strategies were employed by Irish machines in cities throughout the country after 1910. The St. Paul case is quite singular, however, because even in the first generation Irish power depended on support from a diverse constituency. See Erie, *Rainbow's End*, 67–106.

49. *MD*, 17 March 1852 and 22 March 1854; *P&D*, 20 March 1860; Regan, "The Irish," 145–46.

50. As a typical example of the style of local Irish politics, Daniel Lawler, a power in local Democratic circles and mayor from 1908–10, made it a practice to attend every Catholic and Protestant celebration, from church dedications to fundraisers. Having schooled himself in the German language, Lawler endeared himself to city Germans by delivering his speeches in their native tongue. See *The Mayors of St. Paul, 1850–1940* (Minnesota WPA Writers' Project, 1940), 53; John Rynda, "A History of the Parish of St. Stanislaus in St. Paul, MN," typescript, 10, St. Stanislaus folder, parish records, AASPM; James J. Byrne, *A History of St. Agnes* (St. Paul, 1953), 23; and Carl Chrislock, "The German-American Role in Minnesota Politics, 1850–1950," in *A Heritage Deferred: The German-Americans in Minnesota*, ed. Clarence A Glasrud (Moorhead, Minn., 1981), 105; Regan, "The Irish," 143.

51. On Republican anti-Catholicism, see Richard Oestreicher, "Urban Working-Class Political Behavior and Theories of American Electoral Politics, 1870–1940," *JAH* 74 (March 1988): 1261–63; and Paul Kleppner, "Voters and Their Roots: The Politics of Rejection," in *The*

Growth of American Politics, 2 vols., ed. Frank Otto Gatell, Paul Goodman, and Allen Weinstein (New York, 1972), 2: 152–55.

52. Benson, *Irish and German Families*, 280. For in-depth discussion of the tariff issue in the Midwest, see Merrill, *Bourbon Democracy*.

53. It is not surprising to find that workers as well as managers opposed regulation. After the establishment of the Interstate Commerce Commission (ICC), the railroad brotherhoods regularly lobbied together with the railroads for favorable rulings. In 1909, P. H. Morrissey, president of the Trainmen's Brotherhood, observed, "It is good business for employees to keep a watch on the fund from which their wages are paid. . . . They are vitally interested in the earnings of the roads." David Montgomery, *The Fall of the House of Labor: The Workplace, the State, and American Labor Activism, 1865–1925* (Cambridge, Mass., 1987), 366.

54. Martin, *James J. Hill*, 158, 184–86, 215; C. W. Johnson, *A Tale of Two Cities: Minneapolis and St. Paul Compared* (Minneapolis, 1885), 43–49, 91; Kane, *Falls of St. Anthony*, 100.

55. In 1877, St. Paul still far outpaced Minneapolis in wholesaling, with $27,815,072 worth of goods sold in St. Paul compared to $8,034,000 in Minneapolis. Kane, *Falls of St. Anthony*, 101.

56. In contrast, Minneapolis reported three breweries, capitalized at $180,000. *Report on the Manufactures of the United States at the Tenth Census, 1880* (Washington, 1883), 412, 434. See also Schmid, *Social Saga of Two Cities*, 35.

57. H. P. Hall, *H. P. Hall's Observations: Being More or Less a History of Political Contests in Minnesota from 1849 to 1904* (St. Paul, 1904), 197.

58. Michael Boyle diary, 10 September 1880, MBP, MHS.

59. Ibid., vol. 7, 2 September 1882, and vol. 5, 18 June 1880.

60. Joel Best, "Looking Evil in the Face: Being an Examination of Vice and Respectability in Saint Paul as Seen in the City's Press, 1865–83," *MH* 50 (summer 1987): 247.

61. Ibid., 249–50; O'Brien, *There Were Four*, 19–20.

62. According to contemporary political observer Harlan Hall, residence in St. Paul was a "usually fatal claim." Hall, *Observations*, 190–91. Only Scandinavian candidates were able to surmount the St. Paul handicap. Not only could they appeal to a statewide Scandinavian majority, the city's Scandinavians tended to favor reform and held themselves aloof from the rest of the city, both socially and geographically, clustering almost exclusively on the remote East Side.

63. Oestreicher, "Urban Working-Class Political Behavior," 1283–84, 1286.

64. Merrill, *Bourbon Democracy*, 174–78.

65. *PP*, 22 April 1885; *Trib.*, 17 April 1885; Merrill, "Ignatius Donnelly," 514; Ridge, *Ignatius Donnelly*, 222; Regan, "The Irish," 143.

66. See, for example, Grace Flandrau, "St. Paul: The Untamable Twin," in *The Taming of the Frontier*, ed. Duncan Aikman (New York, 1925), 151.

67. For a colorful rendition of nineteenth-century Minneapolis politics and its relationship with the city elites, see A. J. Russell, *Fourth Street* (Minneapolis, 1917).

68. For example, see the case of Boston in Paula M. Kane, *Separatism and Subculture: Boston Catholicism, 1900–1920* (Chapel Hill, N.C., 1994).

69. Mary Hill, 1 May 1899; 30 and 31 August 1886, MMHD, JJHRL. Interpretative guides at the J. J. Hill house relate the legend of the kitchen floor.

70. Celia Tauer to Henry Forstner, 2 January 1911 and 3 September 1910, CF, MHS.

71. The family usually moved to the farm at North Oaks at the beginning of May, where they often remained until the chill of November drove them back to the city. MMHD.

72. Tauer to Forstner, 14 August 1910, CF.

73. Claire Strom, "James J. Hill: Empire Builder as Farmer," *MH* 54 (summer 1995): 249–50; Jarchow, *Amherst H. Wilder*, 197.

74. MMHD, 1886–99.

75. Washburn to Hill, 29 May 1882, general correspondence file, B12, JJH, JJHRL; see also Wills, "Tangled Webs," 272.

76. *Formal Opening of the West Hotel*, commemoration program reproduced in Goodrich Lowry, *Streetcar Man: Tom Lowry and the Twin City Rapid Transit Company* (Minneapolis, 1978), 64–72.

77. The directors of the Soo Line were the most prominent power brokers in Minneapolis.

Marion Daniel Shutter, ed., *History of Minneapolis*, 3 vols. (Chicago, 1923), 1:282–83 (for biographical sketches of the directors, see vols. 2–3); Hill to George Stephen, 11 and 18 May 1886, vol. P14, JJH LB; Stephen to Hill, 23 May 1886, general correspondence file, B9, JJH.

78. Hill's assessment here was remarkably prescient, though decades premature. Not until the opening of the Panama Canal in 1914 was Minneapolis' milling dominance seriously threatened. As export trade became an increasingly important part of the market, Buffalo's more strategic location gave it the advantage, allowing it to surpass Minneapolis as the milling capital by the mid-twenties. Nonetheless, though the milling operations migrated, control of the industry remained in Minneapolis, since by 1929, Minneapolis firms owned more than 85% of the milling capacity in Buffalo. Schmid, *Social Saga of Two Cities*, 16.

79. Henry D. Minot to John S. Kennedy, 21 May 1886, Letterpress Books, RR series, vol. R28–R29, reel 41, JJH.

80. Kane, *Falls of St. Anthony*, 86–87, 116, 147; Folwell, *History of Minnesota*, 3: 186–87.

81. S. S. Simrall to Hill, 31 December 1885, quoted in Martin, *James J. Hill*, 263.

82. Undeniably, Minneapolis also played a role in this distancing act, since Minneapolis elites tended to look down on St. Paul society, considering it inferior in both culture and wealth. Moreover, St. Paul capitalists who ventured into Minneapolis partnerships all too often found them a poor investment. Profit eluded the St. Paul men in their various ventures, but inexplicably, once they pulled out, the enterprises seemed to turn to gold for their former Minneapolis partners. See Lowry, *Streetcar Man*, 58–59, and Kane, *Falls of St. Anthony*, 48–49, 70–80.

83. Marvin R. O'Connell, *John Ireland and the American Catholic Church* (St. Paul, 1988), 21, 39–40.

84. Ibid., 42–52.

85. Ibid., 53–58. Though the archbishop technically was not the superior of the sisters, according to the history of the Sisters of St. Joseph, the nuns most often treated his "guidance" as law. Hurley, *On Good Ground*, 222–23. I am indebted to Sister Peronne Marie Thibert of the Convent of the Visitation for information about the archbishop's elimination of internal hierarchies within the order.

86. James P. Shannon, *Catholic Colonization on the Western Frontier* (New Haven, Conn., 1957); O'Connell, *John Ireland*, 88–114; Daniel P. O'Neill, "The Development of an American Priesthood: Archbishop John Ireland and the Saint Paul Diocesan Clergy, 1884–1918," *JAEH* 4 (spring 1985): 35–50; Joseph Guillamette, one of Ireland's last seminarians, interview by the author, 14 July 1996, St. Paul, tape recording, side 1.

87. Lindley, *James J. and Mary T. Hill*, 79–80; Martin, *James J. Hill*, 61.

88. Given the size of his fortune, Hill was, by any standard, a meager philanthropist, evidenced in his donation books, meticulously kept from 1880–1915. The conditions of his gift to the St. Paul Seminary are laid out in detail in the trust agreement that conveyed the funds. Seminary files, JJH.

89. MMHD, 1885–1918.

90. Martin, *James J. Hill*, 63–64; O'Connell, *John Ireland*, 116–17.

91. The historian Sister Helen Angela Hurley asserts that Ireland did indeed incur Mary Hill's enduring disfavor. Hurley, *On Good Ground*, 222.

92. MMHD; Martin, *James J. Hill*.

93. Shannon, *Catholic Colonization*, 46, 90–91.

94. Lowry, *Streetcar Man*, 104, 117; Virginia Brainard Kunz, *St. Paul: Saga of an American City* (Woodland Hills, Calif., 1977), 66–69; O'Connell, *John Ireland*, 571 n. 2.

95. Johnson, *Tale of Two Cities*, 85; Charles W. Johnson, *Another Tale of Two Cities: Minneapolis and St. Paul Compared* (Minneapolis, 1890), 13.

96. Ireland to Hill, 22 April 1893, quoted in O'Connell, *John Ireland*, 381; *NC*, 23 March 1894, quoted in Benson, *Irish and German Families*, 217.

97. Ireland to Hill, telegram, 9 May 1893, quoted in O'Connell, *John Ireland*, 382.

98. Hill to Samuel Hill, telegram, 19 May 1893, quoted in Martin, *James J. Hill*, 404; O'Connell, *John Ireland*, 381–85.

99. O'Connell, *John Ireland*, 378–79; trust agreement for the St. Paul Seminary, 24 September 1895, legal documents file, B2, SSP, JJHRL. One telling clause of the trust agreement man-

dated that the seminary remain in perpetuity under the control of the archdiocese. If it were to be turned over to the management of a religious order (which Hill would have far less ability to influence), the trust automatically would be revoked.

100. Boyle diaries, 25 August 1876; 15 May 1881; 13 February 1878. Boyle's patron, Constantine McConville, later became a partner in the firm and became president in 1910. McConville obituary, *CB*, 23 November 1918, 2.

101. Boyle diaries, 2 April 1880; 18 April 1878; 18 November 1877; 25 April 1880; 7 May 1881; 11 October 1878; 5 July 1880; 17 November 1881; 28 January 1878; 4 November 1880; official Program of the Tenth Annual Regatta of the Minnesota Boat Club, 1883, MBP. See also O'Brien, *There Were Four*, 52–53.

102. McCarthy to Bill, 28 August 1922, FAB; O'Brien, *There Were Four*; Donnelly diary, 1887, quoted in Ridge, *Ignatius Donnelly*, 232.

103. Boyle diaries, 31 May 1881, and 26 February 1880.

104. Boyle diaries, which cover the years 1876–1890 and 1918–1941, and the biographical sketch included with his papers delineate his career in detail, as well as his deep longing to move up in society.

105. Boyle diaries.

106. On the myth of the mournful exile, see Miller, *Emigrants and Exiles.*

107. Joan M. Allen, *Candles and Carnival Lights: The Catholic Sensibility of F. Scott Fitzgerald* (New York, 1978); Andrew Turnbull, *Scott Fitzgerald* (New York, 1962).

108. Town and Country Club roster, 1 June 1915, T&C Records, MHS. A tally of Irish surnames does not, of course, take into consideration the considerable number of young women from Irish families who married into non-Irish families.

Chapter 3: Delivering the Goods

1. *The Story of the Town and Country Club* (St. Paul, 1947), 8, 23.

2. Ibid., 23.

3. Calvin E. Schmid, *The Social Saga of Two Cities: An Ecological and Statistical Study of Social Trends in Minneapolis and St. Paul* (Minneapolis, 1937), 70–79; Judith A. Martin and David A. Lanegran, *Where We Live: The Residential Districts of Minneapolis and St. Paul* (Minneapolis, 1983), 30–34; David A. Lanegran and Ernest R. Sandeen, *The Lake District of Minneapolis: A History of the Calhoun-Isles Community* (St. Paul, 1979), 32–35; Charles Rumford Walker, *American City: A Rank-and-File History* (New York, 1937), 129–36.

4. Schmid, *Social Saga of Two Cities*, 77–79; Goodrich Lowry, *Streetcar Man: Tom Lowry and the Twin City Rapid Transit Company* (Minneapolis, 1978). On streetcar suburbanization, see Kenneth T. Jackson, *Crabgrass Frontier: The Suburbanization of the United States* (New York, 1985), 103–56.

5. In her monograph on the Minneapolis labor movement, Elizabeth Faue defines the nature of community in Minneapolis in these terms; however, her analysis becomes problematic when applied to St. Paul. Elizabeth Faue, *Community of Suffering & Struggle: Women, Men, and the Labor Movement in Minneapolis, 1915–1945* (Chapel Hill, N.C., 1991). On working-class migration and community stability, see John Bodnar, *The Transplanted: A History of Immigrants in Urban America* (Bloomington, Ind., 1987).

6. Ernest R. Sandeen, *St. Paul's Historic Summit Avenue* (St. Paul, 1978), 7–10. On fiscal conservatism, see Thomas D. O'Brien, *There Were Four of Us, or Was It Five* (St. Paul, 1936), 98–99. On the Victorian boulevard, see Jackson, *Crabgrass Frontier*, 75–76.

7. Andrew Turnbull, *Scott Fitzgerald* (New York, 1962), 18–23.

8. Such city-planning schemes, with private interests underlaying public development and beautification efforts, were common currency in nineteenth-century urban development. For a classic example, see Roy Rosenzweig and Elizabeth Blackmar, *The Park and the People: A History of Central Park* (Ithaca, N.Y., 1992), 78–91.

9. Edward Kagin, *James Wallace of Macalester* (Garden City, N.Y., 1957), 84–85; Lane-

gran and Martin, *Where We Live*, 89–90; Billie Young and David Lanegran, *Grand Avenue: The Renaissance of an Urban Street* (St. Cloud, Minn., 1997), 18–20.

10. For instance, one typical block near Macalester College in the 1910s was home to the families of a doctor, milkman, railroad clerk, lawyer, grocer, and several renters who came and went in the three duplexes that shared the block with single-family homes. Marguerite Lux Lethert, interview by the author, St. Paul, 24 July 1997, tape recording, side 1.

11. Celia Tauer, maid in the household of James J. Hill, commonly passed a Sunday afternoon in this manner with her fellow servants and their beaus. Tauer to Henry Forstner, 26 April 1910, CF, MHS. It is also worth noting that while the St. Paul Cathedral was under construction between 1905 and 1918, literally hundreds of workmen not only worked at the site every day but also traveled to and fro, lounged on the manicured boulevard, and chatted with local domestic workers. CF.

12. Florence Milton McCarthy diary, 20 July 1910, privately held; Tauer to Forstner, 25 January 1911, CF.

13. On the important role that Catholic parishes played in creating stable, enduring neighborhoods, see John T. McGreevy, *Parish Boundaries: The Catholic Encounter with Race in the Twentieth-Century Urban North* (Chicago, 1996), 7–28. For a vivid evocation of the Catholic geography of St. Paul, see Patricia Hampl, *Virgin Time* (New York, 1992); and "Parish Streets," quoted in McGreevy, *Parish Boundaries*, 21–22.

14. Maude Pohl to Joseph Lethert, 5, 13, and 16 October, 1 December 1909; 8 and 31 January, 29 March, and 18 December 1910; Lethert to Pohl, 11 April 1910, letters in the author's possession. On the Theis family, I rely on recollections of my grandmother, Celia Theis Lux.

15. Pohl to Lethert, 13 October 1909; James J. Byrne, *A History of St. Agnes: A Condensed Chronicle* (St. Paul, 1953). On the interclass nature of ethnic neighborhoods, see Bodnar, *Transplanted*, 117–43.

16. *Golden Jubilee: St. Louis Church* (St. Paul, 1959), 1–2. Accounts of interparish visiting practices appear in Michael Boyle diaries, Mary Hill diaries, and Forstner papers. For the Holy Thursday observance, I rely on personal childhood memories.

17. Pohl to Lethert, 15 and 29 March 1910; Tauer to Forstner, 26 April 1910.

18. David Vassar Taylor, "The Blacks," in *They Chose Minnesota: A Survey of the State's Ethnic Groups*, ed. June Drenning Holmquist (St. Paul, 1981), 75–81; and Evelyn Fairbanks, *Days of Rondo* (St. Paul, 1990). St. Paul's black community bears a striking resemblance to the African American community in Chicago before the Great Migration of World War I. See James R. Grossman, *Land of Hope: Chicago, Black Southerners, and the Great Migration* (Chicago, 1991). In St. Paul, however, no wave of immigrants disrupted the established workings of the community, and it retained this configuration until its destruction by urban renewal in the 1960s.

19. William D. Green, "Race and Segregation in St. Paul's Public Schools, 1846–69," *MH* 55 (winter 1996–97): 142.

20. "Othello and Desdemona," *Disp.*, 3 September 1888.

21. *Thirteenth Census of the United States*, vol. 2: *Population* (Washington 1913), 991; Taylor, "The Blacks," 74; "Minnesota Organizing," *New York Age*, 26 November 1887.

22. Taylor, "The Blacks," 80.

23. It has only recently come to light, thanks to the assiduous detective work of independent historian David Riehle, that James was black. No mention of his race occurs in either the *Union Advocate* or the local dailies. A brief mention in the *Western Appeal*, St. Paul's African American newspaper, put Riehle on the trail of this astonishing fact, which awaits in-depth interpretive analysis.

24. Sister Helen Angela Hurley, *On Good Ground: The Story of the Sisters of St. Joseph in St. Paul* (Minneapolis, 1951), 103, 153.

25. *Diamond Jubilee: St. Peter Claver Church, St. Paul, Minnesota, 1892–1967* (n.p., n.d.), 6–11. Though the membership of St. Peter Claver never challenged that of the other black churches—in 1910, the parish counted about four hundred members—this missionary effort still supported the cause of black advancement. In 1910, Ireland ordained Stephen Theobald to the priesthood, the first black priest in the state and one of only a handful in the country. "Father Theobald," *America* 47 (23 July 1932): 368–69.

26. Taylor, "The Blacks," 77; Mary Ann Schwantes (niece of Ann and Henry Houck), interview by the author, St. Paul, 4 July 1998, tape recording, side 2.

27. John G. Rice, "The Swedes," and Carlton C. Qualey and Jon A. Gjerde, "The Norwegians," in *They Chose Minnesota*, ed. Holmquist, 251, 262, 223.

28. The reorganization of city government is delineated in *St. Paul City Directory* (St. Paul, 1915), 17–18.

29. James P. Shannon, "Bishop Ireland's Connemara Experiment," *MH* 35 (March 1957): 205–9. Rudolph J. Vecoli, "The Italians," in *They Chose Minnesota*, ed. Holmquist, 453–54; Nils M. Hokanson, "I Remember Swede Hollow," *MH* 40 (winter 1969): 362–71; Polly Nyberg and Jerome Bette, "Swede Hollow: A Community's Love Affair with Its Past," *Common Ground* (fall 1974): 4–8.

30. Quoted in Hokanson, "I Remember Swede Hollow," 368–70.

31. This social ordering appears as a sharp contrast to ethnic enclaves that developed in cities, where single immigrant groups settled in large numbers, such as Italian Harlem. But even in most of those neighborhoods, ethnic homogeneity was seldom total. See Robert Orsi, *Madonna of 115th Street: Faith and Community in Italian Harlem, 1880–1950* (New Haven, Conn., 1985).

32. Angelo "Tony" Vruno, interview by the author, 24 July 1996, St. Paul, tape recording, side 2, Gentile Yarusso, "La Scola Lincoln," unpublished manuscript, p. 1, MHS.

33. Rudolph J. Vecoli, "The Italians," in *They Chose Minnesota*, 450, 453. On Minneapolis as a recruiting center for casual labor, see David L. Rosheim, *The Other Minneapolis or A History of the Minneapolis Skid Row* (Maquoketa, Iowa, 1978), 22–86; and O. E. Rolvaag, *The Boat of Longing* (New York, 1933; rpt., St. Paul, 1985).

34. Nyberg and Bette, "Swede Hollow," 7; Vecoli, "The Italians," 453; Yarusso, p. 2; Vruno interview, sides 1 and 2.

35. Ethel McClure, *More Than a Roof: The Development of Minnesota Poor Farms and Homes for the Aged* (St. Paul, 1968), 20–108; *St. Paul City Directory*, 115–19; James Michael Reardon, *The Catholic Church in the Diocese of St. Paul: From Earliest Origin to Centennial Achievement* (St. Paul, 1952), 325; Marilyn J. Chiat, "Work and Faith and Minnesota's Jewish Merchants," *RCH* 28 (spring 1993): 7–8; "A History of Neighborhood House," pp. 2–4, typescript, B2, D-PP, MHS.

36. Evidence of immigrant conflict with the Americanizing clergy can be found in parish files of St. Ambrose (Italian) and St. Stanislaus (Czech) parishes, AASPM. On Swedes, Hokanson, "I Remember Swede Hollow," 371. On immigrants clinging to old ways, *PP*, 2 January 1910, 7.

37. Vruno interview, side 1.

38. Vecoli, "The Italians," 453.

39. On the intersection of the forces of capital and the agency of historical actors in explaining social change, see David Harvey, *The Condition of Postmodernity: An Enquiry into the Origins of Cultural Change* (Cambridge, 1989).

40. Susan E. Williams, " 'A Wild Hurrah': The Great Northern Celebration of 1893," *MH* 48 (fall 1982): 119; *PP*, 7 January 1893, 1.

41. *Disp.*, 2 January 1893, 8 and 9 June 1893; Albro Martin, *James J. Hill and the Opening of the Northwest* (New York, 1976; rpt., St. Paul, 1991), 396–98; Williams, " 'Wild Hurrah,' " 120–21.

42. Martin, *James J. Hill*, 414–15.

43. Ibid., 415; Nick Salvatore, *Eugene V. Debs: Citizen and Socialist* (Urbana, Ill., 1982), 119–20.

44. It seems reasonable to suspect that, in addition to the recorded donations, other money or favors may have informally changed hands, as it did regularly in Hill's behind-the-scenes political machinations. For recorded donations, see JJH Donation Book, 1880–1894, JJHRL; gift to Knights of Labor appears on pp. 4–5. On Hill and NP officials, Shelton Stromquist, *A Generation of Boomers: The Pattern of Railroad Labor Conflict in Nineteenth-Century America* (Urbana, Ill., 1993), 253–54.

45. The Knights, whose influence in the labor movement had been declining steadily since the late 1880s, experienced a brief resurgence in membership during the strike. One assembly in St. Paul gained 225 new members at a single meeting held during the strike. Salvatore, *Eugene V. Debs*, 120–21.

46. Stromquist, *Generation of Boomers*, 254–55; Salvatore, *Eugene V. Debs*, 121, 370 n. 35.

47. Correspondence between the officers of West Publishing, one of St. Paul's most well-

capitalized firms, attests to the damage a transportation shutdown presented. During the Pullman strike in July 1894, West faced potential shortages in coal, paper, metal, and leather and, furthermore, felt a negative impact on collections. For the city's smaller businesses, the impact would have been even more immediately disastrous. Homer Clark to Charles Ames, secretary of West Publishing, 5 and 6 July 1894, Homer Clark folder, B18, CWA, MHS.

48. Salvatore, *Eugene V. Debs*, 122–23.

49. Ibid., 121–22.

50. Martin, *James J. Hill*, 426; Salvatore, *Eugene V. Debs*, 123.

51. Matthew Josephson, *The Robber Barons: The Great American Capitalists, 1861–1901* (New York, 1934), 406–7, 416–17.

52. Martin, *James J. Hill*, 426. For a full account of the Pullman strike, see Salvatore, *Eugene V. Debs*, 126–46.

53. Stromquist, *Generation of Boomers*, 261–65, 274.

54. In 1936, *Fortune* magazine stated unequivocally, "The Panama Canal killed St. Paul." "Revolt in the Northwest," *Fortune*, April 1936, 186. With the opening of the canal and regulations imposed by the Interstate Commerce Commission, it became cheaper to ship freight from Seattle to New York via the canal and then forward it west by rail than it was to ship the same load by rail from Seattle to Ohio. See Walker, *American City*, 22. For the effect of new technology, mail-order businesses, and chain stores on regional centers, see William Cronon, *Nature's Metropolis: Chicago and the Great West* (New York, 1991).

55. *UA*, 2 January 1920, 4, and 20 March 1947, 1. I am grateful to David Riehle and Barbara Kucera, editor of the *Advocate*, for additional biographical information on Guiney.

56. Though no firm numbers are available on membership in the Knights, it is instructive to note that more than one thousand members turned out to hear Grand Master Workman Terrence Powderly in 1885. George B. Engberg, "The Knights of Labor in Minnesota," *MH* 22 (December 1941): 371, 376–77.

57. Engberg, "Knights of Labor," 389–90; Carl H. Chrislock, *The Progressive Era in Minnesota, 1899–1918* (St. Paul, 1971), 115–16.

58. In 1899, the total manufacturing output for St. Paul was $30,060,000; for Minneapolis, it was $94,410,000. Schmid, *Social Saga of Two Cities*, 18–19. Schmid provides graphic evidence of the growing disparity between the two cities in every category. See also Lucile M. Kane, *The Falls of St. Anthony: The Waterfall That Built Minneapolis* (St. Paul, 1987), 101, 115, 147.

59. Out of a total of 599 manufacturing or wholesaling establishments, 29 employed more than one hundred people; only 7 employed more than two hundred (including the Twin City Rapid Transit Company, which was Minneapolis-owned). In contrast, 482 establishments employed less than fifty persons. *BOL, 1901–1902*, 20–50.

60. "Revolt in the Northwest," 116.

61. St. Paul recorded 22,942 wage earners in 1902; Minneapolis recorded 36,576, of whom 13,140 (36%) claimed union membership—an increase of nearly 24% from 1900. *BOL, 1901–1902*, 50, 97, 452–53.

62. On the employers' campaign against the unions, the most comprehensive source is William Millikan, *A Union against Unions: The Minneapolis Citizens Alliance and Its Fight against Organized Labor, 1903–1947* (St. Paul, 2001). I am grateful to Mr. Millikan for sharing his work with me in manuscript form. Chapters 1–3 deal particularly with this era in Minneapolis labor relations. On the milling strike, see also William C. Edgar, *Medal of Gold: A Story of Industrial Achievement* (Minneapolis, 1925), 225–33.

63. As examples of pressure applied to maintain Minneapolis employer unity, in a 1907 machinists' strike, the alliance provided financial support to striking employers. In cases of employers who continued to waver, the Citizens Alliance threatened to put them out of business. Similarly, during a building trades strike in 1911, the Alliance threatened to withhold materials from any builder who signed a union contract. William Millikan, *Union against Unions*, mss.d. 52; see also W. Millikan, "Maintaining Law and Order: The Minneapolis Citizens Alliance in the 1920s," *MH* 51 (summer 1989): 219–33; Millikan, "Defenders of Business: The Minneapolis Civic and Commerce Association versus Labor during W.W. I," *MH* 50 (spring 1986): 2–11;

Lois Quam and Peter J. Rachleff, "Keeping Minneapolis an Open-Shop Town: The Citizens Alliance in the 1930s," *MH* 50 (fall 1986): 105–17; David Paul Nord, "Hothouse Socialism: Minneapolis, 1910–1925," in *Socialism in the Heartland: The Midwestern Experience*, ed. Donald Critchlow (Notre Dame, Ind., 1986), 133–66; and Walker, *American City*, 188.

64. "The Men and Products of St. Paul," *Third Annual St. Paul Almanack* (St. Paul, 1915), 60.

65. The "live and let live" plan is referred to repeatedly in both labor and business publications. For examples, see *UA*, 18 December 1903, and 5 January 1917, 3.

66. Comparative wage rates and working hours appear in the annual reports of the Bureau of Labor.

67. *UA*, 15 June 1917, 1.

68. Pamphlet charging the Golden Rule Department Store with unfair labor practices, B2, WM, MHS.

69. *UA*, 5 January 1917, 3.

70. Ibid., 23 February 1917, 8. These arguments were largely persuasive among union workers. According to one retired teamster, he and his friends seldom went to Minneapolis: "People really felt that they should spend their money at home and not somewhere else . . . because if you go to Minneapolis and spend it, it will be gone. It won't turn over eight times like it will in St. Paul." Gordon "Mock" Larson, interview by the author, 27 July 1996, St. Paul, tape recording, side 2.

71. In Seattle in the 1920s, a weakened labor movement turned to similar consumer-based strategies when it lacked the strength to challenge employers directly. But there, where the balance of power clearly was on the side of business, the strategy did not have the clout it wielded in St. Paul. See Dana Frank, *Purchasing Power: Consumer Organizing, Gender, and the Seattle Labor Movement, 1919–1920* (Cambridge, Mass., 1994).

72. *UA*, 24 and 31 July 1903.

73. *BOL, 1901–1902*. On features in the *Advocate* aimed at women, see all issues, 1901–5.

74. Minutes of the "preliminary meeting for the organization of a Citizens' Association of St. Paul," CASP, MHS. (The minutes for this meeting are undated, but a second "preliminary" meeting was held on 22 July 1903.)

75. Typewritten draft of membership solicitation for the Citizens' Association, 12 November 1903, p. 2, CASP. The boycott was a long-established strategy in the St. Paul labor movement, grounded in ethnic as well as community tradition. Adapted from a mode of Irish peasant resistance to landlord exploitation, the boycott was a familiar and effective means of protest for Irish St. Paulites. On the Irish origins of boycott, see Richard Schneirov, *Labor and Urban Politics: Class Conflict and the Origins of Modern Liberalism in Chicago, 1864–97* (Urbana, Ill., 1998), 123.

76. Membership solicitation letter, p. 2, CASP.

77. Minutes of the Meeting of the Executive Committee, 29 September 1903, p. 3, CASP.

78. *UA*, 25 September 1903, 5; Minutes of the Meeting of the Executive Committee, 29 September 1903, p. 2, CASP.

79. It is not surprising that organized labor found Parry "unspeakable." At the 1903 convention of the National Association of Manufacturers, Parry had declared trade unionism to be "a system that coerces and impoverishes the worker, ruins the capitalist, terrorizes our politicians and destroys our trade—a system which seems to be hopelessly and irredeemably bad, a bar to all true progress, a danger to the state and a menace to civilization." *Proceedings of Annual Convention of the National Association of Manufacturers, 1903*, quoted in Millikan, *Union against Unions*, mss.d. 41. For examples of *UA* strategies, see 25 September 1903, 7; 16 October 1903, 7; and 6 November 1903, 1.

80. Minutes of the Executive Committee, 16 October 1903, 2–3, CASP.

81. J. W. Cooper, J. H. Beek, and George M. Gibbs, Report to the Citizens' Association of St. Paul, 5 November 1903, 1–7; and Minutes of the Meeting of the Executive Committee on the same date, CASP.

82. *UA*, 20 November 1903, 1.

83. Ibid., 20 November 1903, 4; 18 December 1903, 4.

84. Ibid., 11 December 1903, 1.

85. Ibid., 25 December 1903, 3; *PP*, 2 December 1903, 1; and 3 December 1903, 4.

86. Minutes of the Meeting of the Executive Committee, 3 December 1903, 2, CASP.

87. The members of the Minneapolis Citizens Alliance had no similar compunctions about utilizing an employers' boycott. In fact, Millikan argues that the threat of boycott against union shops "was probably the most effective tool to enforce employer unity." Millikan, *Union against Unions*, mss.d. 55.

88. Harrison E. Salisbury, "The Victorian City in the Midwest," in *Growing Up in Minnesota: Ten Writers Remember Their Childhoods*, ed. Chester G. Anderson (Minneapolis, 1976), 51.

89. From the 1880s until the time of his death in 1918, Archbishop Ireland was a prominent figure at every important civic event—from visits of presidents to the annual Labor Day celebration to seeing off the troops for the Spanish-American and world wars. For examples, see Marvin R. O'Connell, *John Ireland and the American Catholic Church* (St. Paul, 1988), 395; *UA*, 11 September 1903, 1; and Franklin F. Holbrook, *St. Paul and Ramsey County in the War of 1917–1918* (St. Paul, 1929), 99.

90. John McCarthy to Fred Bill, 28 August 1922, FAB Papers, MHS; O'Brien, *There Were Four*, 19.

91. Hurley, *On Good Ground*, 198, 224. By 1905, the Catholic Church had established five high schools, two colleges, a music conservatory, an industrial school, two homes for "friendless girls," two orphanages, one hospital, and two homes for the aged, in addition to twenty-three parishes—most with schools attached—spreading across every ward of the city, and the imposing St. Paul Seminary at the western boundary. In contrast, Minneapolis housed two Catholic high schools, two homes for delinquents, a home for the aged, one hospital, and sixteen parishes, almost all of these located in working-class neighborhoods. Reardon, *History of the Catholic Church*, 581–97, 653–68, 373–87.

92. O'Connell, *John Ireland*, 104–13.

93. Minute book of the St. Paul chapter of the Father Mathew Society, 1872, B1, CTAU, AASPM.

94. O'Connell, *John Ireland*, 109.

95. Ibid., 110.

96. Minutes of the Father Mathew Society, 1871–72; Constitution and By-Law of the St. Paul Clerical Total Abstinence Society, B1, CTAU.

97. Brochure of the Crusader's Total Abstinence Society, n.d.; Total Abstainers membership card, n.d.; programs of the Crusader's Society, 1893–1902; "The Business Outlook," pamphlet of the Crusader's Total Abstinence Society, n.d., 1–3. Crusader's Society folder, B1, CTAU.

98. Draft of dedication speech, general correspondence file, JJH Papers; Willis James, New York financier and director of the Great Northern, to Hill, 10 September 1895, quoted in Martin, *James J. Hill*, 453.

99. Ireland received considerable publicity for his role in this episode, though the critical advocate for the Knights is acknowledged to have been Cardinal James Gibbons of Baltimore. Jay P. Dolan, *The American Catholic Experience: A History from Colonial Times to the Present* (Garden City, N.Y., 1985), 330–32; Henry J. Browne, *The Catholic Church and the Knights of Labor* (Washington, D.C., 1949), 182–274; O'Connell, *John Ireland*, 229–39. Dolan notes that by the turn of the century, the Catholic Church was generally supportive of the AFL. With the widespread participation of Catholics in the labor movement, to do otherwise would have been institutional suicide. *American Catholic Experience*, 311–12, 333–34.

100. O'Connell, *John Ireland*, 238. Ireland, speech delivered at the Baltimore Cathedral, 1889, quoted in Hurley, *On Good Ground*, 205.

101. O'Connell, *John Ireland*, 394.

102. Ibid.; Ireland, "Personal Liberty and Labor Strikes," 1901, reprinted in "The Morals and Law Involved in Labor Conflicts," pamphlet published by the American Anti-Boycott Association, n.d., 7–14.

103. *UA*, 31 July 1903, 1, 4.

104. Ibid., 7 August 1903, 1.

105. Ibid., 31 July 1903, 4.

106. Ibid., 14 August 1903, 1.

107. Ibid., 11 September 1903, 1, 4.

108. Daniel P. O'Neill, "The Development of an American Priesthood: Archbishop John Ireland and the Saint Paul Diocesan Clergy, 1884–1918," *JAEH* 4 (spring 1985): 39.

109. Ibid., 33–55.

110. The debate between Ryan and Hillquit, entitled "Socialism: Promise or Menace," appeared in monthly installments between October 1913 and April 1914.

111. Francis L. Broderick, *Right Reverend New Dealer: John A. Ryan* (New York, 1963), 36–111; quoted on 59.

112. John P. Ryan, *Social Doctrine in Action* (n.p., n.d.), 28, quoted ibid., 75.

113. In 1910, 15% of those residing in the Eighth Ward, where St. Agnes parish was located, were foreign-born German Americans. *Thirteenth Census*, 2: 1018. See also, *Byrne, History of St. Agnes*; Pohl/Lethert correspondence.

114. Diaries of Louise Lindeke Weyerhaeuser, WF, MHS; and correspondence of Margaret Weyerhaeuser Jewett. As an example, see Margaret Jewett to James Jewett, 1 October 1904, B1, JRJ, MHS.

115. On the reciprocal obligations of paternalism, see Mary Lethert Wingerd, "Rethinking Paternalism: Power and Parochialism in a Southern Mill Village," *JAH* 83 (December 1996): 872–902.

116. In 1910, approximately 42% of the Swedish and Norwegian-born population was clustered in the first, second, and third wards of the upper and lower East Side, with another 12% residing in the far northwestern Tenth Ward, separated from heavily Scandinavian northeast Minneapolis only by municipal boundary. *Thirteenth Census*, 2: 1018. The 1915 St. Paul City directory lists thirty churches, of various denominations that are self-defined as Scandinavian, three weekly Scandinavian-language newspapers, and more than two dozen Scandinavian associations located on the East Side. *R. L. Polk & Company City Directory of St. Paul, 1915*, 97–132. On Scandinavian attitudes toward Catholics and St. Paul cultural practices, see Larson interview, side 1.

117. "A New Synagogue," *Disp.*, 3 September 1888; *CB*, 24 November 1918. Programs from the Hibernians and the Crusader's Society can be found, respectively, in JM, MHS, and CTAU, AASPM. Additional programs abound in the individual parish records of AASPM. The Michael Boyle diaries (MBP) provide evidence of the long-standing nature of city-wide participation in Irish events; see, for instance, the entry dated 26 February 1880.

118. O'Brien, *There Were Four*, 58–60; Ann Regan, "The Irish," in *They Chose Minnesota*, ed. Holmquist, 145–46; St. Vincent de Paul folder, parish records, AASPM. On the Hill servants, see Tauer to Forstner, 17 March and 26 April 1910, 2 January 1911, CF.

119. *Chinese and Japanese in the United States, 1910* (Washington D.C., 1914), 38; *St. Vincent's Parish Twentieth Anniversary, 1889–1909* (St. Paul, 1909), 42–44.

120. O'Brien, *There Were Four*, 63–69.

121. Ibid., 17–18, 23.

122. James Manahan to A. Ross Hill, 24 January 1910; Manahan to Pierce Butler, 30 January 1912; John Dumpley to Manahan, 7 April 1910. Programs from the Ramsey County Bar Association, St. Patrick's Day celebrations, and the Ancient Order of Hibernians also provide evidence of broad-based Irish participation. All documents located in correspondence file, B3, JM.

123. Kathryn Manahan Hoxmeier, manuscript of unpublished biography of her father, James Manahan, 204, B9, JM; *PP*, 26 September 1911, 1.

124. Hoxmeier manuscript, 147–48, 211–12.

125. Grace Flandrau, "St. Paul: The Untamable Twin," in *The Taming of the Frontier*, ed. Duncan Aikman (New York, 1925), 153. In a 1936 article, *Fortune* magazine made much the same point. But from an outsider's perspective, the qualities that St. Paulites celebrated as virtues made the city small, cramped, and petty, "an embittered invalid." See "Revolt in the Northwest," 190.

126. "Men and Products of St. Paul," 60. This protectionist attitude was a source of complaint for some people in the business community. See the draft of a letter to the board of directors of the Commercial Club of St. Paul, 1916 (neither signature nor specific date noted), B15, HDF, MHS.

127. Larson interview; *UA*, 12 October 1917.

128. Manahan to Will Owen Jones, *Nebraska State Journal*, 16 December 1911, correspondence folder, B3, JM; Hoxmeier manuscript, 153–54.

129. *Annual Report of City Officers of the Various Departments, City of St. Paul, Minnesota,*

1905, 16; Joel Best, "Looking Evil in the Face," *MH* 50 (summer 1987), 241–51; Schmid, *Social Saga of Two Cities*, 32, 35–36; O'Brien, *There Were Four*, 27.

130. Carl H. Chrislock, *The Progressive Era in Minnesota, 1899–1918* (St. Paul, 1971), 31–32; Paul Maccabee, *John Dillinger Slept Here: A Crooks' Tour of Crime and Corruption in St. Paul, 1920–1936* (St. Paul, 1995), 13–14; reporter Fred Haeberlin, quoted in Maccabee, *John Dillinger*, 13; Don Boxmeier, "Lust's Lost Way?" *PP*, 17 July 1999, 1, 6E.

131. Maccabee, *John Dillinger*, 3, 8–12; Regan, "The Irish," 143.

132. Maccabee, *John Dillinger*, 9–11; *UA*, 18 December 1903, 7, and 4 April 1917, 1.

Chapter 4: Raising the Flag

1. *PP*, 3 August 1914, 4; Carl H. Chrislock, *The Progressive Era in Minnesota, 1899–1918* (St. Paul, 1971), 68–70.

2. For an overview of the divided nature of American opinion about the war, see David M. Kennedy, *Over Here: The First World War and American Society* (New York, 1980), 3–44.

3. Ibid., 24, 66–72; Chrislock, *Progressive Era in Minnesota*, 93–100.

4. These winter carnivals were staged on a scale comparable to New Orleans' Mardi Gras, drawing thousands of out-of-town visitors, with hundreds of events, countless parades, and a massive ice palace that soared 106 feet into the air, described by *Northwest Magazine* in 1888 as "the most strangely beautiful structure that had up to that time been erected on any part of the globe." Judith Yates Borger, "This Is Where the Fun Begins," in *Saint Paul Winter Carnival: 100th Anniversary History, 1886–1986* (1986), 6–12. For a contemporary account of events, see Michael Boyle diaries, 3–29 January 1887, MBP, MHS.

5. In his study of public patriotic commemoration, historian John Bodnar notes, "Cultural leaders orchestrate commemorative events to calm anxiety about change or political events, eliminate citizen indifference toward official concerns, promote exemplary patterns of citizen behavior, and stress citizen duties over rights. They feel the need to do this because of the existence of social contradictions, alternative views, and indifference that perpetuate fears of societal dissolution and unregulated political behavior." John Bodnar, *Remaking America: Public Memory, Commemoration, and Patriotism in the Twentieth Century* (Princeton, N.J., 1992), 15. Bodnar's observation is equally pertinent in the context of civic loyalty, the *raison d'être* for the St. Paul Winter Carnival.

6. Henry P. Wickham, manager, St. Paul Outdoor Sports Carnival Association, to Edna E. Smith, *National Magazine*, 17 October 1916; Wickham to H. R. Galt, managing editor, *St. Paul Pioneer Press*, 29 September 1916, correspondence files, B1; "The St. Paul Carnival," *Madison Independent Free Press*, 9 February 1917, scrapbook, B12, SPOSCA, MHS.

7. *1886–1961, 75th Anniversary of the Fun-Filled Saint Paul Winter Carnival* (St. Paul, 1961). For evidence of Louis Hill's golfing and recreational travel schedule, see MMHD, 1910–20. For a description of Hill's disengagement from business, see "Revolt in the Northwest," *Fortune*, April 1936, 114, 190.

8. *De Luxe Souvenir View Book: St. Paul Outdoor Sports Carnival, Jan. 27– Feb. 5th, 1916*, (St. Paul, 1916), 1–3.

9. Borger, "This Is Where the Fun Begins," 13; *De Luxe Souvenir View Book; Souvenir Program Northern Pacific Carnival Marching Club: St. Paul Outdoor Sports Carnival* (1916); Wickham to Miss Lula B. Howes, 16 October 1916, B1; list of participating organizations, floats, and marching units, B12, SPOSCA.

10. *De Luxe Souvenir View Book*, 1–2.

11. Wickham to Ray C. Johns, St. Paul Athletic Club, 11 March 1916; H. D. Fields to Outdoor Sports Carnival Association, 18 January 1916; John A. Lethert to A. W. Lindeke, St. Paul Association of Commerce, 5 August 1916; Lethert to secretary of the Carnival Club, 14 October 1916, B1, SPOSCA.

12. The working-class nature of these insurance claimants is determined by the addresses accompanying their claims. Louis Hill to Wickham, 13 February 1916; V. E. Bradford, Maryland Casualty Company, to Wickham, 12 February 1916; John A. Burns, Assistant Corporation

Counsel, City of St. Paul, to Wickham, 24 March 1916; Miss B. Thorbus to carnival manager, 7 February 1916; Charles A. Lethert, attorney for Miss Clara Hannig, to Carnival Association, 23 February 1916; Lawler and Mulally, attorneys for John O'Donnell, to Wickham, 14 February 1916; Frank Drill, attorney for Alice Holmquist, Anna Danielson, and Ellen Danielson, to Carnival Association, 24 February 1916; Wickham to Louis Hill, 24 April 1916; Bradford to Wickham, 25 April 1916, correspondence file, B1, SPOSCA.

13. Paul N. Myers, vice president, H. L. Collins Co., to St. Paul Association of Commerce, 30 June 1916; Wickham to J. C. Hardy, manager, Northwestern Telephone Company, 16 October 1916, correspondence file, B1, SPOSCA.

14. "Forward," *Official Souvenir View Book, 1917;* correspondence file, B1, SPOSCA; Borger, "This Is Where the Fun Begins," 15–16. For a vivid evocation of the 1917 ice palace, see F. Scott Fitzgerald, "The Ice Palace," in *The Short Stories of F. Scott Fitzgerald*, ed. Matthew J. Bruccoli (New York, 1989), 48–69.

15. *Official Souvenir Book; UA*, 2 February 1917, 4.

16. *UA*, 2 February 1917, 1, 5; "History of the Saint Paul Winter Carnival," manuscript, p. 4, B1, SPWCA, MHS; *Report of a Survey of the School System of Saint Paul, Minnesota* (St. Paul, 1917), 438–40; Borger, "This Is Where the Fun Begins," 16.

17. Solicitor's journal, B12, SPOSCA. After 1917, the Winter Carnival was shelved until 1937, when internal stresses again prompted its resurrection as a means of allaying civic tensions.

18. *DN*, 25 March 1917, 6.

19. See Chrislock, *Progressive Era in Minnesota*, 70–71, 96–98.

20. *Red Wing Daily Republican*, 5 August 1914, 7, quoted in Chrislock, *Progressive Era*, 71; Albro Martin, *James J. Hill and the Opening of the Northwest* (New York, 1976; rpt., St. Paul, 1991), 605.

21. Martin, *James J. Hill*, 604–8. Chrislock, *Progressive Era*, 97. It is unlikely that the bank had many German American customers. In 1915 the Union of German War Veterans, meeting in St. Paul, had resolved to do no business with banks that sold Allied bonds. German Americans in the city generally patronized the German-owned American National Bank, headed by Otto Bremer, the city's most prominent brewer. John Christine Wolkerstorfer, "Nativism in Minnesota in World War I: A Comparative Study of Brown, Ramsey, and Stearns Counties, 1914–1918" (Ph.D. diss., University of Minnesota, 1973), 126.

22. Letter to the board of directors of the Commercial Club of St. Paul, 1916 (specific date not noted), HDF, B15, MHS.

23. Edmond D. DeLestry, "Local Industries in the War," in *St. Paul and Ramsey County in the War of 1917–1918*, ed. Franklin F. Holbrook (St. Paul, 1929), 192–93.

24. Chrislock, *Progressive Era in Minnesota*, 222 n.12.

25. *UA*, 6 February 1917, 1, 8.

26. *DOL, 1915–1916*, 164–75; *DOL, 1917–1918*, 151–71; Chrislock, *Progressive Era in Minnesota*, 113–16.

27. *MJ*, 13 March 1917, 1; Franklin F. Holbrook and Livia Appel, *Minnesota in the War with Germany* (St. Paul, 1928), 44–46.

28. Holbrook and Appel, *Minnesota in the War with Germany*, 44. Throughout 1916 and 1917, both the *Union Advocate* and *the Catholic Bulletin* published numerous articles warning of the dangers of socialism.

29. *DN*, 1 April 1917, 6; Holbrook, *St. Paul and Ramsey County in the War*.

30. Businessmen's concern over the city's image dates from the outbreak of the European war. Though the St. Paul Patriotic League was not formally unveiled until 1917, thirty-three prominent city businessmen, all members of the St. Paul Association, had established a local branch of the National Security League (NSL) by December 1915. Through participation in the NSL, they worked to shape public opinion in favor of intervention. On original members of the NSL, see Grant VanSant, St. Paul NSL secretary, to Donald Cotton, 13 December 1915, correspondence folder, B1, DRC Papers, MHS. On the origins and business agenda of the NSL, see Robert D. Ward, "The Origin and Activities of the National Security League, 1914–1919," *MVHR* 57 (June 1960): 51–65.

31. Charles Farnham to James Clark, 13 April 1917, B1, PLSP, MHS.

32. *St. Paul Dispatch*, 2 March 1917, 1; Farnham to Clark, 13 April 1917, B1, PLSP.

33. The files of the Patriotic League Papers contain many letters from Farnham regarding display of the flag. No lapse was beneath his notice.

34. S. E. MacKean to Farnham, 19 March 1917; Farnham to Clark, 13 April 1917, B2, PLSP.

35. Farnham to Clark, 13 April 1917. Farnham's correspondence reveals a strong pattern of intimidation. See B2, PLSP.

36. Membership subscription lists, B1, PLSP.

37. Farnham to W. T. Francis, 10 April 1917, B2, PLSP.

38. Francis to Farnham, 13 April 1917, B2, PLSP.

39. John Swanson to Farnham, 24 March 1917 and 2 April 1917; Farnham to Swanson, 3 April 1917, B1, PLSP.

40. Wolkerstorfer, "Nativism in Minnesota," 121, 141–42. *St. Paul City Directory* (St. Paul 1915), 100–101. St. Paul Lutherans were divided into Swedish, Norwegian, German, Danish, and English congregations.

41. Farnham to C. L. Abbott, 25 April 1917, B2, PLSP.

42. *The More Important Accomplishments of the Saint Paul Association since the Reorganization in 1916*, pamphlet, B14, HDF.

43. Group meetings folder, B1, PLSP.

44. Holbrook and Appel, *Minnesota in the War*, 46–47.

45. Ibid., 47–48; *Disp.*, 6 March 1917. For a more sympathetic portrayal of Wallace, see Edwin Kagin, *James Wallace of Macalester* (Garden City, N.Y., 1957), 211–22.

46. *Disp.*, 7 March 1917.

47. Group membership folder, B1, PLSP; *CB*, 20 January 1917, 4; James Michael Reardon, *The Catholic Church in the Diocese of St. Paul: From Earliest Origin to Centennial Achievement* (St. Paul, 1952), 659–60.

48. Wolkerstorfer, "Nativism in Minnesota," 140; Thomas J. Rowland, "Irish-American Catholics and the Quest for Respectability in the Coming of the Great War, 1900–1917," *JAEH* 15 (winter 1996): 5.

49. Ireland, quoted in Rowland, "Irish-American Catholics," 8–9. For a discussion of the Americanism movement in the Catholic Church and Ireland's role therein, see Philip Gleason, "'Americanism' in American Catholic Discourse," in Gleason, *Speaking of Diversity: Language and Ethnicity in Twentieth-Century America* (Baltimore, 1992), 272–300.

50. John Ireland to C. W. Ames, 18 April 1917, telegram quoted in Wolkerstorfer, "Nativism in Minnesota," 140.

51. John Ireland, quoted in Marvin R. O'Connell, *John Ireland and the American Catholic Church* (St. Paul, 1988), 517.

52. Colman Barry, *The Catholic Church and German Americans* (Milwaukee, 1953); and Philip Gleason, *The Conservative Reformers: German-American Catholics and the Social Order* (Notre Dame, Ind., 1968); O'Connell, *John Ireland*; Rowland, "Irish-American Catholics."

53. O'Connell, *John Ireland*, 216–39; Colman J. Barry, *Worship and Work* (Collegeville, Minn., 1956), esp. 175–82.

54. N. I. Lowry to H. W. Libby, secretary of Minnesota Commission of Public Safety, 21 October 1918, agents' correspondence file, MCPS, MHS; See also Mary Wingerd, "The Americanization of Cold Spring: Cultural Change in an Ethnic Community" (honors' thesis, Macalester College, 1990), 114.

55. See, for instance, "Catholics in War," *CB*, 20 January 1917.

56. For parish activities, I rely on the 1917 issues of the *Catholic Bulletin*—a fragmentary source, since not all parish activities were listed there.

57. Grace Holmes Carlson, interview by Carl Ross, 9 July 1987, transcript, pp. 2–3, 5, radical history collection, MHS.

58. Ibid.

59. "To the Men and Women of the Irish Race in America," petition, located in Patrick O'Donnell correspondence folder, B1, MCO'D, MHS; Chrislock, *Progressive Era in Minnesota*, 99–101.

60. Correspondence among a diverse group of Irish politicians and civic leaders can be found in Manahan's correspondence files, JM, MHS.

61. It is notable that no such self-censorship occurred in Minneapolis, where the *Northwest Standard,* official paper of the Ancient Order of Hibernians, was published. The *Standard* carried regular editorials supporting the cause of Home Rule and denouncing British imperialism. In Minneapolis, where the Irish were heavily concentrated in the working class (and absent from positions of power), Irish politics, as expressed by the *Standard,* were outspokenly opposed to the war. The *Standard,* with a limited readership, ceased publication in 1920. Ann Regan, "The Irish," in *They Chose Minnesota: A Survey of the State's Ethnic Groups,* ed. June Drenning Holmquist (St. Paul, 1981), 143.

62. Werner Sollors, ed., *The Invention of Ethnicity* (New York, 1989). See also Benedict Anderson, *Imagined Communities: Reflections on the Origin and Spread of Nationalism* (London, 1991). On the political nature of the invention of ethnicity, see Kathleen Neils Conzen, David A. Gerber, Ewa Morawska, George E. Pozzetta, and Rudolph J. Vecoli, "The Invention of Ethnicity: A Perspective from the U.S.A.," *JAEH* 12 (fall 1992): 4–5. Correspondence between Patrick O'Donnell, the Minneapolis director of the AOH, and Clan na Gael's national office, attests to the feeble presence of that organization in St. Paul. See the Patrick O'Donnell correspondence folder, B1, MCO'D. I am grateful to David Emmons for assistance in deciphering the cryptic code employed by the Clan.

63. *CB,* 27 January 1917, 3.

64. Farnham to Clark, 13 April 1917; *PP,* 4 March 1917; Carl I I. Chrislock, *Watchdog of Loyalty: The Minnesota Commission of Public Safety during World War I* (St. Paul, 1991), 42–47; *Important Accomplishments of the Saint Paul Association;* D. A. Mudge to Farnham, March 1917 (n.d.), B2, PLSP.

65. W. G. Johnson to secretary of the Patriotic League, 11 March 1917, B2, PLSP; *DN,* 11 March 1917, 6.

66. Maurice Pitman, 26 March 1917, B2, PLSP.

67. Farnham to Alfred Jacques, U.S. District Attorney, 27 March 1917, B2, PLSP.

68. Quoted in Holbrook, *St. Paul and Ramsey County in the War,* 11.

69. The appropriation, as passed by the legislature, was reduced to $1 million. Even cut by half, this was a fairly stunning allocation of funds, when the state's total expenditures from its revenue fund in 1917 were less than $11 million. *Annual Report of the State Treasurer of Minnesota for the Fiscal Year Ending July 31, 1917,* 17.

70. Chrislock, *Watchdog of Loyalty,* 52–55, 89–93.

71. Ibid., 53; *Trib.,* 4 April 1917, 1; Farnham to Clark, 13 April 1917.

72. The thick web of influence that linked the Public Safety Commission to Minneapolis business interests is well documented in William Millikan, *A Union against Unions: The Minneapolis Citizens Alliance and Its Fight against Organized Labor, 1903–1947* (St. Paul, 2001), mss.d., esp. 130–33.

Chapter 5: Taking Aim

1. On the Minnesota Employer's Association and the Chamber of Commerce, see William Millikan, *A Union against Unions: The Minneapolis Citizens Alliance and Its Fight against Organized Labor, 1903–1947* (St. Paul, 2001), mss.d. 59–83.

2. *MJ,* 4 April 1917, 16.

3. Charles Rumford Walker, *American City: A Rank-and-File History* (New York, 1937), 1–2, 21; Calvin E. Schmid, *Social Saga of Two Cities: An Ecological and Statistical Study of Social Trends in Minneapolis and St. Paul* (Minneapolis, 1937), 14, 20.

4. The Chamber of Commerce was the official name of the grain exchange. The general business booster organization was called the Minneapolis Civic and Commerce Association.

5. James Manahan, *Trials of a Lawyer* (St. Paul, 1928), 206; Robert L. Morlan, *Political Prairie Fire: The Nonpartisan League, 1915–1922* (Minneapolis, 1955; rpt., St. Paul, 1985), 6–7; Walker, *American City,* 19–20.

6. Manahan, *Trials of a Lawyer,* 209–12; Morlan, *Political Prairie Fire,* 18–21. See also Charles Edward Russell, *The Story of the Nonpartisan League: A Chapter in American Evolution* (New York, 1920).

7. Morlan, *Political Prairie Fire,* 76–100.

8. Ibid.

9. David Paul Nord, "Hothouse Socialism: Minneapolis, 1910–1925," in *Socialism in the Heartland: The Midwestern Experience*, ed. Donald Critchlow (Notre Dame, Ind., 1986), 133–66.

10. Ibid., 140–41.

11. John McGee to Knute Nelson, 15 November 1916, quoted in Carl H. Chrislock, *Watchdog of Loyalty: The Minnesota Commission of Public Safety during World War I* (St. Paul, 1980), 63.

12. David Paul Nord, "Socialism in One City: A Political Study of Minneapolis in the Progressive Era" (master's thesis, University of Minnesota, 1972), 116.

13. Ibid., 112–14.

14. On proprietary attitudes of elites, see Rufus Rand (grandson of the founder of the state's largest gas company), interview by Charles Walker, 1935, handwritten notes, CRW, MHS. See also "Revolt in the Northwest," *Fortune*, April 1936, 116, 118; and Walker, *American City*.

15. Minneapolis Trades and Labor Assembly, quoted in Nord, "Socialism in One City," 115; Millikan, *Union against Unions*, mss.d. 113–20.

16. Undercover agent reports, NIB, MHS.

17. Melvyn Dubofsky, *We Shall Be All: A History of the Industrial Workers of the World* (Chicago, 1969), 315. Dubofsky remains the definitive work on the IWW.

18. I base these estimates on membership lists and numerous surveillance reports conducted by the Pinkerton and Burns detective agencies, the Minnesota Commission for Public Safety, and the local Northern Information Bureau. See agents' reports file, MCPS, and NIB.

19. Handbill, 1 April 1915, correspondence file, NIB; Luke Boyce, Northern Information Bureau, to F. R. Bigelow, president, St. Paul Fire & Marine Ins. Co., 27 January 1926, retainer file, NIB.

20. As Melvyn Dubofsky notes, federal prosecution of IWW leaders in 1918 followed a similar thread and condemned "a philosophy, an attitude, and an organization" rather than making a case for any specific crime. Dubofsky, *We Shall Be All*, 435.

21. Copious reports in the agents' files of the MCPS and the NIB demonstrate conclusively that the commission had no substantive evidence of subversive activity by the IWW.

22. *DOL, 1913–1914*, 215, 218; *DOL, 1915–1916*, 176–90. The 1914 report lists a total of 360 members in Minneapolis and 67 in St. Paul but does not include the membership of the AWO, which may have numbered several thousand. In 1919, after years of concentrated repression, agents under cover in the IWW claimed that the AWO had approximately 30,000 members. Luke Boyce to J. F. Gould, the American Committee, 28 October 1919, American Committee file, NIB Records.

23. *DOL, 1915–1916*, 166. For a detailed chronology of the miners' strike, see Robert Troger Schultz, "Beyond the Fall: Class Conflict and Social, Cultural, and Political Change, Minnesota, 1916–1935" (Ph.D. diss., University of Minnesota, 1991), 25–57; *DOL, 1915–1916*, 169.

24. John E. Haynes, "Revolt of the 'Timber Beasts': The IWW Lumber Strike in Minnesota," *MH*, 42 (spring 1971): 163–65. See also Schultz, "Beyond the Fall," 58–80, and Dubofsky, *We Shall Be All*, 330; *Daily Virginian* (Virginia, Minn.), 1 January 1917, quoted in Schultz, "Beyond the Fall," 66.

25. Harrison E. Salisbury, "The Victorian City in the Midwest," in *Growing Up in Minnesota: Ten Writers Remember Their Childhoods*, ed. Chester Anderson (Minneapolis, 1976), 61.

26. John McGee, testimony to the National Committee on Military Affairs, 18 April 1918.

27. Trade Union Reports and Correspondence, B115.H.17.8.F, LID; agent's report, 18 February and 7 March 1918, NIB; M. Churchill, director of military intelligence, to Bruce Bielaski, Department of Justice, 11 October 1918, Military Intelligence Files, microfilm, WL.

28. *UA*, 2 February 1917, 1; 25 April 1917, 8.

29. *Minnesota Votes: Election Returns by County for Presidents, Senators, Congressmen, and Governors, 1857–1957* (St. Paul, 1977), 98, 100.

30. Jay P. Dolan, *The American Catholic Experience: A History from Colonial Times to the Present* (Garden City, N.Y., 1985), 336.

31. Ireland, quoted in Marvin R. O'Connell, *John Ireland and the American Catholic Church* (St. Paul, 1988), 225. On Ireland's support for labor, see Dolan, *American Catholic Experience*, 312–13.

32. According to archdiocesan historian James Reardon, Ireland had realized that "if all

Catholics, and especially all Irish Catholics, belonged to the Democratic party, they would wield no influence in government circles when that party was not in power. He decided to throw his lot in with the Republicans in order that there would be some one at court to plead the cause of the Catholic Church and defend her interests when they held the reins of power and dispensed patronage." Reardon, *The Catholic Church in the Diocese of St. Paul: From Earliest Origin to Centennial Achievement* (St. Paul, 1952), 424. For a similar interpretation, see Sister Helen Angela Hurley, *On Good Ground: The Story of the Sisters of St. Joseph in St. Paul* (Minneapolis, 1951), 204. This explanation, whether or not it reflected Ireland's actual political motivations, is entirely consistent with his demonstrated strategy of maintaining a balance between competing factions.

33. Francis L. Broderick, *Right Reverend New Dealer: John A. Ryan* (New York, 1963), 36–92; *UA*, 30 January, 30 October, 20 November, and 27 November 1914; *Proceedings of the 31st Convention of the Minnesota State Federation of Labor*, 67, quoted in Broderick, *Right Reverend New Dealer*, 85.

34. Grace Holmes Carlson, interview by Carl Ross, 9 July 1987, transcript, p. 1, radical history collection, MHS.

35. Aileen Kraditor, *The Radical Persuasion, 1890–1917: Aspects of the Intellectual History and the Historiography of Three American Radical Organizations* (Baton Rouge, La., 1981), 16–17.

36. Ibid. Kraditor provides voluminous evidence of socialist rhetoric that lavishes contempt on working people's values, especially on their religious beliefs. See, for example, 136–37.

37. Schmid, *Social Saga of Two Cities*, 20–21; *Fortieth Annual Report of the Chamber of Commerce of Minneapolis* (1922), 142; Inspection Reports for the Cities of St. Paul and Minneapolis, 1917–1918, B126.J.2.3, LID, MHS.

38. Morlan, *Political Prairie Fire*, 18–20; *Accomplishments of the Saint Paul Association*, 1916, and minutes of the board of directors' meetings, St. Paul Association folder, B14, HDF, MHS.

39. E. M. McMahon to Hiram Frankel, 16 September 1918, Saint Paul Association folder, B14, HDF.

40. On Minnesota politics, see Carl H. Chrislock, *The Progressive Era in Minnesota, 1899–1918* (St. Paul, 1971). Woodrow Wilson and the national Democratic Party had virtually the same attitude toward the Nonpartisan League as did St. Paul Democrats. Throughout the war, while the Nonpartisan League was relentlessly persecuted in Minnesota, the president continued to speak highly of the League and its president, Arthur Townley. Wilson actively courted League support, viewing its nonpartisan position as potential votes for the Democratic Party.

41. *UA*, January–April 1917.

42. John McGee to Knute Nelson, 11 April 1917, quoted in Chrislock, *Watchdog of Loyalty*, 55.

43. Ibid.

44. Joseph A. Burnquist, *Minnesota and Its People*, 4 vols. (Chicago, 1924), 4:140–43; Chrislock, *Watchdog of Loyalty*, 68–73.

45. Burnquist was elected from the thirty-third congressional district, which encompassed St. Paul's heavily Swedish, working-class First and Second Wards.

46. At the 1916 convention of the Minnesota Federation of Labor, a resolution was introduced calling for Burnquist's impeachment. After a heated discussion, delegates settled for a request that the Department of Labor investigate the strikes. Chrislock, *Watchdog of Loyalty*, 72.

47. John Lind to William Folwell, 12 December 1924, quoted in Millikan, *Union against Unions*, mss.d. 133.

48. William Millikan, "Defenders of Business: The Minneapolis Civic and Commerce Association versus Labor during W.W. I," *MH* 50 (spring 1986): 6.

49. West Publishing, publisher of law books, was the largest concern in the city engaged in the printing or publishing trade. In 1917, it employed 267 men and 367 women. Inspection reports for the City of St. Paul, 1917–1918, accidents and inspections file, B126.J.2.3, LID.

50. *UA*, 3 August 1917, 4.

51. On Ames's business interests, see Ames and Winter, West Publishing, and Homer Clark folders, B3, CWA, MHS. Within weeks after the commission went into operation, Thomas Winter would become head of its intelligence bureau, a particularly powerful position.

52. Lind had run for office over the years as a Republican, a Democratic-Populist, and then

as a Democrat. Even as a Democrat, however, he continued to support progressives of either party.

53. Chrislock, *Progressive Era in Minnesota*, 11–14; Millikan, *Union against Unions*, mss.d. 134–36.

54. Chrislock, *Watchdog of Loyalty*, 82–83. Burnquist, *Minnesota and Its People*, 4: 525–26.

55. In addition to his corporate law practice, Tighe also had multiple business interests in the city and was a member of the Lafayette Club, a recreational enclave of the Minneapolis elite. Albert Nelson Marquis, ed., *The Book of Minnesotans* (Chicago, 1907), 513–14. See also Chrislock, *Watchdog of Loyalty*, 83–85, 89–93.

56. Tighe to Lind, 13 February 1918, JNL, MHS. As James Scott notes, modern social-engineering projects often take advantage of the social disruptions created by war. James C. Scott, *Seeing Like a State: How Certain Schemes to Improve the Human Condition Have Failed* (New Haven, Conn., 1998).

57. Burnquist to Sigurd Qvale, 25 April 1917, quoted in Chrislock, *Watchdog of Loyalty*, 85.

58. John S. Pardee to A. F. Ferguson, 14 August 1917, Pardee folder, correspondence with counties file, MCPS.

59. *UA*, 2 March 1917, 1; 16 April 1917, 8.

60. Ibid., 16 February 1917, 4.

61. Ibid., 1 June 1917, 1, 3.

62. Creel, quoted in Morlan, *Political Prairie Fire*, 157.

Chapter 6: The First Volley

1. Carl H. Chrislock, *Watchdog of Loyalty: The Minnesota Commission of Public Safety during World War I* (St. Paul, 1991), 54–55.

2. Ireland, quoted in Marvin R. O'Connell, *John Ireland and the American Catholic Church* (St. Paul, 1988), 517; *Disp.*, 9 February 1917; Franklin F. Holbrook and Livia Appel, *Minnesota in the War with Germany*, 2 vols. (St. Paul, 1928), 2: 13–15; Franklin F. Holbrook, ed., *St. Paul and Ramsey County in the War of 1917–1918* (St. Paul, 1929), 11–12.

3. David Paul Nord, "Socialism in One City: A Political Study of Minneapolis in the Progressive Era" (master's thesis, University of Minnesota, 1972), 128–31.

4. Holbrook and Appel, *Minnesota in the War*, 2: 12–16.

5. *Disp.*, 18 April 1917, 1, and 19 April 1917, 1; Chrislock, *Watchdog of Loyalty*, 66–68; Holbrook and Appel, *Minnesota in the War*, 2:15–16.

6. *DN*, 6 April 1917, 13; St. Paul Trades and Labor Assembly to Carl Van Dyke, 13 April 1917, B 1, TLA, MHS.

7. *UA*, 20 April 1917, 1.

8. Ibid.

9. Ibid., 27 April 1917, 1.

10. Ibid., 4 May 1917, 1, 8.

11. Quoted in Holbrook, ed., *St. Paul and Ramsey County in the War*, 169.

12. Ibid.

13. T. Jackson Lears, *No Place of Grace: Antimodernism and the Transformation of American Culture, 1880–1920* (1983; rpt., Chicago, 1994), 97–140.

14. Captain John F. Snow, "Benefits of Military Life," in *Company "C": First Infantry Minnesota National Guard, Its History and Development* (St. Paul, 1905), 23; National Guard folder, B1, DRC, MHS.

15. Roster, *Company "C,"* 92–95; Patricia Willie Brady and Sister Paula McCarthy, *Milton and McCarthy Family History* (St. Paul, 1989).

16. James Michael Reardon, *The Catholic Church in the Diocese of St. Paul: From Earliest Origin to Centennial Achievement* (St. Paul, 1952), 660; Thomas Rowland, "Irish American Catholics and the Quest for Respectability in the Coming of the Great War, 1900–1917," *JAEH* 15 (winter 1996).

17. David M. Kennedy, *Over Here: The First World War and American Society* (New York, 1980), 180; Scott Fitzgerald to Mollie McQuillan Fitzgerald, quoted in Andrew Turnbull, *Scott Fitzgerald* (New York, 1962), 79–80 (emphasis in the original).

18. Kennedy, *Over Here*, 147–48.

19. Ibid., 48.

20. Donald Cotton, untitled report, 27 April 1917, St. Paul Association folder, DRC.

21. Kennedy, *Over Here*, 103–5, 147–49.

22. Ibid., 147–49; Wilson quoted, ibid., 148.

23. William Watts Folwell, *A History of Minnesota*, 4 vols. (St. Paul, 1926), 3:556.

24. Official Bulletin of the Saint Paul Association, quoted in Milton J. Blair, "The Civic-Commercial Organization: Review of Efficient War Time Service to a Community, as Exemplified by the Saint Paul Association," *Western Magazine*, December 1917, 206.

25. Max H. Hermann to Public Safety Commission, 29 May 1917, St. Paul Association folder, correspondence with counties, B8, MCPS.

26. John Pardee to Hermann, 1 June 1917, ibid.

27. MCPS minutes, 24 April 1917, quoted in Chrislock, *Watchdog of Loyalty*, 97.

28. As early as 1905, the fees from liquor licenses were the second-largest source of revenue for the municipal coffers, totaling $384,000—86% of all licensing revenues, more than six times the total of all other licenses and fines collected, and 7% of its total revenues. *Annual Report of City of St. Paul, Minnesota, 1905* (St. Paul, 1906), 87–94.

29. *DN*, 8 October 1917, 10.

30. On the military's campaign for vice control, see Kennedy, *Over Here*, 185–87.

31. Holbrook, ed., *St. Paul and Ramsey County in the War*, 230–33.

32. *DN*, 3 September 1917, 1.

33. Holbrook, ed., *St. Paul and Ramsey County in the War*, 232–33.

34. Circular of the Minnesota Commission of Public Safety, quoted in Sr. John Christine Wolkerstorfer, "Persecution in St. Paul—The Germans in World War I," *RCH* 2 (1976): 5.

35. *Trib.*, 20 April 1918, clippings file, 98–99, D-PP, MHS.

36. Kennedy, *Over Here*, 64–68; Wilson quoted ibid., 67.

37. On nativism, see John Higham, *Strangers in the Land: Patterns of American Nativism, 1860–1925* (New York, 1970); and Maldwyn Allen Jones, *American Immigration*, 2d ed. (Chicago, 1992), 196–211.

38. *Report of the Minnesota Commission of Public Safety*, quoted in Folwell, *History of Minnesota*, 3, 588; June Drenning Holmquist, ed., *They Chose Minnesota: A Survey of the State's Ethnic Groups* (St. Paul, 1981), 1–3; and Sr. John Christine Wolkerstorfer, "Nativism in Minnesota in World War I: A Comparative Study of Brown, Ramsey, and Stearns Counties, 1914–1918" (Ph.D. diss., University of Minnesota, 1973), 14–15.

39. Chrislock, *Watchdog of Loyalty*, 56.

40. *Thirteenth Census of the United States Taken in the Year 1910* (Washington, 1913), 18, 36, 618.

41. Calculated from *Minnesota Census, 1905* by Hildegard Binder Johnson, "The Germans," in *They Chose Minnesota*, ed. Holmquist, 164.

42. Paul A. Schons, "German Social Clubs and Organizations, in *A Heritage Fulfilled: German Americans*, ed. Clarence A. Glasrud (Moorhead, Minn., 1984), 133–41; Johnson, "The Germans," 171–73; *DN*, 7 October 1917, society section, 2; Michael Boyle diaries, 15 October 1878, MBP, MHS.

43. Holbrook, *St. Paul and Ramsey County in the War*; Wolkerstorfer, "Persecution in St. Paul," 12; Virginia Brainard Kunz, *St. Paul: Saga of an American City* (Woodland Hills, Calif.: 1977), 100–104.

44. "Patriotic Americans of German Origin," manuscript notes, RL, MHS. Wolkerstorfer, "Nativism in Minnesota," 165; *PP*, 24 October 1917, 1, and 18 July 1917, 6; *Golden Jubilee Book, St. Agnes Parish*, 37–38, quoted in Wolkerstorfer, "Nativism in Minnesota," 133.

45. Correspondence between Robert Auerbach/Rice and Hiram Frankel, Home Guard folder, B8, HDF, MHS; see also Wolkerstorfer, "Persecution in St. Paul," 12.

46. Wolkerstorfer, "Persecution in St. Paul," 5.

47. In contrast, rural Stearns County, the most German county in the state, had an exceptionally placid record in Safety Commission files. Unified in their German Catholicism, county residents maintained a public silence, presenting an outward appearance of conformity—while the internal life of the communities went on in its accustomed way. See Mary Wingerd, "The Americanization of Cold Spring: Cultural Change in an Ethnic Community" (honors' thesis, Macalester College, 1990), 103–18.

48. Agent C.H. report, 31 May 1917 and 1 June 1917. Agent C.H. folder, agents reports, B8, MCPS.

49. Ibid., 1 June 1917.

50. Ibid., 1, 2, 5, and 6 June 1917.

51. John Pardee to S. H. Bingham, 27 August 1917; Pardee to Lincoln Steffens, 5 July 1917; Pardee to E. M. Morgan, 24 July 1917, Pardee correspondence folder, B8, MCPS.

52. *DN*, 14 April 1917, 1, and 28 July 1917, 1.

53. Chrislock, *Watchdog of Loyalty*, 116–17. Reports from the various detective agencies are filed in agents' reports files, MCPS; see also, intelligence reports handwritten by McGee, especially one dated 8 July 1917. On the APL, see Emerson Hough, *The Web* (Chicago, 1919), 310–23.

54. G. H. Richards, secretary, Minnesota Bankers' Association, to association members, 2 May 1917, Pardee correspondence folder, correspondence with counties file, MCPS.

55. *Trib.*, 20 April 1918, 1.

56. Chrislock, *Watchdog of Loyalty*, 99–102.

57. Holbrook and Appel, *Minnesota in the War*, 2: 14–15; Chrislock, *Watchdog of Loyalty*, 101.

58. See Stearns County folder, correspondence with counties file, MCPS; and Wingerd, "Americanization of Cold Spring," 109–12.

59. Hough, *The Web*, 312–13.

60. Robert Rice to Major Kelsey Chase, 25 July 1918, Home Guard folder, B8, HDF.

61. John Wagener to Minnesota Commission of Public Safety, 6 August 1917, Ramsey County folder, correspondence with counties file, MCPS.

62. Walter Butler to Charles March, 8 June 1917, Order #8 folder, correspondence files, MCPS.

63. C.H. Reports, 12 June and 19–23 June 1917, TGW folder, agents' reports, MCPS. N.E.K. Reports, 2–5 June 1917, N.E.K. folder, agents' reports file; agent "E" to T. G. Winter, 16 August 1917, ESS folder, agents' reports file; L. Benshoof to H. W. Libby, 22 October 1917; A. C. Gooding to Libby, 9 October 1917, correspondence with counties file, MCPS.

64. O. R. Hatfield to Burnquist, 12 July 1917, Secret Service folder, agents' reports file, MCPS.

65. Hatfield to Winter, 17 July 1917, ibid.

66. *UA*, 31 August 1917, 4.

67. E.T.O. Report, 1 June 1917; O. R. Hatfield to T. G. Winter, 18 July 1917; C.H. report, 10 June 1917; #27 Report, 21 August 1917; C.M.R. Report, 1 June 1917, agents' reports files, MCPS.

68. E.T.O. Reports, 4–5 July 1917, agents' reports files, MCPS.

69. Holbrook, ed., *St. Paul and Ramsey County in the War*, 44–46, 20, 25–26.

70. Ibid., 175–78; Holbrook and Appel, *Minnesota in the War*, 2: 199–202.

71. *The More Important Accomplishments of the Saint Paul Association*, B8, HDF.

72. Ibid.; *UA*, 26 May 1917, 4, and 15 June 1917, 1.

73. *UA*, 15 June 1917, 1, 3 and 24 August 1917, 4.

74. Ibid., 15 June 1917, 1, 3. Announcements of union social activities appear in every issue of the *Advocate* throughout the summer of 1917.

75. Ibid., 17 August 1917, 4.

76. Ibid.

77. *DN*, 3 September 1917; *UA*, 31 August 1917.

78. *UA*, 31 August 1917, and 7 September 1917, 5.

79. Ibid., 7 September 1917, 1, 5, and 31 August 1917, sec. 1, pp. 1, 8; *DN*, 3 September 1917, 1.

80. *UA*, 7 September 1917, 1, 5.

Chapter 7: The War of St. Paul

1. See Carl H. Chrislock, *Watchdog of Loyalty: The Minnesota Commission of Public Safety during World War I* (St. Paul, 1991), 133–43; and Chrislock, *The Progressive Era in Minnesota, 1899–1918* (St. Paul, 1971), 140–44.
2. Transcript of examination of NPL lecturer James S. Ingalls, in hearing before Charles Ames, 2 January 1918, 222–37, Townley hearings file, B1, D-PP, MHS; also, Robert L. Morlan, *Political Prairie Fire: The Nonpartisan League, 1915–1922* (Minneapolis, 1955; rpt., St. Paul, 1985), 110; Chrislock, *Progressive Era in Minnesota*, 147.
3. Pt. 6, p. 23, and pt. 3, p. 16, Townley brief, p. 16, NPL folder, B1, D-PP.
4. *UA*, 21 September 1917, 1.
5. The price determined by regulation was $2.20 at Chicago and $2.17 at Minneapolis, for No. 1 grade wheat. According to historian Robert Morlan, however, grain was most often graded at No. 3 or No. 4; after transportation and storage charges, the farmer netted approximately $1.85. The corporate historian of General Mills (formerly Washburn-Crosby) set the wartime price paid by that company at $1.50. Morlan, *Political Prairie Fire*, 141; William C. Edgar, *Medal of Gold: A Story of Industrial Achievement* (Minneapolis, 1925), 292.
6. Using wage and price levels of 1913 as an index of 100, in 1916–17 wages in Minnesota rose to 126, while prices increased to 149; in 1917–18, prices outpaced wages even further, 185 to 126. U.S. Bureau of Labor Statistics, quoted in Franklin F. Holbrook, ed., *St. Paul and Ramsey County in the War of 1917–1918* (St. Paul, 1929), 234.
7. *UA*, 7 September 1917, 1.
8. Ibid., and 21 September 1917, 1, 4.
9. *Disp.*, 18 September 1917.
10. Ibid., 18 and 19 September 1917, D-PP clippings file, 12–15.
11. *Disp.*, 20 September 1917, 1.
12. *UA*, 21 September 1917, 4.
13. Morlan, *Political Prairie Fire*, 143–46; Chrislock, *Watchdog of Loyalty*, 170–73; Holbrook, ed., *St. Paul and Ramsey County in the War*, 243–47; Holbrook and Livia Appel, *Minnesota in the War with Germany*, 2 vols. (St. Paul, 1928), 1:46–8.
14. *MJ*, 21 September 1917, 18; *PP*, 22 September 1917.
15. *MJ*, 23 September 1917, 12.
16. Ames to John Lind, 17 October 1917, NPL folder, B1, D-PP.
17. *Windom Reporter*, 5 October 1917, D-PP clippings file, 16.
18. *PP*, 22 September 1917; *MJ*, 21 September 1917, 18 (my emphasis).
19. Holbrook, ed., *St. Paul and Ramsey County in the War*, 246–48.
20. Ibid., 248.
21. *DN*, 3 September 1917, 6.
22. Robert Troger Schultz, "Beyond the Fall: Class Conflict and Social, Cultural, and Political Change, Minnesota, 1916–1935" (Ph.D. diss., University of Minnesota, 1991), 84–129; and William Millikan, *A Union against Unions: The Minneapolis Citizens Alliance and Its Fight against Organized Labor, 1903–1947* (St. Paul, 2001), mss.d. 151–77.
23. On Lowry's connections with the Citizens Alliance, see Millikan, *Union against Unions*, mss.d.153. On the public ownership campaign, see David Paul Nord, "Hothouse Socialism: Minneapolis, 1910–1925," in *Socialism in the Heartland: The Midwestern Experience*, ed. Donald Critchlow (Notre Dame, Ind., 1986), 133–66.
24. Goodrich Lowry, *Streetcar Man: Tom Lowry and the Twin City Rapid Transit Company* (Minneapolis, 1978), 94–95, 139–40.
25. Ibid., 139–40, 81; Marion Daniel Shutter, *History of Minneapolis, Gateway to the Northwest*, 3 vols. (Chicago, 1923), 2: 397.
26. The Twin Cities' union membership totaled 33,070: 13,558 in St. Paul and 18,346 in Minneapolis, along with 1,166 with Twin Cities affiliations. The joint locals were bookbinders, electrical workers, elevator constructors, granite cutters, lithographers, pattern makers, photo

engravers, plate-glass and art-glass workers, plasterers and cement finishers, sheetmetal workers, sign writers, and tile layers. *DOL, 1917–18*, 167–72.

27. Millikan, *Union against Unions*, mss.d. 152–54.

28. Estimates on union membership vary widely among sources. The State Department of Labor and Industries reported a membership of 650 but consistently tended to underreport union strength. The figure I use comes from the ardently probusiness *Pioneer Press*, which was unlikely to inflate actual numbers. See *PP*, 26 November 1917.

29. Millikan, *Union against Unions*, mss.d. 152–54; Langum quoted ibid., 154.

30. *DN*, 6 October 1917, 1.

31. On the same editorial page where the *Advocate* made an impassioned case for the carmen, it excoriated the IWW, pronouncing that "by its open advocacy of revolt, sedition and sabotage, the I. W. W. organization has forfeited the right to exist. It is an enemy of true liberty and of the cause of human progress." *UA*, 5 October 1917, 1; *DN*, 5 October 1917, 1, 6.

32. *UA*, 5 October 1917, 1, 4.

33. *DN*, 5 and 6 October, 1917, 1.

34. Millikan, *Union against Unions*, mss.d. 155; *DN*, 6 October 1917, 1 and 7 October 1917, 2, 3; *MJ*, 6 October 1917, 1.

35. *DN*, 7 October 1917, 1–2.

36. Ibid.; *PP*, 7 October 1917, 1.

37. *PP*, 7 October 1917, 1; *DN* and *PP*, 7–11 October.

38. *UA*, 5 October 1917, 5. Assuming that the value of the St. Paul line was one third that of the Minneapolis company (a conservative estimate), the TCRT's St. Paul operation had a value of nearly $10 million. *Report of the Value of the Properties of the Minneapolis Street Railway Company*, vol. 1 (Minneapolis, 1916).

39. As social theorist James Scott observes, "To be a part of a crowd or mob was another way of being anonymous, whereas to be a member of a continuing organization was bound to expose one to detection and victimization." See James C. Scott, *Domination and the Arts of Resistance: Hidden Transcripts* (New Haven, 1990), 150.

40. In his analysis of the 1863 New York City draft riots, historian Iver Bernstein demonstrates a powerful example of the appropriation of public protest to express multiple grievances. See Bernstein, *The New York City Draft Riots: Their Significance for American Society and Politics in the Age of the Civil War* (New York, 1990).

41. *DN*, 7 October 1917, 1.

42. Ibid., 1–2.

43. *PP*, 7 October 1917, 1; *DN*, 7 October 1917, 1.

44. *PP*, 7 October 1917, 1.

45. Ibid., 8 October 1917, 1; *DN*, 8 October 1917, 2.

46. *DN*, 8 October 1917, 2.

47. Ibid., 9 October 1917, 4.

48. Ibid., 1; *UA*, 12 October 1917, 1.

49. *DN*, 9 October 1917, 1. Millikan has argued that St. Paul labor militancy had the capacity to defeat the TCRT. As he notes, the resolution of the strike by the Safety Commission was primarily an act of damage control in favor of the TCRT. See Millikan, "Defenders of Business: The Minneapolis Civic and Commerce Association versus Labor during W.W. I," *MH* 50 (spring 1986): 12.

50. Ames was already feeling the pressure of labor's militancy. On October 2, the typographical union had petitioned Governor Burnquist to remove Ames from the commission "because of his unrelenting hostility to organized labor." See *UA*, 12 October 1917, 1.

51. Chrislock, *Watchdog of Loyalty*, 188–89.

52. *DN*, 9 October 1917, 4; *PP*, 10 October 1917, 1; Holbrook, ed., *St. Paul and Ramsey County in the War*, 238.

53. *DN*, 11 October 1917, 2.

54. Ibid., 6.

55. Arrest records are compiled from *DN*, 7–10 October 1917; Fineout quoted 10 October, p. 2.

56. *UA*, 12 October 1917, 4.

57. *DN*, 11 October 1917, 1.

58. Millikan, *Union against Unions*, mss.d. 157; *DN*, 11 October, 1.

59. B. J. Randolph to Winter, 25 July 1917; Winter to W. J. Smith, 14 October 1917, BJR folder, agents' reports file, MCPS, MHS.

60. Millikan, *Union against Unions*, mss.d. 158, and "Defenders of Business," 12; Chrislock, *Watchdog of Loyalty*, 191.

61. Schultz, "Beyond the Fall," 96. The *Union Advocate* reports similar petitions from numerous St. Paul unions throughout October and November.

62. Millikan, *Union against Unions*, mss.d. 158; Chrislock, *Watchdog of Loyalty*, 191–92, "Report of Special Committee" quoted p. 192.

63. Minutes of MCPS meeting, 20 November 1917, MCPS; Chrislock, *Watchdog of Loyalty*, 192–93; Millikan, *Union against Unions*, mss.d. 158–61.

64. Millikan, "Defenders of Business," 13. In 1917 Minneapolis was estimated to be 95% nonunion. Millikan, *Union against Unions*, mss.d. 161.

65. Millikan, "Defenders of Business," 13.

66. On the IWW, see *UA*, 26 October 1917, 3; on support of the railroad brotherhoods, 5 October 1917, 4; for examples of attacks on Ames, 3 August 1917, 4, and 12 October 1917, 1.

67. On NPL support for streetcar strikers, see "'Townley's False Statements," 20; Ames to John Lind, 17 October 1917, NPL folder, B1, D-PP.

68. Holbrook, ed., *St. Paul and Ramsey County in the War*, 180; *DN*, 12 October 1917, 1.

69. On December 26, 1917, the government took control of the railroads for the duration of the war. See David M. Kennedy, *Over Here: The First World War and American Society*, 252–55. On Hill's recreational travel schedule, see MMHD, 1910–20, JJHRL; and "Revolt in the Northwest," *Fortune*, April 1936, 114, 190.

70. *UA*, 23 November 1917, 3, and 30 November 1917, 4; Schultz, "Beyond the Fall," 99.

71. *UA*, 30 November 1917, 1.

72. Ibid., 4. According to the 1918 yearbook of the Saint Paul Association, the city hosted forty-four conventions in 1918. Most comprised only a few hundred participants and lasted between one and three days. The AFL was the only national organization to choose St. Paul for its convention, an event scheduled for more than twice as long as the next largest booking and (by multiplying conventioneers by number of days) one that would top other attendance figures by more than seven thousand attendees. Figures compiled from "A Review of the Activities of the Saint Paul Association during the Year 1918," 13, B3, CWA, MHS.

73. Lowry to Louis W. Post, 1 December 1917, quoted in Millikan, *Union against Unions*, mss.d. 162.

74. Burnquist to Post, 1 December 1917, quoted in Millikan, "Defenders of Business," 14.

75. *UA*, 7 December 1917, 4.

76. James Manahan, *Trials of a Lawyer* (St. Paul, ca. 1928), 225.

77. Schultz, "Beyond the Fall," 105–6; Chrislock, *Watchdog of Loyalty*, 194–95; Holbrook, ed., *St. Paul and Ramsey County in the War*, 239–40.

78. Millikan, "Defenders of Business," 14–15.

79. *UA*, 14 December 1917, 1.

80. Ibid.

81. Ibid. Union suspicions may well have been correct. Though no corroborating evidence exists of agents provocateur in the crowd that day, apparently the Safety Commission used a similar tactic to entrap the Nonpartisan League. A St. Paul teacher innocently reported to the commission that "she knows four men who are receiving $200 and $250 a week to attend Nonpartisan League meetings & incite the farmers to pro-German activities by misrepresentation." Very likely, the commission itself was paying these agents. See Mrs. Nels Strand Jr. to Public Safety Commission, 13 October 1917, miscellaneous papers folder, B1, D-PP papers. That this handwritten communication found its way into the files of the St. Paul daily is another indication of the close complicity between the conservative newspaper and the commission. No mention of Mrs. Strand's allegation appeared in the paper.

82. Schultz, "Beyond the Fall," 106–7; Millikan, *Union against Unions*, mss.d. 162–63; Holbrook, ed., *St. Paul and Ramsey County in the War*, 239–40.

83. Manahan, *Trials of a Lawyer*, 226–28; Chrislock, *Watchdog of Loyalty*, 195; *UA*, 28 December 1917, 1.

84. *UA*, 7 December 1917, 4, and 28 December 1917, 1.

85. Manahan, *Trials of a Lawyer*, 229–32; *UA*, 8 February 1918, 1, 8.

86. *Disp.*, 1 February 1918, 4.

87. Chrislock, *Watchdog of Loyalty*, 195; Vivian Irvin, quoted in *UA*, 7 December 1917, 1. On Irvin's background, see *The Mayors of St. Paul, 1850–1940* (WPA Writers' Project, n.d.), 58–59.

88. Holbrook, ed., *St. Paul and Ramsey County in the War*, 238–39; Schultz, "Beyond the Fall," 103.

89. Minutes of St. Paul Association Meeting, 26 May 1918, B14, HDF, MHS; *Review of the Activities of the St. Paul Association*, B3, CWA.

90. Charles Ames to George T. Slade, first vice president, Northern Pacific Railway., 28 September 1917, "Railroads in Time of War" folder, MCPS papers; W. P. Kenney to St. Paul Association, 21 June 1918, Home Guard folder, B8, HDF.

91. E. M. McMahon to John Pardee, 5 July 1917; Pardee to McMahon, 7 July 1917; McMahon to Pardee, 9 July 1917, St. Paul Association folder, MCPS. A partial list of association responsibilities in September 1917 included the Military Industrial Co-operation Committee, Military Affairs Committee, Invention and Research Committee, Public Information Committee, Commercial Economy Committee, Advisory Council, Women's Auxiliary Committee, Food Conservation Committee, Fuel Conservation Committee, War Industries Board, Liberty Loan Committee, Ramsey County Red Cross Committee, plus numerous parades, pageants, mass meetings, and recruitment events. Donald Cotton, war director for Ramsey County, to C. W. Ames, 26 September 1917, correspondence with counties file, MCPS. See also *A Review of the Activities of the St. Paul Association*.

92. *UA*, 14 December 1917, 1.

93. *CB*, 8 December 1917, 4.

94. Ibid.

95. Ibid., 10 November 1917, 1; Sr. John Christine Wolkerstorfer, "Nativism in Minnesota in World War I: A Comparative Study of Brown, Ramsey, and Stearns Counties, 1914–1918" (Ph.D. diss., University of Minnesota, 1973), 166–67; James J. Byrne, *A History of St. Agnes* (St. Paul, 1953), 27.

96. Daniel P. O'Neill, "The Development of an American Priesthood: Archbishop John Ireland and the Saint Paul Diocesan Clergy, 1884–1918," *JAEH* 4 (spring 1985): 35–50.

97. *CB*, 8 December 1917, 4.

98. McGee, quoted in Millikan, *Union against Unions*, mss.d. 164; Burnquist, quoted in Schultz, "Beyond the Fall," 111.

99. Chrislock, *Watchdog of Loyalty*, 87–88.

100. "A Crisis in the Northwest," *Survey*, December 29, 1917, 359.

101. *UA*, 7 December 1917, 1; Chrislock, *Watchdog of Loyalty*, 196–97.

102. *New Ulm Review*, 6 June 1917, 2, quoted in Chrislock, *Watchdog of Loyalty*, 88.

103. The other members of the commission tried to persuade Lind to return, recognizing the value of his moderate cachet. He refused, declaring they had "no one to fight except organized labor," and formally resigned from the commission in March. Chrislock, *Watchdog of Loyalty*, 199, 201–4. Lind to William Folwell, quoted 201.

104. *UA*, 7 December 1917, 1; *PP*, 6 December 1917. See also Schultz, "Beyond the Fall," 113.

105. Manahan, *Trials of a Lawyer*, 226; *UA*, 7 December 1917, 1.

106. *UA*, 7 December 1917, 4, and 21 December 1917, 4.

107. Chrislock, *Watchdog of Loyalty*, 198; Millikan, *Union against Unions*, mss.d. 165.

108. *UA*, 7 December 1917, 1, and 14 December 1917, 1.

109. Millikan, *Union against Unions*, mss.d. 166–77.

110. Kennedy, *Over Here*, 143.

111. *UA*, 21 December 1917.

112. McGee, quoted in Millikan, *Union against Unions*, mss.d. 167–68.

113. J. H. Walker (member of the president's mediation commission) to union official Joseph Colgan, quoted in Millikan, *Union against Unions*, mss.d. 167. On the NWLB, see Kennedy, *Over Here*, 266–67; Joseph A. McCartin, *Labor's Great War: The Struggle for Industrial Democracy and the Origins of Modern American Labor Relations, 1912–1921* (Chapel Hill, N.C., 1997), 90–93; Melvyn Dubofsky, *The State and Labor in Modern America* (Chapel Hill, N.C., 1994), 71–74.

114. Millikan, *Union against Unions*, mss.d. 169–71.

115. *Trib.*, 20 April 1918, 1.

116. Tighe to Lind, 13 February 1918, quoted in Chrislock, *Watchdog of Loyalty*, 203.

117. Emerson Hough, *The Web* (Chicago, 1919), 313–16; Holbrook, ed., *St. Paul and Ramsey County in the War*, 226–27.

118. Minutes of SPA meetings, 17 May 1918 and 4 January 1919, B14, HDF; Holbrook, ed., *St. Paul and Ramsey County in the War*, 192–203; Holbrook and Appel, *Minnesota in the War*, 2:223–25.

119. Holbrook, ed., *St. Paul and Ramsey County in the War*, 182–83; Holbrook and Appel, *Minnesota in the War*, 2:210.

120. *CB*, 13 April 1918, 1.

121. Sr. John Christine Wolkerstorfer, "Persecution in St. Paul—The Germans in World War I," *RCH* 2 (1976): 8.

122. Holbrook and Appel, *Minnesota in the War*, 2:204, 211.

123. L. G. Glaser, Report to Commission, 18 September 1918, MCPS papers; see also Wolkerstorfer, "Nativism in Minnesota," 158–59.

124. Holbrook, ed., *St. Paul and Ramsey County in the War*, 19–20, 91, 131.

125. *UA*, 11 January 1918, 1, and 1 February 1918, 1; Schultz, "Beyond the Fall," 126–27.

126. *PP*, 20 March 1918.

127. See Morlan, *Political Prairie Fire*.

128. William Mahoney, speech delivered at the Farmer-Labor conference in 1923, reprinted in James M. Youngdahl, ed., *Third Party Footprints: An Anthology from Writings and Speeches of Midwest Radicals* (Minneapolis, 1966), 190.

129. George Herrold and Katherine Spear, "Foreign Born Population Studies, St. Paul Minnesota" (St. Paul, 1934), 3, 7. The city's aggregate population figures, which rose by twenty thousand between 1910 and 1920, do not indicate a pattern of outmigration. *Thirteenth Census of the United States, Taken in the Year 1910*, vol. 2: *Population* (Washington 1913), 994; *Fourteenth Census of the United States, Taken in the Year 1920*, vol. 3: *Population* (Washington, 1923), 507.

130. Holbrook, ed., *St. Paul and Ramsey County in the War*, 229–32.

131. John A. Hawgood, *The Tragedy of German-America: The Germans in the United States of America during the Nineteenth Century—and After* (New York, 1940), 297. For an example of German cultural persistence, see Wingerd, "The Americanization of Cold Spring: Cultural Change in an Ethnic Community" (honors' thesis, Macalester College, 1990).

132. In contrast, Swedish-born residents (the next-largest group of foreign-born), who had not sustained the same sort of cultural damage, remained concentrated in the First Ward, though there was some movement to the Tenth and Eleventh Wards. Herrold and Spear, "Foreign Born Population Studies," 7–8.

133. David Montgomery, *The Fall of the House of Labor: The Workplace, the State, and American Labor Activism, 1865–1925* (Cambridge, Mass., 1991), 347–48.

134. *Minnesota Leader*, 8 April 1918, quoted in Morlan, *Political Prairie Fire*, 189.

Chapter 8: Vying for Power

1. *CB*, 13 February 1918, 2; 9 March 1918, 5; 27 April 1918, 4; 13 July 1918, 4.

2. On the *Bulletin's* editorial policy, see James Michael Reardon, *The Catholic Church in the Diocese of St. Paul: From Earliest Origin to Centennial Achievement* (St. Paul, 1952), 396.

3. *CB*, 28 April 1918, 1; 4 May 1918, 1, 4; 8 June 1918, 1; 13 June 1918, 1, 2. On p. 1 of the 13 June edition, the *Bulletin* published the text of a resolution Lindbergh had introduced in the

House of Representatives in 1916, which demanded investigation of the alleged political activity of the Catholic Church in American political affairs.

4. *DN*, 18 June 1918, 6. That Lindbergh's alleged anti-Catholicism was the determining factor to defeat him in St. Paul is borne out by the fact that David Evans, designated as the Farmer-Labor candidate (though the Farmer-Labor Party was not formally established until 1921), carried the city in the general election. Carl H. Chrislock, *The Progressive Era in Minnesota, 1899–1918* (St. Paul, 1971), 164–81.

5. *CB*, 5 October 1918, 1, 5, and 12 October 1918, 1.

6. Ibid.; *UA*, 27 September 1918, 4; *Disp.*, quoted in "Secular Press Tributes," *CB*, 14 December 1918.

7. In 1914, St. Paul had replaced its ward-based common council of assemblymen and aldermen with a commission form of municipal government, with six councilmen, elected on an at-large basis.

8. *UA*, 15 February 1918, 1; 8 March 1918, 1.

9. Ibid., 8 August 1918, 1; 15 March 1918, 3.

10. Ibid., 4 May 1918, 1, 4.

11. *UA*, 7 June 1918, 5; 9 November 1918, 8.

12. *Minnesota Votes: Election Returns by County for Presidents, Senators, Congressmen and Governors, 1857–1977* (St. Paul, 1977), 183; Chrislock, *Progressive Era in Minnesota*, 181.

13. *UA*, 29 November 1918, 8. For candidate profiles and election results, see *UA*, 31 April 1918, 5; 4 October 1918, 1, 8; 8 November 1918, 1, 8.

14. Mahoney biography, *UA*, 24 January 1994; Mahoney, "Open Letter to Organized Workers," 1914, B2, WM, MHS.

15. *UA*, 20 September 1918, 2; 29 November 1918, 8.

16. Mahoney to H. E. Soule, 12 April 1920, B1, WM; Mahoney, interview by Richard Leekley, 26 July 1940, typewritten notes entitled "Labor Politics 1918," RL, MHS. According to Mahoney, "a deal had been made" with the MFL. Lawson quoted in *PP*, 12 March 1920, 1.

17. *UA*, 23 January 1920, 1; Mahoney to the editor of the *Minnesota Union Advocate*, 1 June 1938, 1–2, B2, WM; *Disp.*, 23 February 1920, 4.

18. Minutes of the Working People's Nonpartisan League, 6 September 1919, 6 December 1919, and 14 February 1920; summaries in RL. See also Richard M. Valelly, *Radicalism in the States: The Minnesota Farmer-Labor Party and the American Political Economy* (Chicago, 1989), 34–35, and Millard L. Gieske, *Minnesota Farmer-Laborism: The Third Party Alternative* (Minneapolis, 1979), 52–53.

19. Minutes of WPNPL, 6 December 1919, 14 February 1920.

20. The Nonpartisan League displayed a similar new interest in women, as demonstrated by Kim E. Neilson, " 'We All Leaguers By Our House': Women, Suffrage, and Red-Baiting in the National Nonpartisan League," *JWH* 6 (spring 1994): 31–50.

21. *DOL, 1917–1918*, 167; Gieske, *Minnesota Farmer-Laborism*, 52; *UA*, 22 June 1917, 5; 27 September 1918, 3.

22. *DOL, 1919–1920*, 155; *UA*, 30 January 1920, 4; 2 April 1920, 5; 30 April 1920, 4; 16 November 1922, 3. Similar efforts were made to organize housewives in cities nationwide. See Dana Frank, *Purchasing Power: Consumer Organizing, Gender, and the Seattle Labor Movement, 1919–1920* (Cambridge, Mass., 1984), 15–39.

23. *DOL, 1919–1920*, 155.

24. *Report of a Survey of the School System of Saint Paul, Minnesota* (St. Paul, 1917), 290; *UA*, 26 April 1918, 4.

25. *UA*, 21 June 1918, 5; 31 April 1918, 4.

26. *UA*, 2 August 1918, 4; 30 August 1918, 4; 18 October 1918, 4; 1 November 1918, 1 (my emphasis).

27. *UA*, 6 September 1918. The railroad men had their own reasons to ally with a broad-based political bloc of labor voters. They were actively engaged in lobbying for the passage of the Plumb Plan, which would put the nation's railroad's permanently in the hands of the federal government—an initiative forcefully backed by the Trades and Labor Assembly. See David

Montgomery, *The Fall of the House of Labor: The Workplace, the State, and American Labor Activism, 1865–1925* (Cambridge, Mass., 1989), 369.

28. South St. Paul was a separate municipality, located across the county line and about ten miles from St. Paul. (Its stockyards and packinghouses played an important part in Minnesota industrial unionism, but that story is beyond the scope of this book.) St. Paulites themselves regarded South St. Paul as an entirely different community—which, indeed, it was. Nonetheless, Department of Labor statistics include South St. Paul with St. Paul proper. Before 1920, this does not appreciably skew the numbers, but during the twenties packinghouse workers unionized, thereby adding appreciably to St. Paul totals.

29. In 1920, St. Paul unions reported ninety-six unions with 26,597 members, as compared to 1916 membership of 11,094 and 85 unions. *DOL, 1919–1920*, 133; *DOL, 1915–1916*, 165.

30. *UA*, 18 October 1918, 2; 22 November, 1918, 1; 29 November 1918, 4; *DOL, 1919–1920*, 138–48. The report acknowledges that its list of strikes is incomplete. Thus, the numbers cited in the text are conservative.

31. Melvyn Dubofsky, *The State and Labor in Modern America* (Chapel Hill, N.C., 1994), 76–77; see also David Brody, *Workers in Industrial America: Essays on the Twentieth Century Struggle*, 2d ed. (New York, 1993), 44–45. For a study of the 1919 strike wave in Seattle, see Frank, *Purchasing Power*, 15–39.

32. William Millikan, *A Union against Unions: The Minneapolis Citizens Alliance and Its Fight against Organized Labor, 1903–1947* (St. Paul, 2001), mss.d. 195–235; *DOL, 1919–1920*, 136–48.

33. Millikan, *Union against Unions*, mss.d. 239.

34. E. M. McMahon to Hiram Frankel, 16 September 1918, SPA folder, B14, HDF, MHS; Robert Rice, correspondence to Frankel, 1917, Minnesota Home Guard folder, B8, HDF, MHS; John Christine Wolkerstorfer, "Persecution in St. Paul—The Germans in World War I," *RCH* 2 (1976): 11–13; docket of the board of directors meeting, St. Paul Association, 4 January 1919, SPA folder, B14, HDF.

35. McMahon to Frankel, 16 September 1918; inaugural address of C. H. Bigelow, 1918; minutes of the executive board of the SPA, 17 May 1918, all located in SPA folder, B14, HDF.

36. Minutes of the board of directors meeting, 13 September 1918, SPA folder, B14, HDF.

37. Minutes of the board of directors meeting, 5 December 1919, SPA folder, B14, HDF.

38. For a national perspective, see Robert K. Murray, *Red Scare: A Study in National Hysteria, 1919–1920* (Minneapolis, 1955).

39. The message of impending revolution infused Northern Information Bureau reports to business clients and correspondence with agencies and individuals throughout 1919 and 1920. Hundreds of documents can be found in the American Committee, Military Intelligence, Walter Newton (U.S. congressman), and correspondence files of the NIB Papers. Boyce claimed to be retained by "practically all the large corporations in the Twin Cities," but because no client lists exist for this period, it is impossible to determine how many St. Paul businesses subscribed to NIB service at this time other than Butler Brothers Construction and Weyerhaeuser Lumber. (Both these firms had substantial interests in northern Minnesota, where IWW activity was more of a factor). See Boyce to J. A. Reid, Charter Oak Detective Services, 18 May 1921, correspondence file, NIB Papers, MHS. Nonetheless, it is almost certain that members of the Minneapolis Citizens Alliance shared this information with St. Paul businessmen who were promoting the establishment of the Alliance in St. Paul.

40. Myers to Frankel, 12 November 1919, SPA folder, B14, HDF.

41. Myers to Frankel, 12 November 1919; "How the Open Shop Came to Saint Paul," *The American Plan* (newsletter of the Ramsey County Citizens Alliance), 1 February 1922, 1, DC Records, MHS.

42. Gieske, *Minnesota Farmer-Laborism*, 52–64.

43. Millikan, *Union against Unions*, mss.d. 239; *Five Years: Showing What Has Been Accomplished in Improving Industrial Relations in Saint Paul* (St. Paul, 1925), n.p., CA, MHS.

44. *Five Years*. In the 1934 Minneapolis teamsters' strike, the union similarly shut down the city without official backing from organized labor. However, in that strike, masterful organizers Vincent Dunne and Carl Skoglund were much more adept at gaining public sympathy. Where

St. Paul teamsters in this dispute promised to "investigate" individual needs for coal, the Minneapolis organizers commandeered coal trucks that continued to operate and simply dumped the load of fuel in working-class neighborhoods—free for the taking. George Dmitri Tselos, "The Minneapolis Labor Movement in the 1930s" (Ph.D. diss., University of Minnesota, 1970), 211.

45. "How the Open Shop Came to Saint Paul," 1.

46. *DN*, 11 January 1920, 1; *UA*, 23 January 1920, 4; 6 February 1920, 4; 12 March 1920, 1; *PP*, 10 March 1920, 6; 13 March 1920, 1, 4; 9 March 1920, 4; see also *PP*, 11 and 12 March.

47. Election broadside, B1, WM.

48. *DN*, 3 January 1920, 1, 3; 5 January 1920, 1. See also *Disp.* and *PP*, January–March, 1920.

49. Notes on the Sound Government Association, RL Papers; "The Red Menace in Minnesota: An Open Letter to Friends of Constitutional Government" (St. Paul, 1923), 30–36.

50. *PP*, 17 March 1920, 1–3, 5.

51. Mahoney, untitled manuscript, B1, WM.

52. Valelly, *Radicalism in the States*, 38; "How the Open Shop Came to Saint Paul," 1.

53. *Five Years*; *PP*, 9 March 1920, 6; "How the Open Shop Came to St. Paul," 1, 3.

54. *The Truth about Organized Labor: An Official Refutation of the Charges Made against Organized Labor* (St. Paul 1921), pamphlet collection, MHS; *UA*, 26 March 1920, 1; *Five Years*.

55. *Five Years*.

56. *UA*, 26 March 1920, 4; Davidson to "My Dear Sir," 25 June 1920, quoted in Millikan, *Union against Unions*, mss.d. 240.

57. Millikan, *Union against Unions*, mss.d. 247–53; *DOL, 1919–1920*, 153–55; *UA*, 12 May 1921, 1; 19 May 1921, 1; 2 June 1921, 1; 14 July 1921, 1; *The Labor World* (Duluth), 27 August 1921, 1.

58. Millikan, *Union against Unions*, mss.d. 241.

59. Broadsides and pamphlets, B1, WM; *UA*, 12 May 1921, 1.

60. Citizens Alliance advertisements, B1, WM; Millikan, *Union against Unions*, mss.d. 243–44, 247; *Five Years*.

61. Gieske, *Minnesota Farmer-Laborism*, 55. Several typewritten manuscripts that Mahoney composed defending his political position in the campaign of 1920 can be found in B1, WM. Of particular interest is the justification entitled "Socialism."

62. Gieske, *Minnesota Farmer-Laborism*, 84–87; Mahoney quoted ibid., 84; Mahoney quoted in *UA*, 17 January 1924, 1; Valelly, *Radicalism in the States*, 38–45. See also David Brody, "On the Failure of U.S. Radical Politics: A Farmer-Labor Analysis," *Industrial Relations* 22 (spring 1983): 149.

Chapter 9: Hard Times in the "Holy City"

1. *PP*, 9 March 1920, 6.

2. The farm crisis was precipitated by a combination of surplus production, reduced national and international demand, higher production costs, decline in farm land value, and farmers' increased debt load—a complex set of conditions that can be traced directly to the wartime economy. Richard M. Valelly, *Radicalism in the States: The Minnesota Farmer-Labor Party and the American Political Economy* (Chicago, 1989), 70–82.

3. *CB*, 12 October 1918, 5.

4. Ibid., 25 November 1918, 2. It was commonly understood that the *Bulletin* served as the voice of John Ireland during his long tenure. A letter from Archbishop Dowling to the editor provides evidence that Dowling would wield similar editorial control: "I expect the Bulletin to use more care & more consideration in discovering what I say and when I think it proper to print it. . . . Let the substance of this letter be your guide." Dowling to Father McGinnis, 24 May 1919, F1, B2, AD, AASPM.

5. *CB*, 2 November 1918, 4; Dowling to Reverend Dear Father, 27 February 1922, F6, B1, AD.

6. Secretary to the archbishop to Reverend Dear Father, 10 April 1922, F6, B1, AD; Joseph Guillamette, interview by the author, St. Paul, 14 July 1996, tape recording, side 1.

7. Petition from the parishioners of St. Stanislaus to Dowling, 1927, St. Stanislaus folder; notes on meeting with St. Ambrose parishioners, undated; Dowling to Mr. Carletta, 7 September 1925, St. Ambrose folder, parish records files, AASPM.

8. Lenten instructions to the clergy of the archdiocese, 1921, F6, B1; typewritten draft of a speech, n.d. (1919 or 1920), F12, B3; Dowling, letter without salutation, F6, B1, AD.

9. Dowling to clergy of the archdiocese, 12 September 1919, F6, B1, AD.

10. Dowling to Reverend Dear Sir, 25 February 1920, F6, B1; Dowling (no salutation), 1921, F12, B3, AD Papers. Numerous pleas for funds can be found in F12, entitled "WWI and European and Near Eastern Relief," B3, AD.

11. *CB*, 9 November 1918, 1; Dowling to Clara Hill Lindley, 2 December 1927, F5, B2, AD.

12. Mahoney to editor of the *UA*, 1 June 1938, B1, WM, MHS; *UA*, 1 June 1918, 8; James Michael Reardon, *The Catholic Church in the Diocese of St. Paul: From Earliest Origin to Centennial Achievement* (St. Paul, 1952), 396.

13. *UA*, 13 February 1920, 5.

14. Valelly, *Radicalism in the States*, 42.

15. "The Shiely Story" (privately printed, 1952); Martin R. Haley, *Building for the Future: The Story of the Walter Butler Companies* (St. Paul, 1956); *UA*, 14 December 1922, 1.

16. Minutes of the WPNPL meetings, 24 January 1920; Mahoney interview, RL Papers, MHS; Millard L. Gieske, *Minnesota Farmer-Laborism: The Third Party Alternative* (Minneapolis, 1979), 85.

17. The rosters of the above-mentioned organizations reveal multiple overlapping memberships.

18. Louis Flynn, interview by the author, 6 May 1996, St. Paul, tape recording, side 1.

19. M. O'Brien to P. J. O'Donnell, 1 January 1920; O'Donnell to Representative Walter J. Newton, undated draft; E. St. J. Condon to O'Donnell, 5 February 1920, correspondence files, B1, MCO'D, MHS. The Clan na Gael, as a quasi-secret brotherhood, left no official local records. Evidence of St. Paul activity is based on coded letters that discussed its later decline. See O'Donnell to James Reidy, 1 February and 21 March 1927, and Reidy to O'Donnell, 24 March 1927, ibid.

20. Gieske, *Minnesota Farmer-Laborism*, 80–82.

21. Mahoney, FLP keynote address, quoted in *DN*, 17 June 1924, 13; Gieske, *Minnesota Farmer-Laborism*, 86–87; Valelly, *Radicalism in the States*, 44–46.

22. Benjamin Gitlow, *I Confess: The Truth about American Communism* (New York, 1939), 207–9; Gitlow, *The Whole of Their Lives: Communism in America—A Personal History* (New York, 1948), 115–17; "1924 St. Paul Convention," notes contained in draft manuscript, RL Papers; Gieske, *Minnesota Farmer-Laborism*, 87.

23. *DN*, 18 June 1924, 1–2; *PP*, 20 June 1924, 4 and 17 June 1924, 1. For full accounts of the convention, see *DN* and *PP*, 16–21 June, 1924.

24. Gieske, *Minnesota Farmer-Laborism*, 87.

25. *DN*, 18 June 1924, 2; *PP*, 18 June, 1, 3; 19 June 1, 3, and 21 June 1924, 8.

26. Gieske, *Minnesota Farmer-Laborism*, 87, 97. Smith easily won heavily Catholic Ramsey County in the 1928 election with 51% of the vote, in contrast to the dismal 38% he garnered in Hennepin County (Minneapolis). *Minnesota Votes: Election Returns by County for Presidents, Senators, Congressmen, and Governors, 1857–1957* (St. Paul, 1977), 21. On the merger of the Farmer-Labor and Democratic Parties, see John Earl Haynes, *Dubious Alliance: The Making of Minnesota's DFL Party* (Minneapolis, 1984).

27. Luke Boyce, Northern Information Bureau report, 30 August 1919, NIB, MHS; Hannon Detective Agency papers, quoted in William Millikan, *A Union against Unions: The Minneapolis Citizens Alliance and Its Fight against Organized Labor, 1903–1947* (St. Paul, 2001), mss.d. 324.

28. H. R. Galt, memo to Mr. Riegel, 16 April 1924, correspondence file, B2, D-PP, MHS.

29. *Five Years: Showing What Has Been Accomplished in Improving Industrial Relations in Saint Paul* (St. Paul, 1925), n.p.; *CB*, 25 November 1918, 2.

30. *Story of the Town and Country Club* (St. Paul, 1947), 26, 31–2; Flynn interview.

31. Reardon, *Catholic Church*, 653–65, 448–52; "What We Have—What We Need," pamphlet produced by the Ireland Educational Fund, F19, B2, AD; contracts files, B7–8, FBIC, MHS.

32. Minutes of the meetings of the board of directors of the Archbishop Ireland Education Fund, 23, 37, journal held at AASPM; Dowling to Lindley, 2 and 11 December 1927, F5, B2, AD.

33. Ireland Fund minute book, 29; contracts files, B7, FBIC; Haley, *Building for the Future*.

34. That the fulfillment of parish pledges was of paramount importance is clear in the hundreds of documents contained in the Ireland Education Fund files, B2, AD. The relationship between pledge fulfillment and labor practices seems quite clear in campaign receipt records. In the first year of the multiyear campaign, St. Paul parishes were on target, with well over $100,000 collected. In contrast, Minneapolis parishes, which had pledged only slightly less than St. Paul, but where the archbishop had little leverage with business leaders, had fulfilled only $50,000 of their pledged amount. Ireland Fund Minutes, 23.

35. See contracts files, B7, FBIC.

36. Between 1922 and 1924 Foley Bros. contracts with the Catholic Church included the chancery building, Cathedral rectory and sacristy, St. Andrew's School, the St. Paul Catholic Orphan's Home, and an addition to the House of Good Shepherd, as well as the multimillion-dollar Nazareth Hall. B7, FBIC.

37. *Five Years*.

38. Sister Helen Angela Hurley, *On Good Ground: The Story of the Sisters of St. Joseph in St. Paul* (Minneapolis, 1951), 250; *Five Years*.

39. W. H. MacMahon, "The Open Shop Movement and the Open Shop Workman," text of a speech, June 1930, 12, WHM, MHS.

40. MacMahon, untitled manuscript, 1929, pp. 8–10, B1, WHM.

41. J. C. Harrington to Patrick O'Donnell, 4 May 1926, correspondence folder, B1, MCO'D; Harrington speech, "The Church and Labor" (rpt., St. Paul: Minnesota Federation of Labor, 1925), 14–15, AASPM collections; Harrington, *Catholicism, Capitalism, or Communism*, quoted in review by Patrick O'Donnell, typescript, pp. 1–2, B1, MCO'D.

42. Dowling to My dear Friend, n.d., F19, B2, AD Papers.

43. MacMahon, typescript of Alliance publication (untitled), 1929, p. 4, B1, WHM.

44. Ibid., 5; MacMahon, "The Open Shop," 8, 11–12.

45. MacMahon, draft of letter to employers, n.d., ca. 1929, B1, WHM.

46. Ibid.

47. Memorandum on Stoltz Dry Cleaners, 8 March 1929; MacMahon, "The Open Shop," 11–12, B1, WHM.

48. Mock Larson, interview by Mary Wingerd, St. Paul, 27 July 1996, tape recording, side 1.

49. Ibid., sides 1 and 2.

50. Ibid., side 1.

51. "Cardozo Erects Barriers against Independent Workmen," *Industrial Freedom* (newsletter of the Citizens Alliance), July 1931, 1, DC Records, MHS.

52. A. W. Lindeke, quoted in "The Twin Cities: An Addendum," *Fortune*, July 1936, 88.

53. John O'Dell, National Secretary of the AOH, to O'Donnell, 6 April 1920; "Counties Organized in the State," 31 December 1924; T. J. Doyle to O'Donnell, 25 May 1926, B1, MCO'D.

54. James Reidy to O'Donnell, 24 March 1927; O'Donnell to Reidy, 1 February 1927, B1, MCO'D.

55. In the mid-1920s, the Minneapolis chapter of the AOH petitioned local merchants to withdraw merchandise and window displays "disrespectful to St. Patrick and the Irish people." Unidentified newspaper clipping, ca. 1925, clippings scrapbook, B1, MCO'D.

56. In his essay "The Odd Couple: Pluralism and Assimilation," Philip Gleason provides an exceptionally helpful analysis of the permutations of assimilation theory. See Gleason, *Speaking of Diversity: Language and Ethnicity in Twentieth-Century America* (Baltimore, 1992), 47–90. For models of assimilation, see Milton M. Gordon, *Assimilation in American Life: The Role of Race, Religion, and National Origins* (New York, 1964), esp. 69–81, and Elliot R. Barkan, "Race, Religion, and Nationality in American Society: A Model of Ethnicity—From Contact to Assimilation," *JAEH* 14 (winter 1995): 39–75.

57. As examples, see Grace Flandrau, "St. Paul: The Untamable Twin," in *The Taming of the Frontier*, ed. Duncan Aikman (New York, 1925), 151–54; and Flynn interview.

58. Kathleen Conzen describes a somewhat similar cultural accommodation between Milwaukee and its German residents, though the circumstances in which it occurred were quite different. See Conzen, *Immigrant Milwaukee, 1836–1860: Accommodation and Community in a Frontier City* (Cambridge, Mass., 1976).

59. Nathan Glazer and Daniel Patrick Moynihan, *Beyond the Melting Pot: The Negroes, Puerto Ricans, Jews, Italians, and Irish of New York City*, 2d rev. ed. (Cambridge, Mass., 1990), 16–17. For a perceptive analysis of Glazer and Moynihan's thesis, see Gleason, *Speaking of Diversity*, 71–72.

60. J. Fletcher Williams, *A History of the City of St. Paul, and the County of Ramsey, Minnesota* (St. Paul, 1876), 83.

61. Flynn interview, side 1.

62. Paul Maccabee, *John Dillinger Slept Here: A Crooks' Tour of Crime and Corruption in St. Paul, 1920–1936* (St. Paul, 1995), 25; Flynn interview, side 1; Angelo Vruno, interview by Mary Wingerd, 24 July 1996, St. Paul, tape recording, side 1.

63. Vruno and Flynn interviews.

64. Maccabee, *John Dillinger*, 25; Abe Gleeman deposition, 1925, pts. 3, 9, 11, 17, Gleeman deposition folder, D-PP.

65. Bennie Gleeman deposition, 1925, pts. 2–3, Gleeman deposition folder, D-PP; Maccabee, *John Dillinger*, 32–33.

66. Bennie Gleeman deposition, 1925, pts. 2–3; Maccabee, *John Dillinger*, 2–3; Larson interview, side 2.

67. Maccabee, *John Dillinger*, 3–4, 188–89; Gleeman deposition, pt. 4; Vruno interview, side 1.

68. Maccabee, *John Dillinger*, 134–41, 64–68, xii, 26.

69. Vruno interview, side 1.

70. Larson interview, sides 1 and 2.

71. Maccabee, *John Dillinger*, 78–80.

72. Bill Green quoted in Maccabee, *John Dillinger*, 11–12; Larson interview, side 1.

73. Marcy Frances McNulty, "Wilbur Burton Foshay: The Saga of a Salesman" (master's thesis, Creighton University, 1964), 32–33, 46–47, 85–87; George Dimitri Tselos, "The Minneapolis Labor Movement in the 1930s" (Ph.D. diss., University of Minnesota, 1971), 34.

74. McNulty, "Foshay," 32–33, 81–82.

75. "They Believed in the Foshay Company," *The Foshay Spotlight*, September 1929; McNulty, "Foshay," 59–60, 85–88.

76. Millikan, *Union against Unions*, mss.d. 354–65; McNulty, "Foshay," 89–92. Foshay's family and friends and the Minneapolis Central Labor Union all claimed that this was a case of revenge rather than simple conservative banking practice, noting that the banking giant had extended liberal credit to Minneapolis Steel & Machinery, Pillsbury, and Washburn-Crosby when the crash caught them temporarily short. In their estimation, the bank easily could have done the same for Foshay. Essentially, the corporation was sound; under receivership, all 110 of its companies operated at a profit and made payments to stockholders and bondholders despite the Depression. Millikan, *Union against Unions*, mss.d. 364; Tselos, "Minneapolis Labor Movement," 61–62; McNulty, "Foshay," 151–52.

77. MacMahon, typescript, 1929, pp. 1, 9, B1, WHM Papers; Thomas J. Kelley, "A Case History of Government in Action: The Newly Restored, Newly Renovated City Hall–County Courthouse," *RCH* 18 (1993): 5; Dane Smith, "The City Hall–County Courthouse and Its First Fifty Years," *RCH* 17 (1992): 9.

78. Smith, "City Hall–County Courthouse," 7–8.

79. Demonstrating the widespread nature of this pressure, the Italian-American Legion of St. Paul, "voicing the sentiment of the Italian people of this city," petitioned the commission to "select the major architect . . . from those now practicing in St. Paul." Kelley, "Case History," 8.

80. Smith, "City Hall–County Courthouse," 15.

81. Ibid., 15–16.

82. Mahoney, "Socialism," p. 1; Laurance Hodgson to Mahoney, 4 May 1934, B1, WM.

83. Mahoney, "Inaugural Address," 7 June 1932; Mahoney to civic organizations, 30 June 1932, B1, WM.

84. William Meikle to Mahoney, 1 July 1932; Max Keller to Mahoney, 14 July 1932, B1, WM.

85. MacMahon to Mahoney, 7 July 1932, B1, WM.

86. Homer Clark to E. A. Goldenweiser, 15 February 1933, B1, WM.

87. City Council files 96831–96834; "Information about the Proposal for a City Owned Electric Plant for Saint Paul," 1933; "Citizens Committee on Public Utilities," 1934; "Inaugural Address," B1, WM. On the stigma attached to relief, see Vruno interview.

88. Maccabee, *John Dillinger;* "Re-elect Mark Gehan," 1936 campaign flyer, B1, WM Papers; "Revolt in the Northwest," *Fortune*, April 1936, 186, 190; Alvin Karpis, *The Alvin Karpis Story* (New York, 1971), 127–46, 161–71.

89. "Re-elect Mark Gehan Mayor of St. Paul," B1, WM Papers; Maccabee, *John Dillinger,* 250–53; "Revolt in the Northwest," 118–19.

90. "Information about the proposal . . ."; Hodgson to Mahoney, 4 May 1934, B2, WM Papers. Among the unethical campaign practices employed against Mahoney, the Gehan for Mayor Volunteer Committee sent out a letter threatening city relief clients with loss of a job, food, and coal if they supported Mahoney. Though Gehan disavowed the letter as "unauthorized," that could hardly obviate the effect of such a threat. Mahoney cited the letter as "a true indication of the malicious campaign being carried on by Mr. Gehan and the so-called anti-Labor ticket." *Disp.*, 16 April 1934.

91. Maccabee, *John Dillinger*, 138–39. No evidence exists that Mahoney was involved in corrupt practices. In fact, a story told by the doorman of the Hollyhocks Club, preferred watering spot of the city's major criminals, suggests quite the opposite. The doorman recalled that in 1933 or 1934, Mahoney knocked on the door of the club but was refused admittance. Mahoney demanded the door be opened, declaring, "I'm the mayor of St. Paul, let me in!" According to the doorman, "He wanted to see the inside of the place, but I never let him in." Judging from all accounts of the illegal gambling club, Mahoney may be one of the few people in St. Paul who was not familiar with the interior of the club by 1933.

92. Hodgson to Mahoney, 4 May 1931.

93. Hodgson to Mahoney, "Re-elect Mark Gehan," and "Elect John. J. McDonough," all items in B1, WM; *The Mayors of St. Paul, 1850–1940* (St. Paul, 1940), 66–73.

Epilogue

1. Charles Rumford Walker, *American City: A Rank-and-File History* (New York, 1937); Philip A. Korth, *The Minneapolis Teamsters Strike of 1934* (East Lansing, Mich., 1995); Farrell Dobbs, *Teamster Rebellion* (New York, 1972).

2. "Revolt in the Northwest," *Fortune*, April 1936, 113.

3. Ibid., 197; George Dimitri Tselos, "The Minneapolis Labor Movement in the 1930s" (Ph.D. diss., University of Minnesota, 1970), 220, 236.

4. Gordon "Mock" Larson, interview by the author, 29 July 1996, St. Paul, tape recording, side 1.

5. "Revolt in the Northwest," 197, 118–19.

6. Ibid., 190. I am indebted to David Emmons for his insight on St. Paul as a cultural island within the state—somewhat similar to what he discovered in his study of Butte, Montana, where residents described their city as "Butte, America."

7. The Holmes sisters were part of a small cohort of radicals to come out of St. Paul's Catholic social justice community. For years, the sisters combined membership in the Communist League (later, the Socialist Workers Party) with devout Catholicism. Dorothy recalled that she often attended daily mass and Communist meetings on the same day, finding nothing inconsistent between Catholicism and Communism. She confided that she was introduced to the works of Karl Marx by one of the nuns who taught her at St. Catherine's College. The particular configuration of St. Paul labor and politics, however, kept her from putting her activist principles into action in her home town. Thus, after classes at St. Catherine's, she would take the streetcar to Minneapolis to work with the labor activists there. Dorothy's sister Grace became a leader in

the Socialist Workers Party, running as its vice-presidential candidate in 1952. Grace's husband, Gilbert Carlson (also a St. Paul Catholic), became deeply involved in Minneapolis labor and radical politics. Dorothy Holmes Schultz, interview by Mary Wingerd, 31 August 1995, Madison, Wisc., tape recording, side 1; Francis Gilligan, interview by the author, 19 August 1995, Hastings, Minn., tape recording, side 2. On the Dunnes, see Dale Kramer, "The Dunne Boys of Minneapolis," *Harper's*, March 1942, 388–98.

8. Alan Altshuler, *A Report on Politics in St. Paul, Minnesota* (Cambridge, 1959), part 1, 8.

9. Altshuler, *Politics in St. Paul*, pt. 1, 1, 2, 5. A companion study of Minneapolis estimates that Catholics composed approximately 25 percent of the city's population in 1957. Altshuler, *A Report on Politics in Minneapolis* (Cambridge, 1959), pt. 1, 5.

10. John McGreevy notes that these were common cultural signifiers among Catholics in the urban north and specifically cites St. Paul. John T. McGreevy, *Parish Boundaries: The Catholic Encounter with Race in Twentieth-Century Urban America* (Chicago, 1996), 20–22. For personal recollections of growing up in St. Paul, see Patricia Hampl, *A Romantic Education* (New York, 1981), and *Virgin Time* (rpt., New York, 1993); Michael J. O'Connell, "Together We Are Better Than We Ever Would Be Alone," *Vision* (fall 1997): 6. As striking evidence of parish stability, the fifty-year reunion of St. Agnes High School's graduating class of 1929 found fully 40% of those who could be located still residing within five miles of the old German, working-class parish. St. Agnes folder, parish records files, AASPM.

11. Altshuler, *Politics in St. Paul*, pt. 1, 3, pt. 2, 13–17.

12. Ibid., pt. 5, 4–5, pt. 2, 3.

13. Ibid., pt. 2, 13–17.

14. Ibid., pt. 5, 2.

15. Ibid., pt. 5, 4–5. In contrast, Minneapolis politics were highly contentious, with business, labor, and political liberals each adhering to a distinct ideological perspective and political rhetoric grounded in class appeals. Altshuler, *Politics in Minneapolis*, pt. 2, 1–23.

16. Altshuler, *Politics in St. Paul*, pt. 2, 12, 17–18.

17. In his biography of Eugene Debs, Nick Salvatore makes the point that Debs's politics were fundamentally influenced by the environment in which he was raised. Separated from his roots in Terre Haute, Indiana, "Debs, of necessity must appear a wistful, would-be hero, an aberration separated from his time and culture," an assessment that has equal application for Eugene McCarthy. Nick Salvatore, *Eugene V. Debs: Citizen and Socialist* (Urbana, Ill., 1982), 3.

18. Altshuler, *Politics in St. Paul*, pt. 2, 17, pt. 1, 5–6, pt. 5, 13. In Minneapolis, religion played a much less significant role, though it was "usually advantageous" for a candidate to be Lutheran. Catholicism neither helped nor hindered a candidate, and the institutional church was "not politically active." Altshuler, *Politics in Minneapolis*, pt. 1, 5, pt. 5, 10.

19. Gilligan interview, side 1. Gilligan's strategies bear striking similarity to those of labor priests in other parts of the country, suggesting that while Gilligan may have worked alone in St. Paul, he had a network of contacts that originated in John Ryan's classroom at Catholic University. See Steve Rosswurm, "The Catholic Church and the Left-Led Unions: Labor Priests, Labor Schools, and the ACTU," in *The CIO's Left-Led Unions*, ed. Steve Rosswurm (New Brunswick, N.J., 1992), 119–37.

20. Altshuler, *Politics in St. Paul*, pt. 2, 10–11, 19–21.

21. Ibid., pt. 2, 17, pt. 5, 1.

22. As Thomas Bender observes, "External forces, including metropolitan markets and governmental bureaucracies, can actually revitalize a traditional local moral order." Thomas Bender, *Community and Social Change in America* (New Brunswick, N.J., 1978; rpt., Baltimore, Md., 1982), 120.

23. *Newsweek*, 6 February 1989, 42–43. For a comparative assessment of St. Paul's fortunes in the post-industrial age, see Anthony M. Orum, *City-Building in America* (Boulder, Colo., 1995). Though Orum makes an astute analysis of certain aspects of the city's resurgence, his conflation of the Twin Cities into a single metropolitan area misses a good deal of the underlying complexity in the relationship between the two cities.

24. I base this interpretation on numerous conversations with non-native St. Paulites. Though this sense of insularity is slowly eroding, it is far from defunct. For example, one Min-

neapolis native who married a St. Paul man has insisted to me that, though she has lived in the same St. Paul neighborhood for more than a quarter of a century, has belonged to the local parish all those years, and sent her children through the local Catholic schools, she still feels like an outsider because she didn't grow up in the city and share the adolescent history of her friends and neighbors.

25. Citizen comments reflected both ethnic and civic defensiveness, ranging from: "He's generalizing that all Irish drink. He's very, very wrong"; to "I think it's a total disgrace. If he has a problem with living in St. Paul, why doesn't he give up the beautiful mansion on Summit Avenue?" Bill Salisbury, "Ventura Plays 'Late Night' for Laughs at St. Paul's Expense," *PP*, 24 February 1999, 1, 5A; Kermit Pattison, "Talk of the Town," *PP*, 25 February 1999, 1, 6A; and Don Boxmeier, "Ventura Should Explore St. Paul's Urban Jumble," ibid., 6A.

26. "Revolt in the Northwest," 112; "Glaring across the River," *The Economist*, 1 November 1997, 31; Kevin Diaz, "Revisiting a Rivalry," *Minneapolis Star-Tribune*, 6 April 1997, D1, 5–6; Ronald D. Clark, "Looking Back," *PP*, 8 December 1996, 20A; Grace Flandrau, "St. Paul: The Untamable Twin," in *The Taming of the Frontier*, ed. Duncan Aikman (New York, 1925), 154.

27. Richard Chin, "St. Paul Happier Than Its Twin City," *PP*, 16 October 1997, 1, 8A. Though St. Paulites demonstrated slightly greater place-based loyalty, 72% of Minneapolitans also rated their quality of life as good or excellent; 44% thought the rivalry with St. Paul was strong as well, and 42% declared that no incentive would induce them to move to St. Paul.

28. Edward L. Ayers and Peter S. Onuf, introduction to *All Over the Map: Rethinking American Regions*, ed. Edward L. Ayers, Patricia Nelson Limerick, Stephen Nissenbaum, and Peter S. Onuf (Baltimore, Md., 1996), 5.

29. "Revolt in the Northwest," 190.

30. In the last decade, a flood of both scholarly and popular literature has challenged the trajectory of urban development and extolled a lost (and often somewhat romanticized) urban ideal. As examples, see Michael Sorkin, ed., *Variations on a Theme Park: The New American City and the End of Public Space* (New York, 1992); and Ray Suarez, *The Old Neighborhood: What We Lost in the Great Suburban Migration, 1966–1999* (New York, 1999).

31. E. P. Thompson, *Whigs and Hunters: The Origins of the Black Act* (New York, 1975). Thompson, *Customs in Common: Studies in Traditional Popular Culture* (New York, 1993); Thompson, *The Making of the English Working Class* (New York, 1966); Lawrence Goodwyn, *Democratic Promise: The Populist Moment in America* (New York, 1976); Sean Wilentz, *Chants Democratic: New York City and the Rise of the American Working Class, 1788–1850* (New York, 1984); David Montgomery, *The Fall of the House of Labor: The Workplace, the State, and American Labor Activism* (Cambridge, Mass., 1989). For a case study of the place-based nature of union consciousness, see Mary Wingerd, "Rethinking Paternalism: Power and Parochialism in a Southern Mill Village," *JAH* 83 (December 1996): 872–902.

32. Arif Dirlik, "Place-based Imagination: Globalism and the Politics of Place," unpublished manuscript in the author's possession, 44.

33. Jackson Lears, "Looking Backward: In Defense of Nostalgia," *Lingua Franca* (December–January 1998): 61.

34. See Harry C. Boyte, *Commonwealth: A Return to Citizen Politics* (New York, 1989).

Index